ADVANCES IN BEHAVIORAL ASSESSMENT OF CHILDREN AND FAMILIES

Volume 2 · 1986

ADVANCES IN BEHAVIORAL ASSESSMENT OF CHILDREN AND FAMILIES

A Research Annual

Editor: RONALD J. PRINZ
Department of Psychology
University of South Carolina

VOLUME 2 · 1986

Greenwich, Connecticut *London, England*

36 Sherwood Place
Greenwich, Connecticut 06836

JAI PRESS LTD.
3 Henrietta Street
London WC2E 8LU
England

ISBN: 0-89232-481-3

Manufactured in the United States of America

CONTENTS

LIST OF CONTRIBUTORS

Russell A. Barkley	Department of Psychiatry University of Massachusetts Medical School
Debora Bell-Dolan	Department of Psychology West Virginia University
Ellen S. Berler	Department of Psychology Florida State University
Karen Linn Bierman	Department of Psychology Pennsylvania State University
Judith Carta	Juniper Gardens Children's Project Bureau of Child Research University of Kansas
Janice Cohen	Department of Psychology University of Waterloo
John D. Cone	Department of Psychology West Virginia University
Granger Dinwiddie	Juniper Gardens Children's Project Bureau of Child Research University of Kansas
Sharon L. Foster	Department of Psychology West Virginia University
Charles R. Greenwood	Juniper Gardens Children's Project Bureau of Child Research University of Kansas

Tamara S. Hoier Department of Psychology
West Virginia University

Frank Kohler Juniper Gardens Children's Project
Bureau of Child Research
University of Kansas

Gina G. Krehbiel Department of Pediatrics
University of Iowa Medical School

Gary Ladd Department of Child Development & Family Studies
Purdue University

Eric J. Mash Department of Psychology
University of Calgary

Richard Milich Department of Psychology
University of Kentucky

Pamela A. Moore Department of Psychology
University of South Carolina

Helen Orvaschel Western Psychiatric Institute & Clinic
University of Pittsburgh School of Medicine

Joseph M. Price Department of Child Development & Family Studies
Purdue University

Ronald J. Prinz Department of Psychology
University of South Carolina

William Roberts Department of Psychology
University of South Carolina

Kenneth H. Rubin Department of Psychology
University of Waterloo

Dan Schulte
Juniper Gardens Children's Project
Bureau of Child Research
University of Kansas

Geraldine A. Walsh-Allis
Western Psychiatric Institute & Clinic
University of Pittsburgh School of Medicine

PREFACE

Advances in Behavioral Assessment of Children and Families is a research annual devoted to applied scientific work in the growing field of behavioral assessment with children. Methodological, theoretical, and practical issues regarding children's psychological functioning are presented with an emphasis on empirical verification and behavioral referents. Assessment of family functioning is included in recognition of the significant impact of family on child behavior. Contributions include comprehensive reports of original data-based research, presentations of individual programs of research, and to a lesser extent critical reviews of selected topics. The series samples a broad range of child assessment topics germane to child clinical psychology, child development, medicine, education, and social work. The first half of each volume has a general topics section covering a variety of child assessment areas. The second half of each volume contains a special topic or theme, such as assessment of children's social skills or assessment of child behavior in the context of family interaction, in order to present in greater depth an important topic being researched by several investigators. In addition to promoting empirical validation of behavioral assessment methods, the series aims to elucidate significant controversial and complex issues associated with the behavioral assessment of specific child problems.

This is the first volume of *Behavioral Assessment of Children and Families* under my editorship. The General Topics section presents four chapters from divergent areas of behavioral assessment. In the first chapter, Cone and Hoier challenge the inclusion of traditional psychometric concepts in a contemporary model of behavioral assessment. Instead, they support a natural science approach that is criterion-referenced, idiographic, inductive, and accuracy oriented. With a family assessment methodology that is compatible with Cone and Hoier's approach, Mash and Barkley describe the Response-Class Matrix, an observational system that assesses interactive sequences of parent-child behavior. Mash and Barkley describe their extensive work with family assessment as well as others' work across several child populations. In a strikingly different area, Greenwood and his colleagues present a comprehensive observational system for eco-behavioral interaction in classrooms. In light of recent national interest in improving education, eco-behavioral observation is a major contribution from the field of behavioral assessment toward this endeavor. The last contribution (Prinz, Moore, and Roberts) is a review of 450 studies of childhood hyperactivity from 1960 to 1984 with respect to assessment methods and related issues.

The specialty topic for Section II of this volume is assessment of social functioning in children. The initial chapter by Price and Ladd outlines the conceptual and procedural issues associated with the assessment of childhood friendships. Price and Ladd are careful to take into account developmental levels in their evaluation and provide a normative backdrop for the subsequent chapters. In a more clinical analysis, Bierman reports her findings relating aggression, a dimension of psychopathology, to rejection, a social status designation. Bierman's careful and innovative work provides a much needed detailed description of the social status subgroups. In a similar vein, Rubin and Cohen use the Revised Class Play, a measure of peer relations, as a vehicle for analyzing social status, peer relations, and behavioral style in a multivariate profile. Of particular note is the use of teacher, peer, observer, and self perspectives to explain social status outcomes in a short-term longitudinal design. From a broader vantage point, Walsh-Allis and Orvaschel review measures of social adaptation and offer appropriate recommendations for improvement of this assessment. Foster, Bell-Dolan and Berler also offer a critical analysis of current methods of assessing social status. They present data from their own studies to help answer sticky but significant questions regarding sociometric measurement. Finally, Krehbiel and Milich competently evaluate several issues pertaining to assessment and treatment of rejected children.

The chapters on childhood social functioning summarize the social status literature in a useful fashion and present new data and formulations. Hopefully, these will permit clinicians and investigators alike to refine their hypotheses and move in new and fruitful directions in the assessment of social status, social skills, and childhood adjustment.

Ronald J. Prinz
Series Editor

ASSESSING CHILDREN:
THE RADICAL BEHAVIORAL PERSPECTIVE

John D. Cone and Tamara S. Hoier

ABSTRACT

Two major conceptual perspectives within contemporary child behavioral assessment are described. It was argued that the cognitive perspective, contrary to being an advance, actually represents a return to traditional clinical assessment with its emphasis on traits, norms, classical psychometric concepts, and hypothetico-deductive, nomothetic models. Evidence is presented for the pervasiveness of these emphases in contemporary child behavioral assessment. A radical behavioral alternative that takes behavior as its subject matter, studies it from a natural science point-of-view, is criterion-referenced, inductive, idiographic, and relies on accuracy as the most important feature of its instruments is described. The use of template matching procedures to assess children's social behavior is shown to involve most of these characteristics. Studies are presented to support the reliability and preliminary experimental validity of template matching, and suggestions are given for future research.

Advances in Behavioral Assessment of Children and Families, Vol. 2, pgs. 1–27.
Editor: Ronald J. Prinz

ISBN: 0-89232-481-3

INTRODUCTION

Behavioral assessment generally, and child behavioral assessment specifically, are relatively young disciplines. As such, they have yet to differentiate themselves fully from traditional clinical assessment. In this chapter we argue that much of contemporary child behavioral assessment carries the trappings of its traditional forebearers. After describing prevalent conceptual perspectives, we identify four areas of difficulty facing child behavioral assessment. We then call for the discipline to assert itself positively, to assume a radical posture characterized by the study of behavior from a natural science point-of-view. We argue that such a discipline should be inductive, idiographic, and criterion-referenced. In addition, we suggest that accuracy should be the principal evaluative criterion applied to its instruments.

Having said all this, we next describe a series of studies developing an assessment technology that incorporates many of these attributes. Template matching procedures are applied in the assessment of children's social skills to show the promise of an approach that is inductive, idiographic, and criterion-referenced. We conclude with a number of suggestions concerning the future development of such procedures.

PREVALENT CONCEPTUAL PERSPECTIVES IN CHILD BEHAVIORAL ASSESSMENT

Perhaps because of its newness child behavioral assessment has achieved no singular conceptual focus. Multiple models have been proposed, organizing different aspects of the enterprise (Bornstein, Bornstein, & Dawson, 1984; Ciminero & Drabman, 1977). With respect to *what* to assess, for example, the A-B-C approach (Bijou, Peterson, Harris, Allen, & Johnston, 1969) divides important events into the behavior (B) of interest and immediately contiguous antecedent (A) and consequent (C) environmental events. Lindsley's (1964) S-R-K-C model adds the schedule or contingency between behavior and consequence (K), and the S-O-R-K-C model of Kanfer and Saslow (1969) adds the biological condition of the organism (O). Other models include Lazarus' (1973) BASIC ID, Nay's (1979) multimethod model and its five "modalities" and Cone's (1978) Behavioral Assessment Grid (BAG).

With the exception of the BAG model, each of these conceptualizations offered a way of guiding the assessor to consider critical variables for individual clients. The BAG was intended simply as a taxonomy for describing research in the field of behavioral assessment and possibly for classifying assessment instruments at some point in the future.

As models to guide assessment practice, some of the approaches are driven by conceptual systems dealing with the causes of behavior generally. The A-B-C, S-R-K-C, and S-O-R-K-C models all derived from an operant perspective with its emphasis on objective quantification of the behavior of interest and its search for causes in immediate *external* environmental antecedents and consequences. Even with the addition of the O component to Lindsley's (1964) earlier formulation, Kanfer and Saslow (1969) were merely acknowledging that behavior occurs in a biological context that might be an important source of antecedent (and consequent) stimulus variables. In this way, Kanfer and Saslow shifted our focus from exclusively external causative events to internal ones as well.

Though Kanfer and Saslow did not explicitly admit cognitive events into their system, the recent upsurge in cognitive behavior modification with children as well as adults has led to the inclusion of cognitions as important phenomena for consideration in child behavioral assessment (Ollendick & Hersen, 1984). Research showing differential intervention effects depending on a child's causal attributions (e.g., Bugental, Whalen, & Henker, 1977; Ollendick, Elliott, & Matson, 1980) can be seen as supporting this logic.

The conceptual orientations prevalent within child behavioral assessment today thus appear to be operant on the one hand, and cognitive on the other. Though some (e.g., Ollendick & Hersen, 1984) advocate the superiority of cognitive conceptualizations, a plausible case can be made for the superiority of operant approaches as well. Without arguing the merits of operant versus cognitive perspectives it can be noted that a radical behavioral view does make room for private events or intraverbal behavior (Skinner, 1957), though it assigns no causative priority to them. Private speech (cognitions) are treated as any other behavior. The task of the assessor is to determine the stimulus events controlling the private speech. This is conceptually no different from the assessor's task when nonprivate (i.e., observable) behavior is at issue.

The cognitive approach seems quite different. Whereas some of its proponents (e.g., Ollendick & Hersen, 1984) refer to cognitive events "such as self-statements, expectancies, and plans" (p. 7) as included within the R term, there is a corresponding tendency to ascribe causal power to them, thus shoving them more toward S or C portions of the model. To assume, for example, that a "perspective taking structure" exists and that deficiencies in it require remedy (Kendall, Pellegrini, & Urbain, 1981) in socially maladroit children suggests some controlling power for perspective taking. Presumably if one could understand the other's perspective better, one could be more socially effective.

Cognitive behavioral assessment with children appears to return us to a tradition within clinical assessment from which behavioral assessment should be differentiated, i.e., a tradition that relies on hypothetical constructs as explanatory phenomena. The assessment of social cognition illustrates this point. Various measures have been developed to tap aspects of the general social cognition construct (Kendall et al., 1981). Measures of perspective-taking ability such as Chandler's (1973) "bystander cartoon" test have been produced and examined for reliability and validity much as any trait measure traditionally has been evaluated.

While the cognitive behavioral assessment literature presents some of the clearest evidence for the tenacity of traditional, trait-oriented assessment in child behavioral assessment, there is other evidence as well. Some of this evidence will be reviewed below. Interest is assessing enduring characteristics of children, the tendency to refer individual scores to the mean of some normative group, the tendency to apply classical psychometric criteria in evaluating measures, and the continued reliance on hypothetico-deductive reasoning in conceptualizing, designing, implementing, and evaluating research seem to get in the way of developing child assessment procedures that are truly behavioral. To set the stage for the major departure from these tendencies we will first consider each of them in more detail.

Traitism

Within behavioral assessment generally, alarm has been expressed over the lingering tendency to conceptualize the process in trait terms (Cone, 1979; McFall, 1977; Rich & Schroeder, 1976).

As McFall (1977) has implied, concern with factor structure, consistency across situations, item equivalence, and response additivity all suggest a trait-based conceptualization of a particular measuring instrument. Indeed, the common practice of reporting internal consistency coefficients for self-report measures is trait-based. The higher the internal consistency, the more each item may be said to be drawn from a common pool of items that reflects a general disposition. In a similar vein, summing item responses to produce a single scale score suggests concern with a general trait or at least a response class.

Obvious examples of this persistence of "traitism" can be found in literatures related to assessing assertion and in references to triple response mode assessment research. Many of the self-report measures of assertion, based on the early work of Wolpe (1969) and Wolpe and Lazarus (1966), contain individual items that only vaguely specify stimulus referents (Rich & Schroeder, 1976). Thus, there appears to be more interest in assessing nonspecific (i.e., general) attitudes than situation-specific, clearly defined behaviors.

The frequent reference to triple response mode assessment and the use of cognitive, motor, and physiological "channels" (Paul & Bernstein, 1973) is further evidence of the persistence of trait logic. In referring to three ways in which fear could be manifested, Lang (1971) was clearly coming from a trait-based view of emotion. Much of the subsequent literature looking at the correspondence among cognitive, motor, and physiological behavior has been similarly predicated on the assumption that these measures are signs of underlying attributes. For example, Odom, Nelson, and Wein (1978) concluded that intervention for phobic disorders should involve first assessing "the response systems that *indicate* fear" (p. 941, emphasis added). Leitenberg, Gross, Peterson, and Rosen (1984) recently observed that "in exposure-based treatments of any supposed anxiety disorder the question arises as to which components . . . change first, and what the relationship is between change in any one *anxiety modality* and another'' (p. 4, emphasis added). Additional examples are not hard to find. Recent texts devoted to behavioral assessment (e.g., Barlow, 1981; Ciminero, Calhoun, & Adams, 1977; Cone & Hawkins, 1977; Haynes, 1978; Hersen & Bellack, 1981; Mash & Terdal, 1981) also include examples of the use of trait logic. There are still even occasional suggestions that behavioral assessors be concerned with demonstrating construct validity (e.g., Haynes, 1978).

Specific areas within the child behavioral assessment literature offer additional examples of trait logic. With respect to hyperactivity for instance, Abikoff and his colleagues (Abikoff, Gittelman-Klein, & Klein, 1977; Abikoff, Gittelman, & Klein, 1980) have noted that a ''simple symptom has limited diagnostic utility'' (Abikoff et al., 1980, p. 562). Haynes and Kerns (1979) suggested that observation systems in this area need to have validity for assessing the hyperactivity ''construct.''

Even clearer examples of lingering traitism in child behavioral assessment are to be found in the use of self-report measures to assess constructs such as depression and anxiety. The Childhood Depression Inventory (Kovacs & Beck, 1977; Kovacs, 1978) is a 27-item scale designed to assess the general dimensions of depression in children between 8 and 13 years of age. Craighead, Kennedy, Smucker, and Peterson (1984) have suggested we consider subtypes of childhood depression. They found 60% of a group of depressed children were also anxious, for example. Finch and Rogers (1984) recently reviewed self-report measures of childhood anxiety, reporting the usual normative, reliability, and construct validity information one is accustomed to examining for trait measures. These authors also reviewed downward extensions of measures of the popular adult dimensions of depression and internal-external locus of control. Each of these lines of research attempts to define a general construct, syndrome, or dimension referred to globally as hyperactivity, anxiety, and so on.

Normism

The tendency to seek the meaning of scores in their comparison with the mean of a group of ''normal'' children is another characteristic of contemporary behavioral assessment. Nowhere is this more evident than in calls for assessors to take a ''normative-developmental perspective'' in evaluating children's behavior (Edelbrock, 1984). While there are good reasons for child behavioral assessors to know the course of normal development, there are usually better criteria for making sense of individual scores than are provided by norms for comparably aged children. This is especially so when intervention is the aim of assessment in the first place. The question to ask when assessing any behavior is what is an effective level of performance (McFall, 1977). In the academic sphere, for example, it is important to know what rate of correct consonant-vowel (CV) pair reading is necessary for a student to move successfully into consonant-vowel-consonant (CVC) reading. Comparing a student's CV rate with the norm for his age or grade seems less desirable than comparing it with a level shown empirically to be associated with high probabilities of success on more complex skills.

In another example, consider the case of a child with a physical handicap who is socially withdrawn. After assessing the child on a number of behaviors known to be associated with high rates of interaction in groups of socially competent children it is found that the child is below average with respect to "verbal initiations," "proximity," and "sharing." The appropriately designed intervention brings the child's performance to normal levels on all three. Subsequent observation reveals other children are still not interacting with our client child. Normal was not enough. Given the physical handicap of our client child, more than normal might have been necessary. A norm-referenced proponent might complain that we used the wrong "normal" reference group. We should have looked at norms for socially successful children who have similar physical handicaps. These are unlikely to be available, however, making obvious the problem with a norm-referenced approach. Any child is going to be different from the group on which the norms were based. When these differences are related to clinically relevant criteria as in the example above, they invalidate our normal reference point.

Perhaps norms are most useful as descriptive benchmarks for group research. When we want to establish the validity of a certain amount of change produced by a particular intervention, for example, it might be helpful to know how the final level of performance achieved by our subjects compares with that of some normal group (Edelbrock, 1984; Robinson, Eyberg, & Ross, 1980). It is unlikely that norms would ever be the most appropriate reference points for selecting intervention targets and judging the effectiveness or social validity of intervention efforts in the single case, however.

Psychometricism

A third problematic tendency in contemporary behavioral assessment, generally, and child behavioral assessment, specifically, is reflected in repeated calls for the application of psychometric criteria to the evaluation of behavioral assessment procedures (Cone, 1977; Johnson & Bolstad, 1973). The following quote is illustrative:

> In reading through the various chapters of Hersen and Bellack (1976), I was struck more by the primitive stage of research in certain areas of behavioral assessment than I was by startling new developments. In some respects, by comparison to the traditional psychometric literature we have a long way to go. . . . Where are the factor analytic studies, item analysis, split half and test-retest reliability determinations? Where are the large sample cross-validity studies (Leitenberg, 1978, p. 138)?

It is probably accurate to say that Leitenberg's questions reflect the apparent majority view that classical psychometric procedures are applicable to evaluating behavioral assessment methods. While it is imperative that we evaluate our methods as Johnson and Bolstad (1973) and others have noted, it is not obvious that classical psychometrics provide the appropriate procedures or criteria. In fact, there is good reason to question their general relevance to a discipline concerned with assessing child behavior (cf. Barrett, Johnston, & Pennypacker, 1986; Cone, 1981). This is so because classical psychometric procedures were designed for a different subject matter altogether. Johnston and Pennypacker (1980) observed that classical psychometric test theory had its origins in the study of measurement error by Legendre in the early 1800s, and the later use of demonstrated variability to *define* "latent entities or characteristics" by Adolph Quetelet. From Johnston and Pennypacker's (1980) historical overview it is not difficult to see that the armamentarium of psychometric procedures developed in the early part of this century was based on the view that important psychological phenomena can be defined in terms of variability in performance. This approach involves thinking up a phenomenon (trait, dimension, construct), developing a scale to assess it, and administering the scale to a group of people (Cone, 1981). Variation in scores on the scale can be taken to support the significance of the phenomenon. Further, this variability becomes the basis for evaluating the adequacy of the measuring device itself since most classical psychometric procedures involve comparisons of differences between scores, e.g., over time, across items, between one measure and another, and so on.

Variability between persons is basic to the definition and assessment of traits and to the evaluation of trait measures. The assessment of *behavior* that is available for visual inspection and independent verification does not depend on variability between persons but instead can rely on concepts worked out for phenomena in the natural sciences. We shall return to this point later.

Hypothetico-deductivism

Perhaps at the base of some of the difficulties mentioned thus far is a certain reluctance among behavioral assessors to abandon hypothetico-deductive philosophical approaches to studying human behavior. Skinner (1938, 1950, 1957) has repeatedly pointed to the advantages of building a science of human behavior inductively. Johnston and Pennypacker (1980) noted that the elaborate, hypothetico-deductive models so highly valued in the early days of behavioral psychology collapsed in the absence of a comparably elaborate data base. Mischel (1968) and others (Peterson, 1968; Vernon, 1964) have documented a similar collapse of the deductive approach to assessment, largely because of the insufficient data base on which it was built.

Much of the activity of behavioral assessors is still driven by deductive reasoning. For example, in predicting that depressed compared to nondepressed individuals would manifest a lower rate of social initiation behaviors Haynes (1978) is suggesting we start from a general construct and work toward the specific. We are interested in depression to begin with, and we conceptualize it as made up of discrete behaviors controlled by antecedent and consequent environmental events. In a similar vein, MacDonald (1978) has noted that "response patterns observed in a test should demonstrate structural fidelity, paralleling the pattern one expects from an a priori conception of the behavior construct under study" (p. 185, emphasis added).

A major difficulty with deductive reasoning is that the prior formulation of response classes (e.g., "aggression," "depression") might constrain our observation to supposed members of the class. Important behavior might then be overlooked.

> The clinical psychologist, aware as he is of the traps of preconception, must constantly try to free himself from a priori considerations, and be ready to generalize afresh from his observations as he finds them (Shapiro, 1961, p. 665).

The failure of traditional assessment to find cross-situationally general classes of behavior should alert us that there are precious few generalities at this point. Attempts to combine responses into classes or constructs on the basis of rational analysis might impede the discovery of empirical aggregates. For example, Wahler (1975) has found that behaviors not only group themselves differently from one setting to another between children, but that they do so *within* children as well. Thus, the behavioral assessment alternative to deductive approaches might be the more tedious, inductive accumulation of data with few a priori assumptions about interrelationships among responses. Voeltz and Evans (1982) have recently provided a comprehensive review of behavior-behavior relationships.

Summary

The problems with traitism, normism, psychometricism, and hypothetico-deductivism just described are a carryover from traditional trait-oriented views of assessment. The history of individual difference measurement in psychology shows quite clearly that its concepts are inconsistent with a natural science view of behavior. They were developed to assess unseen phenomena assumed to account for differences in human performance and have led to a measurement tradition that seems entirely inappropriate for a discipline whose subject matter is behavior itself.

As Barrett et al. (1986) have observed, the methodology of behavioral assessment is only tenuously related to clear conceptualizations of behavior itself. At best it appears unrelated to natural science perspectives on behavioral phenomena.

A RADICAL BEHAVIORAL ALTERNATIVE

Up to now, behavioral assessment has been stuck in defining itself largely in the form of contrasts with traditional assessment. As a result we know a lot about what behavioral assessment is not. It was probably reasonable, in the beginning, to be clear about what the field was not, but as anti-war activist David Harris has noted in another context,

> A politics defined by its negation is never free of that negation. If the negation were to cease, so would the politics. Life exists as an *is,* not as an *is not* (Martyna, 1979).

In this spirit it seems time for behavioral assessment to define itself as an *is*. In this section we outline six characteristics of a ''radical'' alternative to contemporary child behavioral assessment.

Behavior as Subject Matter

Behavioral assessment can be defined as at least the objective description of specific human responses that are controlled by contemporaneous environmental events and whose variability is directly related to the variability of their environment. From a radical behavioral view we can say that child behavioral assessment is concerned with behavior itself. Behavior can be defined as:

> that portion of the organism's interaction with its environment that is characterized by detectable displacement in space through time of some part of the organism and that results in a measurable change in at least one aspect of the environment (Johnston & Pennypacker, 1980, p. 48).

When defined in this way behavior can be seen to have ''many of the characteristics of matter in motion, and the same principles of measurement are applicable'' (Johnston & Pennypacker, 1980, p. 73).

Natural Science Perspective

Measurement in the natural sciences requires counting phenomena in terms of units that are standard and absolute and are not defined by variability in the subject matter being studied. In the physical sciences standard units exist for measuring distance, mass, and time. These are combined to define additional units such as velocity and density. As Johnston and Pennypacker (1980) have noted, such units of measurement have anchors in natural phenomena. For example, time and length can be defined in terms of certain wavelengths of light and ''atomic vibrational phenomena.''

Once it is accepted that behavior is comparable to matter in motion it is reasonable to apply measurement principles worked out for matter to behavior as well. Such dimensional characteristics of behavior as frequency, latency, duration, and intensity can all be assessed in terms of the same absolute and standard units employed with other forms of matter.

Inductive

Earlier, we suggested that behavioral assessors return to the more tedious, movement-by-movement, *inductive* gathering of information about behavior. The reasons for doing so may need some elaboration. Wahler (1975) found behaviors that cluster together for a child in school may be members of different clusters for that same child at home. Wahler and Fox (1980) noted during baseline observations that one child behavior that was consistently negatively correlated with parents' reports of aggressive actions was solitary play. When attempts to reduce aggressive behavior by strengthening incompatible prosocial responses failed, the intervention focus shifted to increasing solitary toy play. Reductions in problem behaviors followed.

By using an inductive approach to baseline data collection, Wahler and Fox "discovered" the systematic covariation between aggressive behavior and solitary play. This relationship was then used to design an effective intervention strategy. If Wahler and Fox had formulated an "oppositional response class" before observing natural covariations, they might not have included solitary toy play and would therefore have missed the relationship that led to the design of the successful intervention (Cone, 1979). Kazdin (1985) has emphasized this point by suggesting that core components of current constructs may in fact be part of larger constellations or intrapersonal systems. These systems may not "fit" any currently defined constructs or syndrome. Further, behaviors may be organized in ways which are counterintuitive, i.e., they bear no topographic or functional relationship. Therefore, inductively determining the structure of repertoires would seem to offer a promising alternative.

Idiographic

The arguments just made for inductive approaches apply to the idiographic-nomothetic distinction as well. The case for building a science of behavior on the intensive study of a few behavers is well known. A similar case in the assessment area was made long ago by Allport (1937) and has been reiterated quite recently by Bem and his associates (Bem, 1982; 1983; Bem & Funder, 1978; Bem & Lord, 1979). As behavioral assessors we are most likely to be concerned with the actions of individual persons. We design interventions for individuals and evaluate their outcome in terms of individual behavior change. In so doing we are appropriately perplexed at how to make use of information that the pretreatment mean of the experimental group was such and such and the pre-post difference was statistically significant. Rather than information derived from group studies that are nomothetic, deductive, and inter-individual based we need information derived from careful study of the individual client, studies that are idiographic, inductive, and that are designed to detect *intra*individual behavioral organization. The work of the clinician faced with understanding and predicting the behavior of individual clients requires a different paradigm from that of the scientist concerned more with general laws relating universal variables among large numbers of people.

Thus, a radical child behavioral assessment takes behavior as its subject matter, studies it from a natural science perspective, is inductive, and is idiographic.

Criterion-referenced

Scores on measures used by radical child behavioral assessors are interpreted in terms of relatively absolute standards of performance rather than by comparing them with the norm of some reference group. In calling for criterion-referenced assessment we are arguing that behavior be interpreted in terms of its effects. Discrepancies between observed and desired effects identify intervention targets. For example, the observed effect of a particular child's academic performance might be a failing grade assigned by the teacher. To know what behavior of the child will lead to a more desirable effect, i.e., a "passing grade," it is necessary to know something about the teacher's concept of "passing grade." While it is possible that the teacher's concept consists entirely of "performance at or higher than one standard deviation below the class mean," this is not necessarily the case. It might require mastery of 60% or more of the material or perhaps performance that is "consistent with other things I know about the student" (e.g., the child's high performance on an intelligence test). Both the last two examples involve a relatively absolute standard of performance that is independent of the average performance of the class. It is in comparing our example child's behavior against this absolute rather than normative standard that we obtain the information necessary to assign meaning to it.

As another example, recall our earlier reference to a handicapped child who seemed withdrawn and devoid of close friends and social interactions. Despite bringing her to average levels of performance viz initiations and sharing, levels which she was observed to transfer to interactions with her own classmates at recess, her initiations were not reciprocated and she failed to establish close friendships. In other words there was still a discrepancy between the observed and desired effects of her performance.

The failure of an intervention designed to increase behaviors to a normative standard in this case might stem from an inadequate assessment of the meaning of interpersonal competence in a child's unique social context. While it might be true that average performers of vocal initiations and sharing responses were found to be judged socially adequate in the research literature, their circumstances may be too remote, too unlike those of our client to be of relevance to her. What is needed is an analysis of the behavior required of the target child to produce social acceptance by *her* peers. The argument that social competence will mean different things in varying social contexts supports the requirement for idiographic analyses mentioned above. The fact that absolute levels of performance can be defined for a given child underlies our argument for a criterion-referenced assessment that assigns meaning to scores in terms of their effects on the environment.

Nowhere is the value of a criterion-referenced approach to child behavioral assessment clearer than in examining the performance of severely handicapped children. To judge such a child's performance as inadequate because it is below normal seems unduly restrictive. This is especially true where "normal" is only indirectly related to a level of performance found effective in a particular environmental context. For example, to judge a paraplegic child's performance inadequate because she does not "walk independently between two objects at least 20 feet apart" might fail to see the purpose behind such items. If the objective is to assess the skill of getting from one place to another, a child who covers the distance in a motorized wheelchair might produce the same effect as one who walks.

From a radical behavioral perspective it is difficult to think of cases where a norm would provide a better point-of-reference for interpreting scores on assessment devices than would a criterion of effective performance that is specific to the setting. Relating individual scores to relatively absolute performance standards requires accurate assessment, a final characteristic of radical behavioral assessment to which we now turn.

Accuracy as the Ultimate Criterion of Measurement Adequacy

When objectively verifiable responses are the subject matter of a discipline, its methods must be sensitive transducers of those responses, i.e., they must portray them accurately. A behavioral assessment that accepts behavior as its subject matter must study behavior with methods shown independently to be appropriate for the task (Cone, 1981). An appropriate measure is one that is known to be accurate for determining certain facts about the behavior in question. The facts of interest to behavioral assessors are (a) whether the behavior occurs, (b) whether it occurs repeatedly, (c) whether it occurs in more than one setting, (d) whether it can be assessed in more than one way, and (e) whether it is related to the occurrence of other events.

To establish the accuracy of an instrument, it is necessary to have (a) an incontrovertible index of the behavior said to be assessible by the instrument, and (b) a set of rules and procedures for using the instrument. A variety of more or less incontrovertible indices has been proposed, including electromechanical switch closures with associated counters, and scripted interactions (Foster & Cone, 1980).

The mathematics of establishing accuracy for an instrument for each of the questions raised earlier have been presented elsewhere (Cone, 1981). In most instances simple agreement measures will suffice. The logic here is that accuracy is the extent to which data obtained with the instrument agree with what is known about behavior as reflected by the independent, incontrovertible index.

Just as in the physical sciences, it is important for behavioral assessors to establish the accuracy of their instruments *before* using them to answer questions about behavior. Without prior calibration, it is impossible to determine whether the behavior is not occurring, not related to other behaviors, or whether occurrence and relatedness are simply not being detected because of inadequacies of instrumentation.

The emphasis on accuracy is one of the most important features distinguishing radical child behavioral assessment from other forms of behavioral assessment that have emphasized the traditional concepts of reliability and validity (cf. Cone, 1977; Johnson & Bolstad, 1973). An accurate instrument must be reliable, though not necessarily valid in the sense of correlating with other variables. However, a reliable instrument may or may not be accurate and it may or may not be valid. Similarly, a valid instrument must be reliable, but it may or may not be accurate. For child behavioral assessment to proceed with the study of behavior from a natural science perspective, it must use measures that are at least known to be accurate.

Summary

It has been argued that it is time for child behavioral assessment to take a more radical stance with respect to the study of children's responding. Specifically, we are calling for the study of behavior from a natural science perspective using approaches that are inductive, idiographic, and criterion-referenced. At the foundation of such an enterprise should be measurement tools shown, independently, to be appropriate (i.e., accurate) for the questions being raised.

In the final section of the chapter we will present a program of research that incorporates many of the characteristics of a radical approach to child behavioral assessment. At the outset we must acknowledge that it is not a pure example. Our work with template matching approaches to assessment has evolved in a somewhat parallel relationship to our developing conceptual orientation. It would have been more satisfying from a scientific point-of-view for the latter to have driven the former. The overlap and the intellectual consistency are reasonably high, however, and should serve to give some idea of the operationalizability of some of the concepts discussed in this section.

TEMPLATE MATCHING AS AN APPROXIMATION TO RADICAL CHILD BEHAVIORAL ASSESSMENT

Origins of Template Matching

As mentioned earlier, nomothetic assessment efforts have been directed toward identifying general patterns or laws of behavior which hold for groups of subjects rather than for individuals (Wiggins, 1973). As one example, multivariate approaches have been used to develop taxonomic frameworks for the classification of child psychopathology (Achenbach & Edelbrock, 1978). Such procedures result in clusters of behaviors found to be statistically associated in large groups of subjects (cf. Weintraub, Prinz, & Neale, 1978). Behaviors found to be related are often later included in scales that are supposed to assess different behavioral constructs or dimensions of adjustment. These scales are often assumed to be applicable to childen generally.

Another nomothetic approach involves contrasted or between-groups comparisons (e.g., Hops, 1983). Groups of different types of children identified via clinical judgments are compared via behavioral rating, checklist, or direct observation measures to identify differences among them. Behaviors showing differences are assumed to underlie differences related to group membership and can be collected together to form scales.

Assumptions underlying nomothetic approaches to the development and application of assessment instruments pose some difficulties when the instruments are applied in the individual case. First, because nomothetic research paradigms assume individual differences within groups account for less variance than those between groups, intra- and intersubject variability is treated as error variance. When parameters of performance are specific to individuals and their significant others, overlooking both forms of variance can miss opportunities to identify important controlling variables for individual cases. Further, focus on between-group differences in the organization of behavior sidesteps the possibility that interbehavioral relationships can be individual specific. The identification of these idiosyncratic clusters of behavior can contribute to the selection of maximally effective targets for intervention (Kara & Wahler, 1977; Kazdin, 1985; Voeltz & Evans, 1982; Wahler, 1975).

Second, nomothetic research often assumes group homogeneity. In the absence of data clearly describing characteristics of subject populations, it is difficult to determine the degree of similarity between a client and the research populations used to develop and validate particular devices (Barlow & Hersen, 1984; Wanlass & Prinz, 1982).

Third, norms are often used to establish the degree of deviance or competence in individuals. The extent to which an individual and his or her significant others are like the subjects included in the research would need to be determined in order to generalize the group findings to the individual case. There is some evidence to suggest the existence of "local norms" which vary among the small groups included in larger subject populations, however (cf. Edelbrock, 1984; Gottman, Gonso, & Schuler, 1976; Greenwood, Walker, Todd, & Hops, 1981; Sainato & Lyons, 1983). Establishing peer norms specifically for a given client would assure the selection of performance criteria that should be achieved within the same set of contingencies operative for both the client and his/her peers (Walker & Hops, 1976).

Finally, statistically significant differences between individuals or groups do not indicate that these differences are clinically significant. Clinical significance involves some type of social validation of change or difference, either via social comparison or subjective evaluation procedures (Kazdin, 1977; Wolf, 1978). Such consumer-based indices of differences are probably of greater value to clinicians and clients than are indices sensitive to almost imperceptible, but statistically demonstrable differences.

As we have suggested in an earlier section, idiographic behavioral assessment diverges from more global nomothetic assessment in several respects. First, idiographic procedures should be sensitive to between-individual variability *and* covariations of behavior within clients and their significant others. Second, client-specific targets for intervention should be the result of an inductive, empirical selection procedure which follows directly from assessment procedures involving judgments by or observations of significant others. Such procedures should result in identifiable client-specific criteria of competent performance which are maximally relevant for the client in settings of interest. Further, scores should be referenced to appropriate criteria, preferably those derived from the client's own social-interpersonal context. In so doing, emphasis should be on the clinical rather than statistical significance of discrepancies between the performance of the client and the client-specific criteria.

A general procedure that potentially meets the requirements outlined above has been proposed by Cone (1979, 1980) in his discussions of template matching. The approach is essentially an extension of the procedure first developed by Bem and his colleagues (Bem, 1982; 1983; Bem & Funder, 1978; Bem & Lord, 1979). In Cone's version of the template matching technique applied to children's social skills, the behavioral requirements of situations are conceptualized in terms of behaviors (template items) important to the social context of the particular client child. Behaviors most characteristic of exemplary performers (i.e., competent peers) in that context are identified. They are collected into templates against which the client is compared. Discrepancies between the client's repertoire and the template indicate targets for intervention.

Examples of Template Matching in Assessing Social Skills

Template matching initially involves deriving a set of client and "expert" profiles or templates that are unique to clients and their significant others. In the research described here, peers produced these templates. We assumed that the judgments of significant social agents in the child's environment form a reasonable basis for the assessment of social skill (Hops & Finch, 1985). While peer assessments have a traditional place in the behavioral literature (cf. Coie, Dodge, & Coppotelli, 1982; Pekarik, Prinz, Liebert, Weintraub, & Neale, 1976; Tuddenham, 1951), little work has been done to explore the reliability and validity of peer assessments obtained on a local or small group basis. Because of their central role in the procedures to be described, we examined these characteristics.

The first investigation addressed the reliability and discriminative validity of templates and client descriptions generated by a group of classroom peers. Twenty-two fourth-grade students in one classroom were interviewed on two occasions eight weeks apart. Each child was asked to identify the three students with whom s/he would most and least like to play at school. After the positive and negative peer nominations were completed, each child described all classmates using a peer assessment checklist that contained the names of all children in the class as columns and 28 specific social behaviors as rows. Half of the items were from the literature on children's social behavior. The others included behavior that might occur in classrooms but that had not appeared as targetted social skills in the literature (e.g., "Puts things away carefully"). From the peer nomination and checklist data it was possible to develop descriptions of children with whom each subject did and did not want to play. Descriptions of most accepted and rejected children were also obtained.

We first examined the temporal consistency of the descriptions provided by the children. For the three classmembers with whom each person most wanted to play, the mean number of times an item was used to describe them was correlated across assessment occasions for the class as a whole. The resulting correlation of .96 ($p < .001$) showed that children described their friends comparably at different times. The temporal consistency of subject's descriptions of children with whom they did *not* wish to play was not as high ($r = .58$, $p < .001$) suggesting more variability in descriptions of rejected children across time. Inspection of the peer nomination data on a rater-by-rater basis indicated that children consistently selected the same children as friends across time but were less consistent when identifying rejected peers. It is possible that children's descriptions of rejected peers varied across time because the children being described also varied. It is also possible that raters had less interaction with rejected children and therefore less experience on which to base the ratings.

The latter explanation seems contradicted by our finding that peer descriptions of social behaviors for the four most positively nominated children (two males, two females) and the two most rejected children (one male, one female) were highly consistent across time. The mean number of times each of the eight items was used by the class at Times 1 and 2 resulted in correlations of .92 and .95 for male and female highly accepted children, respectively, and .93 and .72 for male and female rejected students, respectively.

The descriptions of these two types of peers can be viewed as "local" norms. To examine discriminative validity, we correlated item use to describe most accepted peers with item use to describe rejected classmates. No relationship was found. Further, when the description of each most rejected child was compared to descriptions of the two most accepted same-sex peers, low and nonsignificant correlations were obtained (−.18 and −.34 for males and .06 and .03 for females at Times 1 and 2, respectively). Thus, a specific classroom group can generate stable and discriminating descriptions of peers who differ in terms of social acceptance in that group.

Taking the analyses further, we were interested in the extent to which a subset of the classroom group would be consistent and discriminating in their descriptions of other children. For this analysis we identified four child "experts" using two criteria: (1) the experts (two males and two females) were those children receiving the highest number of positive nominations from their peers, no negative nominations from same-sex peers, and relatively few negative nominations from peers of the opposite sex; (2) the experts were chosen by two "client" children as "desired playmates" (peers with whom the clients wished to play at school). For this analysis, "client" children were defined as the male and female receiving the most negative peer nominations and no positive nominations. The first criterion for selecting experts was based on research evidence suggesting that children with high social status can determine the norms or frame of reference of peers most readily (Putallaz & Gottman, 1981). The second criterion assured us that our informants were significant others of the client children, i.e., persons with whom the clients wished to play. Three of the four experts met both of these criteria.

The male client selected one male and one female expert as desired playmates. The female client chose both females. A second male expert who did not meet both criteria was used to permit comparisons of templates and client descriptions generated by male and female expert pairs. Peer status for the experts and clients remained constant in that the number and type of nominations were generally comparable from Time 1 to Time 2. A minor exception involved one female expert who received fewer negative nominations from male peers at Time 2 compared to Time 1. Experts' status as significant others (desired playmates) for the clients also remained constant over time.

As with the local norms, we examined the temporal consistency of the descriptions of the three selected friends for each expert by correlating item use at Times 1 and 2. The correlations ranged from .63 to .81 (mean = .71, all $p < .001$). Experts' descriptions of the male and female client children were less temporally consistent. Phi coefficients of item use by each expert to describe clients at Times 1 and 2 ranged from −.03 to .60 (absolute value of the mean = .25). We also explored the degree to which pairs of experts converged in terms of item use to describe their friends and same-sex clients. Correlations of item use when describing three friends were .63 and .73 for males and .56 and .39 for females at Times 1 and 2, respectively. These moderate levels would be expected because, although each expert consistently chose the same children as friends, pairs of experts chose different children. Interexpert correlations of item use when describing clients of the same sex were .50 and .04 for males and −.22 and −.16 for females at Times 1 and 2, respectively.

Individual informants were consistent with themselves when using a checklist to generate templates. However, three of four experts did not use the checklist consistently to describe clients across time. One possible explanation for the poor reliability of informants' descriptions of clients was suggested by interactional data collected concurrently during this study. Observed informants did not play with the clients. Therefore, they had limited opportunity to sample the behavior of those children. In contrast, informants did play with the children they described as best friends. This play history may have contributed to the differential stability of template descriptions for accepted over rejected peers.

In summary, these early findings suggest that 4th grade classroom peers as a group can be consistent and discriminating in their use of checklist items. Individual children were also consistent when describing their friends. However, templates generated by same-sex experts were only moderately comparable. Individual children used fewer descriptors and were more variable when describing specific clients across time. Experts might be a potential source of template profiles (i.e., descriptions of children with whom they like to play) but they may be less useful as sources of descriptive information about client children for purposes of template matching.

Encouraged by these results we next sought to improve the reliability of individual informants and to make the procedure even more inductive. A larger pool of descriptors was included to sample a wider range of critical social behaviors. We chose a Q-sort and rank ordering procedure for interviewing informants that required more discriminating decisions than were required by the checklist used previously.

Specifically, valued social behaviors were identified by individual elementary school children from a 50-item pool of social behaviors. These selected template behaviors were then manipulated in a multiple-baseline across subjects design to answer the following questions: (1) Does a child informant, when asked to use a Q-sort procedure to describe a valued peer, consistently select the same behaviors from a broad pool of items? (Intrasubject consistency). (2) Do same-age, same-sex children differ from one another in terms of the behaviors they identify as most valued in their friends? (Intersubject consistency). (3) When specific behaviors identified via a Q-sort procedure are systematically manipulated, are increases in frequency relative to baseline associated with increases in peer ratings and interactive behaviors? (Experimental validity).

During the first phase, four volunteer elementary-school third- and fourth-grade girls participated as paid subjects. All subjects were described by their classroom teachers as average or above in terms of popularity.

Three home interviews were conducted over a ten-day period with each child. The children described a best friend in terms of 50 behavioral descriptors (25 positive and 25 negative items), that were derived from the social skills literature and from previous interviews with other elementary school students. Each child sorted descriptors into piles labeled "very much like my friend" and "not like my friend." Items in the "not like my friend" pile were eliminated, and sorting continued until ten items remained. Each child then rank ordered the ten-item set in terms of how well an item described her friend. The three highest ranked descriptors in each child's set were identified as the template for that child.

Intrasubject consistency of item use was assessed by comparing the template obtained from each child on the three different occasions. Consistency between sets was computed using simple percent agreement values. Thus, if Items 12 and 25 fell into one child's three-item template set at Times 2 and 3, agreement would be 66%. For Subject 1 a mean of 78% (range 66–100%) was obtained. For Subjects 2 and 3 mean agreement was consistently 66% and 100%, respectively, at Times 1, 2, and 3. For Subject 4 mean agreement was 44% (range = 33–66%). Subject 4 included the same two of three items in template sets generated at Times 2 and 3 (agreement = 66%), however, seeming to become more consistent over time.

Intersubject consistency was examined by calculating percent agreement for template sets generated by pairs of subjects. Percent agreement scores were computed between girls at Times 1, 2, and 3 in the same manner as described above for the assessment of intrasubject consistency. Three of the subjects shared one or two items in their template sets when dyadic comparisons were made. At Time 1, agreement on item inclusion in the template sets of the four subjects was fairly comparable (mean agreement at Time 1 = 56%, range = 33–66%). At Times 2 and 3, one subject diverged from the others in terms of items she included in her template sets. Therefore, mean agreement among all subjects at Times 2 and 3 dropped to 28% (range = 0–66%). If the divergent subject is excluded from the analysis for Times 2 and 3, mean agreement for the other three subjects is 46% (range = 33–66%).

Thus, the template generation procedure highlighted between-subject differences as well as similarities in terms of behavioral preferences. Individual children can select behaviors to generate templates consistently when using a Q-sort and rank order procedure. There was less consistency between than within subjects. Nonetheless, three of the four subjects were comparable in terms of items they considered to be critical in their friends (i.e., "Shares," "Says nice things to me, compliments," and "Says I did well, praises").

In the second phase, a multiple-baseline across subjects design was used to assess the experimental validity of the template behaviors identified in the first phase. The three behaviors (shares, compliments, and praises) were manipulated in two child confederates. Subject-confederate dyads played together for several ten-minute play sessions. Systematically produced changes in the frequencies of the template behaviors constituted the independent variable. Ratings obtained from subjects and observational data obtained from videotapes of subject-confederate play sessions constituted the dependent variables.

The four girls from the first phase participated as subjects in play sessions with two fraternal twin third-grade confederates. The confederates, who were not previously acquainted with the subjects were trained to enact one of two roles in the play sessions. In the "social neutral" role (baseline condition), confederates oriented toward, smiled at, talked to, and remained in proximity with the subjects. They did not perform any template behaviors in the social neutral role. In the template role (experimental condition), confederates performed cued template behaviors, which they were free to "fit" into the stream of ongoing interaction with their respective subjects. In the experimental condition, confederates increased the frequency of each template behavior at least 200–300% per session over baseline. The impact of manipulations of the template behaviors was assessed with sociometric ratings and observations of interactive behavior.

Ratings of the likeability of the confederates by the subjects generally increased from baseline to the experimental condition. The increase was not statistically significant, however, possibly due to a ceiling effect in the baseline condition. Furthermore, rating increases were obtained for only three of four subjects. Thus, exposure to preferred behaviors in confederates did not improve subjective evaluations of confederates by the subjects in every case.

The template behaviors had several effects on the observed behavior of the subjects, however. Interactive behavior for subjects and confederates increased over baseline levels. Subjects performed more template behaviors in the experimental condition, indicating reciprocation of the specific behaviors generated by the confederates. Subjects responded more frequently to template-behavior initiations than to other types of initiations used by confederates.

Taken together, the two investigations of informant-based template matching support the psychometric acceptability of using checklist procedures to generate templates with third- and fourth-grade children. The Q-sort and rank ordering procedure is useful and psychometrically acceptable if individual informants are to be interviewed to identify critical social behaviors. Further, it appears that three of the individual children we interviewed extensively in Study 2 identified behaviors which were important antecedents for their own behavior in interactions with a peer confederate. These behaviors were also effective antecedents for a fourth subject who included those items in her ten-item sets across time but did not consistently include them in her template sets.

Children in Studies 1 and 2 used different sets of behaviors to describe their friends. Two of three template behaviors in Study 2 had also been included in the 28-item checklist used in Study 1. It is interesting to note that the three items most highly associated with peer nominations by the class and informants in Study 1 were not selected by subjects in Study 2. One might speculate the differences in preferred behaviors identified as most critical by different groups of subjects may have been the result of between-classroom differences, not just a function of the checklist vs. Q-sort format. This would support the radical behavioral argument for an idiographic approach.

Further research efforts in the area of social competence might explore the comparability of templates generated at different ages, by different sexes, and in different classroom settings. As Putallaz (1982) points out, if generic and local norm social skills exist, it would be useful to know which are which when selecting targets for individual children. Our finding of only moderate overlap in items selected by individual children argues for the further exploration of child-specific templates as well.

Greenwood et al., (1981) provided a normative description of social interaction within a large sample of 17 preschools, 29 classrooms, and 461 children. Classroom means varied in terms of number of interactions per minute, variability which they attributed to class differences such as locality, size, physical space, and program structure. Their findings support the existence of local norms within classrooms, at least in preschool settings and indirectly provide a rationale for assessing interactional norms for peer groups specific to client children referred for low interaction rates or social withdrawal.

Our first study showed that children as a group used many fewer descriptors to describe the most rejected children than to describe popular children. A Q-sort procedure such as that used in Study 2 might lead to better descriptions from peers of children with whom they do not have much interaction. It is possible, however, that peer informants who do not interact with a client cannot provide useful client descriptions. It might be necessary to interview someone who knows the child well, such as siblings or other family members who have experience observing the client in social situations with peers. Care will be necessary, however, less the integrity of the template matching strategem be violated. A basic assumption of the approach is that the most important targets for change will be those most relevant to the social context in which the client is having problems. If inadequate peer interactions is the area of concern, peers would seem the most relevant persons to provide descriptions. The comparative validity of different sources for client descriptions is in need of careful study.

In a related vein, research as to the treatment validity of behaviors identified by matching client descriptions against a locally derived template also should be investigated. Few investigations have compared the relative effectiveness of interventions involving targets identified via different assessment procedures. A treatment study that compares the effects of changing targets identified via template procedures and nomothetic approaches would certainly be a logical next step in this area.

Future Development of Template Matching Procedures

We have proposed that assessment procedures should involve accurate and sensitive transduction of behavior. While results of systematic manipulations of template behaviors in Study 2 indirectly support the accuracy of subjects' *selection* of specific behaviors, we have not examined the accuracy of our measures per se. Informants' reports of behavior occurring more frequently need to be compared with direct observation and other criteria, for example.

The use of the verbal behavior of children's peers to formulate templates in the present research was a convenient means of beginning work in this area. It is likely that templates might be more satisfactorily composed of specific motor behavior directly observed in appropriate social contexts. For example, rather than ask children to describe what their best friends do, one could observe the friends and determine their behavior directly. Performance criteria or behavioral templates identified via direct observation have also been proposed by others (e.g., Strain, Odom, & McConnell, 1984).

In closely related research Matson (1981) described an assessment procedure that targeted child and peer-specific levels of avoidance and withdrawal behavior for three excessively fearful children. Teachers identified a classroom peer who was not fearful of "safe" strangers for each subject. Thus, an "expert" peer was identified for each subject against whom the clients could be compared. Both clients and "expert" peers were then assessed in a series of situations in which they were in contact with designated "safe" unfamiliar adults. Levels of self-reported fear, speaking to the stranger, and approach toward the stranger were assessed for each client-expert pair separately. The assessment procedures identified criterion levels for each subject on the target behaviors. Criterion levels varied from subject to subject as a function of the performance of the expert peer. Using this assessment procedure, Matson was able to match client performance to that of more appropriate peers during treatment and found treatment effects were maintained at six-month follow-up.

Similarly, Carden-Smith and Fowler (1983) identified and assessed four mainstreamed exceptional children and five normal classmates to determine the degree to which the children differed in terms of rate and form of behavior problems in school. The exceptional child whose behavior most closely approximated that of the normal peers continued to receive services in a regular classroom on follow-up. The three exceptional children who differed from normal peers were later placed in self-contained classrooms. Both of these studies (and there are others) show the value of defining performance criteria on the basis of local norms.

CONCLUSION

After rejecting the trait logic, reliance on norms, use of classical psychometric concepts, and hypothetico-deductive, nomothetic models of contemporary child behavioral assessment the case was made for a more "radical" approach. We have argued for a perspective that takes behavior as its subject matter, studies it from a natural science perspective, is inductive, idiographic, criterion-referenced, and views the accuracy of its instruments as their principal criterion of adequacy. Using template matching as an example, we showed that target behaviors idiosyncratic to specific children could be identified reliably using informants who were part of the child's own social context. Moreover, we showed that individual informants, while stable in their production of relevant behaviors over time, showed only moderate agreement as to what should constitute the relevant set. Thus, peers who are part of one child's social context will not necessarily value the same behaviors as peers who are members of another child's social context. Selecting target behaviors from a pool of items available from the group-based, nomothetic research literature might have minimal to no relevance for individual client children.

That the template matching approach has some experimental validity was also shown. By systematically increasing template behaviors over baseline rates in confederates, increased interaction between subject children and confederates was produced.

These early findings support the value of pursuing inductive, idiographic, criterion-referenced template matching approaches further. What are needed now, are studies of the comparability of informant-based and direct observation-based template generation procedures, and the usefulness of different sources of descriptive information about the client child. The extension of idiographic assessment strategies such as template matching into other areas of child behavior is also needed.

For example, development of templates of "good" and "poor" performers in different medical programs (e.g., insulin administration, dyalysis programs) might be developed. Profiles of incoming patients could be developed and compared against the templates for each program in order to place patients in programs with the greatest likelihood of success. In a related vein, profiles of exceptional children in special education preschool programs could be developed. These could be compared to profiles of successful children in receiving classrooms into which target children might be placed.

Ideally, idiographic assessment procedures such as template matching offer a means to make client-specific intervention decisions. Data-based and inductively driven approaches to assessment of individual children such as these will make a significant and unique contribution to the area of behavioral assessment in general, and to assessment of children in particular.

REFERENCES

Abikoff, H., Gittelman, R., & Klein, D. F. (1980). Classroom observation code for hyperactive children: A replication of validity. *Journal of Consulting and Clinical Psychology, 48,* 555–565.

Abikoff, H., Gittelman-Klein, R., & Klein, D. F. (1977). Validation of a classroom observation code for hyperactive children. *Journal of Consulting and Clinical Psychology, 45,* 772–783.

Achenbach, T. M., & Edelbrock, C. S. (1978). The classification of child psychopathology and analysis of empirical efforts. *Psychological Bulletin, 85,* 1275–1301.

Allport, G. W. (1937). *Personality: A psychological interpretation.* New York: Holt.

Barlow, D. H. (Ed.), (1981). *Behavioral assessment of adult disorders.* New York: Guilford Press.

Barlow, D. H., & Hersen, M. (1984). *Single case experimental designs: Strategies for studying behavior change* (2nd ed.). New York: Pergamon Press.

Barrett, B. H., Johnston, J. M., & Pennypacker, H. S. (1986). Behavior: Its units, dimensions, and measurement. In S. C. Hayes & R. O. Nelson (Eds.), *The conceptual foundations of behavioral assessment.* New York: Guilford Press.

Bem, D. J. (1982). Assessing situations by assessing persons. In D. Magnusson (Ed.), *Toward a psychology of situations: An interactional perspective.* Hillsdale, NJ: Erlbaum.

Bem, D. J. (1983). Further deja vu in the search for cross-situational consistency: A response to Mischel and Peake. *Psychological Review, 90,* 390–393.

Bem, D. J., & Funder, D. C. (1978). Predicting more of the people more of the time: Assessing the personality of situations. *Psychological Review, 85,* 485–501.

Bem, D. J., & Lord, C. G. (1979). Template matching: A proposal for probing the ecological validity of experimental settings in social psychology. *Journal of Personality and Social Psychology, 37,* 833–846.

Bijou, S. W., Peterson, R. F., Harris, F. R., Allen, K. E., & Johnston, M. S. (1969). Methodology for experimental studies of young children in natural settings. *The Psychological Record, 19,* 177–210.

Bornstein, P. H., Bornstein, M. T., & Dawson, B. (1984). Integrated assessment and treatment. In T. H. Ollendick & M. Hersen (Eds.), *Child behavioral assessment* (pp. 223–243). New York: Pergamon.

Bugental, B. D., Whalen, C. K., & Henker, B. (1977). Causal attributions of hyperactive children and motivational assumptions of two behavior-change approaches: Evidence for an interactionist position. *Child Development, 48,* 874–884.

Carden-Smith, L. K., & Fowler, S. A. (1983). An assessment of student and teacher behavior in treatment and mainstreamed classes for preschool and kindergarten. *Analysis and Intervention in Developmental Disabilities, 3,* 35–57.

Chandler, M. J. (1973). Egocentrism and antisocial behavior: The assessment and training of social perspective-taking skills. *Developmental Psychology,* 9, 326–337.

Ciminero, A. R., & Drabman, R. S. (1977). Current developments in the behavioral assessment of children. In B. B. Lahey & A. E. Kazdin (Eds.), *Advances in clinical child psychology, Vol. 1* (pp. 47–82). New York: Plenum.

Ciminero, A. R., Calhoun, K. S., & Adams, H. E. (Eds.), (1977). *Handbook of behavioral assessment.* New York: Wiley.

Coie, J. D., Dodge, K. A., & Coppotelli, H. (1982). Dimensions and types of social status: A cross-age perspective. *Developmental Psychology, 4,* 557–570.

Cone, J. D. (1977). The relevance of reliability and validity for behavioral assessment. *Behavior Therapy, 8,* 411–426.

Cone, J. D. (1978). The behavioral assessment grid (BAG): A conceptual framework and a taxonomy. *Behavior Therapy, 9,* 882–888.

Cone, J. D. (1979, March). *Inductive behavioral assessment.* Paper presented at the meeting of the Southeastern Psychological Association, New Orleans.

Cone, J. D. (1980, November). *Template matching procedures for idiographic behavioral assessment.* Paper presented at the meeting of the Association for the Advancement of Behavior Therapy, New York.

Cone, J. D. (1981). Psychometric considerations. In M. Hersen & A. S. Bellack (Eds.), *Behavioral assessment: A practical handbook* (2nd ed.). New York: Pergamon.

Cone, J. D., & Hawkins, R. P. (1977). *Behavioral assessment: New directions in clinical psychology.* New York: Brunner/Mazel.

Craighead, W. E., Kennedy, R. E., Smucker, R., & Peterson, A. (1984). *Maladaptive cognitive coping styles in childhood and adolescent depression and conduct disorders.* Paper presented at the meeting of the Association for the Advancement of Behavior Therapy, Philadelphia, PA, November.

Edelbrock, C. (1984). Developmental considerations. In T. H. Ollendick & M. Hersen (Eds.), *Child behavioral assessment* (pp. 20–37). New York: Pergamon.

Finch, Jr., A. J., & Rogers, T. R. (1984). Self-report instruments. In T. H. Ollendick & M. Hersen (Eds.), *Child behavioral assessment* (pp. 106–123). New York: Pergamon.

Foster, S. L., & Cone, J. D. (1980). Current issues in direct observation. *Behavioral Assessment, 2,* 313–338.

Gottman, J. M., Gonso, J., & Schuler, P. (1976). Teaching social skills to isolated children. *Journal of Abnormal Child Psychology, 4,* 179–197.

Greenwood, C. R., Walker, H. M., Todd, N. M., & Hops, H. (1981). Normative and descriptive analysis of preschool freeplay social interaction rates. *Journal of Pediatric Psychology, 6,* 343–367.

Haynes, S. N. (1978). *Principles of behavioral assessment.* New York: Gardner Press.

Haynes, S. N., & Kerns, R. D. (1979). Validation of a behavioral observation system. *Journal of Consulting and Clinical Psychology, 47,* 397–400.

Hersen, M., & Bellack, A. S. (1976). *Behavioral assessment: A practical handbook.* New York: Pergamon.

Hersen, M., & Bellack, A. S. (1981). *Behavioral assessment: A practical handbook* (2nd ed.). New York: Pergamon.

Hops, H. (1983). Children's social competence and skill: Current research practices and future directions. *Behavior Therapy, 14,* 3–18.

Hops, H., & Finch, M. (1985). Social competence and skill: A reassessment. In B. H. Schneider, K. H. Rubin, & J. Ledingham (Eds.), *Peer relationships and social skills in childhood: Issues in assessment and training.* New York: Springer-Verlag.

Johnson, S. M., & Bolstad, O. D. (1973). Methodological issues in naturalistic observation: Some problems and solutions for field research. In L. A. Hamerlynck, L. C. Handy, & E. J. Mash (Eds.), *Behavior change: Methodology, concepts, and practice.* Campaign, IL: Research Press.

Johnston, J. M., & Pennypacker, H. S. (1980). *Strategies and tactics of human behavior research.* Hillsdale, NJ: Lawrence Erlbaum Associates.

Kanfer, F. H., & Saslow, G. (1969). Behavioral diagnosis. In C. M. Franks (Ed.), *Behavior therapy: Appraisal and status* (pp. 417–444). New York: McGraw-Hill.

Kara, A., & Wahler, R. G. (1977). Organizational features of a young child's behaviors. *Journal of Experimental Child Psychology, 24,* 24–39.

Kazdin, A. E. (1977). Assessing the clinical or applied importance of behavior change through social validation. *Behavior Modification, 1,* 427–451.

Kazdin, A. E. (1985). Selection of target behaviors: The relationship of the treatment focus to clinical dysfunction. *Behavioral Assessment, 7,* 33–47.

Kendall, P. C., Pelligrini, D. S., & Urbain, E. S. (1981). Approaches to assessment for cognitive behavioral intervention with children. In P. C. Kendall & S. D. Hollon (Eds.), *Assessment standards for cognitive behavioral intervention.* New York: Academic Press.

Kovacs, M. (1978). *Children's Depression Inventory.* Unpublished manuscript, Univ. of Pittsburgh, Pittsburgh.

Kovacs, M., & Beck, A. T. (1977). An empirical-clinical approach toward a definition of childhood depression. In J. G. Schulterbrandt & A. Raskin (Eds.), *Depression in childhood: Diagnosis, treatment, and conceptual models.* New York: Raven Press.

Lang, P. J. (1971). The application of psychophysiological methods to the study of psychotherapy and behavior modification. In A. E. Bergin & S. L. Garfield (Eds.), *Handbook of psychotherapy and behavior change.* New York: John Wiley.

Lazarus, A. A. (1973). Multimodal behavior therapy: Treating the "Basic Id." *Journal of Nervous and Mental Disease, 156,* 404–411.

Leitenberg, H. (1978). Review of *Behavioral assessment: A practical handbook.* M. Hersen & A. S. Bellack (Eds.). *Behavior Modification, 2,* 137–139.

Leitenberg, H., Gross, J., Peterson, J., & Rosen, J. C. (1984). Analysis of an anxiety model and the process of change during exposure plus response prevention treatment of bulimia nervosa. *Behavior Therapy, 15,* 3–20.

Lindsley, O. R. (1964). Direct measurement and prosthesis of retarded behavior. *Journal of Education, 147,* 62–81.

MacDonald, M. L. (1978). Measuring assertion: A model and method. *Behavior Therapy, 9,* 889–899.

Martyna, W. (1979). Beyond "liberation": From resistance to responsibility, a context for the sexes. *The Graduate Review est,* 1–5.

Mash, E. J., & Terdal, L. G. (Eds.), (1981). *Behavioral assessment of childhood disorders.* New York: Guilford.

Matson, J. L. (1981). Assessment and treatment of clinical fears in mentally retarded children. *Journal of Applied Behavior Analysis, 4,* 287–294.

McFall, R. M. (1977). Analogue methods in behavioral assessment: Issues and prospects. In J. D. Cone & R. P. Hawkins (Eds.), *Behavioral assessment: New directions in clinical psychology.* New York: Brunner/Mazel.

Mischel, W. (1968). *Personality and assessment.* New York: Wiley.

Nay, W. R. (1979). *Multimethod clinical assessment.* New York: Gardner Press.

Odom, J. V., Nelson, R. O., & Wein, K. S. (1978). The differential effectiveness of five treatment procedures on three response systems in a snake phobia analog study. *Behavior Therapy, 9,* 936–942.

Ollendick, T. H., Elliott, W. R., & Matson, J. L. (1980). Locus of control as related to effectiveness in a behavior modification program for juvenile delinquents. *Journal of Behavior Therapy and Experimental Psychiatry, 11,* 259–262.

Ollendick, T. H., & Hersen, M. (Eds.), (1984). *Child behavioral assessment.* New York: Pergamon Press.

Paul, G. L., & Bernstein, D. A. (1973). *Anxiety and clinical problems: Systematic desensitization and related techniques.* Morristown, NJ: General Learning Press.

Pekarik, E. G., Prinz, R. J., Liebert, D. E., Weintraub, S., & Neale, J. M. (1976). The Pupil Evaluation Inventory: A sociometric technique for assessing childrens' social behavior. *Journal of Abnormal Child Psychology, 4,* 83–97.

Peterson, D. R. (1968). *The clinical study of social behavior.* New York: Appleton-Century-Crofts.

Putallaz, M. (1982, November). *The importance of the peer group for successful intervention.* Paper presented at the annual meeting of the Association for the Advancement of Behavior Therapy, Los Angeles, CA.

Putallaz, M., & Gottman, J. M. (1981). An interactional model of children's entry into peer groups. *Child Development, 52,* 986–994.

Rich, A. R., & Schroeder, H. E. (1976). Research issues in assertiveness training. *Psychological Bulletin, 83,* 1081–1096.

Robinson, E. A., Eyberg, S. M., & Ross, A. W. (1980). The standardization of an inventory of child conduct problem behaviors. *Journal of Clinical Child Psychology, 9,* 22–28.

Sainato, D. M., & Lyons, S. R. (1983, December). *A descriptive analysis of the requirements for independent performance in handicapped and nonhandicapped preschool classrooms.* Paper presented at the Handicapped Children's Early Education Projects Conference, Washington, DC.

Shapiro, M. B. (1961). The single case in fundamental clinical psychological research. *British Journal of Medical Psychology, 34,* 255–262.

Skinner, B. F. (1938). *The behavior of organisms.* New York: Appleton-Century-Crofts.

Skinner, B. F. (1950). Are theories of learning necessary? *Psychological Review, 57,* 193–216.

Skinner, B. F. (1957). *Verbal behavior.* New York: Appleton-Century-Crofts.

Strain, P. S., Odom, S. L., & McConnell, S. (1984). Promoting social reciprocity of exceptional children: Identification, target behavior selection, and intervention. *Remedial and Special Eduation, 5,* 21–28.

Tuddenham, R. D. (1951). Studies in reputation: III. Correlates of popularity among elementary school children. *Journal of Educational Psychology, 42,* 257–276.

Vernon, P. E. (1964). *Personality assessment: A critical survey.* New York: Wiley.

Voeltz, L. M., & Evans, I. M. (1982). The assessment of behavioral interrelationships in child behavior therapy. *Behavioral Assessment, 4,* 131–165.

Wahler, R. G. (1975). Some structural aspects of deviant child behavior. *Journal of Applied Behavior Analysis, 8,* 27–42.

Wahler, R. G., & Fox, III, J. J. (1980). Solitary toy play and time out: A family treatment package for aggressive and oppositional children. *Journal of Applied Behavior Analysis, 13,* 23–39.

Walker, H. M., & Hops, H. (1976). Use of normative peer data as a standard for evaluating classroom treatment effects. *Journal of Applied Behavior Analysis, 9,* 159–168.

Wanlass, R. L., & Prinz, R. J. (1982). Methodological issues in conceptualizing and treating childhood isolation. *Psychological Bulletin, 82,* 39–55.

Weintraub, S., Prinz, R. J., & Neale, J. M. (1978). Peer evaluations of the competence of children vulnerable to psychopathology. *Journal of Abnormal Child Psychology, 6,* 461–473.

Wiggins, J. S. (1973). *Personality and prediction: Principles of personality assessment.* Reading, MA: Addison-Wesley.

Wolf, M. M. (1978). Social validity: The case for subjective measurement or how applied behavior analysis is finding its heart. *Journal of Applied Behavior Analysis, 11,* 202–214.

Wolpe, J. (1969). *The practice of behavior therapy.* New York: Pergamon.

Wolpe, J., & Lazarus, A. A. (1966). *Behavior therapy techniques.* New York: Pergamon.

ASSESSMENT OF FAMILY INTERACTION WITH THE RESPONSE-CLASS MATRIX

Eric J. Mash and Russell A. Barkley

ABSTRACT

This chapter describes the development and use of the Response-Class Matrix (RCM), a standardized observational recording procedure designed for the behavioral assessment of dyadic family interactions in a structured clinic or playroom setting. Findings are presented from studies that have used the RCM to assess parent-child interactions in clinical populations of hyperactive (ADDH), physically abused, developmentally delayed and language delayed children, and in populations of normal children from intact and separated families. Characteristic patterns of play and task interactions are described for each population, as are relationships between observed interactions and other family characteristics such as stress, self-esteem and perceptions of the child. The RCM has also been employed as an

Advances in Behavioral Assessment of Children and Families, Vol. 2, pgs. 29–67.
Editor: Ronald J. Prinz

ISBN: 0-89232-481-3

outcome measure, and in this regard is sensitive to the effects of stimulant medications and behavior therapy.

It is concluded that standardized behavioral assessment procedures, such as the RCM, are important if the comparability of findings across settings and studies is to be increased. Unlike most idiosyncratic behavioral assessments which have tended to confound method and setting variance, standardized behavioral assessments are especially sensitive to the effects of settings as moderator variables. It is recommended that the development of standardized behavior categories and assessment situations, which can be used in an idiographic and flexible manner for specific populations, should help to increase the frequency and reliability of use for observational procedures in applied contexts. The importance of computer technologies in achieving this goal is discussed.

INTRODUCTION

The Response-Class Matrix (RCM) (Mash, Terdal, & Anderson, 1973, 1981) is a standardized observational recording procedure, designed for the behavioral assessment of dyadic social interaction in a structured clinic or laboratory playroom setting. Although the RCM was originally developed to evaluate mother-child interactions in populations of young developmentally delayed and handicapped children, its use has since been extended to encompass a broad range of populations and situations. As a result, the RCM is one of a few behavioral assessment observational procedures that has received continuing and widespread use.

This chapter describes the development and uses of the RCM, and highlights general issues pertinent to behavioral assessment of children and families. Findings from studies that have utilized the RCM are selectively reviewed.

While direct observation has been touted as the hallmark of behavioral assessment with children and families (Kent & Foster, 1977; Mash & Terdal, 1976; 1981), only a few observational systems have received frequent use (see for example, Forehand & McMahon, 1981; Mash, Terdal, & Anderson, 1973; Reid, 1978; Wahler, House, & Stambaugh, 1976), and there has been little uniformity of use or standardization of observation measures. Unlike traditional psychometric approaches to child assessment where certain tests have gained widespread popularity (e.g., Palmer, 1970), observational measures in behavioral assessment have evolved in an idiosyncratic and mostly unsystematic fashion. Lack of standardization has resulted from theoretical emphasis on individualized assessments in behavior therapy and practical constraints associated with utilizing observational procedures in an applied context (Nelson, 1983).

From a theoretical perspective, a fundamental theme underlying the growth and development of behavioral assessment has been the emphasis on idiographic analysis (Baer, Wolf, & Risley, 1968; Kanfer & Hagerman, in press; Kanfer & Saslow, 1965; Mash & Terdal, 1974). In the context of idiographic analysis, standardized assessments such as the RCM might be insufficiently sensitive to the unique behavioral characteristics of individuals assessed in clinical settings. However, the use of standardized observational measures does not preclude the possibility of idiographic analysis, particularly for individuals exhibiting a class of problems. This is especially true when measures are standardized in the context of situations which have either predicted or established importance for the individual(s) involved. The approach being advocated here is that standardized assessments may be used in an idiographic manner with individuals exhibiting similar problems in similar situations (Lambert, Christensen, & DeJulio, 1983). In contrast to the proliferation of idiosyncratic and non-standardized behavioral assessments, this approach enhances the comparability of findings across settings and studies, makes situation-appropriate measures more accessible to clinicians and researchers, and establishes the strengths and limitations of an assessment procedure for specific functions and purposes.

One of the more perplexing aspects of behavioral assessment with children and families has been the discrepancy between idealized descriptions of observational procedures and their actual use in practice. Behavioral clinicians use observational assessments infrequently because such procedures are seen as impractical and time consuming in applied settings, unacceptable to clients, and frequently unavailable (Ford & Kendall, 1979).

The lack of readily available standardized measures has contributed to the cost ineffectiveness of behavioral observation, for on each occasion the clinician is faced anew with the problem of what to observe, how to observe, how often to observe, where to observe, and how to interpret the findings.

Standardized procedures that can effectively deal with a circumscribed set of questions, however, provide greater clinical utility for behavioral assessors. The fact that the procedure has known properties and an existing data base to reference is likely to increase efficiency and yield. The RCM findings to be reviewed in this chapter are intended to illustrate this point.

RESPONSE-CLASS MATRIX

Early Use and Development

The RCM code was designed to be used in two structured observation situations, play and assigned tasks, which were intended to elicit behaviors relevant for describing the relationships between handicapped children and their mothers. Observations were conducted in a clinical-training facility during a one-day multi-disciplinary evaluation that resulted in situational constraints. To elicit interactions of interest in a brief period of time, a structured observation situation was chosen over less structured naturalistic observation. Since the observed population exhibited a relatively restricted and homogeneous behavioral repertoire, behavioral codes were selected to reflect classes of responses rather than behaviors highly specific to individual children. Since the observers were clinical staff with limited time commitment, the code was simplified in procedure and content so that a minimal training time was needed for reliable use. The procedural format minimizes the time needed for data summarization, provides easy data access and a graphic display of results, and thus permits immediate feedback to parents and trainees.

The early considerations in the development of the RCM are important in understanding its strengths and weaknesses. As shall be described in this chapter, since the time of its initial development the RCM has been shaped, molded, modified, and bent to accommodate to the specific theoretical concerns and practical needs of individual investigators. These adaptations have involved extensions to nondevelopmentally delayed and nonhandicapped populations including hyperactive children (Cunningham & Barkley, 1979), language delayed children (Cunningham, Siegel, & Offord, 1985), abused children (Mash, Johnston, & Kovitz, 1983), nonproblem children (Mash & Johnston, 1982), and children in divorcing families (Copeland, in press). The RCM has also been used with a much wider age range of children than originally proposed including infants as young as eight months (Hanzlik & Stevenson, 1984) and youngsters as old as twelve years (Cunningham, Siegel, & Offord, 1985). Finally, the study of family interaction with the RCM has gone beyond the mother-child sub-system to include fathers (Tallmadge & Barkley, 1983), peers (Siegel, Cunningham, & van der Spuy, 1985), and siblings (Tarver-Behring, Barkley, & Karlsson, 1985).

Description of the RCM

Categories

In its original and most frequently used format, the RCM consists of two coding sheets. The Child's Consequent Behavior Record includes six child behaviors (compliance, independent play, question, negative, interaction and no response) that could occur in response to seven possible antecedent behaviors (command, command-question, question, praise, negative, interaction, no response) on the part of another member of the interaction dyad, usually the mother. The Mother's Consequent Behavior Record includes the same seven maternal behaviors, that could occur in response to six child antecedent behaviors (compliance, independent play, competing behavior, negative, interaction and no response). The RCM categories are intended to be exhaustive in describing the interaction, and complete category definitions are included in the RCM coding manual (see Mash & Johnston, 1979a; Mash et al., 1981, pp. 419–436).

The inclusion of particular categories in any code system reflects some a priori hypotheses regarding what behaviors are important to assess. In the case of the RCM the categories were consistent with a behaviorally-oriented approach to working with developmentally delayed children, and were selected to reflect the interactional features of maternal control, reward strategies, and responsiveness to the child, and child compliance, play and responsivity to the mother. It was presumed, and confirmed in later studies (Cunningham, Reuler, Blackwell, & Deck, 1981; Terdal, Jackson, & Garner, 1976), that the deficits of developmentally delayed children would necessitate greater maternal directiveness thereby highlighting issues of control and compliance. Assessment of the mother and child's play and interactional initiative are assumed to be important both as an index of the mother's involvement with her child and in relation to the possible implications of play for the child's cognitive development.

Mash & Johnston (1979a) made minor category changes for their work with hyperactive and abused children. "Question" was added as an antecedent child behavior category, and the single "interaction" category for both mother and child was sub-divided into two categories: verbal interaction and non-verbal interaction.

Copeland (in press) modified the RCM categories for her work with recently separated mothers and their children. "Offers help" and "asks for help" were added as antecedent and consequent categories for both mother and child (these would have previously been coded as either interaction or question). A category labelled "strategy" was added to describe suggestions "implying flexibility in responding, requiring a series of responses, a nonspecific response, or statements of a general rule about the situation."

Other RCM category modifications have been made for the study of peer (Cunningham, Siegel, & Offord, 1985) and sibling interactions (Mash & Johnston, 1983a). Independent play was divided into verbal and non-verbal categories and the category "looks at" was added. Categories of special interest have been added to the matrix by other investigators such as Hanzlik and Stevenson (1984) who coded "physical contact" in a study of developmentally delayed infants.

Coding Procedures

One RCM observer records the behavior of the child as an antecedent and the mother's behavior as a consequent while the second observer records the mother's antecedent behavior and the child's consequent behavior. Each 10-second observation is followed by a 5-second period for marking the matrix cell corresponding to the dyadic interchange for the immediately preceeding interval. With this system, dyadic interchanges are being sampled as events.

This coding procedure permits a description not only of the overall proportions of each behavior category as reflected in the row and column totals of each matrix, but also of the specific reactions of mother or child to specific antecedent behaviors of the other. Such reactions are reflected as conditional probabilities, for example, the likelihood that a mother would respond positively to her child's compliance. Assessment of these dyadic sequences is useful for evaluating behavioral treatment goals (e.g., reducing a child's competing behavior) and additionally engender social learning hypotheses regarding the changes needed in order to achieve these goals (e.g., reduce the probability of mother's interaction and positive response to competing behavior).

Summary Measures

A variety of summary measures from the RCM have been reported (e.g., Cunningham & Barkley, 1979), and an even larger number have been presented in unpublished manuals (e.g., Mash & Johnston, 1979b report over a hundred such measures). The summary measures have generally been of two general classes with sub-types within each class. The first class includes (a) row and column totals reflecting overall proportions of occurrence for each antecedent and consequent behavior category for mother and child, and (b) combinations of row or column totals which reflect supra-ordinate categories such as maternal control (e.g., commands + command-questions + questions). These types of measures have been the ones most often reported in published papers, reflecting their higher frequencies of occurrence.

Some caution should be exercised in interpreting the supra-ordinate categories across investigations since overall categories such as "positive interaction" may be based upon the inclusion of different individual categories from study to study. Greater consistency across studies would be helpful, and in fact this point applies to the use of observational codes in behavioral assessment more generally.

The second class of summary measures includes (a) conditional probabilities based upon individual cell totals divided by row or column totals, e.g., 10 complies to 20 commands yields a 50 percent compliance-to-command ratio; and (b) a wide range of cell combinations designed to reflect specific interactional occurrences. In general, these types of summary measures are likely to be less stable than the overall measures just described since they are based upon lower frequencies of behavior and may be highly susceptible to minor variations in behavioral occurrence. Care must be exercised in interpreting these latter summary measures, especially when describing low frequency behaviors.

Observer Training

In the initial report by Mash, Terdal and Anderson (1973) interobserver agreement measures ranging from 78% to 96% following 4 to 6 hours of training were reported. Later reports (Mash & Johnston, 1982; Cunningham & Barkley, 1979) have provided estimates of training time ranging from twenty to twenty-five hours. The recommended training protocol typically involves a sequence in which observers read the coding manual, participate in a discussion of the code system, practice coding from written material to ensure basic understanding of the codes and their definitions, code and discuss videotaped parent-child interactions in groups, code videotapes individually until a satifactory level of reliability has been achieved, and participate in weekly booster sessions involving practice and discussion. Training is sequenced such that later stages come to increasingly resemble the conditions under which observations are to be made (see Garner & Jackson, 1978, and Mash & Johnston, 1979c for examples of semi-standardized training protocols).

Observer Reliability

The most frequently reported reliability measure has been inter-observer agreement taken as the number of agreements regarding category occurrence/number of agreements on occurrence + number of disagreements on occurrence. Some investigators (Hanzlik & Stevenson, 1984) have employed Kappa in order to appropriately correct for chance agreements. While reported agreement measures have usually exceeded 80%, there have been minor variations from study to study in the methods used to calculate observer reliabilities. Measures have been reported for overall agreement, agreement for individual behavior categories, and less frequently, for cell-by-cell agreement. It should be pointed out that such cell-by-cell agreement measures are appropriate for the summary measures based on conditional probabilities which have been reported in a number of studies to be described. Many studies with the matrix have depended on a "core group" of highly experienced observers. In some cases reliability during training or during weekly booster sessions has been taken as an estimate of reliability for the data being reported. There is a need for investigators utilizing the RCM to be more consistent in the manner in which reliability is calculated and reported and it is especially important that the agreement measures being presented are consistent with the types of dependent measures being described.

SITUATIONAL CONTEXT

Observational Analogues

With few exceptions (e.g., Hanzlik & Stevenson, 1984; Mash, Lazere, Terdal, & Garner, 1973) the RCM has been used in clinic or laboratory playroom situations designed to elicit behaviors that are relevant for understanding the dyad being assessed. Such structured observational assessments (Hughes & Haynes, 1978) have a long but often maligned history of use in behavioral assessment. Although presumed to be more efficient and convenient than observations in the natural environment, analogue observation raises the issue of generalizability to behavior in the home. The early work of Tharp and Wetzel (1969) and the highly influential work of Patterson (1982) directed behavioral assessors to the natural environment as the appropriate arena for assessment and as the primary source for criterion validity data. Reported correlations between analogue and home assessments have, in general, been discouragingly low (Mash, 1984).

However, behavior in the natural environment need not be the only criterion for the validity of an observational analogue. Home observations as they are typically carried out are ambiguous with respect to situational context. Since such observations likely represent an averaging of behaviors across situations, the signal to noise ratio is high and larger samples of behavior are needed to adequately sample interactions of interest. Although some home observations are made under specifiable stimulus conditions such as "having dinner," or "going to bed," the family is often artificially placed together at a time and place conforming to observational demands. Additionally, the constraints that accompany home observations such as observers in the living room, all family members present, no television, and limited telephone use, raise serious questions regarding the veridicality of such measures of interaction as a "truer" sample than that obtained in a clinic-playroom analogue.

The validity and utility of assessments with the RCM have been demonstrated. The interactions of mothers and children with particular types of problems are differentiable from those shown by nonproblem and other-problem comparison groups. Behavior in the observational analogue has been shown to correlate with other important criterion measures such as maternal characteristics (e.g., stress and self-esteem) and child characteristics (e.g., reactions to divorce), and to be sensitive to the effects of both behavioral and psychopharmocological interventions. Playroom observations have been helpful for generating clinical hypotheses concerning appropriate targets for treatment in therapy and in this regard have demonstrated their validity for treatment (Mash, 1979, 1985; Nelson, 1983).

Play and Command Situations

The two most frequently used analogues with the RCM have been "free play" and "command" situations. Free play instructions to parents have shown a good deal of consistency across studies, although even here there do appear to be minor variations in instructions both within and across investigators. Mothers are typically instructed to "play with your child as you would at home, as you would when you have some free time." Instructions to mothers have varied with respect to emphasis on availability of toys (e.g., "play with these toys" vs. "toys are available") and designation of free time (e.g., "you've got your work done and you have some free time," "you have some time with nothing else going on," or "you don't expect to be interrupted"). Findings in the play situation appear to be robust for these minor instructional variations.

Toys available in the play situations differed across clinics and laboratories primarily as a reflection of the need to include age-appropriate materials. However, other variations have reflected the introduction of specific play materials (e.g., etch-a-sketch) designed to prompt interactive rather than independent activity, and in this regard could produce interactions quite different from those where such toys were not available.

The command analogue places demands on mother and child, with the goal of prompting behavior related to control issues, compliance, and strategies of reward and punishment. The types of tasks have varied considerably as a result of age-appropriateness of materials and requests, and from a sensitivity to specific population characteristics (e.g., such as instructions to perform self-help skills in retarded children versus requests to delay performance in an impulsive group). RCM findings appear to be robust in relation to most variations, but some task instructions may seriously interfere with the comparability of studies. For example, it was initially thought that having a hyperactive child play independently in a particular location while his mother was busy with another task would constitute an ecologically valid situation. Contrary to expectation, the hyperactive children either complied totally or not at all, resulting in a bimodal distribution with large variability and spuriously high rates of compliance for many hyperactive children. Furthermore this manipulation dramatically reduced the overall amount of dyadic interaction.

Situational Variations

Several situational factors could influence RCM assessment findings. Almost all studies have utilized a sequence of situations going from play to task interactions. This sequence is presumed to reflect a natural occurrence in that the first task is often to pick up the toys that have been played with, and the transition from free play to task provides a contrast that reinforces the more demanding nature of the task situation. However, it is conceivable that behaviors during task situations that do not involve this type of transition might be quite different.

The size of the playroom has varied across studies, with room sizes ranging from 6½′ × 13′ (Pollard, Ward, & Barkley, 1984) to 18′ × 19′ (Mash & Johnston, 1982). For hyperactive children, variations in room size may influence observed behavior, since studies in which smaller playrooms have been used have typically shown fewer between group differences for play situations. Although this issue has not been investigated systematically, it may be easier for mothers to exert direct control over play interactions with hyperactive children when they are in close proximity. On the other hand, a large room can increase activity in young hyperactive children and thereby necessitate a greater use of prohibitions, directions and control in order to redirect the child to play materials. This illustrates the potentially important interactions between the assessment procedure and population characteristics, since it is conceivable that playroom size may not be nearly as salient in structuring play interactions for normal and retarded children as for hyperactives.

Another factor that has varied across studies has been the duration of play and command situations. The modal time has been 15 minutes in free play and 15 minutes of tasks but times have ranged from 10 to 30 minutes, with command situations longer than play. The length of a particular session is frequently confounded with content, such that longer task sessions may include either a greater number or variety of tasks (e.g., ones that take longer to complete). Longer sessions providing larger behavior samples will enhance reliability of findings. However, 15 minutes provides a sample of behavior that is consistent across studies and brief enough to be well-suited to the clinical context.

In most studies, mother-child interactions were videotaped for later coding. The degree of obtrusiveness varied greatly with video cameras placed in the room or concealed. In the latter case, mothers always give informed consent whereas children may not always be aware of being videotaped. Although instructions to mothers are often explicit, the instructional set for the child is often unclear or left up to the mother. Apart from the potential differential reactivity effects associated with varying degrees of awareness of being observed, it has also been our general impression that reactivity effects may vary across populations. Hyperactive children in our playroom, when compared with normals, seemed to get caught up in the immediacy of the situation, e.g., toys, commands, furniture, and seemed far less concerned about such ''meta-features'' of the situation as what was behind the one-way glass and who was watching them. Lower socioeconomic status abusive mothers seemed much less inhibited in the playroom situation (e.g., some mothers spontaneously prepared their lunch during the assessment), in contrast with middle class mothers of nonproblem children for whom social desirability was more of a factor. These subjective impressions highlight the possibility that the reactivity of our measures may not be the same across populations and this issue requires further attention and study.

REVIEW OF FINDINGS

Studies of Clinical and Normal Groups of Children

Investigators interested in the interaction patterns in clinical and normal groups of children have employed the RCM to evaluate social exchanges between parents and children, teachers and children, and between the clinical groups of children and their siblings or normal peers. In many cases, the results of these investigations have helped to increase our understanding of the clinical conditions of interest.

Attention Deficit Disorder with Hyperactivity

Hyperactivity, or Attention Deficit Disorder with Hyperactivity (APA, 1980: DSM-III), is one of the most prevalent psychopathological disorders of childhood, occurring in approximately 3 to 5 percent of the childhood populations and accounting for as much as 40% of the referrals to child guidance centers in the United States. The initial studies of ADDH children with the RCM (Cunningham & Barkley, 1979) extended the previous findings of Campbell (1973, 1975) who had compared groups of hyperactive children with groups of learning disabled, impulsive, and normal children, and found differences between these groups in their mother-child interactions during structured task situations.

Cunningham and Barkley (1979) observed the interactions of 20 ADDH and 20 normal boys with their mothers during a 15-minute free play and a 15-minute structured task situation using the RCM. Results for play indicated that mothers of ADDH boys initiated fewer social interactions and their children were less likely to respond to initiations. While the ADDH and normal boys did not differ in overall percentage of interaction, the mothers of ADDH boys were less likely to respond to interactions when they occurred. No differences were noted in the degree to which ADDH and normal boys played independently of their mothers, but mothers of ADDH boys showed less attention and encouragement of their children's play and were more likely to react with commands and controlling behavior than were mothers of normal boys. Even in the play situation, mothers of ADDH boys provided twice as many commands to their children as mothers of normal boys, and the ADDH boys were significantly less compliant with these commands than normals. The RCM revealed a pattern of reciprocal unresponsiveness in the general social interactions of ADDH children and their mothers during play. Mothers of ADDH boys spent considerably more time than normals attempting to manage and control the behavior of their children even during independent child play. The hyperactive boys were much less likely than normals to respond compliantly to the mothers' management efforts.

In the task situation, hyperactive boys were considerably less compliant with commands and spent a significant amount of time engaged in activities that competed with compliance (e.g., off-task). These boys sustained their compliance for shorter periods of time than normal boys, perhaps as a result of short attention span or impulsivity. The mothers of ADDH boys gave significantly more commands and directions, and provided less approval and praise for child compliance.

A series of subsequent studies replicated these findings with ADDH children (Barkley, Karlsson, & Pollard, 1985; Befera & Barkley, 1985; Mash & Johnston, 1982; Tallmadge & Barkley, 1983) and with children described as having low self-control on Kendall and Wilcox's (1979) *Self-Control Rating Scale* (Copeland, 1985b). However, the differences between ADDH and normal children for free play interactions have been inconsistent across studies. Some studies (Mash & Johnston, 1982; Befera & Barkley, 1985) found greater directiveness by mothers of ADDH children in free play while another (Barkley, Karlsson, & Pollard, 1985) did not. Nevertheless, reliable and significant differences between ADDH and normal dyads emerge during the task situation, especially concerning decreased compliance by the ADDH children and heightened use of commands by their mothers.

Mash and Johnston (1982) compared groups of younger (mean age 4.1 years) and older (mean age 8.4 years) ADDH children with normal children. Results generally supported those of Cunningham and Barkley (1979) and also revealed significant age-related differences for many of the interaction categories. Younger ADDH boys were significantly more deviant from normals than were older ADDH boys, although even in the older group there were heightened rates of maternal commands and child noncompliance. Results suggested that ADDH children more clearly approximated normal levels of social behavior in their mother-child interactions with increasing age but despite these improvements, they continue to remain identifiable from normals in important interaction categories (e.g., compliance to commands).

Barkley, Karlsson and Pollard (1985) also evaluated age-related changes in the mother-child interactions of ADDH boys. A total of 60 ADDH and 60 normal boys were evenly subdivided into 5 age levels (years 5, 6, 7, 8, and 9) and observed with their mothers in play and task situations. The findings are shown in Tables 1 and 2. In play, the findings were similar to previous studies in showing that mothers of ADDH boys initiated fewer interactions with their

Table 1. Measures of Mother-Child Interactions During Free Play for Hyperactive and Normal Children

	Hyperactive		*Normal*		
Measure	*Mean*	*S.D.*	*Mean*	*S.D.*	*Group Signif.*
Mother Initiates Interaction	55.6	13.6	65.3	16.8	.01
Child Responds	85.9	8.7	87.8	10.8	—
Mother Questions	9.6	5.2	10.1	7.4	—
Child Responds	84.9	16.2	89.8	17.4	—
Mother's No Response	25.7	14.3	21.0	17.6	—
Mother Rewards	1.6	3.5	1.2	2.6	—
Mother Commands	6.6	5.9	3.2	3.3	.01
Child Complies	81.6	27.6	90.8	21.7	.05
Mother Negative	0.7	2.0	1.7	12.9	—
Child Initiates Interaction	71.3	15.4	79.5	19.5	.01
Mother Responds	82.8	8.2	88.7	6.9	.01
Child's No Response	0.4	1.0	2.2	12.5	—
Child Negative	0.6	1.5	0.1	0.7	.01
Child's Independent Play	26.4	15.3	17.6	16.1	.01
Mother Attends to Play	32.1	19.0	36.0	28.0	—
Mother Controls Play	7.3	10.5	2.4	7.8	.05

Note: All measures are percent occurrence or conditional percentages (indented). From "Effects of age on the mother-child interactions of ADDH and normal boys" by R. A. Barkley, J. Karlsson, & S. Pollard, 1985, *Journal of Abnormal Child Psychology, 13*. Reprinted with permission from Plenum Publishing Corp.

Table 2. Measures of Mother-Child Interactions During the Task Period for Hyperactive and Normal Children

Measure	*Hyperactive*		*Normal*		*Group signif.*	*Age signif.*
	Mean	*S.D.*	*Mean*	*S.D.*		
Mother Initiates Interaction	42.4	15.9	58.1	13.7	.01	.05
Mother Questions	6.4	7.3	7.0	5.7	—	—
Mother's No Response	15.5	10.4	12.9	9.2	—	.01
Mother Rewards	2.6	3.0	2.8	3.0	—	—
Mother Commands	32.1	16.1	19.8	10.9	.01	.01
Child Complies	90.0	12.1	96.8	6.0	.01	.05
Mother Negative	2.4	2.8	0.5	0.9	.01	—
Mean Compliance Duration	4.4	2.9	6.9	3.7	.01	.01
Child Compliance	89.1	9.2	97.8	3.3	.01	—
Mother Responds Positively	52.9	16.0	69.6	11.7	.01	.05
Mother Responds Negatively	32.8	15.9	19.1	10.1	.01	.01
Child Competing or Off-Task Behavior	8.5	7.6	1.7	2.8	.01	—
Mother Responds Positively	27.7	30.6	31.6	43.5	—	—
Mother Responds Negatively	49.9	37.1	23.6	39.1	.01	.05
Child Negative	1.9	3.1	0.6	1.4	.05	—

Note: From "Effects of age on the mother-child interactions of ADDH and normal boys" by R. A. Barkley, J. Karlsson, & S. Pollard, 1985, *Journal of Abnormal Child Psychology, 13*. Reprinted with permission from Plenum Publishing Corp.

children, were less responsive to their children's interactions, gave more commands, and responded with greater control over their children's play than mothers of normal boys. The ADDH boys exhibited significantly less compliance, more negative behavior, more independent play, and fewer interactions with their mothers than normal boys. Unlike the Mash and Johnston (1982) study, no age-related changes in interactions were found for free play. During the task period, however, significant effects of age were noted in addition to the commonly observed group differences. Older boys in both groups were better able to sustain their compliance to commands than younger boys. The mothers of older boys gave fewer commands, responded with less control over their compliance, and spent more time observing their children than mothers of younger boys. In contrast to the Mash and Johnston (1982) study, no significant group by age interactions were observed, suggesting that the older ADDH boys remained as deviant from normals as the younger ADDH boys despite age related improvements in both groups.

Although normal, biologically unrelated groups of children have been commonly employed as comparison groups in this area of research, another useful control group is the normal siblings of ADDH children. A sibling comparison reduces differences in the characteristics of mothers that might affect interaction patterns, and any emerging differences are more attributable to child characteristics.

Tarver-Behring, Barkley, and Karlsson (1985) compared a small group (N = 16) of ADDH boys with their normal male siblings during mother-child interactions. Few differences between ADDH boys and their brothers were found. ADDH boys were less compliant and more "off-task" during both play and tasks than the siblings, and their mothers provided less praise and approval to the ADDH boys for compliance. In spite of the small number of observed behavioral differences, mothers rated their ADDH boys as significantly more problematic across a variety of home situations relative to their brothers.

Mash and Johnston (1980) also observed mother-child and mother-sibling interactions in 22 matched pairs of four to nine year old ADDH and normal siblings. Consistent with the Tarver-Behring et al. (1985) study, few hyperactive-sibling differences were found for mother-child interactions, although the mother-child interactions of both ADDH children and their siblings differed from nonrelative normals. During play, ADDH children and siblings initiated less interaction with their mothers, were less responsive to questions, and engaged in more independent play than either normal children or their siblings. Mothers of ADDH children were more negative to both the target child and sibling and more likely to ignore the children when they were playing independently. Both the ADDH child and sibling exhibited higher rates of noncompliant and negative behavior during the task situation and were especially likely to respond negatively to questions from their mothers when compared with normals. During the task situation, mothers were significantly less responsive to both the ADDH child and his sibling when compared with normals. In spite of the fact that both the ADDH child and sibling exhibited equivalent rates of negative and noncompliant behavior during the task situation, mothers tended to be more directive and negative with their ADDH child. Such a finding is consistent with the notion that one child in the family may be singled out as deviant in spite of the high correlations that have been shown to exist between problem-child and sibling rates of deviancy (e.g., Arnold, Levine, & Patterson, 1975).

The RCM has also proven useful in the study of sex differences in the mother-child interactions of ADDH relative to normal children. Befera and Barkley (1985) studied 30 ADDH and 30 normal children subdivided equally by sex in play and task situations. Few group differences were found during play interactions and these were significantly associated with child gender. In general, ADDH boys differed from normal boys for compliance and the extent of maternal interactions received, while ADDH girls did not differ in this respect from normals. In contrast to prior research, few group differences were noted during the task situation, perhaps because the tasks differed from those employed previously. Only one difference for ADDH boys and girls emerged: mothers provided more praise to ADDH boys than to ADDH girls or normal children.

Tallmadge and Barkley (1983) used the RCM to study possible interactional differences between fathers versus mothers of ADDH children. The play and task interactions of 18 ADDH boys were contrasted with those of 18 normal boys. As expected, substantial differences were found between ADDH and normal boys, particularly during task performance. However, mothers and fathers in both groups did not differ in their interaction patterns. Yet, within the ADDH group, mothers faced more noncompliance with their boys than did fathers. This finding is consistent with the clinical complaints of many mothers that ADDH boys behave better for fathers (Barkley, 1981) and with behavior problem checklist ratings showing that fathers perceive their ADDH children as less problematic (Mash & Johnston, 1983b).

As noted previously, several studies have modified the RCM for coding the interactions of ADDH children with other children as opposed to their parents. Mash and Johnston (1983a) observed the interactions of ADDH children with their siblings and contrasted these patterns with those of normal child-sibling dyads. The dyads were observed while playing with the mother absent and in a mother-supervised task situation. There were virtually no differences between the target children and their siblings during either situation or in either group. However, relative to normal child-sibling dyads, ADDH child-sibling dyads had higher levels of negative behavior or conflict. The highest levels of conflict were observed in dyads with a younger ADDH child.

Cunningham, Siegel and Offord (1985) also used a modified version of the RCM to study the social interactions of ADDH children with their peers. Interactions were observed during free play, a cooperative task, and a simulated school situation where each child worked on assigned academic tasks independently at separate desks. Three age groups of children were used: 4–6 year-olds, 7–9 year-olds, and 10–12 year-olds. A number of situation and age-related differences between the groups were noted. Like the studies of parent-child interactions of ADDH children, the modified version of the RCM used here proved quite sensitive to differences in the social interaction patterns between ADDH and normal children.

To summarize, the RCM has been employed extensively in studies of social interactions in ADDH children. These studies have identified abnormal interaction patterns in these children, when contrasted with normals, for mother-child, father-child, child-sibling, and child-peer interactions. Such studies have greatly expanded the empirical data base available on these patterns where previously, clinical reports served as the primary sources of information. The matrix format of the RCM has also permitted the analysis of contingent relationships in these social exchanges providing a clearer picture of the antecedent and consequent events surrounding the social behavior of ADDH children. These studies also indicate that the types and amount of interaction are greatly influenced by the situation in which the interactions occurred (e.g., free play vs. task).

Physically Abused Children

The RCM has also been employed to investigate the mother-child interactions of physically abused and nonabused children (Mash, Johnston, & Kovitz, 1983). Eighteen abused and 18 nonabused children were observed with their mothers in a clinic playroom situation during play and task conditions. Parents completed the Child Behavior Checklist (Achenbach & Edelbrock, 1983) as a measure of perceived behavioral problems in their children. Abusive mothers rated their children as more problematic on both the Internalizing and Externalizing dimensions of the checklist. These profiles were quite similar to those seen in ADDH children. However, the abused children did not differ significantly from normals in their behavior during either play or task conditions. Yet, the mothers of the abused children gave more commands and directions to their children during the task period.

The results of this study suggest that physically abusive mothers perceive their children as deviant and react to them as such despite the absence of observed behavioral differences from normal children. Prior descriptions of abused children based only on parent interviews and ratings have suggested that such children may differ from normals in their behavior. Such discrepant findings support the need for multi-method behavioral assessments, including direct observation, in both research and clinical studies of parent-child interaction.

Developmentally Delayed Children

In one of the earlier studies to utilize the RCM with clinically referred children, Terdal, Jackson, and Garner (1976) studied the mother-child interactions of 42 developmentally delayed (DD) children and 40 normal children during play and task. Each group was further subdivided into three age levels based upon mental age. Within the DD group, these were children with a mean mental age of 2-years 1-month (low mental age group), 4 years (middle group), and 6-years 9-months (high group), respectively. The normal children were subdivided into three similar age groupings based upon their chronological age.

In free play, children in the low DD group were less responsive to the interactions and questions of their mothers and were less compliant to commands than children in other two DD groups or the normal children. The lack of child responsiveness to mothers was not related to a similar lack of responsiveness by the mothers to their DD children as the mothers in the low DD group were just as responsive to the interactions of their children as mothers in the other DD and normal groups. In the task setting, the low DD children were again less compliant and less able to sustain their compliance to commands than were the other groups. The mothers of these low DD children gave more commands to their children than mothers in the other DD and normal groups.

It is interesting to note that the low DD children were similar to ADDH children in exhibiting less compliance to commands during play and tasks and less maintenance of compliance during tasks than normals. Mothers in both groups also gave more commands and directions relative to normals. These similarities suggest that the difficulties in the interactions of young DD children may stem more from delays in attention span, impulse control, and the regulation of activity levels than from intellectual retardation.

Hanzlik and Stevenson (1984) used the RCM with an added category of "physical contact" to compare the interactions of DD and DD with cerebral palsy infants with two groups of normal infants matched for either mental age or chronological age. The mean mental age for the DD and DD with cerebral palsy groups was approximately 12-months, and their corresponding mean chronological age was 21-months. Interactions were observed during a free play situation in the home. Mothers in both groups of DD infants were more directive than mothers of non-delayed infants and DD infants showed lower overall levels of behavior and less verbal interaction when compared with CA matched controls. Physical contact was more frequent for cerebral palsied infants and their mothers than for all other groups. These results are consistent with the Terdal et al. (1976) findings with respect to maternal directiveness and child nonresponsiveness, and extend these results to a population of younger children than those previously studied, and to interactions in the home. In addition, it was shown that the physical limitations imposed on the DD cerebral palsied children's interactions with their mothers were related to differences in mother-child interactions between the two DD groups. The cerebral palsied DD children showed less independent play and more physical contact, and their proximity to mothers was associated with higher levels of responsiveness when compared with DD infants without physical impairment.

Cunningham, et al. (1981) observed the parent-child interactions of 18 normal and 18 retarded children. The normal and retarded children were well matched on mental age, sex, and socioeconomic status. Each group of children was subdivided into low and high mental age levels (i.e., those below versus those above a mental age of 28-months). The retarded children initiated fewer social interactions, responded less to the social interactions initiated by their mothers, and spent more time engaged in play independent of their mothers than did the normals. The mothers of the retarded children were more directive during both play and task periods, were more controlling of their children's independent play, and were less likely to initiate interactions with their children than were mothers of normal children. Within the retarded group, mothers of higher mental age children were less responsive to their children's interactions than were those in the lower mental age group. Across both normal and retarded children, those with higher mental ages initiated more interactions, and were more compliant than children with lower mental ages. These findings are consistent with those of the Terdal et al. (1976) and Hanzlik and Stevenson (1984) studies. In general, mothers of retarded children spend a greater amount of time attempting to manage and control their children's behavior than do mothers of normal children who spend more of their time socializing with their children. With increasing mental age, the compliance and responsiveness of both groups of children improve.

Children of Divorced Parents

Anne Copeland at Boston University has conducted a series of studies describing the interactions of a nonclinical sample of divorced mothers and their children. Given the prevalence of divorce in North American society, concern has arisen over the manner in which divorce might affect children's psychological adjustment. An important aspect of this adjustment and of the family's general reorganization following divorce are the specific types of patterns of interactions between divorced parents and their children.

In one study (Copeland, in press), 61 children between 6- and 12-years whose parents had separated or divorced within the past year were observed interacting with their mothers in a clinic laboratory playroom during three conditions: (1) 10 minutes of free play with toys, (2) 10 minutes of a tower building with blocks task during which the child was blindfolded, and (3) 10 minutes of an art project. Several parent and child behavior categories were collapsed into more general ones due to the low frequency of occurrence for certain behaviors (e.g., question and interaction were now scored as a single category of interaction, commands and strategy were now scored as control, etc.). Children were compared by age (6 to 8 years vs. 9 to 12 years), gender, and length of time since parental separation (1 to 5 months vs. 6 to 12 months).

As in the studies of ADDH and DD children, a number of measures were related to the child's age. Younger children were more negative and their mothers gave more commands, provided more praise, and were more responsive to their children's interactions. Of greater interest, however, was the finding that age and length of parental separation yielded significant interaction effects for many of the dependent measures. In general, the mother-young child dyads were more positive toward each other with greater length of parental separation while the opposite was true of mother-older child dyads. Furthermore, as length of separation increased, the differences between the interaction patterns of mothers with younger versus older children diminished. However, the opposite was true of the younger and older children, whose behavior patterns were similar shortly after separation but were quite different with longer separations. No significant main effects related to the sex of the child were found. These findings indicate that families continue to experience reorganization of social interaction following parental separation and that the age of the child and the time since separation are significant variables affecting these patterns.

In a second study, employing data obtained from the same sample, Copeland (1985a) observed 56 children between 6- and 12-years of age interacting with their mothers who had been separated from 1 to 12 months. Results again indicated no main effects related to the child's sex. Separate analyses were then done in which each sex group was further subdivided on the basis of the amount of child behavior problems and illnesses. Mothers who rated their sons as having more behavior problems were more negative and directive toward them. However, no differences were found in the boys' observed behavior during the playroom tasks. Boys who had more illnesses were more interactive with their mothers and more responsive to their mothers' interactions than were those having fewer illnesses. In contrast, no differences were found between girls rated as having more versus fewer behavior problems in their mother-child interactions, and the findings for frequency of illness were the opposite of those for boys. Girls with more illnesses were less interactive with their mothers who were also less responsive. Results suggest that the number of child behavior problems and child illnesses affect the interaction patterns of mothers and children in divorced families but that these variables operate differently depending upon the sex of the child. Since control groups of mother-child dyads from nondivorced families were not employed in either of these studies, it is difficult to determine whether these interaction patterns are similar to those occurring in intact families.

Language Delayed Children

Cunningham, Siegel, van der Spuy and Bow (1985) observed the mother-child interactions of younger (28–50 months) and older (51–60 months) language delayed (LD) and normal boys in a play and task situation. During play, younger LD children interacted less frequently than older LD children or normals. In addition, both groups of LD children were less likely to re-initiate interaction and more likely to ignore their mothers following intervals of maternal non-interaction. No differences were observed between LD and normal children during the task situation. The only maternal behavior that differed between the LD and normal groups in either situation was a lower frequency of questions by mothers of LD children during the task situation. However, further analyses suggested a number of relationships between level of language comprehension and interactional behavior. Furthermore, within the LD group children who were rated as having more behavior problems were less compliant during play and tasks. The few significant differences between LD and normal mother-child interactions that were observed in this study suggests that the RCM may have limited utility with a general population of LD children. On the other hand, for LD children who are also experiencing behavior problems, the RCM may be useful in identifying important features of the interaction that may set the context for the expression of language difficulties.

In another study by the McMaster group, Siegel, Cunningham and van der Spuy (1985) observed the peer interactions of LD and normal preschool boys during play and structured task situations. Children were assigned to three dyadic groupings where: both children were LD, both children showed normal language, or the dyad was mixed with an LD and normal child. In mixed dyads, the normal children gave more commands during tasks and in both play and tasks asked more questions and were generally more dominant and controlling than their LD counterparts. There were fewer differences in the behavior of normal or LD children when matched with a child of similar language ability. During play and tasks, normal children were less likely to respond positively to the compliance of an LD versus normal social partner. In the task situation LD children were more likely to control and less likely to ignore interactions by an LD versus normal peer. In general, it would appear that the RCM may be sensitive to some of the dominance and control dimensions associated with peer interaction in children with differing levels of language ability.

Normal Children

Many of the studies described have included normal children for purposes of comparison. The use of the RCM with children of different ages and sexes has provided considerable normative information on parent-child interaction patterns. While the absolute levels of various social behaviors across studies can be expected to vary as a function of differences in the nature of the observation settings, the types of tasks parents and children were required to perform, and modifications to the categories of the RCM in several studies, there is surprising consistency in the patterns of observation. As such, the studies of normal children provide a rich source of normative interactional data which might be used for behavioral assessment in some of the ways described by Hartmann, Roper, and Bradford (1979) and Mash and Terdal (1981).

Studies of mothers interacting with their normal children, especially mother-son interactions, have been reported extensively (Barkley, Karlsson, & Pollard, 1985; Befera & Barkley, 1985; Cunningham & Barkley, 1979; Cunningham et al., 1981; Mash & Johnston, 1982; Tallmadge & Barkley, 1983) and will receive the greatest discussion here. During play situations with provided toys in which mothers are instructed to play with their children as they might do at home, maternal social behavior mostly consists of socializing in which few commands or directions are given and very little praise or reprimand is provided. The percentages of total social exchanges during free play in which mothers initiate such general "chatty" interactions toward their children range from 39.3 to 65.8 with most studies finding at least 50% of the interactions falling into this category. On more than 80% of these occasions, the children respond with general interactions or questions indicating a high degree of child responsivity. The next most common activity of normal mothers is to actively observe the play of their children without interference (coded as No Response). This accounts for approximately 11 to 21% of the observation intervals. The third most frequent type of maternal social behavior (which in some studies occurred more often than the No Response category) was asking questions, accounting for 10 to 25% of the social exchanges of normal mothers. Commensurate with the high degree of responsivity of the children to their mothers, the studies found that between 77 and 96% of these questions were answered. Commands and directions were rarely given by mothers during free play, accounting for only 1 to 13% of the interactions, with the highest amount occurring between mothers and very young children (mental age below 2.5 years). Even so, when commands were given, the children complied frequently and responded in the directed fashion to 73 to 90% of the commands. Mothers were likely to praise their children 1 to 3% of the time and to behave negatively toward them (reprimand, yell, punish) only about 1% of the time. In general, mothers of normal children behave quite pleasantly toward their children during play, often engaging their children with general, nondirective verbal statements or questions to which the children are quite responsive. Rates for commands, reprimands, and, surprisingly, praise are low.

Observed base rates of maternal behavior have certain implications for parent training in child behavior management skills. Several programs (Barkley, 1981; Forehand & McMahon, 1981) expressly instruct parents of behavior problem children to decrease their rates of questions to children and to increase their rates of praise and attention. The present review suggests that if this is done with the belief that this makes these parents more like those of normal children, such is not the case, as normal parents rarely use praise during play interactions and frequently use questions as a vehicle of social exchange. While such training may still be important for the benefit of the behavior problem child, it should probably not be promoted as an ultimate outcome measure presumed to "normalize" parent-child exchanges in problem dyads.

Normal children observed during play interactions apparently spend a majority of their time engaged in general social exchanges, conversation, and other nondisruptive behavior. Normal children initiate such general interactions approximately 54 to 79% of the time and, like the children themselves, their mothers prove highly responsive to these exchanges, reciprocating with general interactions of their own in 84 to 92 percent of these transactions. The second most frequent activity of normal children is to play independently of their mothers, which they do approximately 13 to 42% of the time. Mothers are likely to respond actively to such play with general comments, interaction, or other facilitating behavior 35 to 54 percent of the time, while intrusive attempts to control, redirect, or otherwise punish such play occur approximately 2 to 11% of the time. Outright negative, stubborn, or obstinate behavior by normal children was found to occur in fewer than 1% of the interactions.

Comparisons across studies for normal mother-child dyads in the task situations are more difficult to make given the diversity of tasks used. What is obvious, however, and not very surprising was a dramatic shift from the nondirective, conversational and play-oriented activity seen during play to a more directive, controlling, and task-oriented pattern of interactions. Although mothers initiated general interactions as much as 50% of the time, their rates of commands and directions increased up to 5 fold accounting for as much as 20 to

30% of their interactions. Normal children remained quite compliant, however, obeying over 80% of the requests immediately (average compliance was approximately 90%). Maternal rates of questioning and passive observation of their children declined, as might be expected given that more time was spent in directing the child's behavior. Levels of maternal negative behavior remained at their same very low rates (less than 1 to 2%) while the amount of praise given doubled over that for free play. Even then, however, praise constituted less than 4% of the mother's interactions. Yet, parents did use their attention contingently, responding positively to child compliance on approximately 40 to 70% of the occasions when it occurred and negatively on fewer than 20% of these occasions. Since the vast majority of the children's activity consisted of compliance, rates of independent play, questions, and general ''chatty'' interactions by the child decreased dramatically during task periods.

Overall, the changes in the patterns of mother-child interactions between free play and task reflect quite nicely the nature of the task demands between the two settings and how responsive both parent and child are to them. Rates of negative behavior by parent and child remain quite low and the impression left is one of a positive yet mission-oriented social exchange in which both participants continue to be responsive to each other as well as to the task demands now imposed upon them by the nature of the setting.

Those studies which have examined related variables for their influence on RCM interactions have found virtually no differences as a function of the sex of the child (Befera & Barkley, 1985) or of the parent (Tallmadge & Barkley, 1983). However, the effects of age have been quite noticeable where studied (Barkley, Karlsson, & Pollard, 1985; Cunningham et al., 1981; Mash & Johnston, 1982; Terdal et al., 1976). With increasing age, normal children during free play become more compliant, less negative, and may play more independently of their mothers. However, developmental changes are most noticeable in task situations. As child compliance increases with age, mothers reduce their amount of commands, reduce their control over compliance, decrease their negative behavior, and increase their time spent observing their child's compliance. The pattern is generally one of increasing child competence and self-control with age, resulting in a corresponding decrease in the need for parental direction and supervision.

Interaction and Collateral Data

The studies reviewed thus far highlight differences between populations of problem children, and children ''at risk'' for problems (children of divorce). Descriptively, they offer information regarding the quantity and quality of interactional difficulties in particular populations and suggest possible targets for treatment. As noted by Hughes and Haynes (1978), few structured observational assessments have examined the relationships between interactional behavior and specific attitudes, roles and values of the parent or child. However, a number of recent RCM studies have been concerned with this relationship between behavior in the observation analogue and other important parent and child characteristics. Interactional data may be viewed with regard to predictive (e.g., how well features of the mother-child interaction predict other characteristics) and criterion (e.g., how well other dimensions of the mother-child relationship predict interaction) validity. Although the nature of these correlations preclude causal analyses, the associations are of interest in suggesting clinical and research hypotheses. In this section, we selectively review some of the associations that have been found between RCM measures and other measures for each of the populations studied.

Attention Deficit Disorder with Hyperactivity

Mash and Johnston (1983b) found that mothers of ADDH children reported higher levels of parenting related stress and lower levels of self-esteem. The relationship between these parental perceptions and interactional behavior was examined by Mash and Johnston (1983c) for both play and command situations. Parental self-esteem, as reflected in the reported value and degree of comfort with the parenting role, was positively correlated with the amount of time mothers interacted with their hyperactive children during play. In contrast, parenting self-esteem as related to perceived skill and competence as a parent was positively related to the amount of control exerted by mothers during the task situation. Mothers reporting higher levels of situational and life stress were less interactive during play and more controlling during the task situation. Multiple regression analyses using child behavior in situ and maternal ratings as predictors of maternal behavior indicated that reports of maternal stress and self-esteem accounted for significant proportions of variance in maternal behavior during task but not play situations.

Within the broader context of behavioral assessment, these findings are a good illustration of how situational variation may serve to structure the interaction in unique ways. In a nondemanding and nonstructured play situation, mothers of hyperactive children may follow their children's lead during interaction. However, the demands of the task situation activate maternal interaction strategies that are influenced not only by their child's behavior in the situation but also by maternal attitudes and beliefs concerning their child. Such hypotheses are worthy of further study and it might be expected that the nature of these types of relationships will vary from population to population. For example, it may be that even in the context of play, mothers of developmentally delayed children will be guided more by internalized attitudes and self-perceptions (e.g., parents should be teachers for their delayed children) and less by their child's behavior. In fact, several studies (Cunningham et al., 1981; Terdal et al., 1976) have shown the interactional style of mothers of developmentally delayed children to be less flexible to changing situational demands, being quite similar in both play and command situations. With few exceptions, recent behavioral assessment studies relating maternal moods and cognitions to behavior have failed to qualify these relationships in terms of situational dimensions. Future studies would benefit from such analyses.

Physically Abused Children

Mash et al. (1983) found that physically abusive mothers reported higher levels of parenting related stress across all three dimensions of the Parenting Stress Index (Abidin, 1983), e.g., child characteristics, maternal characteristics, and life stress, when compared with a group of nonabusive mothers. Abusive mothers who reported higher levels of child-related and relationship-related stress were less responsive to their children during play and task situations and were less likely to praise their children during tasks. Abusive mothers who were more depressed and socially isolated asked fewer questions and were less negative during play, and were also less responsive and praising during the task situation. These findings are suggestive of a passive interactional style. Yet, depressed and socially isolated abusive mothers also tended to initiate more interactions with their children during play. It is possible that such mothers may turn toward their children as interactional partners as a substitute for the more mature adult relationships characteristic of less isolated parents. Finally, abusive mothers who reported more health problems tended to be more directive and less interactive with their children during the task situation. As was the case for the hyperactive population, the findings with abusive mothers indicate that factors outside the parent-child relationship may have indirect but important associations with how mothers interact with their children, and that these associations may vary with the types of situation in which interactions are assessed.

Developmentally Delayed Children

Cunningham et al. (1981) examined the relationship between RCM measures and the relative complexity of maternal and child speech in mixed groups of retarded and normal children with high (over 28 months) and low (under 28 months) mental ages. For both high and low mental age children the relative complexity of mothers' speech (mother's mean length of utterance in syllables/child's mean length of utterance of syllables) was greater for both children and mothers who were less responsive and interactive, and for mothers who gave more commands. A second language measure, the match between the mothers expressive speech and the child's comprehension skills was found to be inversely related to child responsiveness and the amount of mother and child interaction, and positively correlated with maternal directiveness in the low MA, group. In the high MA, group this measure was positively correlated with maternal use of questions. The authors conclude that "less responsive children may fail to provide adults with sufficient information as to the level of language they can comprehend. Adults consequently, may fail to adjust their language complexity accordingly, a response which is likely to contribute to the child's unresponsiveness to adult interactions and requests'' (p. 69).

Children of Divorced Parents

Copeland and her associates have carried out a number of studies with recently (less than 12 months) separated or divorced mothers of six to twelve year old boys and girls that have examined the relationship between aspects of the mother-child interaction and such things as maternal child-rearing attitudes, mood, self-esteem, reported physical symptoms, and post-separation adjustment. Employing the same sample described earlier, Copeland and Barenbaum (1983) observed 62 mother-child pairs in play and task situations, and found that maternal child-rearing attitudes of open expression (affection and communication) and hostility, as measured by Block's (1965) Child Rearing Practices Report, were correlated with several RCM summary measures for boys but not for girls. Mothers reporting higher levels of hostility were more nonresponsive to their sons during both play and structured task situations, and used less praise in the task situation. These mothers also had sons who were less interactive during play and more likely to respond negatively to their mothers interactions during structured tasks. Mothers reporting higher levels of communication and affection had sons who were more likely to initiate interaction, ask fewer questions, and less likely to respond negatively to their mothers' interaction.

These findings suggest (1) that the relationships between child-rearing attitudes and interaction in recently separated mothers may be moderated by the sex of their child, a finding which is consistent with other studies, (2) that negative child rearing attitudes may have greater cross-situational consistency since measures of hostility were more highly correlated with behavior for all situations, and (3) that positive child rearing attitudes may be more strongly associated with behavior during unstructured play situations.

Copeland, Eisenstein, and Reiner (1984) examined the relationship between children's reactions to divorce and interactional measures during play and task. Children of mothers who were less interactive during play reported greater feelings of guilt over their parents divorce. Children with more externalizing problems on the teacher-completed *Child Behavior Checklist* (Achenbach & Edelbrock, 1983) had mothers who were less interactive and more controlling during play. This latter finding is of interest since it is one of the few studies that has looked at the relationship between reports of behavior outside the home and mother-child interaction in the playroom.

Language Delayed Population

Cunningham, Siegel, van der Spuy, Clark, and Bow (1985) examined the relationships between parent-child interaction and measures of both child and maternal language for a population of two to six year old language delayed boys. Children with greater delays in language comprehension interacted less frequently, re-initiated fewer interactions, were less responsive to questions, and less compliant to commands during free play. Mothers of children with greater delays in language comprehension also gave more commands to their children. In contrast to these associations between interactional behavior and language comprehension, no significant relationships between mother or child interaction and measures of the child's language expression were found.

In an analysis similar to that by Cunningham et al. (1981) with retarded children, the relationship between the discrepancy in mother's and child's language complexity and interactional measures was examined. This discrepency was greatest in dyads where children exhibited lower rates of questions and interactions, less responsiveness to maternal interaction and questions, and where mothers gave more commands. It would appear that language delayed children are providing insufficient feedback to permit mothers to adjust their speech accordingly, and that less calibrated language during interaction may also induce a less responsive interactional style.

This study also found that language delayed children were perceived by their mothers as more problematic than non-delayed children, and that maternal reports of behavior problems on the Preschool Behavior Questionnaire (Behar & Stringfield, 1974) were inversely related to the amount of compliance by the child during both free play and task situations. This finding is interesting in that it again illustrates the population-specific nature of many of the relationships being described. In the language delayed and ADDH groups there was good correspondence between mothers perceptions of their children as problematic and their child's actual behavior. In contrast, in the study with abusive mothers (Mash et al., 1983) there was little correspondence between maternal perceptions and child behavior. The important issue then is not whether maternal reports are a reliable index of the child's problem, but rather what is the nature of the relationship between various types of maternal perceptions and behavior under specifiable conditions in particular populations of children and parents?

TREATMENT OUTCOME STUDIES

Populations

Several studies have evaluated the effects of interventions for clinic-referred children using various forms of the RCM. The effects of stimulant medication with ADDH children, and of parent training in child management skills for parents of ADDH, behavior problem, and DD children have been studied.

Treatment Studies with ADDH Children

Stimulant drugs, particularly Ritalin (methlyphenidate), are the most commonly used interventions with ADDH children. Given the problematic social interactions of ADDH children an analysis of the manner in which stimulant drugs alter these social interaction patterns was conducted. Barkley and Cunningham (1979) used the RCM to evaluate the effects of a single daily dose of Ritalin on the mother-child interactions of 20 ADDH children during play and tasks. In play, ADDH children showed less competing or off-task behavior and were able to sustain their compliance for longer periods of time while on medication. Their mothers gave fewer commands, and were more attentive to play and interaction during the drug as compared to the placebo condition. In the task setting, ADDH children were more compliant with commands, better able to sustain their compliance to tasks, and played more independently of their mothers while on medication. Their mothers decreased their commands, increased their approval of compliance, and were less negative during the drug versus placebo condition.

Similar findings were noted in a study of identical twin boys with ADDH using single case reversal designs to evaluate the effects of Ritalin on mother-child interactions (Cunningham & Barkley, 1978). Improvements in compliance and maternal commands similar to these were also reported recently by Pollard, Ward, and Barkley (1984). The results suggest that the improvement in attention span and reduction in activity level directly resulting from the Ritalin treatment (See Barkley, 1977; Cantwell & Carlson, 1978 for reviews) translate into greater compliance with commands in ADDH children. As a result, mothers reduce the level of directiveness they provide to their children.

In a much larger study, Barkley, Karlsson, Strzelecki, and Murphy (1984) examined the effects of two different doses of Ritalin on the mother-child interactions of three different age levels (mean ages 5, 7, and 9.5 years, respectively) of ADDH children. Few age or drug effects were noted during play, but numerous main effects for age and drug conditions were found for the task condition. The age effects were similar to those reported by Mash and Johnston (1982) in that ADDH children in the two older versus younger groups were more compliant and less negative while their mothers were less directive. Both doses of Ritalin (0.3 mg/kg and 1.0 mg/kg daily doses) increased child compliance equally, while only the higher dose resulted in significant reductions in maternal directiveness and negative behavior toward the children. The lack of any age by drug condition interactions suggests that the effects of medication were consistent across the three age groups studied here.

Barkley, Karlsson, Pollard, and Murphy (1985) replicated this study using two higher dose levels of Ritalin and five age levels of ADDH children (years 5, 6, 7, 8, and 9). Again, no effects for age or drug condition were found during the free play setting but several were reported in the task setting which were consistent with those described above. Once again, no significant age by drug condition interactions were reported.

These drug studies have been significant in demonstrating that the effects of Ritalin on the behavior of ADDH children result in improvements in their social behavior toward their parents, especially during task situations. In turn, the mothers reduce their negative and controlling responses to their children and in some cases even increase the level of praise and approval during the drug conditions. In general, Ritalin results in a more normal interaction pattern in these dyads. Such findings have severely undercut the notion that the behavior of ADDH children is the result of their parents' poor behavior management skills and instead suggest that the directive and negative behaviors of parents are more a reaction to than a cause of misbehavior. The use of the RCM in these studies, with its scoring of contingent relations between parent and child behaviors, has provided stronger support for this interpretation than could have been achieved with a scoring system based on behavioral categories scored independently of their antecedents and consequents.

Recently, Cunningham, Siegel, and Offord (1985) used the RCM in a modified form to evaluate the effects of two doses of Ritalin on peer interactions for three age groups of ADDH boys. The results tend to parallel those seen in the studies of Ritalin and mother-child interactions. The drug resulted in increased attention to tasks, decreased activity level, and decreased dominating and controlling behavior by ADDH boys toward their peers. Similar changes were noted in the peers' behavior toward the medicated ADDH boys (e.g., less controlling and dominating behavior toward the ADDH children). The findings suggest that medicated ADDH children are likely to behave more normally toward peers and are more likely to be accepted by peers than they are when their medication is withdrawn.

The RCM has also been used to assess the effects of parent training in child management skills on the parent-child interactions of ADDH children. Pollard et al. (1984) used a multiple baseline across subjects design to assess the effects of both parent training and Ritalin, separately and combined, on the mother-child interactions of 3 ADDH boys. Both treatments resulted in declines in maternal commands and improved durations of compliance by the children as well as declines in ratings of behavioral problems in the home. The combination of treatments proved no more effective than either treatment alone, although only the parent training program significantly increased mothers' use of contingent praise for compliance in the ADDH children. This study is important in showing that rates of behavior for certain of the RCM behavioral categories remain relatively stable over repeated observations, yet are sensitive enough to detect changes in behavior related to both drug and behavior therapy interventions.

Treatment Studies with Behavior Disordered Children

Glogower and Sloop (1976) employed the RCM to evaluate the results of two types of group parent training in child behavior modification skills on parents of clinic-referred behavior disordered children. A sample of 8 mothers were divided into two treatment groups, one receiving training in both the general principles of behavior modification as well as specific assistance with designing methods for use with selected problem behaviors. The second group received only the assistance with designing methods for problematic target behaviors and no training in general behavioral principles.

Both groups showed improvements in their knowledge of behavior modification principles, in their ability to generalize these principles to new hypothetical child behavior problems, and in their actual interactions with their children as observed during free play and task situations in a clinic playroom. However, mothers who received training in both general principles and specific methods acquired somewhat greater knowledge of these principles, showed significantly greater generalization of these principles to hypothetical child management problems, and had more compliant children during play and task observations. Mothers in the combined training program were also less likely to give commands during free play and were more likely to use praise contingent upon child compliance during tasks. As in the studies with ADDH children, this study further demonstrates the sensitivity of the RCM to the effects of differing treatments.

Treatment Studies with Developmental Delayed Children

Several studies have used the RCM to evaluate the results of parent training programs for families with children having severe developmental disabilities. In a case study, Seitz and Terdal (1972) used the RCM with a 4-year-old retarded and hyperactive child to evaluate the effects of a therapy program consisting of a therapist modeling appropriate play interaction while the mother observed and was provided with feedback from a second therapist. Following this treatment, the child was more likely to reciprocate interaction and the mother was less likely to respond negatively to off-task behavior during play. The child was also more compliant in the task situation and the mother increased her use of praise. These changes in child behavior also occurred during interactions between child and therapist suggesting generalized change. This case study, although largely uncontrolled, does demonstrate the clinical uses of the RCM in identifying target behaviors and the use of particular summary measures for the assessment of outcomes for an individual case.

Mash, Lazere, Terdal, and Garner (1973) evaluated treatment effects for four mildly retarded children ranging in age from 4 to 9 years. Three mothers (observers) watched a fourth mother (demonstrator) interacting with her child while a therapist provided ongoing feedback. This was followed by a discussion with all the mothers that emphasized child management skills. Following ten sessions, observation in the task situation indicated that all children increased their rates of compliance relative to controls and this was associated with a reduction in maternal directiveness. The observer mother-child dyads tended to show greater improvement than the "demonstrator" mother and there was some support for changes in home behavior as assessed by the RCM.

Mash and Terdal (1973) evaluated the effects of a group parent training program that was designed to teach mothers of retarded children (Mean I.Q. = 50) effective play skills. Five groups of mothers of retarded children (8–10 mothers per group) and a group of nontreated mothers were observed interacting with their children in a play situation before and after the ten-session program. Mothers who participated in the program reduced their directiveness and questions while increasing their rates of interaction. At the same time, their children were more responsive to commands, questions and interaction than they had been prior to the program. It was also shown that mothers were more likely to respond positively to the child's compliance and interaction following treatment. Such findings suggest some of the contingent and specific behavioral changes that may be mediating the more general changes in frequencies that were observed.

In a well-controlled study Tavormina (1975) used a modified RCM procedure to evaluate the effects of two types of parent training programs for mothers of retarded (modal I.Q. less than 50) children. Mother-child interactions were observed during a free play and task situation following either behavioral or reflective group counselling. No significant changes were observed from pre- to post during play interaction. However, during the tasks the behavioral group showed significant gains in the total amount of appropriate interaction relative to the reflective group and to controls. The reflective group also improved on this overall measure who compared with controls but not as much as the behavioral group. This pattern of improvement in task interaction was shown for several of the other measures.

The studies just described indicate that the RCM may be sensitive to changes associated with a variety of behaviorally oriented treatments for retarded children. Changes have been observed following group and individual parent training, and following the use of child management programs emphasizing both discussion and modeling procedures. Findings from the Tavormina (1975) study indicate that the RCM may be less sensitive to changes following less behaviorally oriented psychological interventions and points up the need for multimethod assessments of treatment outcome.

Treatment Studies with Language Delayed Children

Cunningham, Siegel, van der Spuy, Elbard, Nielson, and Richards (1983) compared a behavioral parenting program with a classroom program (modeled after the work of Reynell) and a community control group for a population of 77 language delayed children. The groups were further subdivided into children who had either a general delay (I.Q. less than 85) or a specific language delay (I.Q. greater than 85). Children were observed during free play and task interactions with their mothers before and after treatment. Parents of both specifically and generally language delayed children in the parent training program showed significant increases in positive interaction, positive responses to their child's interaction and compliance, and decreases in commands and intrusive questions. However, only the generally delayed children showed behavior changes indicative of increased compliance and responsiveness to maternal questions. The specifically delayed children who were in the classroom program showed pre to post increases in positive interaction, questions, and responsiveness to maternal questions and interactions. Although the mothers of these children had received no direct training they reduced commands and showed concomitant increases in positive interaction and responsiveness to the child's interaction and compliance. For the generally delayed group in the classroom program neither parents or children showed any changes in interaction. Few changes were observed in children or parents who were in the community control group. These findings underscore again the sensitivity of RCM measures to differing types of interventions and populations.

FUTURE DIRECTIONS

The work described in this chapter represents a beginning effort to utilize a standardized structured observational procedure for the behavioral assessment of family interactions. In spite of the seemingly large number of research studies that have used the RCM, and likely an even larger number of clinical applications, the RCM data provide only a glimpse into the potential strengths and weaknesses associated with the use of such standardized measures in behavioral family assessment. In this section, we will outline the implications of our work in relation to possible future directions for the use of structured observational procedures in behavioral assessment.

Situational Specificity

Perhaps the most compelling consistency in the work just reviewed is the situation-specific nature of our assessment findings. Situational influence manifested itself in a variety of ways: (1) social interchanges differed dramatically as a function of the way in which the immediate context was structured, as exemplified by the pronounced play versus task differences in interaction; (2) situational effects were almost always mediated by population characteristics and some contexts proved more sensitive to the interactional difficulties of a particular problem population versus another; (3) the pattern of relationships between interactional behavior and extra-setting characteristics, such as maternal mood and cognitions, varied with the situation in which behaviors were observed; (4) the effects of treatment were dependent on the context for assessment, and differing treatments impacted on behavior in different settings.

An emphasis on situational specificity is certainly not new in behavioral assessment. However, the use of the standardized RCM procedure highlighted situational influences in the way that standardized tests magnify individual differences. Idiosyncratic behavioral assessments frequently confound the effects of varying methods with those of varying contexts, and as a result the effects of situations on performance may not be as readily apparent.

The range of situations in which the RCM has been employed in family assessment has been rather restricted, for the most part limited to play and task transactions. However, even in this narrow range we have noted the great variability in instructions, playroom characteristics, and playroom materials from study to study. It is likely that such variability has been even greater in clinical uses of the instrument. If our structured observational assessments are to be sensitive to the subtleties and complexities of situational influences as suggested by the RCM findings, observations need to be extended to a much wider range of relevant and well-standardized contexts.

In this regard, it would be extremely useful to develop a Catalog of Standard Assessment Situations that includes a wide range of analogues appropriate for different populations and ages of children. Descriptions could include standard instructions, detailed lists of playroom materials, session lengths, and population-specific norms for performance in the situation. Ideally, these situations would be empirically validated such that guidelines as to the types of situations that are most useful for particular assessment purposes might be provided. For example, task situations seem well suited for evaluating the effects of Ritalin on the social behavior of ADDH children. Although the empirical validation would take some time, even the provision of standardized descriptions of analogues having conceptual significance would be a first step towards producing the necessary validation information. Moreover, such descriptions would serve to increase the comparability of findings across studies, increase the availability of analogue situations for researchers and clinicians, and serve to avoid unnecessary and redundant descriptions of situational manipulations in published articles (e.g., rather than describing each analogue it would be possible to state simply that analogue "103.2" from the Catalog of Standard Assessment Situations was used). In devising such a taxonomy of representative situations it should be apparent that the "analogue" versus "naturalistic" dichotomy that has been perpetuated in the behavioral assessment literature is both arbitrary and illusory. The question is not whether we have a "true" sample, but rather whether or not the assessment situation samples aspects of behavior that are relevant for particular purposes.

Standard Behavior Categories

The studies reviewed demonstrate the adaptability of the RCM codes across settings and populations. Such adaptability is based upon the use of global categories intended to reflect "classes" of behavior (Kazdin, 1982). The use of such behavior classes as "interaction" or "negative" behavior has a number of advantages: (1) it permits the comparison of populations where the topography of specific behaviors in a particular class are quite different; (2) it allows for comparisons across different ages of children where response topographies are also predictably different; (3) such response classes are useful as treatment outcome measures, especially over long time periods. For example, while rates of negativity in the same child at ages 4 and 9 may be equivalent, an outcome measure that was overly specific (e.g., crying) may not reflect this stability.

On the negative side, the RCM categories were not empirically derived and the functional equivalence and possible covariations of specific behaviors within the more general categories have yet to be established. Moreover, while the general categories are helpful in elaborating some of the major interactional features, the specificity and qualitative differentiation required for particular clinical or research applications may be lacking. It would, however, be possible to provide greater flexibility in RCM use by differentiating the more global categories into smaller units and incorporating these units into the matrix as, for example, was done with the verbal and non-verbal interaction categories in some of the studies described. At a more general level it would seem that even greater flexibility in observation might be achieved by elaborating a variety of behaviors that could be used as needed in the matrix or some other format.

Idealistically, in order to accomplish this flexible use of behavior categories it would first be necessary to develop standardized observational descriptions of family interaction, and a taxonomy for grouping various behavior categories into a hierarchical format. For example, the interaction category might be subdivided into verbal and nonverbal, then social versus solitary, then prosocial versus agonistic, and so forth. The development of a Dictionary of Observational Categories that provided standard definitions and scoring criteria at each level of category differentiation would mean that behavioral assessors employing observational codes would begin to speak a common language. The fact that definitions of the same categories have varied from one code system to another in idiosyncratic behavioral assessments, have made direct comparison of findings from one study to another nearly impossible. Advantages of standardized definitions would be similar to those described in the discussion of standardized situations.

A second prerequisite for flexible category use is a set of decision rules concerning the types of categories that would be most useful for answering particular questions with particular populations and situations. Such decision rules could be based upon theoretical, empirical and practical considerations.

Admittedly, we are a long way from the observational assessment precision being proposed, but if these possibilities are to be realized a necessary first step is the development of standardized code definitions.

Population Specificity

Findings from RCM studies over a range of populations indicate that patterns of interaction and the assessment sensitivity of particular situations and categories varied in relation to the nature of the child or family difficulty. Although the between-population interactional differences were not precise enough to make reliable differential diagnoses, they did suggest that idiographic analysis at the level of commonly occurring family and childhood disorders represents a potentially more efficient behavioral assessment strategy than similar analyses on a case-by-case basis. The RCM, and measures like it, appear useful in illuminating the way in which specific problems (e.g., attentional difficulties, developmental or language delay) structure interactions in specific settings, and make comparisons across populations feasible. The inclusion of groupings of categories in our assessments that were especially sensitive to the unique problems of children with different disorders would retain the advantages of standardized assessment while providing the flexibility of assessment needed to generate the population-specific information required in many clinical and research studies.

Multimethod–Multilevel Assessment

The reported relationships between RCM observational measures and verbal reports by parents and children have provided insights into how such perceptions and attitudes may affect the interactions and vice versa. Disagreements between verbal report and observational data have in the past been taken as reason to doubt the validity of one data source (usually verbal report) versus the other. However, such a lack of correspondence is more likely an indication that different, but equally significant, aspects of family functioning are being measured. The demonstrated relationships between family attitudes and interactional behavior and the situational specificity of these relationships further support the need for multi-method behavioral assessments.

The fact that extra-setting variables, such as family stress, were associated with observed interaction in the analogue setting is indicative of the importance of assessing more remote system variables on the parent-child relationship. The findings with the RCM reinforce the need for a multi-level systems-analysis that examines the interrelationships between proximal (e.g., marital relationship, sibling relationship) and distal (e.g., community support) family sub-systems as they affect observed interaction between family members in particular situations.

Practical Issues

A major reason for the development of the RCM in its current format was its presumed ease of use in both clinical and research contexts. Numbers and types of categories, design of scoring sheets, embeddedness in a playroom analogue, and coding procedures were all intended to increase RCM applicability in the clinical context. While it is true that behavioral assessors have not made extensive use of observational procedures in practice, it was our view that the RCM procedure had a greater potential for use than other multi-category home-based observational procedures. To some extent this has proven true. However, it is quite possible that the assumptions upon which the RCM was based are no longer applicable in light of technological advances that have been made in the use of high speed microprocessors to gather and analyze observational data. Observational data can now be gathered in the most complex of formats and still be easily translated into clinical use.

The major requirements here are the widespread availability of the computer technologies and the resources and trained personnel needed to use them. While it is unlikely that most individual practitioners will be able to meet these requirements, there is little need for them to do so, and in fact such an approach would likely be very inefficient and unreliable. We are at the point in our behavioral observational assessments where clinical research laboratories that have the special resources to deal with the complex observational data sets should be developed, that function in a manner analogous to the testing laboratories that are now relied upon so extensively by medical practitioners. Such laboratories would have an available staff of highly trained observers, access to multiple coding systems, the data analytic programs and empirically derived interpretive skills necessary to deal with complex information, and the capability to provide immediate feedback and/or ongoing assessments of treatment outcome. This type of approach is already beginning to develop on an informal level, where some behavioral centers are now coding tapes that are sent to them from other geographical areas, utilizing the complex observational procedures they have developed and for which they have an already trained staff and appropriate resources.

The potential advantages of this general approach to assessment are enormous, since the reliability, validity, and complexity of analysis underlying clinical decision-making and treatment outcome evaluation can be increased immeasurably. It would seem that the potential savings to researchers or clinicians in not having to purchase or develop resources would make the enterprise economically viable. Moreover, the precision of interpretation in a network of such observational laboratories would increase in an exponential fashion as new information permitted better decision-making based upon a rapidly expanding data base. In this type of assessment framework, the usefulness of any particular observational code system may be short-lived, since the built in feedback loops should result in a continuous revision, refinement and updating of procedures.

ACKNOWLEDGMENTS

The Response-Class Matrix (RCM) was developed in 1969 at the Crippled Children's Division of the University of Oregon Health Sciences University. The format represented the efforts of many individuals including Leif Terdal, Kay Anderson, Ann Garner, Joan Buell, Russell Jackson, Richard Lazere, and Vaughn Hardesty. Since its initial development the procedural refinement and use of the RCM is the result of ongoing work by Ann Garner, Russell Jackson, Leif Terdal, Charles Cunningham, Anne Copeland, Linda Siegel, and Charlotte Johnston. We are greatly indebted to this group of people for their generous sharing of information and helpfulness in the preparation of this chapter.

The work described in this chapter was supported, in part, by grants from Canada Health and Welfare, Alberta Mental Health Research Fund, and a Social Sciences and Humanities Research Council of Canada Leave Fellowship to E. J. Mash and by NIMH grant No. MH32334-01 to R. A. Barkley.

The authors are also grateful to the many committed observers, students and research assistants who have contributed in some measure to the work described in this chapter. Finally, we would like to thank the hundreds of parents and children who have so unselfishly provided us with brief glimpses into their lives so that we might improve our understanding of troubled families and enhance our ability to help them.

REFERENCES

Abidin, R. R. (1983). *Parenting stress index.* Charlottesville, VA: Pediatric Psychology Press.

Achenbach, T. M., & Edelbrock C. (1983). *Manual for the Child Behavior Checklist and revised Child Behavior Profile.* Burlington, VT: Authors.

American Psychiatric Association. (1980). *Diagnostic and statistical manual of mental disorders* (3rd ed.). Washington, DC: Author.

Arnold, J., Levine, A., & Patterson, G. R. (1975). Changes in sibling behavior following family intervention. *Journal of Consulting and Clinical Psychology, 43,* 683–688.

Baer, D. M., Wolf, M. M., & Risley, T. R. (1968). Some current dimensions of applied behavior analysis. *Journal of Applied Behavior Analysis, 1,* 91–97.

Barkley, R. A. (1977). A review of stimulant drug research with hyperactive children. *Journal of Child Psychology and Psychiatry, 18,* 137–165.

Barkley, R. A. (1981). *Hyperactive children: A handbook for diagnosis and treatment.* New York: The Guilford Press.

Barkley, R. A., & Cunningham, C. E. (1979). The effects of Ritalin on the mother-child interactions of hyperactive children. *Archives of General Psychiatry, 36,* 201–208.

Barkley, R. A., Karlsson, J., & Pollard S. (1985). Effects of age on the mother-child interactions of ADDH and normal boys. *Journal of Abnormal Child Psychology, 13,* 631–638.

Barkley, R. A., Karlsson, J. Pollard, S., & Murphy, J. (1985). Developmental changes in the mother-child interactions of hyperactive boys: Effects of two dose levels of Ritalin. *Journal of Child Psychology and Psychiatry, 26,* 705–715.

Barkley, R. A., Karlsson, J., Strzelecki, E., & Murphy, J. (1984). Effects of age and Ritalin dosage on the mother-child interactions of hyperactive children. *Journal and Consulting and Clinical Psychology, 52,* 750–758.

Befera, M., & Barkley, R. A. (1985). Hyperactive and normal girls and boys: Mother-child interactions, parent psychiatric status, and child psychopathology. *Journal of Child Psychology and Psychiatry, 26,* 439–452.

Behar, L. B., & Stringfield, S. (1974). A behavior rating scale for the preschool child. *Developmental Psychology, 10,* 601–610.

Block, J. H. (1965). *The Child-Rearing Practices Report (CRPR): A set of Q items for the description of parental socialization attitudes and values.* Berkley, CA: Institute of Human Development, University of California.

Campbell, S. B. (1973). Mother-child interaction in reflective, impulsive and hyperactive children. *Developmental Psychology, 8,* 341–349.

Campbell, S. B. (1975). Mother-child interaction: A comparison of hyperactive, learning disabled, and normal boys. *American Journal of Orthopsychiatry, 45,* 51–57.

Cantwell, D. P., & Carlson, G. A. (1978). Stimulants. In J. Werry (Ed.), *Pediatric psychopharmacology* (pp. 171–207). New York: Brunner/Mazel.

Copeland, A. P. (in press). An early look at divorce: Mother-child interactions in the first post-separation year. *Journal of Divorce.*

Copeland, A. P. (1985a). Individual differences in children's reactions to divorce. *Journal of Clinical Child Psychology, 14,*11–19.

Copeland, A. P. (1985b). Self-control ratings and mother-child interaction. *Journal of Clinical Child Psychology, 14,* 124–131.

Copeland, A. P., & Barenbaum, N. B. (1983). *Some correlates of child-rearing attitudes.* Paper presented at the meeting of the American Psychological Association, Los Angeles, August.

Copeland, A. P., Eisenstein, J. L., & Reiner, E. M. (1984). *Relationships between mothers' and children's post-separation adjustment.* Paper presented at the meeting of the American Psychological Association, Toronto, Canada, August.

Copeland, A. P., Reiner, E. M., & Eisenstein, J. L. (1984). *Effects of Type A behavior on mother-child interactions.* Paper presented at the meeting of the American Psychological Association, Toronto, Canada, August.

Cunningham, C. E., & Barkley, R. A. (1978). The effects of Ritalin on the mother-child interactions of hyperkinetic twin boys. *Developmental Medicine and Child Neurology, 20,* 634–642.

Cunningham, C. E., & Barkley, R. A. (1979). The interactions of normal and hyperactive children with their mothers in free play and structured tasks. *Child Development, 50,* 217–224.

Cunningham, C. E., Reuler, E., Blackwell, J., & Deck, J. (1981). Behavioral and linguistic developments in the interactions of normal and retarded children with their mothers. *Child Development, 52,* 62–70.

Cunningham, C. E., Siegel. L. S., & Offord, D. R. (1985). A developmental dose-response analysis of the effects of methylphenidate on the peer interactions of Attention Deficit Disordered boys. *Journal of Child Psychology and Psychiatry, 26,* 955–971.

Cunningham, C. E., Siegel, L. S., van der Spuy, H. I. J., Clark, L., Elbard, H., Nielson, B., & Richards, J. (1983). *The effects of parenting, classroom and community programs on the parent-child interactions, language and cognitive development of language delayed preschoolers.* Paper presented at the meeting of the Association for the Advancement of Behavior Therapy, Washington, DC, November.

Cunningham, C. E., Siegel, L. S., van der Spuy, H. I. J., Clark, M. L., & Bow, S. J. (1985). The behavioral and linguistic interactions of specifically-language-delayed and normal boys with their mothers. *Child Development, 56,* 1389–1403.

Ford, J. D., & Kendall, P. C. (1979). Behavior therapists' professional behaviors: Converging evidence of a gap between theory and practice. *The Behavior Therapist,* 2(5), 37–38.

Forehand, R., & McMahon, R. (1981). *Helping the noncompliant child.* New York: The Guilford Press.

Garner, A., & Jackson, R. (1978). *Response-Class Matrix: Outline of The Waverly course.* Unpublished manuscript, Oregon Health Services University, Crippled Children's Division, Portland, OR, October.

Glogower, F., & Sloop, E. W. (1976). Two strategies of group training of parents as effective behavior modifiers. *Behavior Therapy, 7,* 177–184.

Hanzlik, J. R., & Stevenson, M. B. (1984). *Mother-infant interaction in families with infants who are developmentally delayed, developmentally delayed with cerebral palsy or developmentally non-delayed.* Unpublished manuscript, Colorado State University, Occupational Therapy Department, Fort Collins, CO.

Hartmann, D. P., Roper, B. L., & Bradford, D. C. (1979). Some relationships between behavioral and traditional assessment. *Journal of Behavioral Assessment, 1,* 3–21.

Hughes, H. M., & Haynes, S. N. (1978). Structured laboratory observation in the behavioral assessment of parent-child interactions. A methodological critique. *Behavior Therapy, 9,* 428–447.

Kanfer, F. H., & Hagerman, S. M. (in press). Behavior therapy and the information processing paradigm. In S. Reiss & R. R. Bootzin (Eds.), *Theoretical issues in behavior therapy.* New York: Academic Press.

Kanfer, F. H., & Saslow, G. (1965). Behavioral analysis: An alternative to diagnostic classification. *Archives of General Psychiatry, 12,* 529–538.

Kazdin, A. E. (1982). Symptom substitution, generalization, and response covariation: Implications for psychotherapy outcome. *Psychological Bulletin, 91,* 349–365.

Kendall, P. C., & Wilcox, L. E. (1979). Self-control in children: Development of a rating scale. *Journal of Consulting and Clinical Psychology, 47,* 1020–1029.

Kent, R. N., & Foster, S. L. (1977). Direct observational procedures: Methodological issues in naturalistic settings. In A. R. Ciminero, K. S. Calhoun, & H. E. Adams (Eds.), *Handbook of behavioral assessment* (pp. 279–328). New York: Wiley.

Lambert, M. J., Christensen, E. R., & DeJulio, S. S. (Eds.). (1983). *The assessment of psychotherapy outcome.* New York: Wiley-Interscience.

Mash, E. J. (1979). What is behavioral assessment? *Behavioral Assessment, 1,* 23–29.

Mash, E. J. (1984). Families with problem children. In A. Doyle, D. Gold & D. S. Moskowitz (Eds.), *Children in families under stress* (pp. 65–84). San Francisco: Jossey-Bass.

Mash, E. J. (1985). Some comments on target selection in behavior therapy. *Behavioral Assessment, 7,* 63–78.

Mash, E. J., & Johnston, C. (1979a). *Revised manual for the Response-Class Matrix: A procedure for recording parent-child interactions.* Unpublished manuscript, University of Calgary, Department of Psychology, Calgary, Canada, January.

Mash, E. J., & Johnston, C. (1979b). *Summary measures for the Response-Class Matrix.* Unpublished manuscript, University of Calgary, Department of Psychology, Calgary, Canada.

Mash, E. J., & Johnston, C. (1979c). *Response-Class Matrix: Training procedures for observers.* Unpublished manuscript, University of Calgary, Department of Psychology, Calgary, Canada.

Mash, E. J., & Johnston, C. (1980). *Behavioral assessment of sibling interactions in hyperactive and normal children.* Paper presented at the meeting of the Association for the Advancement of Behavior Therapy, New York, November.

Mash, E. J., & Johnston, C. (1982). A comparison of the mother-child interactions of younger and older hyperactive and normal children. *Child Development, 53,* 1371–1381.

Mash, E. J., & Johnston, C. (1983a). Sibling interactions of hyperactive and normal children and their relationship to reports of maternal stress and self-esteem. *Journal of Clinical Child Psychology, 12,* 91–99.

Mash, E. J., & Johnston, C. (1983b). Parental perceptions of child behavior problems, parenting self-esteem, and mothers' reported stress in younger and older hyperactive and normal children. *Journal of Consulting and Clinical Psychology, 51,* 86–99.

Mash, E. J., & Johnston, C. (1983c). The prediction of mothers' behavior with their hyperactive children during play and task situations. *Child and Family Behavior Therapy, 5,* 1–14.

Mash, E. J., Johnston, C., & Kovitz, K. (1983). A comparison of the mother-child interactions of physically abused and non-abused children during play and task situations. *Journal of Clinical Child Psychology, 12,* 337–346.

Mash, E. J., Lazere, R., Terdal, L., & Garner, A. (1973). Modification of mother-child interactions: A modeling approach for groups. *Child Study Journal, 3,* 131–143.

Mash, E. J., & Terdal, L. (1973). Modification of mother-child interactions: Playing with children. *Mental Retardation, 11,* 44–49.

Mash, E. J., & Terdal, L. G. (1974). Behavior therapy assessment: Diagnosis, design, and evaluation. *Psychological Reports, 35,* 587–601.

Mash, E. J., & Terdal, L. G. (Eds.). (1976). *Behavior therapy assessment: Diagnosis, design, and evaluation.* New York: Springer.

Mash, E. J., & Terdal, L. G. (1981). Behavioral assessment of childhood disturbance. In E. J. Mash & L. G. Terdal (Eds.), *Behavioral assessment of childhood disorders* (pp. 3–76). New York: The Guilford Press.

Mash, E. J., Terdal, L. G., & Anderson, K. (1973). The Response-Class Matrix: A procedure for recording parent-child interactions. *Journal of Consulting and Clinical Psychology, 40,* 163–164.

Mash, E. J., Terdal, L. G., & Anderson, K. (1981). The Response-Class Matrix: A procedure for recording parent-child interactions. In R. A. Barkley, *Hyperactive children* (pp. 419–436). New York: The Guilford Press.

Nelson, R. O. (1983). Behavioral assessment: Past, present, and future. *Behavioral Assessment, 5,* 195–206.

Palmer, J. O. (1970). *The psychological assessment of children.* New York: Wiley.

Patterson, G. R. (1982). *Coercive family process.* Eugene, OR: Castalia Publishing Company.

Pollard, S., Ward, E. M., & Barkley, R. (1984). The effects of parent training and Ritalin on the parent-child interactions of hyperactive boys. *Child and Family Behavior Therapy, 5,* 51–69.

Reid, J. (Ed). (1978). *A social learning approach to family intervention, Vol. II.: Observation in home settings.* Eugene, OR: Castalia Publishing Company.

Seitz, S., & Terdal, L. (1972). A modeling approach to changing parent-child interactions. *Mental Retardation, 10,* 39–43.

Siegel, L. S., Cunningham, C. E., & van der Spuy, H. I. J. (1985). Interactions of language delayed and normal preschool boys with their peers. *Journal of Child Psychology and Psychiatry, 26,* 77–83.

Tallmadge, J., & Barkley, R. A. (1983). The interactions of hyperactive and normal boys and their mothers and fathers. *Journal of Abnormal Child Psychology, 11,* 565–579.

Tarver-Behring, S., Barkley, R. A., & Karlsson, J. (1985). The mother-child interactions of hyperactive boys and their normal siblings. *American Journal of Orthopsychiatry, 55,* 202–209.

Tavormina, J. B. (1975). Relative effectiveness of behavioral and reflective group counseling with parents of mentally retarded children. *Journal of Consulting and Clinical Psychology, 43,* 22–31.

Terdal, L., Jackson, R., & Garner, A. M. (1976). Mother-child interactions: A comparison between normal and developmentally delayed groups. In E. J. Mash, L. A. Hamerlynck, & L. C. Handy (Eds.), *Behavior modification and families* (pp. 249–264). New York: Brunner/Mazel.

Tharp, R. G., & Wetzel, R. J. (1969). *Behavior modification in the natural environment.* New York: Academic Press.

Wahler, R. G., House, A. E., & Stambaugh, E. E. (1976). *Ecological assessment of child problem behavior: A clinical package for home, school, and institutional settings.* New York: Pergamon.

ASSESSMENT AND ANALYSIS OF ECOBEHAVIORAL INTERACTION IN SCHOOL SETTINGS

Charles R. Greenwood, Dan Schulte, Frank W. Kohler, Granger I. Dinwiddie, and Judith J. Carta

ABSTRACT

The purpose of this chapter is to describe and illustrate an ecobehavioral interaction approach to school performance. Ecobehavioral interaction is defined as the quantification of both changing situational factors and temporally related child responses within the context of direct observational assessment in natural settings. The chapter discusses conceptual issues concerning the assessment of ecobehavioral interaction and presents an example of this methodology based upon data collected with the Code for Instructional Structure and Student Academic Response (CISSAR) (Stanley & Greenwood, 1981). Development of the code is

Advances in Behavioral Assessment of Children and Families, Vol. 2, pgs. 69–98.
Editor: Ronald J. Prinz

ISBN: 0-89232-481-3

reviewed, as are studies demonstrating the validity and reliability of the system. Studies using the code are used to illustrate a line of programmatic research focused on the discovery and refinement of procedures for decreasing academic retardation in inner-city, disadvantaged children.

INTRODUCTION

An emerging trend in behavioral assessment is analysis of ecology-behavior interaction. The assessment of ecobehavioral interaction is based upon recordings of the momentary interactions of environmental stimuli and a person's behavior. Traditional forms of child behavior assessment have focused mostly on the characteristics and behaviors of the child (McReynolds, 1979). Assessment of child status alone, however, does not shed light on the immediate or historic conditions within a child's ecology that may contribute to child growth and development (Bijou, 1981). Thus, the dynamic interrelationship between child behavior and the environment remains largely unknown (Bronfenbrenner, 1979; Brophy, 1979).

Although the early natural science approaches to behavior analysis included theoretical conceptualizations of ecobehavioral interaction (Barker, 1961; Kantor, 1959; Skinner, 1953), empirical data have been forthcoming only in the last 10 years. Computer-assisted observation systems have enabled applied researchers to gather and analyze complex information on the structure, sequence, and function of ecobehavioral phenomena. A premiere example is the coercive theory of aggression developed by Patterson and his colleagues (Patterson, 1982) based on sequential analysis of child-adult interaction records. Sequential analysis of interactions allows the investigator to identify dependencies between the behaviors of interacting persons in natural settings based upon conditional probabilities. Patterson (1974) was able to identify a .65 probability relationship between the event class, *parent command* followed six seconds later in time by child *yell.* Although limited only by the length of the data record, it is quite possible to study the distal impact of particular stimuli or setting events upon specific interaction patterns like the one between parent and child just mentioned. For example, Karpowitz, and Johnson (1981) examined the relationship between parent's social stimuli and child behavior at 10 vs. 30 second time intervals. They concluded that the immediately preceding parent stimulus (10 seconds earlier) was most predictive of child response. Other researchers are currently applying these methods of interactional assessment and analysis to families, (Biglan, Hops, Sherman, Friedman, Arthur, & Osteen, 1984; Hops et al., 1984), family therapy, (Wahler & Graves, 1983), language development, (Hart & Risley, 1984), peer social interaction, (Greenwood, Todd, Hops, & Walker, 1982; Kohler, 1984), and classroom instruction, (Brophy, 1979; Greenwood, Delquadri, Stanley, Terry, & Hall, 1985).

Definition of Ecobehavioral Assessment

Ecobehavioral assessment is designed to reveal sequential and concurrent interrelationships between environmental stimuli and a child's responding. Ecobehavioral assessment extends the sequential assessment method commonly referred to as "social interaction" (Cairns, 1979; Lamb, Suomi, & Stephenson, 1979; Patterson, 1982) by including physical stimuli with less emphasis on social stimuli. In our classroom work, the term "ecobehavioral" refers to the measurement of a broad constellation of stimulus events. We have assessed the subject matter, instructional materials, physical grouping, teacher location, and teacher behavior in order to discover the forces that affect children's classroom performance.

In ecobehavioral assessment, ecological and behavioral variables are sampled in close temporal relationship. By alternately sampling ecological and behavioral variables, changes in environmental stimuli and behavior are systematically recorded in sequence. For example, the teacher's behavior is recorded in an interval just preceding the recording of the student's behavior. In this fashion, the sequence *teacher instruct,* followed by *student read aloud* may be recorded. By alternately sampling the teacher, then the student, the contextual basis for student behavior is included within the record for later analysis.

Limitations Imposed by Traditional Observational Assessment

A substantial observational literature in education is devoted to complex assessments of classroom climate, school ecology, and teacher-student interaction, and has even included the use of interaction matrices to interrelate teacher and student events (e.g., Flanders, 1970). However, in most of these observational studies, the variables were not defined as observable events, interobserver reliability was either inadequate or not reported, the data were presented in a static manner that ignored sequential relationships, and the observation codes were not oriented theoretically toward the scientific investigation of direct environment-behavior influences (for a notable exception, see Brophy, 1979).

In applied behavior analysis and social learning theory, there is a stronger tradition requiring adequate observational reliability in behavior change studies. However, traditional behavioral assessment has proven effective within the context of specific behavior change experiments. By focusing on the subject's behavior without assessing the environment, existing observational codes have not quantified the settings and stimuli within which behavior changes take place. Nonecological assessment methods fail to illuminate the natural conditions that create developmental deficits and behavior problems addressed by behavior analysts. As Patterson (1982) has aptly pointed out "a science can be only as good as its assessment methodology." Assessment of behavioral events in the absence of ecological variables is insufficient for prediction and control of many behavioral phenomena. Without information on natural controlling relationships and subsequent tests of their causal status, problems such as school failure and lack of behavior change maintenance will remain unsolved. The structure and function of setting events or stimulus controls in applied behavior analysis is an under-researched area (Wahler & Fox, 1981). We argue that this is largely the result of methodological obstacles associated with the use of interactive assessment in applied settings.

However, wide expression of setting events in research studies also is limited by the traditional need to maintain experimental control. Consequently, setting events have a long history in behavior analytic research of being considered troublesome, as confounding rather than independent variables (Foster & Cone, 1980; Rogers-Warren & Warren, 1977). Many of the most prized functional relationships have been established within narrowly defined setting conditions. Setting events/conditions establish a context for functional relationships to operate (Larsen, & Morris, 1983; Larsen, Morris, & Todd, 1984; Leigland, 1984; Michael, 1982). Furthermore, setting events are variables which affect stimulus-response or response-consequence relationships. For example, reinforcement can only strengthen behavior under specific conditions of deprivation and subject history. Changing these contexts may in turn change the functional relationship. Unfortunately, we often do not know how functional relationships hold up within extremes of setting variation in the natural environment. The classic example of this point, for which we have yet to supply an adequate answer, is, how schedules of reinforcement strengthen and maintain behavior in natural settings.

Much of the current knowledge about behavior change is based upon data for which setting variation was simply ignored. Many setting factors may be reflected as variability in baseline and treatment data and remain unexplained because we choose not to assess them. Setting variations very likely enhance or retard subjects' performance (Greenwood et al., 1985). Interactive ecobehavioral assessment is one method which can represent immediate and delayed setting factors in applied research.

Benefits of an Ecobehavioral Interaction Approach

The solutions to many social problems (e.g., academic retardation) may require a more fundamental understanding of ecobehavioral process that begins with a comprehensive ecobehavioral interaction approach to assessment. The recording of ecological variables permits description of natural stimuli, normative rates of occurrence, and probability relationships to behavior. As noted by Barker (1961) and Bronfenbrenner (1979), there is no definitive data base on human behavior and its settings. An ecobehavioral approach also facilitates important experimental research on resulting developmental impacts or outcomes (e.g., academic achievement). Base rates and base probabilites on ecobehavioral variables can be established for use in subsequent experimental evaluations of specific interventions. Examination of the conditional relationships between ecological variables and behavior may enable identification of particular ecological arrangements correlated with high levels of criterion behaviors. By identifying these arrangements in high performing subjects, it may be possible to test these natural arrangements for function when introduced into the environments of lower performers. Experiments testing these specific ecobehavioral hypotheses with low performers could yield information concerning their causal status. Structural information from the ecobehavioral code that defines standard and effective treatment formats could be used to study treatment by teachers over time and consequently analyze factors that either interfere with or facilitate standard implementation.

Purpose of this Chapter

The purpose of this chapter is to illustrate an ecobehavioral interaction approach to the assessment of children's school performance. This approach relies on direct observation of ecobehavioral interaction within elementary classroom settings. The approach and resulting data have evolved from studies investigating the problem of low academic achievement and retardation among inner-city children (Greenwood, Delquadri, & Hall, 1984; Greenwood, Dinwiddie, Terry, Wade, Stanley, Thibadeau, & Delquadri, 1984; Hall, Delquadri, Greenwood, & Thurston, 1982). The aim of the chapter is to discuss our ecobehavioral interaction observation system, the Code for Instructional Structure and Student Academic Response (CISSAR) (Greenwood, Delquadri, Stanley, Sasso, Whorton, & Schulte, 1981; Stanley & Greenwood, 1981), in terms of the code's design, reliability, validity, data analysis, and application within programmatic research.

CODE DEVELOPMENT FOR ASSESSMENT OF CLASSROOM ECOBEHAVIORAL INTERACTION

An ecobehavioral interaction approach to classroom assessment was the outgrowth of years of research in which we addressed both problems of low achievement and child misbehavior in inner-city schools based upon the principles of applied behavior analysis. However, after some major successes developing effective behavioral assessment and interventions (Greenwood, Hops, Delquadri, & Guild, 1974; Walker, Hops, & Figenbaum, 1976; Hall & Copeland, 1972; Hall, Lund, & Jackson, 1968), we really had very little information concerning the natural instructional conditions correlated with these problems (Hall et al., 1982). Moreover, we had no data and little confidence in the fidelity with which natural school personnel could and/or would carry out effective procedures without the direct support of the researchers/developers. Although our procedures manipulated ecological and instructional variables (e.g., academic tasks, instructional sequences, time in instruction, etc.), in addition to reinforcement contingencies, we collected systematic information only on teachers' use of reinforcing consequences and praise.

Our informal observations of instructional programs developed by teachers often revealed a minimal amount of academic structure. We frequently had to engineer a student's academic program in addition to supplying a contingency management solution (Hall et al., 1982). We found students incorrectly placed in materials which were often badly programmed. It was also evident that we needed baseline data that reflected the momentary temporal relationships between a student's behavior and instructional setting events, discriminative stimuli provided by the natural program. We hypothesized that children were academically delayed and remained so over their educational experience because the instructional program made relatively few active demands on them. For example, it was not uncommon for the low reading group, scheduled last to meet with the teacher, to miss reading altogether because the teacher failed to adhere to the schedule. When reading groups did meet, there was often little opportunity for each child to respond to questions and read aloud. As a result, the natural program failed to develop students' academic repertoire. It was events such as these that we wished to address through ecobehavioral assessment.

Issues in the Design of Ecobehavioral Assessment

In addition to resolving traditional observational code design issues (e.g., selection of target behaviors, method of sampling, observer prompting, unit of analysis), a well-conceived ecobehavioral coding system must specify the subject units of observation, the ecological events (e.g., activities, tasks, teacher behavior), and an appropriate sequential sampling procedure.

Subject Units for Observation

An ecobehavioral coding system could focus on individual children, peers, parents, other adults, or teachers as the subject units of observation. Since our major goal is the specification of ecobehavioral determinants of classroom behavior, we have focused on the individual child as the conceptual unit of observation and analysis. As a result, CISSAR ecobehavioral codes are data intensive in sampling the behavior and ecology of each target child. This orientation requires that all ecological variables, including physical as well as peer, parent, and teacher social behaviors, are recorded but only in relation to the target child.

Coding systems that repeatedly sample different target children during a single recording session may not be appropriate for examining ecobehavioral relationships because ecological factors sampled across children might not adequately represent the determinants of a specific child's behavior. Repeated sampling of several target children in the same session also constrains the amount of data available for each child. In CISSAR, ecological variables are recorded by one observer in reference to one single target student who is the unit of analysis.

Selection of Ecological and Behavioral Codes

The content validity of the CISSAR codes was established in a sequence of steps that involved: (a) determination of events within the ecobehavior dichotomy, (b) preparation of behavioral definitions or codes for each event, (c) determination of the content validity of each code, (d) confirmation through observational tryouts, (e) calibration of interobserver reliability, and (f) revision and reconfirmation through additional tryout. These steps were subsequently followed by an observation study to generate additional validity and reliability information on the completed system (Hall et al., 1982).

Ecological codes. The original version of the CISSAR code contained four ecological categories (i.e., activities, tasks, structure, and teacher location). A fifth category, teacher behavior, was added shortly thereafter. These categories were selected as variables most likely to influence student behavior during classroom instruction, as noted in other codes and research reports (Cobb, 1971, 1972; Cobb & Hops, 1971; Greenwood, Stokes, & Hops, 1974; Wahler, House, & Stambaugh, 1976) and based on our classroom experience. The ecological codes are summarized in Table 1. *Activities* were defined as the subjects of instruction. ''Reading'' and ''social studies'' instruction are two examples of the 12 codes. *Tasks* were defined as the specific materials or teacher commands being used to occasion student responding. ''Readers'' and ''teacher-student discussion'' are examples of two of the eight task codes. *Structure* was defined as the seating arrangement and peer proximity during instruction and included ''individual,'' ''small group,'' and ''entire group'' arrangement codes. The six *Teacher position* codes represented the teacher's location in the classroom in reference to the target student (e.g., ''in front'' or ''to the side''). *Teacher behavior* was organized into five codes reflecting behaviors such as ''teaching,'' ''approval,'' and ''disapproval'' statements.

Our preliminary observations indicated that activity, task, and structure codes changed slowly in comparison with teacher location, teacher behavior, and student behavior codes. For example, when the activity code was math, the task lecture, and the structure entire group, students could receive a 30 minute lesson concerning addition. During this time, the teacher moved through several locations and shifted teaching behaviors frequently. Similarly, student behavior also changed from attention to writing followed by reading silently. Consequently, activity, task, and structure variables did not have to be recorded as frequently as teacher position, teacher behavior and student behavior codes to provide representative estimates.

Student behavior codes. Student behavior in the CISSAR code had to be more detailed and include more specific response definitions than in any of our previous work. In the past we had used molar behavioral codes consisting of consol-

Table 1. CISSAR Categories, Codes, and Descriptions

	Ecological Categories		
Activity:	The subject of instruction		
Ac	Arts/crafts	M	Mathematics
Bm	Business/management	R	Reading
Ct	Can't tell	Sc	Science
Ft	Free time	Ss	Social studies
H	Handwriting	S	Spelling
L	Language	Tn	Transition
Task:	The curriculum materials or the stimuli set by the teacher to occasion responding		
Fp	Fetch/put away	Rr	Readers
Ll	Listen to lecture	Tsd	Teacher-student/discussion
Om	Other media	Wb	Workbook
Pp	Paper/pencil	Ws	Worksheet
Structure:	Grouping and peer proximity during instruction		
Eg	Entire Group	Sg	Small Group
I	Individual		
Teacher position:	Teacher's position relative to the student and/or group observed		
AS	Among students	IF	In front
AD	At desk	O	Out of room
B	Behind	S	Side of student
Teacher Behavior:	Teacher's behavior		
A	Approval	OT	Other talk
D	Disapproval	T	Teaching
NR	No response		
	Student Behavior Categories		
Academic response:	Specific, active response in relation to academic tasks		
AGP	Academic game play	RS	Read silent
ANS	Answer question	TA	Talk academic
ASK	Ask question	W	Write
RA	Read aloud		
Task management:	Prerequisite or enabling response		
AT	Attention	PA	Play appropriate
LM	Look for materials	RH	Raise Hand
M	Move		
Competing responses:	Responses that compete or are incompatible with academic or task management behavior		
DI	Disrupt	LA	Look around
IL	Inappropriate locale	TNA	Talk non-academic
IP	Inappropriate play	SS	Self-stimulation
IT	Inappropriate task		

idated response classes (e.g., on-task or total appropriate behavior) so productively, but found these inappropriate because display of specific responses was not possible. Alternately, specific responses like write, read aloud, and academic talk, offered a precise molecular means of examining momentary ecobehavioral effects, hence the development of 19 behavior codes.

The organization of the behavior codes was also important. Cobb's (1972) work demonstrated that specific combinations of student behaviors were better predictors of achievement than was an on-task composite score. He organized his best achievement predictors (i.e., attention, volunteer, and look around) into a composite category he termed "academic survival skills." Following Cobb's validation procedures, we demonstrated that writing, reading silently, and reading aloud were the best single predictors of achievement in the CISSAR code, and that our academic response composite defined by the sum of occurrences for seven academic response codes (see Table 1), was the best composite predictor of achievement (Greenwood et al., 1981). Thus, organizing the individual student behavior codes into the three categories of academic response, task management, and competing, inappropriate behavior provided the needed flexibility to examine both molecular and molar ecobehavioral relationships.

A case example is presented to illustrate this precision. A first grade child was referred because he refused to do school work, slept in class, disrupted the class, and was off-task most of the time. Our first assessment of the child covered the entire school day and revealed a competing behavior composite score of 63.5% (see Table 2). By the time we were able to conduct a second assessment, the principal had placed the student into another classroom with a different teacher. Our second assessment indicated a 34.2% level of competing behavior, half the level of the first assessment, but more than double the 14.1% first grade mean for this school (N = 13 students). Several other points were evident. First, the activities each day (the contexts for his behavior) also differed according to the teacher's schedule. For example, handwriting and language instruction occurred during the first and third observation periods but not during the second. Second, there was considerable cross-situational consistency in the student's high competing behavior levels during baseline. For example, competing behavior scores for math, handwriting, and language, were 100%, 53.2%, and 87.8% respectively on the first day.

During the reading and math periods, we implemented as the first intervention, the CLASS program (Contingencies for Learning Academic and Social Skills), which is a behavior management program using individual and dependent group-oriented reinforcement contingencies (Hops, Walker, Fleischman, Nagoshi, Omuri, Skindrud & Taylor, 1978). The student's composite levels of competing behavior dropped to 11.7%, 10.6%, and 5.5% during the first intervention period of three consecutive days. While the CLASS program was only applied in reading and math activities, the child's competing behavior also decreased during other activities in the day. For example, competing behavior

Table 2. Intervention Effects on the Percentage of Time Spent Engaged in Competing Behavior Displayed by CISSAR Activities and Experimental Conditions for a First Grade Student

Activities	*Conditions*						
	Baseline		*Intervention 1*			*Intervention 2*	
	Observation Days						
	01	*02*	*03*	*04*	*05*	*06*	*07*
Math	100.0	0.0	2.5	0.0	2.0	39.4	57.7
Reading	5.0	34.2	4.7	5.0	2.1	28.3	7.9
Handwriting	53.2	—	25.0	23.6	—	—	—
Language	87.8	—	15.6	7.0	9.5	—	32.5
Transition	54.5	5.6	16.4	3.7	0.0	29.3	7.7
Bus/Manage	19.1	45.4	0.0	3.3	1.4	36.1	41.7
Spelling	—	—	6.9	0.0	0.0	—	—
Soc/Study	—	—	—	2.2	16.9	—	—
Arts/Crafts	—	—	—	—	0.8	44.5	—
Free Time	—	—	—	—	0.0	100.0	—
Science	—	—	—	—	6.2	—	—
Competing/Composite	63.5	34.2	11.7	10.6	5.5	37.3	30.8

Note: — = Activity did not occur. Intervention applied during reading and math only.

during transitions and in business management activities dropped to 0.0 and 1.4 by observation 4, the lowest levels observed for these two activities.

In the second intervention period the teacher assumed responsibility for operating the CLASS program. To our initial disappointment, the student's composite competing behavior during this intervention had reversed to the pretreatment baseline levels of 37.3% and 30.8% during observations 5 and 6. The student's behavior when analysed by individual response codes however, demonstrated several important points not reflected in this composite score. Most importantly, the student's writing behavior reported in Table 3 remained high in the teacher intervention compared with the earlier baseline and first intervention levels. The academic-response composite also was notably high during both intervention phases. Examination of specific behaviors indicated that the reversal was a result of the child looking around (LA) more often, but the child was also engaging in more writing (W) and silent reading (RS) during this last phase. Without the profile of specific codes, it would not have been possible to detect the child's qualitative improvement over baseline during the teacher-administered stage of the program.

Table 3. Intervention Effects on Individual Behaviors

Behaviors	*Baseline*		*Treatment 1*			*Treatment 2*	
	01	*02*	*03*	*04*	*05*	*06*	*07*
				Academic Responses			
W	1.8	4.5	19.7	21.7	8.8	25.0	17.3
AGP	0.0	0.0	0.0	0.3	2.2	0.0	0.0
RA	0.0	5.1	2.2	1.5	1.2	1.6	3.3
RS	0.3	8.2	9.2	9.1	3.6	19.1	15.2
TA	0.4	0.0	2.1	2.4	2.1	0.4	1.2
ANS	0.3	0.7	0.8	1.2	1.5	0.5	0.8
ASK	0.0	0.0	0.2	0.1	0.0	0.3	0.4
Composite	2.7	18.5	34.3	36.3	19.6	37.0	38.2
				Task Management			
AT	31.3	41.8	49.8	47.6	70.0	18.8	24.3
RH	1.0	5.5	2.9	3.8	3.2	0.9	1.5
LM	0.8	0.0	0.8	0.3	0.3	4.6	3.7
M	0.7	0.0	0.5	1.3	1.2	1.4	1.5
PA	0.0	0.0	0.0	0.0	0.0	0.0	0.0
Composite	33.7	47.3	54.0	53.0	74.9	25.7	31.0
				Competing Behavior			
DI	2.3	0.0	0.0	0.0	0.0	0.0	0.2
PI	12.2	5.8	2.1	4.0	0.5	6.5	6.2
IT	1.2	0.0	2.0	0.1	0.6	0.0	0.0
TNA	2.7	2.7	0.4	0.5	0.3	2.2	5.0
IL	34.5	0.0	0.6	0.1	2.7	1.8	0.4
LA	8.6	22.6	5.4	5.4	1.2	25.4	18.5
SST	1.9	3.1	1.2	0.4	0.2	1.3	0.6
Composite	63.5	34.2	11.7	10.6	5.5	37.3	30.8

Sampling Procedure

The relating of contemporaneous events and the encoding of sequences between events is made possible through sampling procedures (Bakeman 1978). Patterson's observation systems (Reid, 1978; Dishion et al., 1983) alternately sample child and parent behaviors within consecutive 6 second intervals. The occurrence of behaviors and the identity of the actor are recorded across intervals. The Peer Interaction Code (Greenwood, Todd et al., 1982) requires observers to record subject and peer responses within 10 second intervals. Interaction sequences including the identities of initiator and responder are encoded in the order of occurrence and continue over time.

The CISSAR system relies on 10 second momentary time sampling of multiple events. An illustration of the coding sheet and the sampling procedure is shown in Table 4. The observer codes the activity, task, and structure in the first 10 second interval, followed by 6 intervals in which the observer codes teacher position, teacher behavior, and student behavior. Since only one event is recorded in each category, CISSAR codes are mutually exclusive and exhaustive. After each set of 7 intervals the pattern is repeated. This sampling pattern takes into account the relative stability of activity, task, and structure events and the rapid changes associated with teacher location, teacher behavior, and student behavior events.

Based upon these CISSAR records, ecobehavioral sequences are created for analysis by computer software. Seven intervals of recorded data yield six ecobehavior sequences for analysis. All six sequences take on the activity, task, structure values coded in the first interval while the teacher position, teacher behavior, and student behavior values are free to vary within each single sequence.

Issues Concerning Scores and Data Analysis

Research questions concerning ecobehavioral data are often directed at several levels, including individual ecological and behavioral codes/categories, ecological arrangements and their relationship to student behavior (ecobehavioral interaction), ecological patterns and sequences over time, and the statistical significance of these relationships.

Ecological and Behavioral Description

Molar description of ecological and behavioral events is based upon the unconditional probability of a specific event or sequence of events $p\ (Ei/Sn)$, where Ei = the frequency of event Ei divided by the total number of event sequences observed or Sn. Molar descriptions do not reveal information about the interrelationships among ecobehavioral events.

Molar descriptions using the CISSAR have been used to compare instruction in inner-city and suburban schools. For example, fourth-grade teachers in inner-city schools used specific instructional tasks significantly more often than teachers in suburban schools. In inner-city schools, fourth-grade teachers were more likely to use media (overhead projectors, films, etc.). In suburban schools, teachers were more likely to assign seatwork and allow students to work independently (Greenwood et al., 1984). When the behaviors of students in these groups were compared, inner-city students were found to emit significantly less active academic responding than suburban students, even when IQ and socioeconomic status were statistically controlled (Greenwood et al., 1981; Stanley & Greenwood, 1983). These molar group differences in classroom ecology and student behavior were helpful in making global comparsions between programs.

Table 4. CISSAR Data Sheet

__:__		R M S H L Sc SS Ac									Rr Wb Ws Pp Ll Om Tsd Fp								Eg Sg I				__:__				______		
START		Ft Bm Tn Ct																					STOP				STOP CODE		
IF	AD	AS	S	B	O	NR	T	OT	A	D	W	G	RA	RS	TA	ANQ	ASK	AT	RH	LM	M	PA	DI	PI	IT	TNA	IL	LA	SST
IF	AD	AS	S	B	O	NR	T	OT	A	D	W	G	RA	RS	TA	ANQ	ASK	AT	RH	LM	M	PA	DI	PI	IT	TNA	IL	LA	SST
IF	AD	AS	S	B	O	NR	T	OT	A	D	W	G	RA	RS	TA	ANQ	ASK	AT	RH	LM	M	PA	DI	PI	IT	TNA	IL	LA	SST
IF	AD	AS	S	B	O	NR	T	OT	A	D	W	G	RA	RS	TA	ANQ	ASK	AT	RH	LM	M	PA	DI	PI	IT	TNA	IL	LA	SST
IF	AD	AS	S	B	O	NR	T	OT	A	D	W	G	RA	RS	TA	ANQ	ASK	AT	RH	LM	M	PA	DI	PI	IT	TNA	IL	LA	SST
IF	AD	AS	S	B	O	NR	T	OT	A	D	W	G	RA	RS	TA	ANQ	ASK	AT	RH	LM	M	PA	DI	PI	IT	TNA	IL	LA	SST

__:__		R M S H L Sc SS Ac									Rr Wb Ws Pp Ll Om Tsd Fp								Eg Sg I				__:__				______		
START		Ft Bm Tn Ct																					STOP				STOP CODE		
IF	AD	AS	S	B	O	NR	T	OT	A	D	W	G	RA	RS	TA	ANQ	ASK	AT	RH	LM	M	PA	DI	PI	IT	TNA	IL	LA	SST
IF	AD	AS	S	B	O	NR	T	OT	A	D	W	G	RA	RS	TA	ANQ	ASK	AT	RH	LM	M	PA	DI	PI	IT	TNA	IL	LA	SST
IF	AD	AS	S	B	O	NR	T	OT	A	D	W	G	RA	RS	TA	ANQ	ASK	AT	RH	LM	M	PA	DI	PI	IT	TNA	IL	LA	SST
IF	AD	AS	S	B	O	NR	T	OT	A	D	W	G	RA	RS	TA	ANQ	ASK	AT	RH	LM	M	PA	DI	PI	IT	TNA	IL	LA	SST
IF	AD	AS	S	B	O	NR	T	OT	A	D	W	G	RA	RS	TA	ANQ	ASK	AT	RH	LM	M	PA	DI	PI	IT	TNA	IL	LA	SST
IF	AD	AS	S	B	O	NR	T	OT	A	D	W	G	RA	RS	TA	ANQ	ASK	AT	RH	LM	M	PA	DI	PI	IT	TNA	IL	LA	SST

Analysis of Ecobehavioral Interaction

Analysis of ecobehavioral interaction is based upon the joint occurrences of ecobehavioral events within sequences. Scores are formed based upon the conditional probability of joint events or the probability of event *Ei* given the ecological arrangement *Ai*, $p(Ei|Ai)$. For example, in a study of ecobehavioral interaction in the classroom (Greenwood et al., 1985) the probability of a student reading aloud (*Ei*) was .35 when the task (*Ax*) was a reader but .02 when the task was a worksheet (*Ay*). This analysis reveals the conditional effects of ecological events upon student behavior.

Molecular descriptions with conditional probabilities have revealed the diversity of specific ecological arrangements students experience within single lessons and the specific academic behaviors associated with each particular arrangement (Greenwood et al., 1985). These analyses identify ecological arrangements which significantly accelerate or decelerate student's academic responding compared with the unconditional response probability. For example, we reported a base probability of .33 for academic responding during spelling in an inner-city sample (Greenwood et al., 1985). The probability of academic responding increased to .62 when the following arrangements of variables occurred: Activity = *Spelling,* Task = *Paper/Pencil,* Structure = *Entire Group,* Teacher Location = *At Desk,* Teacher Response = *Not Teaching*. In contrast, the probability of academic responding decreased to .04 when the following arrangement occurred: Activity = *Spelling,* Task = *Teacher/Student Discussion,* Structure = *Entire Group,* Teacher Location = *In Front,* Teacher Response = *Teaching*.

Analysis of Ecological Arrangements

Sequential analysis of ecological arrangements reveals the pattern of change in the classroom environment during teaching and instruction. This analysis is based upon sequence by sequence changes in ecological arrangements over time. Such analysis is completed by counting the frequency with which any arrangement is observed to follow a specific arrangement one sequence later in time or lag = 1. Analyses of this type reveal which events are likely to follow a target event. These results have indicated that some instructional arrangements remain stable, an event follows itself into the subsequent sequence with a high probability. For example, it was found in one observation that the arrangement of Activity = *Reading,* Task = *Paper/Pencil,* Structure = *Entire Group,* Teacher Position = *Among Students,* Teacher Behavior = *Teaching* followed itself in time (lag = 1) 126 of 131 possible times, $p = .96$. This is a picture of the students engaged in a sustained lesson in which they refer to a paper and pencil task.

This same analysis has revealed dynamic changes in teacher location and behavior rarely seen in behavior analytic studies. In a study by Arreaga-Mayer, Dorsey, Carta, and Verna (1984), a teacher was instructed to move among students and give contingent social praise for peer tutoring behaviors. They found that Teaching was most likely to be followed by Teaching one sequence later with a probability of .60. Approval was the behavior most likely to succeed Teaching with a probability of .25. It also was shown that Approval was followed by another occurrence of Approval at a probability of .44 or by Teaching at .30.

The lag = 1 transition matrix of another student in the Arreaga-Mayer et al. (1984) study is found in Table 5 and illustrates in greater detail the points just discussed. The upper panel contains the ecological transition frequencies, the lower panel contains the conditional probabilities based upon these frequencies. As can be seen, the variations in classroom ecology during spelling were restricted to teacher position and teacher behavior as the activity, task, and structure were unchanged. The teacher moved from among students, to in front of the target student, then behind the student, and then to the student's side. Teacher behavior changed from teaching to approval. The probabilities in the diagonal of Table 5 demonstrated that the teacher tended to remain in the same location and to continue her behavior (teaching = .57, approval = .47) into the next sequence. It also was demonstrated that the teacher was likely to return to among students and continue her teaching behavior following a change to approval (.37) or a change to in front of the class and teaching (.67). In contrast to most data concerning improvements in teacher's rates of teacher praise and approval, these data portray the likelihood of the teacher actually distributing approval while teaching.

Statistical Analysis

The statistical analysis of sequential data has been extensively covered elsewhere (cf. Allison & Liker, 1982; Wampold & Margolin, 1982) and the reader is referred to these excellent sources. However, it should be noted that these analyses are relatively new and many issues remain to be addressed (Allison & Liker, 1982). Several procedures that we have found useful include (a) tests of conditional vs. unconditional probabilities in order to identify ecological arrangements that accelerate or decelerate student's academic behavior, (b) tests of probabilities between groups of subjects in order to compare academic behavior differences, and (c) tests of lag = 1 transition probabilities reflecting the stability or variability in the instructional ecology over time.

Until recently, these tests were conducted using the formula for the difference between proportions. Thus, z-tests (Allison and Liker, 1982) or X^2 tests (Castellan, 1979) have been used. According to Gardner and Hartmann (1984) and Gardner, Hartmann, and Mitchell (1982) however, these tests can be adversely affected by dependencies within the data of each interactant (serial dependency) and between the interactant data (joint dependency). They recommended screening the data for serial correlation prior to conducting these analyses and in its presence, interpreting z or X^2 with caution. They further suggested the use of

Table 5. Ecological Transition Matrix for a Student Whose Teacher is Using Systematic Consequences During Spelling Instruction

Ecological Transition Frequencies

Antecedent (T_1) AC TA ST TP TB	Subsequent (T_{+1}) 1	2	3	4	5	6	7	8	Total
1 S PP EG AS T	27	12	6	1				1	47
2 S PP EG AS A	11	14		2	2			1	30
3 S PP EG IF T	5	1	2						8
4 S PP EG B T	2	1							3
5 S PP EG B A		2							2
6 S PP EG IF A	1								1
7 S PP EG S A							1		1
8 S PP EG S T	1								1
Total	47	30	8	3	2	1	1	1	93

Conditional Probabilities

AC TA ST TP TB	1	2	3	4	5	6	7	8
1 S PP EG AS T	.57	.26	.13	.02				.02
2 S PP EG AS A	.37	.47		.07	.07			.03
3 S PP EG IF T	.62	.13	.25					
4 S PP EG B T	.67	.33						
5 S PP EG B A		1.00						
6 S PP EG IF A	1.00							
7 S PP EG S A							1.00	
8 S PP EG S T	1.00							

Note: Table abbreviations are as follows: T_1 = Antecedent at time one. T_{+1} = Subsequent at time two.

Markov procedures as alternate analyses. Wampold and Margolin (1982) recommended use of nonparametic tests based upon runs and game theory, which they argue are not affected by this problem. It appears that the procedures suggested by Gardner and Hartmann and the nonparamentrics discussed by Wampold and Margolin are the current solutions to this problem. However, the extent to which these confounding dependencies affect ecobehavioral interaction data, as they do social interaction data, remains to be demonstrated.

Issues Concerning Reliability and Interobserver Agreement

Test-Retest Reliability

In a recent evaluation of reliability, 17 children were observed for two entire days, with a month in between. Only 12 of 53 (22%) codes produced mear values significantly different ($p < .05$) at the test phase than at the retest occasion. The test-retest correlations ranged from .35 to .93 over codes (*Mn* = .88).

Stability

Another study examined the number of days required to form representative (stable) scores. We only tested the stability of activity and student behavior because these two categories represented the slowest and fastest changing categories. The stability coefficients were based on daily observations of 12 students in one elmentary school. The objective was to determine the number of days required to form representative estimates. The criterion was based upon four observation days randomly conducted over four consecutive weeks for each student and was theoretically representative of one month. CISSAR scores based upon four days were correlated with scores based upon one, two, and three days.

Results of the one day comparison indicated that activities accounted for 57% of the variance in the four day criterion while student behavior accounted for 92% of the variance. In the two day comparison, activities accounted for 77%, increasing to 84% in the three day comparison. Student behavior declined slightly by 1% in variance accounted for at two days, increasing only 3% at three days. Thus, two or three days of data formed better activity estimates while student behavior was well estimated based upon only one day. These data suggested that schedule changes from day to day clearly have an impact on estimates of activity scores. However, these effects had little effect upon student behavior estimates. In our work, we have used one or two day samples depending upon the questions to be addressed. When accuracy in estimating activities is essential, two days are used. The variables that we did not assess in this study, (i.e., tasks, structure, teacher position and teacher behavior), we assume fall within the extremes of estimates for activities and student behavior.

Interobserver Agreement

Interobserver agreement checks are made on a systematic basis in all studies in which CISSAR is used. During research to estimate entire day ecobehavioral variables (Greenwood et al., 1984), we have conducted both short and long-duration sampling of agreement. Agreement studies based upon half-day observations to estimate reliability on slow changing CISSAR variables (e.g., activity), for example, have produced correlations ranging from .58 to 1.00 for codes with sufficient data. Short duration checks to estimate reliability on rapidly changing CISSAR variables (e.g., student behavior), have been based on 14 minute checks and have produced correlations ranging from .73 to 1.00 for codes with sufficient data.

Agreement checks are conducted by two observers, using a single audio interval timer with double earphone jacks to synchronize and pace their recording of the same student. Observers sit four to six feet apart during their checks to prevent them from influencing each other's recording. For observer training and for monitoring of agreement over time, percent agreement [(# agreements/ # agreements + # disagreements) × 100] is calculated for each code within each category based upon analysis of occurrence and nonoccurrence intervals. These data are used for specific feedback to observers and to the observer coordinator for quality control. Table 6 summarizes percent agreement data from a recent evaluation. Percent agreement means ranged from 86.3% to 99.1% over all code categories. In complex codes, percent agreement levels of 70% or higher have been suggested as adequate (Jones, Reid, & Patterson, 1975).

In studies in which sequential scores are to be reported, the agreement on sequences is assessed. In some cases we have assessed the agreement on ecological sequences (i.e., Activity, Task, Structure, Teacher Position, Teacher Behavior) by comparing two observers' records sequence by sequence for exact agreement. If one coded event in the sequence differs, a disagreement is tallied. Cohen's Kappa (Cohen, 1960) is used to compute an agreement statistic which controls for chance levels of agreement. The mean Kappa produced in one such analysis was .69 for ecological sequences and .72 for student behavior within each sequence. The ranges were from .36 to .95 on ecological sequences and from .51 to .89 on student behavior. A Kappa level of .60 or greater has been suggested as adequate (Hartmann & Woods, 1982, p. 126).

Some methodologists (Hartmann, 1977; Hartmann & Woods, 1982) have suggested that reliability for conditional probabilities should be computed on the probability scores produced for sequences instead of on interval or sequence agreements. To examine reliability in this manner, 21 paired records were combined within a single record to yield a large sample of arrangements (sequences). Interobserver agreement (Pearson *r*) for ecological occurrence was .74 across arrangements. Comparably large correlations were found .96, .78, .94 for writing, attention, and the academic composite codes respectively.

Table 6. Percent Agreement Summary[a]

CISSAR Category	*Mean Agreement*	*SD*	*Min*	*Max*
Activities	99.1	4.2	58.0	100.0
Tasks	96.9	7.5	58.0	100.0
Structure	99.2	2.9	83.0	100.0
Teacher Position	94.1	8.0	31.0	100.0
Teacher Behavior	92.1	8.7	55.0	100.0
Student Behavior	86.3	11.7	32.0	100.0
Overall	91.8	6.3	70.0	100.0

Note: [a] Agreement data are based upon 190 fourteen min. agreement checks produced by 10 observers during the 1981–82 school year.

Issues Concerning Validity

Concurrent Validity

Concurrent validity is the correlation between two measures assessed at the same point in time. A positive correlation between achievement test scores and select CISSAR academic response codes has been reported in several studies (Greenwood, 1985; Greenwood et al., 1981; Stanley & Greenwood, 1983). Greenwood et al. (1981) and Stanley and Greenwood (1983) reported that two groups of fourth graders, one attending suburban schools (n = 48) and the other attending inner-city schools (n = 45), differed significantly on reading achievement and IQ but also differed with respect to observed academic responding (inner-city students were lower on all three variables). CISSAR academic responding scores for suburban students were 5% higher than inner-city students based upon an entire day of observation, $F(1,91) = 9.37, p = .003$. The correlation between achievement scores and the academic-response composite in this study was .45 ($df = 91, p < .01$) for reading, and .21 ($df = 91, p < .05$) for math. Within the inner-city group these correlations were .40 in reading ($df = 43, p < .01$) and .09 in math ($p > .05$). Similar figures in the suburban groups were .40 ($df = 46, p < .01$) and .25 ($p > .05$).

These findings were recently replicated in a first grade sample of inner-city (n = 82) and suburban students (n = 23) (Greenwood, 1985). Even as early as October of the first grade, these two groups differed significantly in mean levels of IQ, reading, language, and mathematics achievement. As in the fourth grade samples, inner-city students performed less well on these standardized tests. CISSAR data taken in these settings also replicated Greenwood et al. (1981), by reflecting a 5% mean difference in students' academic responding, $F(1,103) = 3.89, p = .05$.

CISSAR observation scores when submitted to stepwise regression analysis have contributed significant variance to the prediction of achievement beyond that accounted by IQ (Greenwood et al., 1981; Greenwood, Delquadri et al., 1982). For example, in an inner-city group, CISSAR scores accounted for an additional 5% to 20% of the total variance for achievement after IQ was forced into the regression equation. Similarly, writing behavior contributed 13% to the prediction of reading achievement. Teacher located "in front" of the class contributed 17% to the prediction of math achievement. Collectively, these studies of the convergence between direct observation and test measures using different methods of analysis provides evidence for the concurrent validity of CISSAR code scores.

Treatment Validity

The CISSAR codes are sensitive to changes in ecological arrangements made by the classroom teacher (Greenwood et al., 1985) and from direct instructional intervention (Greenwood, Delquadri, & Hall, 1984; Greenwood et al., 1984), thus demonstrating treatment validity.

Validity due to teacher variations in ecological arrangements. In a cross-validation study (Greenwood et al., 1985), we sought to identify ecological arrangements that accelerated or decelerated students' academic behavior. It was generally true that arrangements using paper and pencil tasks increased the probability of academic responding in spelling, while teacher-student discussion tasks decreased this probability. In Title I fourth grade samples, it was demonstrated that the probabilities of academic responding were highest, .62, .60, and .74, during the following arrangements: *S PP EG AD NR* (Spelling, Paper/Pencil, Entire Group, At Desk, No Response), *S PP SG S T* (Spelling, Paper/Pencil, Small Group, Side of Student, Teaching), *S PP SG O NR* (Spelling, Paper/Pencil, Small Group, Out of Room, No Response). These probabilities were also significantly larger than the base probability of .33 in spelling.

The probability of an academic response was lowest, .09, .04, and .00, all significantly below the base probability, during the arrangements *S TSD EG IF T* (Spelling, Teacher-Student Discussion, Entire Group, In Front, Teaching), *S TSD, SG, AS, T* (Spelling, Teacher-Student Discussion, Entire Group, Among Students, Teaching), and *S TSD EG AS T* (Spelling, Teacher-Student Discussion, Entire Group, Among Students, Teaching).

These data demonstrated differential behavioral effects as a function of natural teacher variations in ecological arrangements. We used this information to explain the overall difference in academic responding between Title I and non-Title I groups (Greenwood et al., 1985). Inner-city Title I teachers spent more time using decelerator arrangements (i.e., those involving teacher/student discussion with academic response probabilities significantly lower than the base probability), than did non-Title I teachers.

Data from Title I reading instruction are presented in Table 7 to demonstrate further the natural ecological effects on student's academic behavior. Arrangements with probabilities greater than .50 were defined as accelerator variables and included *R RR SG AS T, R PP SG AS T, R WS SG AS T,* and *R RR SG S T.* These arrangements involved students in the use of readers, worksheets, or paper/pencil tasks. Students were also taught in small groups, with the teacher among them or next to them engaged in teaching behavior. Decelerator reading arrangements were *R LL SG AS T* and *R OM EG AS T.* These arrangements involved the students in lecture or media in either small or entire group arrangements while the teacher was among the students engaged in teaching behavior. The decelerators of academic response, however, were accelerators of student attention (.81 and .88). Accelerator arrangements involving readers increased the probability of silent reading and academic talk (*R RR SG AS T* or *R RR SG S T*) while those involving worksheets or paper/pencil (*R WS SG AS T* and *R PP SG AS T*) raised the probability of student's writing.

Table 7. Classroom Ecological Arrangements and Conditional Academic Response Probabilities for Title I Students During Reading Instruction

Ecological Arrangements [(Ai|Sn) × 100]						*Conditional Probabilities for Student Academic Responding [p(Ri|Si)]*								
AC	*TA*	*ST*	*TP*	*TB*	*%*	*W*	*AGP*	*RA*	*RS*	*TA*	*ANQ*	*ASK*	*Composite*	*AT*
R	RR	SG	AS	T	13.9	.054			.199	.261	.013	.030	.557[a]	.321
R	WS	SG	AS	T	7.5	.342			.149	.035		.005	.531[a]	.337
R	TSD	SG	AS	T	11.2	.030		.030	.163	.027		.010	.297	.586
R	RR	SG	S	T	3.0					.663			.663[a]	.188
R	WB	SG	AS	T	12.7	.167		.006	.235	.006	.006		.420	.396
R	PP	SG	AS	T	8.4	.487				.181	.009	.004	.681[a]	.230
R	LL	SG	AS	T	3.2	.034		.023	.023		.046	.011	.137[d]	.805
R	OM	EG	AS	T	4.1								.000[d]	.883
R	OM	EG	S	T	3.4	.391							.391	.554
R	(Base)				100.0	.155	—	.033	.138	.017	.016	.002	.361	.502

Notes: [a]accelerator arrangement defined as significantly greater than the base probability.
[d]decelerator arrangement defined as significantly less than the base probability.

Another study (Greenwood & Patterson, 1985) evaluated the effects of individualized materials used in activity centers and peer tutoring on the ecobehavioral interaction in an inner-city second grade classroom. Observation of one child is summarized for morning and afternoon segments in Table 8. The instructional format for the class was peer tutoring during the morning in reading, math, and spelling and activity centers in the afternoon where students completed individualized assignments.

These data demonstrated, compared to base probabilities, that peer tutoring in the morning significantly increased the already high level of academic responding in reading, math, and spelling. In the afternoon period, work in activity centers increased academic responding significantly higher than the entire after-

Table 8. Effects of Peer Tutoring and Activity Centers on Classroom Ecological Arrangements and Conditional Academic Response Probabilities for One Student

Ecological Arrangements					*Conditional Probabilities for Student Academic Responding*									
Morning Peer Tutoring Versus Baserates														
AC	*TA*	*ST*	*TP*	*TB*	*%*	*W*	*AGP*	*RA*	*RS*	*TA*	*ANQ*	*ASK*	*Composite*	*AT*
R	RR	SG	AS	T	46.5	.180		.380	.340	.070			.927	.030
													*	
Reading (Base)					100.0	.107		.279	.284	.060	.014		.744	.228
M	PP	SG	AS	T	60.3	.309		.309	.149	.165			.927	.074
													*	
Math (Base)					100.0	.263		.205	.173	.135			.776	.205
S	PP	SG	AS	T	61.3	.326		.316	.137	.168			.947	.053
													*	
Spelling (Base)					100.0	.245		.219	.116	.155			.735	.252
Morning (Base)					100.0	.191		.202	.188	.102	.006		.689	.265
Afternoon Activity Centers Versus Baserates														
AC	*TA*	*ST*	*TP*	*TB*	*%*	*W*	*AGP*	*RA*	*RS*	*TA*	*ANQ*	*ASK*	*Composite*	*AT*
R	PP	SG	AS	T	50.0	.464			.294	.033			.791	.144
Reading (Base)					100.0	.337		.026	.275	.062	.007		.707	.199
M	PP	SG	AS	T	63.7	.633			.190	.051			.874	.089
Math (Base)					100.0	.597			.218	.032			.847	.097
Afternoon (Base)					100.0	.375		.016	.224	.054	.040		.669	.196

Note: * = $p < .05$.

noon base level. Both morning and afternoon periods contributed to consistently high academic responding.

These studies illustrated the CISSAR code's sensitivity to natural teacher variations in the instructional program. This was demonstrated in comparisons across divergent samples (Greenwood, et al., 1985) and for a single student as a result of teacher variation of the program (Greenwood & Patterson, 1985).

Validity due to direct instructional intervention. In three studies comparing classwide peer tutoring methods vs. teacher-developed instruction, we demonstrated using single-subject experimental designs that tutoring produced changes in the instructional ecology, student behavior, and performance on weekly mastery tests (Greenwood et al., 1984). Specifically, peer tutoring was accompanied by clear changes in CISSAR ecological factors (i.e., increased use of paper/pencil and worksheet tasks) and student's behavior (i.e., more frequent writing and talk about learning tasks), as well as a coincidental improvement in weekly performance tests for spelling, math facts, and vocabulary items. In comparison, the major tasks used by students during teacher-developed instruction were teacher-student discussion and media. These were tasks accompanied by increased attention but poorer performance on weekly mastery tests.

We reported similar results for experimentally controlled group evaluations of classwide peer tutoring applied to reading (Greenwood, Delquadri, & Hall, 1984). During a standard reading period, peer tutoring students increased their use of reader tasks from 14% before the program to 62% and 61% at two observations completed while the program was in use. The control group in different classrooms received the regular basal reading program and were observed using reader tasks at a 31% level for preassessment and at levels 9% and 12% during follow-up assessments. The experimental group improved academic responding from 33% to 61% and 65% during the tutoring program while the control group remained unchanged (47%, 39%, and 45%). Oral reading accounted for the increased responding of the experimental group (32%) during the program compared with the control group (4.4%). These ecobehavioral changes during instruction covaried with decreased rates of oral reading errors in assessments made by teachers following tutoring sessions. Collectively, these research studies illustrated convergence of ecological, student behavior, and academic outcome data within experimental designs and demonstrated that ecobehavioral variables covaried directly with causal manipulations of specific instructional procedures. This was additional evidence supporting the treatment validity of the code.

Contribution to Programmatic Research

The ecobehavioral interaction approach we have presented can provide a powerful process variable for studies of child behavior. When used in programmatic research, data describing what children do in a specific situation inspires hypotheses that can be tested for function and generality. The identification of the lower academic response levels for inner-city students and this behavior's ecology is a case in point. Our efforts in programmatic research have been directed at the dual problems of achievement and academic retardation in relation to the ecology of inner-city schools. In our research, examination of ecobehavioral interaction differences among academically delayed and nondelayed children provided a starting point. A careful sifting of these data led to an understanding of what current behavioral repertoires a specific environment supports, the setting events, discriminative stimuli, and reinforcing consequences which are and are not operating in these interactions.

For example, a lower level of daily academic behavior for inner-city students, we have argued, reflects a developmental lag for the inner-city students which is a function of the school program and ecobehavioral interaction within the classroom. We have projected these differences in daily academic responding to be on the order of 11- to 13-minutes of academic behavior per day, the equivalent of 33 school days when compounded over the school year (Greenwood et al., 1981). This finding has been replicated in 1983–84 with students at the first grade level. What is particularly surprising is the fact that this difference at first and fourth grades persists in the natural environment even though special arrangements (e.g., Title I labs), are routinely provided by school personnel to enhance academic instruction.

The analysis of ecobehavioral interaction data revealed that this performance difference was related to Title I classroom environmental arrangements (i.e., frequent uses of media, lecture, and teacher/student discussion) and corresponding lower levels of academic responding (Greenwood et al., 1985). Ecological arrangements that accelerated academic responding were those in which readers, worksheets, and paper/pencil tasks were used. In non-Title I schools, fourth grade students spent more time engaged in sustained study and seatwork, while teachers remained at their desks correcting papers and making no direct responses to students. These ecobehavioral differences, favoring the non-Title I groups, suggested the basis for subsequent investigations of the causal nature of new procedures. These procedures (e.g., peer tutoring), were designed to establish high academic response levels when introduced into the lives of children exhibiting lower achievement levels. Rather than simply assigning inner-city students increased seatwork tasks, we opted to use peer tutors with reader or worksheet tasks, in order to prompt even higher levels of academic responding. Studies and replications at this level of research refined our knowledge concerning individual behavioral control by systematically manipulating these variables. Our efforts then turned towards evaluating this intervention for its ability to remove the lag in academic responding among inner-city students.

Any procedures that we developed could not be solely dependent upon the classroom teacher nor could they require expensive media or electronic technology resources. The procedures had to be ecologically valid, taking advantage of persons and stimuli normally present in classroom settings. The procedure required more than contingency management. A dynamic mechanism was necessary for presenting frequent task response trials and providing frequent response opportunities for all students including the lowest functioning ones. These requirements led to the analysis of peer tutoring and the eventual development of classwide peer tutoring.

Early peer tutoring studies (Hall et al., 1982) demonstrated that direct trials provided by peer tutors increased academic responses. An error correction procedure was developed that could be effectively applied by the tutor. This involved having the tutee practice the correct response immediately following an error (Delquadri, 1978). The next problem was finding a way to extend this procedure to all children in the classroom. Our prior data had demonstrated wide individual variability in mean academic responding, ranging from 4% to 42% across students. Instructional procedures were needed that could effectively reduce this range and ensure that all students would engage in the academic task.

Delquadri, Greenwood, Stretton, and Hall (1983) reported the successful application of a classwide peer tutoring approach in spelling. The tutoring program was designed to increase the student's opportunity to spell words aloud and in writing. This was accomplished through the use of peer tutors and group and individual reinforcement contingencies. In the classwide peer tutoring program, the class was divided into tutoring pairs (including one triad if an odd number of students were present) and each pair randomly assigned to each of two teams. The teams compete to obtain the highest point totals based upon the performance of individual team members while they are tutees.

Students who are tutees orally spell and write the words presented by the tutors. Tutors present words to be spelled, apply an error correction procedure when errors occur, and administer contingent points for each written word. Delquadri et al. (1983) reported that even students who made more than 12 spelling errors on a weekly test improved to fewer than 3 errors after four 20 minute daily tutoring sessions. Subsequent studies of classwide peer tutoring in reading and in other subject matters have demonstrated that the procedure is effective increasing student responding and engagement with academic tasks (Greenwood et al., 1984). When this procedure was used, the range across students in academic responding was reduced and the mean increased such that all the students spent over 45% of the session engaged in academic behavior. These improvements were functionally related to achievement gain (Delquadri et al., 1986; Greenwood, Delquadri, & Hall, 1984; Greenwood et al., 1984).

This set of programmatic research studies using ecobehavioral assessment has demonstrated a developmental progression from study to study. In each case ecobehavioral assessment has enabled the discovery of important factors and relationships, has produced procedures and studies to test these factors, and has confirmed functional relationships between process and outcome variables. The most recent work underway by our group is the development of additional ecobehavioral coding systems. Rotholz et al. (1985) has developed a version of the CISSAR with ecological codes for assessing features of special education settings and setting events for moderate and severely handicapped students. These include variables such as the person directly instructing a child, if other than the teacher (e.g., aides and peers), and teaching structure (e.g., 1 to 1 teaching), in addition to physical structure (e.g., small group). New student response coding features include multiple recording of concurrent student responses. Carta and Greenwood (1985); Carta, Greenwood, and Atwater (1985) have recently developed a code with ecobehavioral variables tailored to the preschool environment. Code categories that measure preacademic tasks and student locations within the classroom are included. Ecobehavioral studies are currently underway using these codes.

CONCLUSION

In contrast to traditional assessment approaches, ecobehavioral interaction allows the structure and pattern of momentary ecology variables (in this case academic instruction) to be displayed and related to behavior. Ecobehavioral assessment is focused on quantification of changing situational factors and subject responses.

While increasingly evident in the literature, the ecobehavioral approach is just beginning to have an impact on work in applied settings. The relative newness of this approach is due to the conceptual and methodological issues reviewed in this chapter, in addition to pragmatic issues. Perhaps most importantly are the increased resources and costs associated with assessments of this type compared with traditional forms of behavioral assessment. Extensive samples of data are required for observational studies of individuals in order to characterize ecobehavioral interaction. These studies require computer assistance for recording, storing, and analyzing the data. The statistical procedures for these data are relatively new with unresolved issues concerning serial correlation and violation of assumptions of independence. These costs may inhibit many applied researchers. In the area of school-based assessment alone, we can point to no examples of ecobehavior interaction being used (e.g., for screening, placement, or progress monitoring, etc). However, with the seemingly endless development of electronic technology and its lower costs, this approach will become more feasible.

The ecobehavioral interaction approach to assessment is a methodology for investigating many of the current issues and problems facing the field. These include (a) setting events and stimulus control (Karpowitz & Johnson, 1981, Larsen & Morris, 1983; Wahler & Fox, 1981), (b) the natural conditions surrounding development of specific behavioral repertoires (Hart & Risley, 1984), (c) maintenance and generalization of social repertoires (Kohler & Greenwood,

1985), and (c) interventions based upon precision interpretations of naturalistic events (Wahler & Fox, 1981; Patterson, 1982). As with other approaches to assessment, the importance of the ecobehavioral approach will be its contribution to our ability to predict and control behavior in applied settings.

ACKNOWLEDGMENTS

The work reported in this manuscript was supported by grants from the Special Education Program, U.S. Department of Education (Nos. G007902271, G007901332, G008300067, and G008300068) and the National Institute of Child Health and Human Development (No. HD03144). However, the opinions reflected in this article are strictly those of the authors and no official endorsement should be inferred.

We are indebted to Dr. Don Moritz, Director of Research and Pupil Personnel Services, and Dr. Lowell Alexander, Director of Special Education, and the Principals, teachers, and students of the Kansas City Public Schools without whose assistance, this work would not be possible. We are also indebted to Dr. R. Vance Hall and Dr. Joe Delquadri for their comments on this paper. Additional thanks are expressed to our graduate students and colleagues at Juniper Gardens. Thanks are also due to Mary Todd for her help preparing the manuscript. Lastly, thanks are expressed to Rebecca Finney for developing the programs used in the CISSAR data analysis system.

Reprints and the CISSAR code may be obtained from Dr. Charles R. Greenwood, Juniper Gardens Children's Project, 1614 Washington Blvd., Kansas City, KS, 66102.

REFERENCES

Allison, P. D., & Liker, J. K. (1982). Analyzing sequential categorical data on dyadic interaction: A comment on Gottman. *Psychological Bulletin, 91,* 393–403.

Arreaga-Mayer, C., Dorsey, D., Carta, J. J., & Verna, G. (1984). Issues related to the ecobehavioral analysis of school problems of minority students. *Monograph of the Bueno Center for Multicultural Education, 5,* 109–132.

Barker, R. R. (1961). *Ecological psychology.* Stanford, CA: Stanford University Press.

Bakeman, R. (1978). Untangling streams of behavior: Sequential analyses of observation data. In G. P. Sackett (Ed.), *Observing behavior: Data collection and analysis methods* (pp. 63–78). Baltimore, MD: University Park Press.

Biglan, A., Hops, H., Sherman, L., Friedman, L. S., Arthur, J., & Osteen V. (1984). *Problem solving interactions of depressed women and their spouses.* Eugene, OR: Oregon Research Institute.

Bijou, S. W. (1981). The prevention of retarded development in disadvantaged children. In M. J. Begab, H. C. Haywood, & H. L. Garber, (Eds.), *Psychosocial influences in retarded performance: Issues and theories in development,* (Vol. 1, pp. 29–46). Baltimore, MD: University Park Press.

Bronfenbrenner, U. (1979). Contexts of child rearing: Problems and prospects. *American Psychologist, 34,* 844–850.

Brophy, J. (1979). Teacher behavior and its effects. *Journal of Educational Psychology, 71,* 733–750.

Cairns, R. B. (1979). *The analysis of social interactions: Methods, issues, and illustrations.* Hillsdale, NJ: Lawrence Erlbaum Associates.

Carta, J. J., & Greenwood, C. R. (1985). A methodology for the evaluation of early intervention programs. *Topics in Early Childhood Special Education, 5,* 88–104.

Carta, J. J., Greenwood, C. R., & Atwater, J. B. (1985). *ESCAPE: Eco-behavioral system for complex assessment of preschool environments.* Kansas City, KS: Juniper Gardens Children's Project, Bureau of Child Research, University of Kansas.

Castellan, N. J., Jr. (1979). The analysis of behavior sequences. In R. B. Cairns (Ed.), *The analysis of social interactions: Methods, issues, and illustrations* (pp. 81–116). Hillsdale, NJ: Erlbaum.

Cobb, J., & Hops, H. (1971). *Coding manual for continuous observations in an academic setting.* Eugene, OR: Center at Oregon for Research in the Behavioral Education of the Handicapped.

Cobb, J. A. (1971). *Manual for coding academic survival skill behaviors and teacher/peer responses.* Eugene, OR: Center at Oregon for Research in the Behavioral Education of the Handicapped.

Cobb, J. A. (1972). Relationship of discrete classroom behaviors to fourth grade academic achievement. *Journal of Education Psychology, 63,* 74–80.

Cohen, J. (1960). A coefficient of agreement for nominal scales. *Educational and Psychological Measurement, 20,* 34–46.

Delquadri, J. (1978). *An analysis of generalization effects of four tutoring procedures on reading responses in eight learning disabled children.* Unpublished doctoral dissertation. Department of Human Development and Family Life, University of Kansas.

Delquadri, J., Greenwood, C. R., Stretton, K., & Hall, R. V. (1983). The peer tutoring game: A classroom procedure for increasing opportunity to respond and spelling performance. *Education and Treatment of Children, 6,* 225–239.

Delquadri, J., Greenwood, C. R., Whorton, D., Carta, J. J., & Hall, R. V. (1986). Classwide peer tutoring. *Exceptional Children, 52,* 535–542.

Dishion, T., Gardner, K., Patterson, G. R., Reid, J., Spryou, S., & Thibadeau, S. (1983). *The family process code: A multidimensional system for observation of family interaction.* Eugene, OR: Oregon Social Learning Group.

Flanders, N. (1970). *Analyzing teaching behavior.* Reading, MA: Addison-Wesley, 1970.

Foster, S. L., & Cone, J. D. (1980). Current issues in direct observation. *Behavioral Assessment, 2,* 313–338.

Gardner, W., & Hartmann, D. P. (1984). On Markov dependence in the analysis of social interaction. *Behavioral Assessment, 6,* 229–236.

Gardner, W., Hartmann, D. P., & Mitchell, C. (1982). The effects of serial dependency on the use of X^2 for analyzing sequential data in dyadic interactions. *Behavioral Assessment, 4,* 75–82.

Greenwood, C. R. (1985, May). *An ecobehavioral interaction approach in behavior analysis: Refinement of issues and data.* Invited address at the Eleventh Annual Convention of the Association for Behavior Analysis, Columbus, OH.

Greenwood, C. R. (1985). Settings or setting events as treatment in special education?: A review of mainstreaming. In M. L. Wolraich & D. Routh (Eds.), *Advances in developmental and behavioral pediatrics,* (Vol 6, pp. 205–239). Greenwich, CT: JAI Press.

Greenwood, C. R., Delquadri, J., & Hall, R. V. (1984). Opportunity to respond and student academic performance. In W. L. Heward, T. E. Heron, J. Trap-Porter, & D. S. Hill, (Eds.), *Focus on behavior analysis in education* (pp. 55–88). Columbus, OH: Charles Merrill.

Greenwood, C. R., Delquadri, J., Stanley, S. O., Sasso, G., Whorton, D., & Schulte, D. (1981). Allocating opportunity to learn as a basis for academic remediation: A developing model for teaching. *Monograph in Behavior Disorders, Summer,* 21–33.

Greenwood, C. R., Delquadri, J., Stanley, S. O., Terry, B., & Hall, R. V. (1982). *Relationships among instructional contexts, student behavior, and academic achievement.* Unpublished manuscript. Kansas City, KS: Juniper Gardens Children's Project, Bureau of Child Research, University of Kansas.

Greenwood, C. R., Delquadri, J., Stanley, S. O., Terry, B., & Hall, R. V. (1985). Assessment of ecobehavioral interaction in school settings. *Behavioral Assessment, 7,* 331–347.

Greenwood, C. R., Dinwiddie, G., Terry, B., Wade, L., Stanley, S., Thibadeau, S., & Delquadri, J. (1984). Teacher- versus peer-mediated instruction: An ecobehavioral analysis of achievement outcomes. *Journal of Applied Behavior Analysis. 17,* 521–538.

Greenwood, C. R., Hops, H., Delquadri, J., & Guild, J., (1974). Group contingencies for group consequences in classroom management. A further analysis. *Journal of Applied Behavior Analysis, 7,* 413–425.

Greenwood, C. R., & Patterson, P. (1985). *Eco-behavioral effects of teacher variations in the instructional program.* Paper presented at the Eleventh Annual Convention of the Association for Behavior Analysis, Columbus, Ohio, May.

Greenwood, C. R., Stokes, J. S., & Hops, H. (1974). *Program for Academic Survival Skills (PASS): Observer training manual.* Eugene, OR: Center at Oregon for Research in the Behavioral Education of the Handicapped.

Greenwood, C. R., Todd, N. M., Hops, H., & Walker, H. M. (1982). Global and specific behavior change targets in the assessment and behavior modification of socially withdrawn preschool children. *Behavioral Assessment, 4,* 273–298.

Hall, R. V., & Copeland, R. (1972). The responsive teaching model: A first step in shaping school personnel as behavior modification specialists. In F. W. Clark, D. R. Evans, & L. A. Hamerlynck (Eds.), *Implementing behavioral programs for schools and clinics* (pp. 125–150). Champaign, IL: Research Press.

Hall, R. V., Delquadri, J., Greenwood, C. R., & Thurston, L. (1982). The importance of opportunity to respond in children's academic success. In E. B. Edgar, N. G. Haring, J. R. Jenkins, & C. C. Pious (Eds.), *Mentally handicapped children: Education and training* (pp. 107–140). Baltimore, MD: University Park Press.

Hall, R. V., Lund, D., & Jackson, D. (1968). Effects of teacher attention on study behavior. *Journal of Applied Behavior Analysis, 1,* 1–12.

Hart, B., & Risley, T. (1984). The 'natural' conditions for learning to talk. In S. Warren (Chair), *Contemporary behavioral perspectives in language acquisition.* Symposium presented at the 10th Annual Convention of the Association for Behavior Analysis, Nashville, TN, May.

Hartmann, D. P. (1977). Considerations in the choice of interobserver reliability estimates. *Journal of Applied Behavior Analysis, 10,* 103–116.

Hartmann, D. P., & Woods, D. D. (1982). Observational methods. In A. S. Bellack, M. Hersen, & A. E. Kazdin (Eds.), *International handbook of behavior therapy* (pp. 109–138). New York: Plenum.

Hops, H., Biglan, A., Sherman, L., Arthur, J., Friedman, L., & Osteen, V. (1984). *Home observations of family interactions of depressed women.* Eugene, OR: Oregon Research Institute.

Hops, H., Walker, H. M., Fleischman, D., Nagoshi, J. T., Omura, R., Skindrud, K., & Taylor, J. (1978). CLASS: A standardized in-class program for acting-out children. II. Field test evaluations. *Journal of Educational Psychology, 70,* 636–644.

Jones, R. R., Reid, J. B., & Patterson, G. R. (1975). Naturalistic observation in clinical assessment. In P. McReynolds (Ed.), *Advances in psychological assessment* (Vol. 3, pp. 42–95). San Francisco: Jossey-Bass.

Kantor, J. R. (1959). *Interbehavioral psychology.* Granville, OH: Principia Press.

Karpowitz, D. H., & Johnson, S. M. (1981). Stimulus control in child-family interaction. *Behavioral Assessment 3,* 161–172.

Kohler, F. (1984). *Social interaction code for the Juniper Gardens peer tutoring game.* Kansas City, KS: Juniper Gardens Children's Project, Bureau of Child Research, University of Kansas.

Kohler, F., & Greenwood, C. R. (in press). *Towards a technology of generalization: The identification of natural communities of reinforcement. The Behavior Analyst.*

Lamb, M. E., Suomi, S. J., & Stephenson, G. R. (1979). *Social interaction analysis*. Madison, WI: University of Wisconsin Press.

Larsen, S. E., & Morris, E. K. (1983). *On the usefulness of the setting event concept in behavior analysis*. Paper read at the Ninth Annual Convention of the Association for Behavior Analysis, Milwaukee, WI.

Larsen, S. E., Morris, E. K., & Todd, J. T. (1984). *Comments on determinism and causality*. Paper read at the Tenth Annual Meeting of the Association for Behavior Analysis, Nashville, TN.

Leigland, S. (1984). On 'setting events' and related concepts. *The Behavior Analyst, 7,* 41–45.

McReynolds, P. (1979). The case for interactional assessment. *Behavioral Assessment, 3,* 237–247.

Michael, J. (1982). Distinguishing between discriminative and motivational functions of stimuli. *Journal of the Experimental Analysis of Behavior, 37,* 149–155.

Patterson, G. R. (1974). A basis for identifying stimuli which control behaviors in natural settings. *Child Development, 45,* 900–911.

Patterson, G. R. (1982). A microsocial analysis of structure and process. In G. R. Patterson, *Coercive family process* (pp. 169–198). Eugene, OR: Castalia Publishing Co.

Reid, J. B. (1978). *A social learning approach to family interaction,* (Vol 2): *A manual for coding family interactions*. Eugene, OR: Castalia Press.

Rogers-Warren, A., & Warren, S. (1977). *Ecological perspectives in behavior analysis*. Baltimore, MD: University Park Press.

Rotholz, D., Whorton, D., Schulte, D., Walker, D., McGrale, J., Norris, M., & Greenwood, C. R. (1985). *CISSAR—special education*. Kansas City, KS: Juniper Gardens Children's Project, Bureau of Child Research, University of Kansas.

Skinner, B. F. (1953). *Science and human behavior*. New York: MacMillan.

Stanley, S. O., & Greenwood, C. R. (1981). *CISSAR: Code for instructional structure and student academic response* (*Observer's manual*). Kansas City, KS: Juniper Gardens Children's Project, Bureau of Child Research, University of Kansas.

Stanley, S. O., & Greenwood, C. R. (1983). Assessing opportunity to respond in classroom environments through direct observation: How much opportunity to respond does the minority, disadvantaged student receive in school. *Exceptional Children, 49,* 370–373.

Wahler, R. G., & Fox, J. J. (1981). Setting events in applied behavior analysis: Toward a conceptual and methodological expansion. *Journal of Applied Behavior Analysis, 14,* 327–338.

Wahler, R. G., & Graves, M. G. (1983). Setting events in social networks: Ally or enemy in child behavior therapy? *Behavior Therapy, 14,* 19–36.

Wahler, R. G., House, A. E., & Stambaugh, E. E. (1976). *Ecological assessment of child problem behavior: A clinical package for home, school, and institutional settings*. New York: Pergamon.

Walker, H. M., Hops, H., & Figenbaum, E. (1976). Deviant classroom behavior as a function of combinations of social and token reinforcement and cost contingency. *Behavior Therapy, 7,* 76–88.

Wampold, B. E., & Margolin, G. (1982). Nonparametric strategies to test the independence of behavioral states in sequential data. *Psychological Bulletin, 92,* 755–756.

MEASUREMENT OF CHILDHOOD HYPERACTIVITY

Ronald J. Prinz, Pamela A. Moore, and William A. Roberts

ABSTRACT

Studies of childhood hyperactivity over the past two decades are reviewed with respect to measurement method and focus. Issues associated with how investigators defined their hyperactive samples are reviewed and analyzed with regard to sources of diagnostic information, behavioral criteria for selection, age of children, chronicity of symptomatology, and responsiveness to stimulant medication. Behavioral observation of hyperactive children is discussed in the context of what has been observed and how the observations have been applied. Outcome measures used for the evaluation of treatment with hyperactive children are discussed. Specific recommendations for improving the clinical and evaluative assessment of problems associated with childhood hyperactivity are offered.

Advances in Behavioral Assessment of Children and Families, Vol. 2, pgs. 99–119.
Editor: Ronald J. Prinz

ISBN: 0-89232-481-3

MEASUREMENT OF CHILDHOOD HYPERACTIVITY

Hyperactivity is a major psychological and psychiatric category used in the classification of childhood problems. Although now subsumed in DSM-III (American Psychiatric Association, 1980) under attention deficit disorder with hyperactivity (ADDH), the basic conceptualization of the disorder has remained relatively constant. The cluster of symptoms commonly associated with childhood hyperactivity include distractibility, poor attention span, perceptual problems, emotional lability, impulsivity, learning problems, and low frustration tolerance, as well as secondary problems involving disturbed peer relations, aggression, sleep disturbance, and negative self-statements. The estimates of prevalence rate for childhood hyperactivity vary according to the behavioral criteria used and the referral source (teacher, parent, physician, psychologist), ranging from as low as one percent (Sandoval, Lambert, & Sassone, 1980) to as high as ten percent (Huessy, Marshall, & Gendron, 1973). The wide range of prevalence estimates has been attributed to sampling problems and related Methodological shortcomings (Bosco & Robin, 1980), differing behavioral criteria for inclusion and exclusion, and differences in who provides the information for diagnosis (Sandoval et al., 1980). A number of investigators have suggested that the hyperactive child population is not homogeneous (Chess, 1960; Langhorne, Loney, Paternite, & Bechtoldt, 1976; Marwit & Stenner, 1972; Ney, 1974; Werry, 1968). Aggression, organicity, learning disabilities, and drug responsiveness have been suggested as dimensions for potential subdivision of the larger hyperactive group. The determination of valid subgroups, however, is highly dependent upon how hyperactivity is measured. Examination of measures of behavioral dimensions of childhood hyperactivity, and the improvement of measurement in this area, are two prerequisites for the determination of subgroups.

The primary purpose of this chapter is to review how dimensions of childhood hyperactivity have been measured. Three aspects of assessment are considered: how samples of hyperactive children are defined in the literature, the method and content of behavioral observation of hyperactive children, and measurement of treatment outcome. The data base was 451 studies reported in psychological, educational, and medical journals between 1960 and 1984 that included children described as hyperactive, hyperkinetic or ADDH but for whom retardation or clear organic dysfunction was not the primary diagnosis.

The primary focus is on what has actually constituted measurement of childhood hyperactivity as reported in empirical literature rather than on an idealized conceptualization of hyperactivity that has permeated the general literature.

DEFINING HYPERACTIVE SAMPLES

Discrepant findings by different investigators and differing estimates for the prevalence of hyperactivity can be attributed in part to variations in how hyperactive samples are defined. While there are several possible contributing sources of variation in definitions of hyperactive samples, the areas considered here are source of diagnosis, behavioral criteria, age variation, chronicity of symptoms, and drug responsiveness.

Source of Diagnostic Information

One of the primary sources of variability in how samples of hyperactive children are selected for studies is the source of information used for the diagnosis. Children who have the potential for a diagnosis of hyperactivity come into contact with several individuals in their environment who could report on their behavior, including parents, siblings, teachers, guidance counselors, peers, physicians, and mental health professionals. Investigators and practitioners can choose who is polled for diagnostic information. The distribution of screening sources for hyperactive samples is described in Table 1. For 25% of the reported studies, no sources of diagnostic information were specified. The proportion of studies failing to specify at least one diagnostic source decreased over time: 39% of the 1960–73 studies compared to only 14% of the 1980–84 studies. The four sources reported by investigators were the child's parents (parental ratings or interviews), the child's teacher (teacher ratings or interviews), physician's examination, and direct observation (either in a naturalistic or contrived setting). As reflected in Table 1, none of the studies prior to 1980 and only 4% of the 1980–84 studies confirmed hyperactivity using four sources. Approximately 15 to 18 percent of the studies tapped three sources. For the entire set of studies, teachers, parents, and physicians were utilized with equally high frequency (195, 153 and 169 studies, respectively). In contrast, direct observation as a screening procedure was used in only 21 of the 426 studies (5%), perhaps because observation requires more time and effort than other screening methods. When observation was used, the screening purpose was usually to exclude children viewed as hyperactive by other sources. For example, Jacob, O'Leary, and Rosenblad (1978) began with 27 children referred by their teachers for treatment of hyperactivity and excluded 7 from the study because observation did not confirm a diagnosis of hyperactivity.

The sources of diagnostic information do make a difference in defining hyperactive samples. In a study of 5,200 children, Sandoval et al. (1980) examined prevalence rates of hyperactivity as a function of the different defining systems of home, school, and physician. Across all grade levels (kindergarten through fifth grade), 1.19% of the children were identified as hyperactive by all three systems. In contrast, children were identified as hyperactive by the school at a rate of 4.78% regardless of whether the parents or physician concurred. If the prevalence rates vary so widely as a function of the defining systems, then it is also likely that the behavioral characteristics of the groups of children vary as a function of the defining sources.

An issue embedded in a discussion of source of diagnostic information is the

Table 1. Screening Sources for Hyperactive Samples

	1960–73 (94)		*1974–79 (176)*		*1980–84 (156)*	
Source	*n*	*%*	*n*	*%*	*n*	*%*
No Sources Specified	37	39%	49	28%	22	14%
One Source Only	24	26%	50	28%	62	40%
T	10		23		34	
PE	10		20		15	
P	4		6		12	
O	0		1		1	
Two Sources	18	19%	50	28%	40	25%
T + P	11		2		19	
P + PE	6		16		8	
T + PE	1		13		10	
T + O	0		1		2	
P + O	0		0		1	
PE + O	0		0		0	
Three Sources	15	16%	27	15%	28	18%
P + T + PE	13		21		21	
P + PE + O	1		2		2	
P + T + O	1		2		1	
T + PE + O	0		2		4	
Four Sources	0	0%	0	0%	4	3%

P = Parent, T = Teacher, PE = Physician's Exam, O = Observation

Note: Of the 451 studies between 1960 and 1984, 25 were excluded from this table because screening methods were referenced in other studies.

problem of cross-situational vs. uni-situational hyperactivity. Schliefer, Weiss, Cohen, Elman, Cvejic and Kruger (1975) addressed the question of whether children who show hyperactivity-related problems at home but not at school belong to the same diagnostic group as children who show the problems in both settings. They found the cross-situationally hyperactive children in general to be more aggressive and slightly more hyperactive. It is difficult to ferret out severity from cross-situationality. Other factors, such as variations in setting demands, discrepant assessment perspectives for teachers versus parents, and the presence or absence of subtle organic problems, complicate the problem of conceptualizing cross-situationality for hyperactive children.

Behavioral Criteria

While source of diagnostic information contributes to variation across hyperactive samples, inexplicit and differing behavioral criteria regardless of course also produce heterogeneity in selected hyperactive samples. Because of the manner in which subject samples are described, it is difficult to compare studies with respect to behavioral criteria for hyperactivity. Generally, investigators tended to emphasize three major areas of symptomatology: motor restlessness, difficulty in sustaining attention, and impulsive or inappropriate social behavior. Descriptions of motor restlessness have included references to excessive running around or crawling, a marked inability to sit still, fidgeting and other indications of unproductive or repetitious movement. Difficulty sustaining attention has been characterized by an inability to finish tasks, a disorganized approach to classroom activities, poor concentration, and a tendency to be easily distracted. Impulsive and inappropriate social behavior refers to noisemaking and calling out of turn in class, frequent interruptions or intrusions into other children's activities, difficulty awaiting one's turn for games or other activities, and fighting with peers.

Investigators typically have not specified exact behavioral criteria for subjects inclusion. More flexible or general criteria have been used instead of requiring every subject to evidence a high degree of motor restlessness, marked inability to sustain attention, and poor social functioning. Instead of operational criteria, some investigators listed a series of symptoms which characterize the group of children. For example, Arnold, Huestis, Smeltzer, Scheib, Wemmer, and Colner (1976) included children in their sample who were "diagnosable MBD with such signs and symptoms as hyperactivity, distractibility, short attention span, incorrigibility, lability, explosiveness, incoordination, perceptual motor dysfunction, and other minor neurologic signs." It is unlikely that all of the children exhibited all of the described symptoms. Children in the sample may have differed with respect to any single symptom (e.g., explosiveness).

Other investigators used cutoff scores from behavioral checklist or rating scales as the basis for inclusion. The rating scale cutoff method does provide a quantitative and systematic means of comparing samples across investigations. However, the problem of behavioral heterogeneity persists even though it is obscured. To illustrate the problem, let us consider the Conners Behavior Rating Scale (CBRS) (Conners, 1973), which has been widely used as a screening instrument. For screening purposes, the CBRS was used with teachers in 82 studies and with parents in 35 studies. Contained within the larger instrument is an abbreviated 10-item scale, referred to as the Hyperkinesis Index, that can be filled out by parents or teachers (see Table 2). The items cut across dimensions associated with a diagnosis of hyperactivity: motor restlessness (items 1 and 2); attentional deficit (items 3, 4, and 5); impulsivity (item 6); emotional lability

Table 2. Conners Abbreviated Parent-Teacher Questionnaire

1. Restless in the "squirmy" sense.
2. Restless, always up and on the go.
3. Fails to finish things.
4. Distractibility or attention span a problem.
5. Easily frustrated in efforts.
6. Excitable, impulsive.
7. Mood changes quickly and drastically.
8. Cries easily or often. (teacher version: Pouts and sulks.)
9. Destructive. (teacher version: Temper outbursts and unpredictable behavior.)
10. Disturbs other children.

Four-point scale: 0 = not at all present
1 = just a little present
2 = pretty much present
3 = very much present

Source: From Goyette, Conners and Ulrich (1978).

(items 7 and 8); and aggression or other inappropriate social behavior (items 9 and 10). Scores on the Hyperkinesis Index can range from 0 to 30. A score of 15, which is two standard deviations above the mean for normal children (Sprague, 1977; Werry, Sprague, & Cohen, 1975), has been used in several studies as the cutting score of defining hyperactivity. Because of the manner in which the instrument is scored and because of the variety of behavioral dimensions, it is possible for one child to have a score above 15 and not show aggression or other inappropriate social behavior, and another child to have a score above 15 and be rated high on aggression and inappropriate social behavior.

The behavioral heterogeneity produced by using a cutting score of 15 with the Conners Hyperkinesis Index was demonstrated in a recent study by Prinz, Connor and Wilson (1981). Of 109 first, second, and third grade children who were rated 15 or above on the Hyperkinesis Index by their teachers, 24% exhibited rates of aggression which differentiated them from their nonhyperactive classmates. The lack of homogeneity with respect to aggression for a group of children rated hyperactive by their teachers is a problem because childhood aggression is clinically and predictively significant. Childhood aggression has been cited as a possible precursor to delinquency (Lefkowitz, Eron, Walder, & Huesmann, 1977; Loney, Kramer, & Milich, 1981), schizophrenia (Watt, Stolurow, Lubensky, & McClelland, 1970; Watt, 1972, 1974; Watt & Lubensky, 1976; Weintraub, Prinz, & Neale, 1978), and other adjustment problems (Robbins, 1966).

To assist in the specification of behavioral criteria for diagnosis of ADDH, Swanson, Nolan and Pelham recently developed the SNAP checklist for parents and teachers to complete (Stephens, Pelham, & Skinner, 1984; Swanson, Nolan,

& Pelham, 1981). The advantage of the SNAP diagnostic checklist is that it specifies each of the subfactors of inattention, hyperactivity, and impulsivity, as described in DSM-III (American Psychiatric Association, 1980). The SNAP checklist has shown significant correspondence with the CBRS Hyperkinesis Index (Swanson et al., 1981). Perhaps the availability of this instrument will help to standardize research diagnostic procedures for ADDH.

Age Variation

The ages of children in the hyperactive samples vary greatly across studies. As seen in Table 3, sample mean ages ranged from 4 to 13 years old with a mean of 8.5 years. This means that some investigators have selected a young sample (as young as kindergarten) while others have targeted an older sample (e.g., seventh grade). The developmental differences between kindergarten and seventh grade children presumably produce behavioral variability and noncomparability across investigations.

Developmental variability also occurred within samples, as reflected by reported age characteristics. Of the 426 studies with 3 or more subjects, 6 failed to report age range. An additional 33 studies appropriately analyzed age as a variable, either by breaking the sample into age groups (e.g., Sostek, Buchsbaum, & Rapoport, 1980) or by analyzing age as a covariate (e.g., Ackerman, Elardo, & Dykman, 1979). Of the 299 studies that reported age range but did not analyze

Table 3. Age Heterogeneity in Hyperactive Samples

Reported Mean Age of Sample	1960 to 1979 (150)	1980 to 1984 (94)
Mean (SD)	8.6 (1.5)	8.4 (1.5)
Range	4 to 13	5 to 13
Reported Age Range of Sample	1960 to 1979 (194)	1980 to 1984 (105)
Mean (SD)	6.1 (2.4)	5.9 (2.1)
Range	1 to 17	1 to 12
Distribution of Age Ranges	Cumulative Percent	Cumulative Percent
Age Range (years)	1960 to 1979 (218)	1980 to 1984 (113)
13 or greater	1%	0%
11 or 12	5%	12%
9 or 10	11%	19%
7 or 8	46%	35%
5 or 6	65%	61%
3 or 4	80%	82%
1 or 2	89%	92%
Age analyzed	100%	100%

Note: Studies with only one or two subjects (16 studies in 1960–1979 and 9 studies in 1980–1984) were not included in the tabulation. Mean age of sample was not reported for 105 studies in 1960–1979 and 42 studies in 1980–1984. Age range was not reported for 61 studies in 1960–1979 and 35 studies in 1980–1984. Studies that divided the sample by age for analysis (24 studies in 1960–1979 and 9 studies in 1980–1984) were not included in the computation of means and standard deviations for mean age and age range.

age as a variable, about three fourths had age ranges that spanned 5 years or greater. The median age span was seven years. As shown in Table 3, recent studies (1980–84) have not included narrower age ranges nor analyzed age groups more often than earlier studies (1960–79).

Age is important to the study of childhood hyperactivity for several reasons. Developmental and psychopathological variables may interact over time. An older hyperactive child who has experienced longer exposure to academic frustration and failure (as a function of attentional problems) may exhibit a different set of behaviors than a younger hyperactive child who has not yet experienced prolonged academic problems. Children who begin to show hyperactivity in third or fourth grade may be qualitatively different, including different etiologies, than kindergarten children beginning to show hyperactivity. Finally, since behaviors, norms, and environmental demands for six year olds are noticeably different than those for twelve year olds, a hyperactive child's behavior must be judged in the context of age appropriateness. Grouping hyperactive children together without regard to age tends to obscure developmental factors.

Chronicity of Symptoms

Another source of variation in the identification of hyperactive children is the temporal requirement for chronicity of symptoms. Certainly, children who show hyperactive/attentional problems for a few years should be distinguished from those who have exhibited the problems for a few months. The DSM-III (APA, 1980) criteria for ADDH include onset before age 7 years and symptom duration of at least six months. Investigators and clinicians alike are faced with the problem of verifying time of onset and chronicity. In addition to the bias of retrospective reporting by parents, there is the issue of deciding what level of reported symptomatology is sufficient to confirm the past existence of the disorder. Of the 451 studies from 1960 to 1984, 89% failed to report any information about the chronicity of symptoms for the hyperactive children in the samples. Recent studies (1980–1984) did not report chronicity information more frequently than did earlier studies, even though formal diagnostic criteria changed to include temporal requirements. In DSM-II (American Psychiatric Association, 1968), the description of Hyperkinetic Reaction of Childhood did not include duration and age of onset criteria, while DSM-III (American Psychiatric Association, 1980) added these criteria for ADDH.

In the studies that reported chronicity information, temporal factors were presented as a requirement met by all children in the sample. The studies fell into three groups. The first set of studies reported a minimum duration of symptoms. For example, Lambert and Hartsough (1984) required a parental report of sustained hyperactive behavior for at least two years for a child to be included in the hyperactive sample. The second set of studies required that a child's history of hyperactivity date back to a specified early age. For example, Firestone and

Prabhu (1983) noted that all of the hyperactive children in their sample met the requirement that chronic inattentiveness, impulsivity, and overactivity was present from the age of three years or younger. The third set of studies imposed the DSM-III temporal criteria of onset before age seven and duration of at least six months (e.g., Greenhill, Puig-Antich, Novacenko, Solomon, Anghern, Florea, Goetz, Fiscina, & Sachar, 1984).

In many of the studies, investigators may have checked but simply failed to report chronicity. For the studies using DSM-III (American Psychiatric Association, 1980), proper application of the diagnostic criteria for ADDH meant verification of duration and onset, even if the investigators failed to report the information in the publication. While it would be a major improvement in the hyperactivity literature, reported confirmation of the two DSM-III temporal criteria may still not provide sufficient information for description of the sample. Onset prior to age seven still leaves a range of four to five years for variation in onset age. Similarly, a minimum duration of six months allows for broad individual differences in chronicity. To solve this issue, investigators will need a uniform method of assessing onset and duration. A validated instrument for this purpose has yet to be proposed and accepted.

Drug Responsiveness

An additional though controversial topic relevant to the defining of childhood hyperactivity is responsiveness to stimulant medication. Favorable response to drug treatment can be used as an additional selection variable, as some investigators have proposed. Laufer and Denhoff (1957) proposed that only the children who responded favorably to stimulant medication were hyperactive because of constitutional, as opposed to environmental, reasons. Favorable and adverse responders are considered by some to represent two distinct groups of hyperactive children with potentially different etiologies and treatment needs (Kinsbourne & Swanson, 1979; Swanson, Kinsbourne, Roberts, & Zucker, 1978). However, even if favorable drug response is not a universally accepted selection criterion, reporting of such information in the description of research samples would certainly facilitate comparisons across studies.

In 89% of the hyperactivity studies from 1960 to 1984, drug responsiveness was not mentioned. There was an increase over time in the use of drug responsiveness as a selection criterion. Only 3% of the 1960–73 studies even mentioned drug responsiveness. For 1974 to 1979, 12% of the studies reported drug response characteristics of the children in the sample, and for most of these studies, favorable response was a requirement for inclusion. A similar pattern occurred for 1980 to 1984 in that 14% of the studies reported drug responsiveness, with some of these studies describing mixed (i.e., favorable and adverse responders) groups while most only included favorable responders in the samples.

Reporting and interpreting drug responsiveness information is problematic because the accuracy of such information depends upon other factors. Some of the children to be studied may not have received stimulant drug treatment prior to evaluation, and for those who had received drug trials in the past, valid indicators of response may not have been available. In either case, drug response information would not be reportable. There would also be practical and ethical issues associated with subjecting every hyperactive child in research studies to a drug response trial. While some have argued the utility of this approach (e.g., Swanson et al., 1978), there is not a concensus that stimulant medication should be seriously considered for all hyperactive children. Nevertheless, reporting of drug responsiveness data, whenever available, serves a useful purpose for comparisons across studies and for sharpening our understanding of individual differences among hyperactive children.

BEHAVIORAL OBSERVATION OF HYPERACTIVE CHILDREN

Methods and Settings

Approximately one fourth of the hyperactivity studies between 1960 and 1984 reported some form of direct observation. Several observational settings and methods were used. The most frequent setting for observation was the classroom, which is not surprising given that much of the problematic behavior of hyperactive children is displayed in school. Play and "work" behaviors were frequently observed in laboratory or clinic playrooms. Typically, the target child was placed alone in the room and observed interacting with environmental stimuli such as toys, puzzles, or academic tasks. Less frequently, laboratory and clinic settings were used for observation of parent-child or child-child interactions.

Six distinct types of observational methods were found in the studies that reported behavioral observation data. (1) The most common type of observational method was frequency counting of discrete behaviors such as hitting (e.g., Patterson, 1965) and crossing a grid marking in the playroom (e.g., Barkley, 1977). (2) Interval-by-interval coding, using ten or fifteen second intervals and recording the occurrence or nonoccurrence of the designated behavior, has also been used relatively frequently. Interval coding has proven particularly useful for recording non-discrete behaviors such as off-task activity (e.g., Drabman, Spitalnik, & O'Leary, 1973) and out-of-seat behavior (e.g., Abikoff, Gittelman-Klein, & Klein, 1977). (3) The Response Class Matrix (see Mash & Barkley, this volume) is an interval coding method that takes into account contingent relationships between parent and child behaviors. In recent hyperactivity studies (e.g., Mash & Johnston, 1982), the Response Class Matrix has been used to observe parent-child interaction. (4) Duration measurement, which typically involves use of a stopwatch or other cumulative recording device, has rarely been used as the sole means of recording observed behavior. (5) In several studies, mechanical devices were used to "observe" behavior. Various types of actometers and pedometers have been attached to children's wrists, ankles, or torso, in order to cumulatively record body and extremity movements during designated activities (e.g., Cunningham & Barkley, 1979). Other investigators (e.g., Sprague, Barnes, & Werry, 1970) have measured fidgeting movements with a mechanical monitor in the seat of a chair. (6) The last method of observation found in hyperactivity studies is that of global ratings. Several studies between 1960 and 1979 included global ratings made by observing professionals or para-professionals regarding dimensions such as activity level (e.g., Alderton & Hoddinott, 1964), ability to stand still (e.g., Small, Hibi, & Feinberg, 1971), and anxiety (e.g., Hoffman et al., 1974). A decrease over time was noted in that global ratings were used for observation of hyperactive children a third as often during 1980–84 as was the case for 1960–79. Finally, in some studies two or more of the methods (frequency count, interval coding, duration, mechanical measure, and global rating) were used in combination to assess different types of behaviors.

Frequency count and interval coding methodology was primarily used in observation of classroom behavior. Mechanical measures and global ratings tended to be employed more in clinic or laboratory settings.

Evidence for adequate reliability was reported in many of the studies using frequency count or interval coding observation (e.g., Abikoff et al., 1977; Drabman et al., 1973), and to a moderate extent for mechanical measurement (e.g., Barkley & Cunningham, 1979). Studies using global ratings typically did not include reports of reliability.

Specific Observational Categories

Several dimensions of child behavior were represented in the hyperactivity studies that used observation. As shown in Table 4, the observed behavioral categories fell into four major groups: movement, task-related dimensions, social interaction, global dimensions. In 51 studies (1960 to 1984), some aspect of either gross or minor motor movement was observed. The most common way of assessing gross motor movement was by counting the number of times a child moved from one quadrant of the room to another. Minor motor movements included fidgeting behaviors, arm movements, and other signs of possible restlessness that a child might display without changing position in the room. During the period 1960 to 1979, 49% of the studies using observation included categories of gross or minor motor movement. Comparatively, 23% of the observational studies from 1980 to 1984 used motor movement categories. This decreased emphasis on motor hyperactivity corresponds to the rise of DSM-III (American Psychiatric Association, 1980) criteria for ADDH, which places greater importance on attentional deficits than motor behavior.

Table 4. Observational Categories Found in Hyperactivity Studies

Behavior Category	*1960–79 (n = 90)*	*1980–84 (n = 30)*
Movement		
Minor Motor Movement		
actometer on wrist or ankle	10	2
seat movements, mechanically measured	8	0
fidgeting	4	2
movements in chair	3	1
tilting or rocking in chair	2	0
movement while in stationary position	2	0
movements directed towards body	2	0
excessive body movement	2	0
fiddling with objects	2	0
gross movements of legs of feet	1	0
flailing arms	1	0
restless motor activity, duration	1	1
repetitive ritualistic behavior	1	1
Gross Motor Movement		
gross motor behaviors	8	1
quadrant changes, grid crossings, or position changes	8	2
pedometer	3	0
ultrasonic or pressure-sensitive measurement	2	0
time spent in locomotion	2	0
total distance moved	1	0
vigorous gross-motor movements, such as running or jumping	1	1
wandering	1	0
quiet (movement-related)	0	1
Task-Related Dimensions		
On-task/Off-task		
on task	11	6
off task	11	13
looking about the room, orienting response, distracted	6	2
attending to teacher	3	1
daydreaming	2	0
task involvement, task persistence	1	1
inappropriate classroom behavior	1	0
In-seat/Out-of-seat		
out of seat, out of workspace	10	5

(*continued*)

Table 4 (continued)

Behavior Category	*1960–79*	*1980–84*
in seat	1	1
Play		
playing	2	1
use of play equipment	2	0
appropriate play, isolate play, cooperative play, proximity play	1	1
Activity Changes		
activity changes	3	3
toy changes	4	1
mean time per activity	1	0
Social Interaction		
Aggression		
aggressive behavior, inappropriate social behaviors, physically aggressive	6	8
disturbing others, interference, disruption	6	4
destructive behavior	2	2
pushing	2	1
threat or verbal aggression to children, namecalling	2	2
threat or verbal aggression towards teacher	2	2
pinching	1	0
hitting	1	2
negative contact	1	6
Vocalization and Noise		
verbalization or vocalization	10	5
noise, nonverbal noise making, disruptive noise	8	2
solicitation of teacher	3	1
private speech, nondirectional verbalization	2	0
communicative activity interfering with school work, inappropriate vocalization	2	0
answering without raising hand	1	1
Interaction, Isolation, and Affect		
physical contact	3	0
isolation, withdrawal	3	2
social initiation, peer interaction	2	1
positive affect, affectionate behavior	2	0
negative affect	2	0

(continued)

Table 4 (continued)

Behavior Category	*1960–79*	*1980–84*
proximity to children	1	0
ignore, bystand	1	1
responsiveness	1	0
Compliance/Noncompliance		
noncompliance, refusal	5	5
compliance	2	5
rule breaking	0	1
Global Dimensions		
activity level	8	2
deviant behavior	4	0
distractibility/concentration, attention	2	2
anxiety	2	0
appropriate or constructive behavior, task application	2	2
depression	1	0
immaturity	1	0
ability to stand still	1	0
cooperation	1	0
self confidence	1	0
excitement	0	1
involvement	0	1
self control	0	1
intensity	0	1
strength of provocation	0	1
locomotion	0	1
fidgeting	0	1
aggression	0	1
impulsivity	0	1
irritability	0	1
talkative	0	1

Note: Each number denotes the number of studies that included the category.

Task-related dimensions were observed in 53 studies. These categories focused on attentional behaviors directed toward or away from specific tasks, such as classroom work, play tasks, or other designated activities. Investigations in classroom settings were particularly concerned with on- and off-task behavior and in- and out-of-seat behavior, while investigations in playroom settings were addressed to the frequency of activity changes (e.g., switching play from one toy to another). While attentional functioning is difficult to operationalize behaviorally, task-related dimensions were probably conceptualized as products of attention (in the case of on-task behavior) and inattention (in the case of off-task behavior). In accordance with the increased interest in attentional performance, 57% of the observational studies for 1980 to 1984 included task-related dimensions compared with 40% for 1960 to 1979.

Categories in studies that observed social interaction mainly included behaviors that interfere with or disturb other children. Of the 41 studies that assessed social interaction with direct observation, 26 included some dimension of aggression. Vocalization, noisemaking, and other categories that suggested disruptiveness were also assessed. Noncompliance, another potentially negative dimension, was also assessed. Positive interactions were much less frequently assessed across studies: examples included positive affect (Whalen, Henker, Collins, McAuliffe, & Vaux, 1979), social initiation (Whalen, Henker, Collins, Finck, & Dotemoto, 1979), and compliance (Barkley & Cunningham, 1979).

Issues

The large variety of observational categories mirrors the behavioral heterogeneity found within and across studies of hyperactive children. Many of the categories focus on the social conduct of the child, and in so doing, pertain more to the symptomatology associated with childhood conduct disorder. Other categories, particularly ones used in the laboratory and clinic settings, emphasize the movement aspect of the childrens behavior, which is suggestive of the classical definition of the term "hyperactivity." The third behavioral aspect of childhood hyperactivity represented among the observational categories is that of attentional deficit. Attentional difficulties were assessed in an indirect manner by observing signs or products of inattention, namely off-task and out-of-seat behavior. However, quadrant changes and other movement categories could also be construed as products of inattention. A child showing the aforementioned problems could be classified as attention deficit with hyperactivity or without hyperactivity, and in addition or instead, could also qualify for a diagnosis of conduct disorder in DSM-III (American Psychiatric Association, 1980). Consequently, the relevant behaviors to observe depend in part on which diagnostic category is being considered.

In addition to content of observation, the problem of representativeness of observational data is an issue of clinical importance. Particularly in clinic settings where one-session observation is the rule rather than the exception, the degree to which the child's observed behavior is representative of the child's typical functioning has not been adequately assessed. If a child were observed in the same playroom on more than one occasion over a few weeks, it is likely that some of the behavioral dimensions would not reflect high stability. Similarly, the relationship between observed behavior in a clinic playroom and observed behavior in another setting (e.g., the home) when only one observation period was assessed per setting might also prove to be tenuous. The degree of correspondence from one observation session to the next, and from one observation setting to another, for hyperactive behavior has not been adequately investigated, despite the large body of literature on childhood hyperactivity. It would also be of clinical and research relevance to determine what factors influence the degree of session and setting behavioral stability for individual children.

Imbedded within the issue of stability is the issue of observational reactivity. The extent to which a child has knowledge of, and reacts to, being observed can in turn affect the representativeness and stability of the observed behavior. In one of the few studies of observational reactivity with hyperactive children, Dubey, Kent, O'Leary, Broderick, and O'Leary (1977) failed to find evidence for reactivity to observation for several different child and teacher behaviors in a laboratory classroom of hyperactive first graders. It is not known whether this finding can be generalized to clinic/laboratory playrooms, where a child would be exposed to a relatively novel environment, or to regular classrooms.

TREATMENT OUTCOME MEASUREMENT

The hyperactivity literature is replete with outcome evaluations of treatment. Treatments included psychostimulant medication, behavior modification, educational intervention, dietary intervention, and to a lesser extent, biofeedback, psychotherapy, and environmental modification. Designs varied greatly and included uncontrolled group and single subject designs, reversal and multiple-baseline designs, control group designs (including no-treatment, attention-placebo, and alternate-treatment control groups), and crossover designs. For the 220 treatment studies identified for the 1960 to 1984 period, types of outcome measures were tallied and summarized in Table 5.

Teacher rating scales have been the most frequently reported outcome measures for hyperactivity. Of the treatment studies from 1960 to 1984 that used a teacher rating scale for outcome evaluation, the CBRS (Conners, 1973) was used in 78% of them. In addition to the ten-item Hyperkinesis Index (mentioned earlier), the teacher CBRS yields factors of conduct problems, hyperactivity, and inattention-passivity, and the instrument has been shown to reflect adequate reliability and validity (Goyette, Conners, & Ulrich, 1978; Zentall & Barack, 1979). Some investigators invented their own scale for the conducted study. A few used the Davids Rating Scales for Hyperkinesis (Davids, 1971; Zentall & Barack, 1979) or the Peterson-Quay Behavior Problem Checklist (Quay, 1977). An alternative to standardized rating scales is ratings of target behaviors that are individually specified for each child. The target behavior approach was used in a few studies.

A new teacher instrument, the Daily Behavior Checklist (DBC) (Prinz et al., 1981), has recently been added to the list of available scales. The DBC involves daily recordings by the teacher for 12 consecutive school days for 22 specific

Table 5. Frequency of Types of Measures Used for Evaluation of Treatment Outcome with Hyperactive Children

Type of Measure	*1960–1973* *(n = 62)*	*1974–1979* *(n = 101)*	*1980–1984* *(n = 57)*	*Total*
Ratings by Teachers	40%	45%	32%	40%
Experimental Task	35%	45%	28%	38%
Ratings by Parents	32%	36%	32%	34%
Standardized Test	37%	25%	19%	27%
Classroom Observation	19%	27%	19%	23%
Laboratory/Clinic Observation	6%	14%	18%	13%
Home Observation	3%	1%	0%	1%

behaviors. The DBC differs from other rating scales of hyperactivity in that occurrences of specific behaviors are recorded daily on a repeated basis over an extended time period (e.g., one week or one month) rather than reported retrospectively in a global manner. Behavioral specificity was emphasized in order to reduce the likelihood of rater bias. While the DBC showed strong correspondence with the Hyperkinesis Index of the CBRS, the instrument also was able to identify high-aggression and low-aggression children among those already selected by the CBRS as hyperactive (Prinz et al., 1981).

In the treatment studies, parental rating scales were also used frequently. The parental version of the CBRS was used in 59% of treatment studies that used parent scales. The second most frequently reported instrument, the Werry-Weiss-Peters Activity Rating Scale (WWPARS) (Routh, Schroeder, & O'Tuama, 1974), was used in 18% of the treatment studies using parental rating scales. The WWPARS characterizes the degree of fidgetiness, excessive activity, and inattentiveness that a child exhibits primarily at home. Barkley (1981) has noted that the WWPARS is correlated with child noncompliance to parental commands but not with performance on laboratory or classroom attentional tasks. The instrument is useful for profiling the situations in which hyperactive behaviors occur.

Instead of the CBRS and WWPARS, some outcome studies used global ratings, target behavior ratings, unpublished instruments, and in a few instances, well known behavior rating scales that do not have a hyperactivity subscale. For teacher and parent ratings of outcome, the CBRS has unquestionably been the most frequently reported scale. Given its multidimensional content (described earlier), behavioral changes in the Hyperkinesis Index of the CRBS noted across outcome studies are difficult to pinpoint because of the composite nature of the instrument. Improvement for a given child could be due to small changes across several content areas (i.e., impulsivity, attention span, aggression, emotional lability, motor hyperactivity) or to large changes in fewer areas. Despite this pitfall, prevalent use of the CRBS has clearly facilitated comparison across studies.

Many treatment studies of childhood hyperactivity have used experimental tasks to assess outcome. Perhaps the most prevalent task has been the Continuous Performance Test, a sustained attentional measure that has several variations (Rosvold, Mirsky, Sarason, Bransome, & Beck, 1956; Sostek, Buchsbaum, & Rapoport, 1980; Sykes, Douglas, Weiss, & Minde, 1971). Several other attentional tasks have been used as treatment outcome measures. Since discussion of the specific tasks is beyond the scope of this review, the reader is referred to Douglas and Peters (1979). In addition to attentional tasks, investigators have administered a variety of performance measures that are related and unrelated to symptomatology of childhood hyperactivity. Of particular note is the lack of consensus about standard tasks for treatment assessment, not to mention marked variation in administration methods for a specific task.

Standardized tests have also been used frequently (in 27% of the treatment studies) as outcome measures. Achievement tests and other tests of academic performance were the most common. Personality inventories were also frequently administered.

Approximately 30% of all hyperactivity treatment studies between 1960 and 1984 included some form of direct behavioral observation to assess outcome. There was a noticeable increase after 1973 in the use of observation as an outcome measure: for 1960–1973, 24% of the outcome studies used observation, compared with 34% of 1974–79 and 32% for 1980–1984. As Table 5 indicates, the classroom was the most frequent setting for observation of outcomes, with laboratory or clinic settings used about half as frequently. Home observation for treatment outcome assessment was rarely used, even though many hyperactive children exhibit pronounced behavior problems at home.

CONCLUSION

Assessment of behavioral dimensions associated with childhood hyperactivity is an essential aspect of diagnostic conceptualization for this population of children. Investigations have varied greatly with respect to inclusion and exclusion criteria, reporting of child characteristics, and observation of behavior. In view of the current state of research with ADDH children, the following recommendations are offered:

1. A diagnosis of ADDH should be confirmed from at least two independent sources, preferably using standardized behavioral criteria such as that found in the SNAP checklist (Swanson et al., 1981).
2. Behavioral observation, particularly if sampled over multiple periods, greatly improves the validity of diagnosis for identified children.
3. To allow accurate interpretation of findings and to facilitate comparison

among studies, published reports of hyperactivity research should describe the age distribution (mean, standard deviation and range), the specific sources of diagnostic confirmation including procedures for obtaining this information available information about drug responsiveness, chronicity of symptoms with information about method of assessing same, and presence or absence of significant secondary features such as aggression, disrupted peer relations, and learning disabilities.

4. ADDH samples with large age ranges, such as a 5 to 12 year old group, tend to obscure developmental factors and to create unwanted variance. Investigators are encouraged to analyze age as a factor by grouping into narrower age groups, or to focus on a narrower age group with a specific purpose in mind.
5. Observations of motor movement and task-related activities, though reliably assessed, have not been explicitly connected to conceptualizations of attentional deficit. A needed research direction is the sharpening of the concept of attentional deficit, with an emphasis on operationalization in observable terms that are valid for diagnosis and outcome evaluation.

REFERENCES

Abikoff, H., Gittelman-Klein, R., & Klein, D. F. (1977). Validation of a classroom observation code for hyperactive children. *Journal of Consulting and Clinical Psychology, 45,* 772–783.

Ackerman, P. T., Elardo, P. T., & Dykman, R. A. (1979). A psychosocial study of hyperactive and learning-disabled boys. *Journal of Abnormal Child Psychology, 7,* 91–99.

Alderton, H. R., & Hoddinott, B. A. (1964). A controlled study of the use of thioridazine in the treatment of hyperactive and aggressive children in a children's psychiatric hospital. *Canadian Psychiatric Journal, 9,* 239–247.

American Psychiatric Association (1968). *Diagnostic and statistical manual of mental disorders (DSM-II).* Washington, DC.

American Psychiatric Association (1980). *Diagnostic and statistical manual of mental disorders (DSM-III).* Washington, DC.

Arnold, L. E., Huestis, R. D., Smeltzer, D. J., Scheib, J., Wemmer, D., & Colner, G. (1976). Levoamphetamine vs. dextroamphetamine in minimal brain dysfunction: Relication, time response, and differential effect by diagnostic group and family rating. *Archives of General Psychiatry, 33,* 292–301.

Barkley, R. A. (1977). The effects of methphenidate on various types of activity level and attention in hyperkinetic children. *Journal of Abnormal Child Psychology, 5,* 351–369.

Barkley, R. A. (1981). *Hyperactive children: A handbook for diagnosis and treatment.* New York: Guilford Press.

Barkley, R. A., & Cunningham, C. E. (1979). The effects of methylphenidate on the mother-child interactions of hyperactive children. *Archives of General Psychiatry, 36,* 201–207.

Bosco, J. J., & Robin, S. S. (1980). Hyperkinesis: Prevalence and treatment. In C. K. Whalen & B. Henker (Eds.), *Hyperactive children: The social ecology of identification and treatment.* New York: Academic Press.

Chess, S. (1960). Diagnosis and treatment of the hyperactive child. *New York State Journal of Medicine, 60,* 2379–2385.

Conners, C. K. (1973). Rating scales for use in drug studies with children. *Psychopharmacology Bulletin (Special Issue, Pharmacotherapy of Children),* 24–84.

Cunningham, C. E., & Barkley, R. A. (1979). The interactions of normal and hyperactive children with their mothers in free play and structured tasks. *Child Development, 50,* 217–224.

Davids, A. (1971). An objective instrument for assessing hyperkinesis in children. *Journal of Learning Disabilities, 4,* 35–37.

Douglas, V. I., & Peters, K. G. (1979). Toward a clearer definition of the attentional deficit of hyperactive children. In G. A. Hale & M. Lewis (Eds.), *Attention and cognitive development* (pp. 173–248). New York: Plenum.

Drabman, R. S., Spitalnik, R., & O'Leary, K. D. (1973). Teaching self-control to disruptive children *Journal of Abnormal Psychology, 82,* 10–16.

Dubey, D. R., Kent, R. N., O'Leary, S. G., Broderick, J. E., & O'Leary, K. D. (1977). Reactions of children and teachers to classroom observers: A series of controlled investigations. *Behavior Therapy, 8,* 887–897.

Firestone, P., & Prabhu, A. N. (1983). Minor physical anomalies and obstetrical complications: Their relationship to hyperactive, psychoneurotic, and normal children and their families. *Journal of Abnormal Child Psychology, 11,* 207–216.

Goyette, C. H. Conners, C. K., & Ulrich, R. F. (1978). Normative data on revised Conners parent and teacher rating scales. *Journal of Abnormal Child Psychology, 6,* 221–236.

Greenhill, M. D., Puig-Antich, J., Novacenko, H., Solomon, M., Anghern, C., Florea, J., Goetz, R., Fiscina, B., & Sachar, E. J. (1984). Prolactin, growth hormone and growth responses in boys with attention deficit disorder and hyperactivity treated with methylphenidate. *Journal of the American Academy of Child Psychiatry, 23,* 58–67.

Hoffman, S. P., Engelhardt, D. M., Margolis, R. A., Polizos, P., Waizer, J., & Rosenfeld, R. (1974). Response to methylphenidate in low socioeconomic hyperactive children. *Archives of General Psychiatry, 30,* 354–359.

Huessy, H. R., Marshall, C., & Gendron, R. (1973). Five hundred children followed from 2nd–5th grade for the prevalence of behavior disorder. *Acta Paedopsychiatrica, 39,* 301–309.

Jacob, R. G., O'Leary, K. D., & Rosenblad, C. (1978). Formal and informal classroom settings: Effects of hyperactivity. *Journal of Abnormal Child Psychology, 6,* 47–59.

Kinsbourne, M., & Swanson, J. M. (1979). Models of hyperactivity: Implications for diagnosis and treatment. In R. L. Trites (Ed.), *Hyperactivity in children: Etiology, measurement, and treatment implications* (pp. 1–20). Baltimore, MD: University Park Press.

Lambert, N. M., & Hartsough, C. S. (1984). Contribution of predispositional factors to the diagnosis of hyperactivity. *American Journal of Orthopsychiatry, 54,* 97–109.

Langhorne, J. E., Jr., Loney, J., Paternite, C. E., & Bechtoldt, H. P. (1976). Childhood hyperkinesis: A return to the source. *Journal of Abnormal Psychology, 85,* 201–209.

Laufer, M., & Denhoff, E. (1957). Hyperactive behavior symptoms in children. *Journal of Pediatrics, 50,* 463–467.

Lefkowitz, M. M., Eron, L. D., Walder, L. O., & Huesmann, L. R. (1977). *Growing up to be violent: A longitudinal study of the development of aggression.* New York: Pergamon.

Loney, J., Kramer, J., & Milich, R. (1981). The hyperkinetic child grows up: Predictors of symptoms, delinquency, and achievement at follow-up. In K. Gadow & J. Loney (Eds.), *Psychosocial aspects of drug treatment for hyperactivity.* Boulder, Colorado: Westview Press.

Marwit, S. J., & Stenner, A. J. (1972). Hyperkinesis: Delineation of two patterns. *Exceptional Children, 38,* 401–406.

Mash, E. J., & Johnston, C. (1982). A comparison of the mother-child interactions of younger and older hyperactive and normal children. *Child Development, 53,* 1371–1381.

Ney, G. N. (1974). Four types of hyperkinesis. *Canadian Psychiatric Association Journal, 19,* 543–550.

Patterson, G. R. (1965). An application of conditioning techniques to the control of a hyperactive child. In L. Ullman & L. Krasner (Eds.), *Case studies in behavior modification* (pp. 370–375). New York: Holt, Rinehart, & Winston.

Prinz, R. J., Connor, P. A., & Wilson, C. C. (1981). Hyperactive and aggressive behaviors in childhood: Intertwined dimensions. *Journal of Abnormal Child Psychology, 9,* 191–202.

Quay, H. C. (1977). Measuring dimensions of deviant behavior: The Behavior Problem Checklist. *Journal of Abnormal Child Psychology, 5,* 277–289.

Robbins, L. N. (1966). *Deviant children grown up.* Baltimore: Williams & Wilkins.

Rosvold, H. E., Mirsky, A. F., Sarason, I., Bransome, E. D., & Beck, L. H. (1956). A continuous performance test of brain damage. *Journal of Consulting Psychology, 20,* 343–352.

Routh, D. K., Schroeder, C. S., & O'Tuama, L. (1974). Development of activity level in children. *Developmental Psychology, 10,*163–168.

Sandoval, J., Lambert, N. M., & Sassone, D. (1980). The identification and labeling of hyperactivity in children: An interactive model. In C. K. Whalen & B. Henker (Eds.), *Hyperactive children: The social ecology of identification and treatment* (pp. 145–171). New York: Academic Press.

Schleifer, M., Weiss, G., Cohen, N., Elman, M., Cvejic, H., & Kruger, E. (1975). Hyperactivity in preschoolers and the effect of methylphenidate. *American Journal of Orthopsychiatry, 45,* 38–50.

Small, A., Hibi, S., & Feinberg, I. (1971). Effects of dextroamphetamine sulfate of EEG sleep patterns of hyperactive children. *Archives of General Psychiatry, 25,* 369–380.

Sostek, A. J., Buchsbaum, M. S., & Rapoport, J. L. (1980). Effects of amphetamine on vigilance performance in normal and hyperactive children. *Journal of Abnormal Child Psychology, 8,* 491–500.

Sprague, R. L., Barnes, K. R., & Werry, J. S. (1970). Methylphenidate and thioridazine: Learning, reaction time, activity and classroom behavior in disturbed children. *American Journal of Orthopsychiatry, 40,* 615–628.

Sprague, R. L. (1977). Psychopharmacotherapy in children. In M. F. McMillan & S. Henae (Eds.), *Child psychiatry: Treatment and research.* New York: Brunner/Mazel.

Stephens, R. S., Pelham, W. E., & Skinner, R. (1984). The state dependent and main effects of methylphenidate and pemoline on paired-associates learning and spelling in hyperactive children. *Journal of Consulting and Clinical Psychology, 52,* 104–113.

Swanson, J., Kinsbourne, M., Roberts, W., & Zucker, K. (1978). Time-response analysis of the effect of stimulant medication on the learning ability of children referred for hyperactivity. *Pediatrics, 61,* 21–29.

Swanson, J., Nolan, W., & Pelham, W. (1981). *The SNAP rating scale for the diagnosis of the attention deficit disorder.* Presented at the Annual Meeting of the American Psychological Association, Los Angeles, California.

Sykes, D. H., Douglas, V. I., Weiss, G., & Minde, K. K. (1971). Attention in hyperactive children and the effect of methylphenidate (Ritalin). *Journal of Child Psychology and Psychiatry, 12,* 129–139.

Watt, N. F. (1972). Longitudinal changes in the social behavior of children hospitalized for schizophrenia as adults. *Journal of Nervous and Mental Disease, 155,* 42–54.

Watt, N. F. (1974). Childhood and adolescent routes to schizophrenia. In D. F. Ricks, A. Thomas, & M. Roff (Eds.), *Life history research in psychopathology,* Vol. 3. Minnespolis: University of Minnesota Press.

Watt, N. F. & Lubensky, A. (1976). Childhood roots of schizophrenia. *Journal of Abnormal Psychology, 85,* 363–375.

Watt, N F., Stolurow, R. D., Lubensky, A. W., & McClelland, D. C. (1970). School adjustment and behavior of children hospitalized for schizophrenia as adults. *American Journal of Orthopsychiatry, 40,* 637–657.

Weintraub, S., Prinz, R. J., & Neale, J. M. (1978). Peer evaluations of the competence of children vulnerable to psychopathology. *Journal of Abnormal Child Psycholgoy, 6,* 461–473.

Werry, J. S. (1968). Studies on the hyperactive child IV: An empirical analysis of the minimal brain dysfunction syndrome. *Archives of General Psychiatry, 19,* 9–16.

Werry, J. S., Sprague, R. L., & Cohen, M. N. (1975). Conners' teacher rating scale for use in drug studies with children-an empirical study. *Journal of Abnormal Child Psychology, 3,* 217–229.

Whalen, C. K., Henker, B., Collins, B. E., Finck, D., & Dotemoto, S. (1979). A social ecology of hyperactive boys: Medication effects in structured classroom environments. *Journal of Applied Behavior Analysis, 12,* 65–81.

Whalen, C. K., Henker, B., Collins, B. E., McAuliffe, S., & Vaux, A. (1979). Peer interaction in a structured communication task: Comparisons of normal and hyperactive boys and of methylphenidate (ritalin) and placebo effects. *Child Development, 50,* 388–401.

Zentall, S. S., & Barack, R. S. (1979). Rating scales for hyperactivity: Concurrent validity, reliability, and decisions to label for the Conners and Davids abbreviated scales. *Journal of Abnormal Child Psychology, 7,* 179–190.

ASSESSMENT OF CHILDREN'S FRIENDSHIPS: IMPLICATIONS FOR SOCIAL COMPETENCE AND SOCIAL ADJUSTMENT

Joseph M. Price and Gary W. Ladd

ABSTRACT

The central purpose of this chapter is to evaluate the potential contributions of friendship to children's social competence and adjustment. The nature of friendship and its functions are examined in light of available theoretical and empirical work. In particular, several sources of evidence illustrating the importance of friendship during childhood are presented, including studies indicating that friends differ from nonfriends or acquaintances along a number of qualitative dimensions. Barriers to a comprehensive understanding of the functions of friendship are also considered,

Advances in Behavioral Assessment of Children and Families, Vol. 2, pgs. 121–149.
Editor: Ronald J. Prinz

ISBN: 0-89232-481-3

including the lack of consistent definitions and assessments of friendship across age levels and investigations.

Current efforts to define, operationalize, and investigate children's friendships, are subsequently reviewed for samples within each of three developmental levels: infants and toddlers, preschoolers, and school-aged children. The purpose of this review is threefold: to explicate the methods typically used to assess friendship at each age level, to identify differences in the definition of friendship as implied by the various assessment procedures, and to evaluate current evidence concerning the potential contributions of friendship to children's social competence and adjustment. Current issues and future directions for research on childrens friendships are also discussed.

INTRODUCTION

Over the past decade, several groups of children have been identified as being "at risk" for childhood and later adjustment problems. Among these groups are children who lack peer acceptance, including those who are rejected by peers. Recently, there has been growing concern for yet another group of children who may be at risk for adjustment difficulties—those who lack close friends (Ladd & Asher, 1985). As Hymel and Asher (1977) found, it is possible for a child to be generally accepted by peers and yet have no close friends. The concepts of social acceptance and friendship may not refer to the same social phenomenon. While social acceptance refers to the degree to which an individual is liked or valued by a group of peers, friendship is a specific relationship between two individuals (Furman, 1982).

The distinction between social acceptance and friendship is further evidenced in the results of an intervention study conducted by Oden and Asher (1977). Although coaching of play skills led to increased social acceptance, the intervention did not help participants gain a higher number of friendship nominations. This pattern was the same at a one-year followup. As Hartup (1975) has cautioned, "the correlates of popularity cannot be used as a data base for formulating assumptions concerning the ontogenetic significance of early friendships" (p. 24).

The growing concern for friendless children is, in part, a product of theoretical and empirical work suggesting that friendships serve essential socialization functions throughout the life span (Dickens & Perlman, 1981), and that children without friends are deprived of experiences that promote social development and adjustment. Hartup (in press) has suggested that peer relationships serve three main functions in the individual's development. First, relationships such as friendships may provide a *context* in which individuals acquire a variety of competencies (e.g., regulation of emotion, self-comparison with equals, and coordination of activities with another). Second, friendships may serve as *resources* for emotional support and security that enable the individual to explore new physical and social environments, and act as a buffer during stressful life events. Third, friendships may function as *precursors* for other relationships. That is, an individual's previous and ongoing friendships may be utilized as important models for the formation of future friendships.

Moreover, in addition to these claims, there is a growing accumulation of empirical evidence to support the contention that friendships do indeed serve important socialization functions across the life-span. The specifics of each of these functions (e.g., the specific competencies learned), and the relative importance of each for the individual is no doubt determined by the person's developmental level and needs. In the adult literature, one of the friendship functions that has received the most attention is the role that friendships play in providing individuals with social or emotional support. Generally, it has been hypothesized that close interpersonal relationships function as a buffer in mitigating the debilitating effects of stress. Several features of close interpersonal relationships are thought to be responsible for this function, one of which is the partner's ability to foster a belief that the individual is loved and cared for, esteemed and valued, and able to rely on the partner for advice and material aid (Cobb, 1976). In support of this hypothesis, there are data to suggest that close friendships may aid in the individual's adjustment to a variety of health problems (e.g., pregnancy complications, recovery from illness), the death of a loved one, and loss of employment (Cobb, 1976).

During adolescence, friendship is important as a source of emotional security, and as a context for social learning. With regard to emotional support, Smollar and Youniss (1982) conducted a series of investigations on the friendship conceptions of children and adolescents, and found that adolescents tend to view their friendships as involving discussions of personal problems and feelings. Based on these findings it may be reasonable to conclude that adolescent friendships serve as a source of emotional support. Moreover, it has been suggested that the closeness of adolescent friendships helps to compensate for the loss of intimacy of family relationships (Dickens & Perlman, 1981). This hypothesis is based on the view that, as the individual matures, the primary source of emotional support may shift from the family to friendships. Based on these findings and hypotheses, some have suggested that adolescents who remain friendless are at risk for a number of adjustment problems (Richey & Richey, 1980).

There is also evidence to suggest that friendships provide adolescents with a context for learning about the self and others. According to a number of personality theorists (e.g., Sullivan, 1953; Erikson, 1968), one of the most important developmental tasks of this period is the elaboration of the various self systems, including self-identity and self-worth. It has been suggested, and there is some empirical work to support this claim, that friendships are the primary context in which these developmental tasks occur (Sullivan, 1953). According to Sullivan, "through mutual interaction, the necessity for thinking of the other fellow as right and for being thought of as right by the other leads to a resolution of the uncertainty as to the real worth of the personality'' (1953, p. 52). This intimacy and open communication leads not only to the validation of the worth of the self, but also to the worth of the friend. Thus, friendships may also foster the development of mutual respect and interpersonal sensitivity. A similar principle emerges from the interview findings of Smollar and Youniss (1982). Not only did adolescents view friendships as relations in which the self is accepted and not judged by the other, but they also conceived of friendships as involving an obligation to maintain the friend's respect. The authors suggested that the primary features of friendships at this age are acceptance and mutual respect.

With regard to children, Hartup (1983) has suggested that the social experiences that occur within friendships are as significant in child development as family events. However, research on the functional importance of friendships, has been limited to preadolescent or adolescent samples. The tendency to focus on these age levels may be attributable to several factors. First, past researchers have been inclined to emphasize the importance of parent/child relations over peer relations during the early periods of childhood. Second, research on children's conceptualizations and expectations of friendship has often been interpreted in such a way so as to suggest that ''true'' friendships may not emerge until middle childhood (Selman, 1981). Finally, theoretical accounts of children's friendships tend to emphasize the importance of friendship during later childhood (preadolescence) (Fine, 1981; Sullivan, 1953; Youniss, 1980).

Although early friendships have received less attention, there is a growing accumulation of theory and data that points to the value of friendships not only during childhood, but also during the later part of infancy. Evidence illustrating the importance of friendship during childhood comes from several sources. First, if social relationships do function as precursors of future relationships, as has been suggested by Hartup (in press), then it could be argued that early friendships provide the templates for construction of preadolescent and adolescent friendships. Thus, children who lack early friendships may be missing out on experiences that prepare them to establish and conduct friendships during later phases of development.

A second source of evidence concerning the importance of childhood friendships is based on the argument that children without friends may be a risk for both present and future functioning. Gottman has suggested that the often cited relationship between peer sociometric status and later adjustment may, in part, be explained by the difficulties experienced by children who remain friendless. Some support for this possibility was provided in a recent investigation by Masters and Furman (1981). Their data revealed that children's selection of specific liked peers was not related to the peers' overall social behavior, but rather to the specific types of interactions between those peers and the individual subjects. The authors concluded that social acceptance is a product of how well a child is able to manage a large number of interpersonal relationships.

The final source of evidence concerning the importance of childhood friendships is derived from evidence indicating that friends differ from nonfriends or acquaintances in the quality of their interactions, knowledge about the other person, and relationships. However, failure to identify friends in a consistent manner across age levels and investigations prohibits a comprehensive understanding of the functions of friendship during childhood. Moreover, this state of affairs is further complicated by the fact that researchers have often chosen to explore different features of friendship across both age levels and investigations.

In view of these issues, a review of recent research and theory on the contributions of friendship during early and middle childhood is in order. The specific purposes of this review are to: (a) organize the existing literature within a developmental framework; (b) provide an overview of the methods currently used to assess friendship within each developmental level; (c) identify differences in the definition of friendship as implied by the assessments used within each level; and (d) evaluate current evidence pertaining to the contribution of friendship to children's social competence and adjustment.

Beyond the contention that friendship is a specific relationship between two people that is distinct from social acceptance, it is useful to explicate some of the characteristics that further define this relationship. First, unlike relationships with parents and siblings, friendships are *voluntary* (Furman, 1982). Children may choose with whom they want to be friends. Even during infancy, children may refuse to interact with playmates provided by parents. Second, since children can choose to terminate a friendship, friendships are *fragile*.

Third, it appears that friendship is manifested in a *variety* of ways. Allen (1981) has suggested that friendship manifests itself in how partners feel about each other (i.e., positive and negative feelings), behave toward each other (i.e., overt interactions), and think about each other (i.e., cognitions). Because friends have positive feelings for one another it can be argued that friendship involves interpersonal attraction. For example friends are often distressed by separation (Hartup, 1975), and this response may imply attachment or some form of affective bond (Hartup, 1976). The behavioral dimension of friendship may be manifested in the types of behaviors children display when they are in the presence of a friend, in terms of quantity (e.g., proximity seeking, time spent in interaction) and quality (e.g., presence of laughing, sharing and helping; Hartup, 1975). Distinctive behaviors may also be evidenced in the process of becoming a friend (e.g., resolving conflicts amicably and disclosing private thoughts and information; Gottman, 1983). Additionally, the cognitive dimension of friendship can be seen in partners' tendencies to apply unique conceptual and linguistic categories to their relationship (Hartup, 1975). Children also possess certain expectations for friendships, such as "loyalty" and "commitment" (Bigelow, 1977).

The fourth and perhaps most distinguishing characteristic of friendship is *reciprocity*. Mannarino (1980) has argued that reciprocity is the most essential component of friendship, and should be included in any definition of friendship. In support of this contention, Hartup (in press) recently concluded that reciprocity is a characteristic common to children's friendship at all ages, in terms of their interactions with friends and their expectations of friendship. What appears to change across levels, however, is the manner and complexity in which reciprocity is manifested in children's expectations and behavioral interactions. These four characteristics of friendship (voluntary, fragile, variety of manifestations and reciprocity) provide a basis for analyzing research efforts to define, operationalize, and investigate children's friendships.

Current research on friendship is reviewed for three age levels: infants and toddlers, preschoolers, and school-age children. Each section discusses the definitions of friendship and procedures for assessment, and examines implications for children's social competence and social-emotional adjustment.

Infants and Toddlers

Before discussing the friendships of infants and toddlers an important question to consider is whether children at this stage of development possess the competencies necessary to form and maintain social relationships with other children.

By 6 months of age, infants possess distinct socially directed behaviors, the most common type being vocalization, followed by smiling and touching peers (Vandell, 1980; Vandell, Wilson & Buchanan, 1980). By the end of the first year, infants not only possess a broad repertoire of peer directed social behaviors (Vandell & Mueller, 1980), but can also engage in sequential interactions with playmates. Although these interactions are often perceived as unrelated and unconnected (Eckerman & Stein, 1982), they are clearly social in nature. Furthermore, the skills necessary to engage in reciprocal play and games emerge during the second year (Vandell & Mueller, 1980). Thus, it appears that by the end of the second year of life, toddlers are capable of engaging in social interactions and social play. Finally, there is also anecdotal evidence to suggest that infants and toddlers tend to prefer some playmates over others. For instance, Vandell and Mueller (1980) found that one pair of toddlers in a play group consistently sought each other out for play activities. Based on these findings, it can be argued that toddlers do in fact possess skills that are conducive to the formation of peer relationships.

Current Assessments of Friendship

At this age level, researchers have typically relied on two forms of assessment to identify children's friendships: verbal reports by a knowledgeable informant (usually an adult), and direct observations of social behavior with peers. In addition to obvious differences in the form of data provided by these sources (i.e., observed versus retrospectively reported interactions), these approaches differ in terms of the specific criteria used to define friendship.

The informant approach has typically required that mothers or teachers identify "friends" from among the child's home or school playmates. Often, the criterion of friendship is that of a consistent or familiar playmate. Lewis, Young, Brooks and Michalson (1975), for example, relied on mothers reports and defined a friend as a child with whom their infant played with at least twice a week over the previous two weeks and at least once a week over the preceding two months.

For the knowledgeable informant procedure, the underlying definition of friendship can be construed as either familiarity to the child or sustained, consistent social contact. Although this representation of friendship may seem limited in scope, it might also be argued that such features accurately represent the true nature of friendship during this period of development. Such an argument might imply that there is little differentiation for infants' and toddlers' peer relationships. Since peer contact is somewhat restricted at this age, any consistent or regular playmate would be considered a friend. Peer familiarity, however, has not always been equated with friendship in the literature on infant social development. For instance, Rubenstein and Howes (1976) asked mothers to identify playmates with whom their child had contact for at least two or three times a week over several months. Rather than referring to these regular playmates as friends, they were labeled familiar peers. While Rubenstein and Howes distinguished between familiarity and friendship, a minimum criterion for children to be considered friends is that they must be acquainted with one another and spend time together.

Occasionally, other adult informants have been used to identify infant's and toddler's friendships. Howes (1983) asked child care teachers to review the children in their group and circle each child's best friend and second best friend. This particular approach appears to involve an implicit friendship criterion, since no specific definition was provided for the teachers. Teachers were allowed to identify children's friends using their own personal definitions of friendship. However, the findings revealed that teacher's ratings corroborated with an alternative behavioral criteria (i.e., mutual initiation preference, complementary and reciprocal play, and expression of positive affect). Ninety-seven percent of the friends identified by the behavioral criterion were also identified by teachers, and all friendship pairs identified by teachers were also identified by the behavioral criterion. Thus, Howes (1983) findings suggested that teachers naturally define friendship in a manner consistent with children's social interaction patterns.

A more time-consuming assessment of infant and toddler friendships involves the direct observation of children's specific social behaviors and social interactions with their peers. Although a wide range of social behaviors could be used to define friendships, there is some consistency across investigations in the types of criteria employed. Most behavioral definitions of friendship for toddlers included one or more of the following categories of behavior: (a) the frequency of positive social interactions (e.g., turn taking, sharing); (b) the extent of positive affect in interactions; (c) the complexity of partner's interactions and/or play; and (d) a mutual preference for interaction.

For instance, in an investigation reported by Vandell and Mueller (1980), several behavioral definitions of friendship were examined. In group and dyadic settings, six male toddlers, who were familiar with one another, were observed at 16, 19, and 22 months of age. The operational definitions included mutual initiation preference, degree of positive interactions (including both positive affect and sharing), and the presence of infant games (e.g., mutual engagement, turn alternation, non-literality, and repetition). Although each of these criteria offers a different definition of friendship, the dimension common to all is reciprocity. While the first criterion reflects reciprocity in children's initiations toward peers, the latter two criteria involve reciprocity in the quality of interactions. Since the children were already familiar with one another prior to assessment, acquaintanceship and regular contact were implied as additional requirements of friendship.

A most interesting finding to emerge from the investigation sighted by Vandell and Mueller (1980), pertained to differences between the dyadic and group settings. In the group setting (i.e., six or seven children present), the mutual initiation and infant games criteria identified only one pair of toddler friends (the same pair), and only at the 22 month assessment interval. However, the positive interaction criterion identified this same pair of friends at all three assessments—16, 19, and 22 months. Alternatively, in dyadic settings (i.e., two children present) each of the three operational definitions identified a friendship at all three times of assessment. Moreover, the three criteria converged in identifying the same dyad.

A possible explanation for these findings is that the more complex dimensions of friendship (i.e., mutual initiation preferences and infant games) did not emerge because toddlers have not acquired the cognitive capabilities needed to coordinate the variety of social phenomena found in group settings. In contrast, dyadic settings may present fewer stimuli to coordinate, making it possible for more complex aspects of friendship to emerge at earlier ages. Rubenstein and Howes (1976) suggested that it may be easier for toddlers to establish interaction patterns with one individual at a time than with several simultaneously. Thus, for infants and younger toddlers, dyadic settings may allow for a more valid assessment of friendships than would larger group settings.

In another observational study of infant friendships, Howes (1983) defined friendship as an affective tie between two children that included mutual preference (i.e., a high probability that a dyadic interaction would follow a social initiation by either partner), mutual enjoyment (i.e., the ability to engage in positive affective exchanges), and interaction skill (i.e., the ability to engage in complementary and reciprocal peer play). Using a convergent approach, it was found that dyads were most likely to fall outside the friendship classification because neither partner had initiated an interaction. When only one criterion was met, it was most likely to be the dyad's success rate in interaction. When only two of the three criteria were met, dyads typically failed to express positive affect. Howes (1983) pointed to the expression of positive affect as the most crucial component of toddler friendship.

Howes (1983) restricted friendship to relationships that are reciprocal in nature, and involve behavioral and affective exchanges. This definition differs from those used in previous investigations (e.g., Lewis et al., 1975) in that positive affect is used to distinguish early friendships from other types of peer relationships (including those that may involve positive interactions and reciprocal play). The presence of positive interactions and reciprocal play may not imply friendship as much as familiarity. Support for this conclusion comes from studies indicating that familiar peers tend to engage in positive social interactions (Rubenstein & Howes, 1976). If this is the case, then the friendship criteria found in some studies (e.g., Lewis et al., 1975) may assess familiarity rather than friendship.

Contributions of Friendships

Although there is a lack of research on the effects of early friendship on children's subsequent social competence and social adjustment, these relationships may provide a socialization context in which children learn and practice positive social interactions and adaptive forms of peer play. Relevant evidence comes from research on the behaviors and interactions that occur between friends as opposed to strangers or acquainted peers.

The nature and direction of any hypothesized relationships between friendship and social competence is important to consider. While the case has been made that friendships contribute to the development of various social competencies, it is also possible that friendships may be an outcome of social competence and social adjustment. In fact, friendship has often been used as an index of social adjustment (Hartup, 1983). Support for this rival hypothesis is found in the aforementioned study by Vandell and Mueller (1980): the same child was found in each of the dyads identified by any of the friendship criteria. Although there was no direct assessment of social skills or competencies, this child may have possessed certain competencies that enabled him to form many different friendships.

However, as the Howes (1983) study suggested, friendships are not reserved for children who evidence a particular level of social competence. Howes suggested that positive affect was the most crucial of the three friendship criteria, and therefore, concluded that the formation of young children's friendships depends not only on children's social skills but also on whether children mutually enjoy being with one another.

In one of the first investigations of early friendships, Lewis et al., (1975) compared the interactions of "friends" and "strangers." The familiarity criterion described in the preceding section was used to select both types of dyads. Each child was observed once with a friend and once with a stranger. Compared with the stranger dyads, friendship dyads evidenced more proximal contacts, positive affect, and imitative behavior. In addition, both offering and sharing behaviors occurred more often in the presence of friends than strangers. In contrast, stranger dyads evidenced three times more negative affect than did friend dyads.

In an effort to extend the results of the first investigation, Lewis et al. (1975) observed 8 1-year-old stranger dyads on three occasions. On the first occasion, the dyads were unfamilar with one another. Prior to the second occasion, the members of each dyad were provided with two or three contacts across a 1-week interval. Two or three additional contacts were provided prior to the third contact. Consistent with the findings of the first study, the investigators found that proximity-seeking behaviors, attempts to offer and share toys, and imitation increased as the infants became more familiar with each other. Although it was not possible to ascertain whether the infants benefited from contacts with the new friends, these relationships provided opportunities for them to practice various social skills. Due to the manner in which friendship was defined, it may be more appropriate to conclude that familiar infants provided each other with opportunities to engage in specific social skills. This interpretation is consistent with the findings of Rubenstein and Howes (1976), in that interactions between familiar peers tended to be of a positive and reciprocal nature.

Strong support for the hypothesis that friendships contribute to early social competence comes from Howes' (1983) investigation of early friendship patterns. Three groups of children from a community based childcare center were observed over the course of a school year. These groups consisted of 7 infants (5–14 months at entry), 8 toddlers (16–23 months at entry), and 9 preschoolers (35–49 months at entry). During each of six assessment intervals, children were observed for two 15-minute periods on separate days. Three categories of friendship were compared: (a) maintained friends (pairs that met the friendship criterion in one of the first three time periods and continued to do so at each subsequent observational time period); (b) sporadic friends (dyads which met the friendship criterion only once or inconsistently); and (c) nonfriends (pairs that never met the friendship criteria).

For children in maintained friendships, significant increases were found over the course of the school year on the number of successful initiations, the number of elaborated exchanges, time spent in complementary and reciprocal peer play, time spent in positive affective exchanges, and the frequency of vocalization. In contrast, sporadic friends evidenced more frequent vocalizations only at time six, and nonfriends did not evidence significant increases on any dimension. Thus, the greatest increase in the complexity of interaction was evidenced within maintained friendships. Based on these findings it appears that maintained (stable) friendships may serve as an important socialization context in which various social interactive skills are acquired.

Preschoolers

Current Assessments of Friendship

Although theories of friendship tend to emphasize the importance of friendship during late childhood and adolescence (e.g., Sullivan, 1953), there has been growing interest in the friendships of preschool children. The interest in friendships of young children has not been accompanied by a consensus regarding the criteria and methods needed to define and assess friendship. Rather, a variety of approaches have been used to assess preschooler's friendships, including methods developed for use in research on infant's and toddler's friendships (i.e., adult's reports of friendships, and direct behavioral observations), and procedures based on sociometric methodology. Of these alternatives, sociometric methodology has been the primary method used to identify children's friendships at this age level.

Despite the popularity of sociometric methods, a number of researchers have relied on adult reports of children's friendships. For example, Gottman (1983), in his investigation of the formation of early friendships, asked mothers to identify their children's best friends. In another study, Schwarz (1972) asked teachers to identify children's friendships and to rate the degree of closeness present in each friendship. Adult reports have also been used in conjunction with other methods, either as a check against the validity of other methods (e.g., Hayes, Gershman, & Bolin, 1980; Howes, 1983) or as one or several sources of information in a battery of measures (e.g., Raupp, 1982).

As was suggested earlier, unless adults are provided with criteria for identifying children's friendships or a definition of friendship, it may be difficult to determine the nature of the relationship that has been targeted for study. However, in instances where a definition of friendship was not provided, there is often evidence to suggest that adult reports may assess the same dimension tapped by behavioral measures. For instance, as was reported earlier, Howes (1983) found that teacher's were able to identify 97% of the friendships identified by several behavioral measures (e.g., mutual initiation preference, complementary reciprocal play, and display of positive affect). In addition, Hayes et al. (1980) reported that parents had identified all of the reciprocal friendship pairs detected by a method that combined children's best friend nominations with the percent of time partners spent in interaction. Apparently, adult reports of friendship are remarkably consistent with certain behavioral measures, especially if the latter methods involve assessment of mutual preference and percent of time spent in interaction. It's possible that in the absence of an explicit criterion, adults rely on these same dimensions to define friendships.

Only a few investigators have used direct behavioral observation as the primary means for identifying friendships among preschoolers (e.g., Hinde, Titmus,

Easton, & Tamplin, 1985; Howes, 1983). Other researchers have combined direct observation with other criteria, either as a means of exploring the validity of alternative measures (e.g., Hayes et al., 1980) or as components in a battery of convergent measures (e.g., Raupp, 1982, 1983). Unlike the majority of behavioral friendship assessments used with infants and toddlers that have focused on specific interactive behaviors and sequences (e.g., mutual initiation preference and complementary reciprocal play), assessment with preschoolers has emphasized global aspects of social interaction such as the types or quality of play (e.g., solitary, parallel and cooperative play). Howes' (1983) investigation of early patterns of friendships is an exception to this trend in that specific social interaction sequences were used in the friendship assessment, possibly because infants and toddlers were also included in the study.

In order to gather data on global aspects of children's social interactions, investigators often observed children during freeplay periods. Children were considered to be friends if they spent a specified percent of time (of the total interaction time sampled) engaged in mutual positive interaction. The amount of time children must spend together to be considered friends varied across studies from 30% (Hinde et al., 1985) to 55% (Raupp, 1983). Efforts to define preschooler's friendships in this manner appear to be based on the premises that friends spend more time with each other than with other familiar peers, that interactions between friends are positive in nature, and that friends are not merely momentary play contacts. Consistent with previous theoretical accounts of the nature of friendship, reciprocity (in this case behavioral reciprocity) is also implied by this definition (Hartup, in press).

The emergence of this form of behavioral assessment with preschoolers may be attributed to factors such as the unique structure of the social environment (i.e., classrooms containing many children) and the opportunity for preschoolers to choose a few preferred playmates from among a larger number of familiar peers. In addition, this behavioral approach appears to parallel some aspects of preschooler's conceptualizations of friendship, namely, the emphasis on common activities (Furman & Bierman, 1983; Hayes et al., 1980).

Alternatively, many investigators have relied on sociometric methodology as a means of identifying friendships with preschool children. Greater use of sociometric methods may be attributable to the cognitive and linguistic advancements children evidence during the preschool years that allow them to conceptualize, reflect on, and describe their friendships. It would appear that these linguistic and cognitive advancements have allowed researchers to acquire infomation directly from the child, thus reducing their reliance on adult report and direct observation.

The sociometric methods used in research on preschooler's friendships can be divided into two broad categories: (1) those that employ a "liking" criterion, and require children to nominate "liked" peers; and (2) those that employ a "friendship" criterion, and require children to nominate peers who are seen as friends (or even best friends). Administration of the former type of sociometric method typically requires that children identify, from pictures of their classmates, three children whom they especially like (e.g., Masters & Furman, 1981). For children to be considered friends, they must reciprocally nominate each other as a liked peer. Paired comparison procedures, in which children are shown all possible pairs of classmates' photographs, have also been used to gather data on peer liking. For each pair of photographs, children are asked with whom they would like to play (Cohen & Melson, 1980). In the latter type of sociometric, children are asked to designate up to three best (e.g., Tuveson & Stockdale, 1981) or favorite (e.g., Raupp, 1982) friends. Typically, a child's first and second choices are used. To be considered friends, a pair of children must have reciprocally nominated each other as their first or second best/favorite friend.

On the surface, it appears that the same definition of friendship underlies these two types of sociometric approaches, namely, mutual liking. However, it is possible that the criteria used in these measures tap differing relationship dimensions. According to some investigators, personal attraction and interpersonal relationships are not equivalent (Dickens & Perlman, 1981). While interpersonal attraction refers to a positive attitude, such as liking, interpersonal relationships refer to some form of continuing association between individuals. When children are asked to nominate "liked" peers, they are being asked to designate individuals for whom they feel some degree of interpersonal attraction. Alternatively, when they are told to nominate friends, they are being asked to designate individuals with whom they have a specific type of relationship. Although liking or interpersonal attraction may be a component of this relationship, recent research on children's conceptions of friendships suggests that children view friendships in a more complicated way, involving more than just liking. A recent investigation by Furman and Bierman (1983), in which multiple methods (i.e., open-ended interviews, picture recognition tasks, and forced-rating tasks) were used to examine developmental changes in children's friendship conceptions, revealed that 4- and 5-year-old children's perceptions of friendship tended to be multidimensional. Whereas most preschoolers mentioned common activities as an important feature of friendship in the open ended interview, the majority also mentioned affection and support. Moreover, results obtained on the rating task indicated that preschoolers saw common activities, affection, and prosocial support as equally important. Thus, from a young child's perspective, a friend is more than just someone who is liked.

Recently, a number of researchers have utilized convergent assessment strategies to identify young children's friendships. To be considered friends, potential dyads must meet pre-established criteria for all of the component measures. For instance, Gershman and Hayes (1983) used both a sociometric measure and behavioral observations of preschool play sessions to identify friends. Pairs of children were considered to be friends if they had reciprocally nominated each other as either best or second best friend, and had spent at least 50% of their time interacting with each other during freeplay.

Raupp (1982) utilized a sociometric measure, observations of behavior during freeplay, and teacher reports of children's best friends. To be considered mutual (i.e., reciprocated) friends, it was necessary for children in any given pair to nominate each other as friends on the sociometric interview, to interact in more than 55% of the scan sample, and to be identified by teachers as best friends. Raupp (1982) identified one-sided friends (i.e., unilateral friendship nomination) acquaintances (children who interacted in less than 2½% of the scan sample, did not nominate each other as friends, and were not identified by teachers as friends) and mixed friends (i.e., children who did not meet all the criteria for friendship) as 3 additional categories of friendship status. Each of these convergent approaches implied that friendship is a multidimensional construct involving affective (interpersonal attraction) and behavioral components. Raupp's approach additionally implied that there are different levels or types of friendship.

Contributions of friendship. As Hartup (in press) has suggested, peer relationships may serve as a socialization context in which certain competencies are learned and as an emotional resource that furnishes children with a sense of security and confidence which, in turn, enables them to explore new environments and form new peer relationships. These relationships among peers may also act as a precursor for other relationships. For young children, friendships may serve these functions and thereby contribute to their social competence and adjustment.

The argument that preschoolers' friendships provide a unique context for socialization rests on the assumption that interactions between friends differ from those of unacquainted or familiar peers. This distinction is important since it is possible that familiarity rather than friendship may alter the nature of children's interactions. Relevant to this point, Doyle, Connelly, and Rivest (1980) recently found that the interactions of familiar children differed from those of unfamiliar peers. Preschoolers were observed during separate play sessions with either a familiar classmate or an unfamiliar child present. Whereas social interaction was more frequent between familiar peers, nonsocial activities occurred more often with unfamiliar peers. Dramatic play occurred almost exclusively in the familiar peer condition, and more object play was found in interactions of familiar as opposed to unfamiliar peers. Positive social behaviors, such as peer directed behavior, success at gaining peer's attention, and success at leading a peer, were more common in the presence of a familiar peer. The authors suggested that these findings may be attributable to the possibility that in previous encounters with one another, which involved mutually shared and understood interactions, familiar peers learned a variety of positive and successful social behaviors. These behaviors, in turn, carried over into subsequent social encounters. Thus, it could be argued that familiarity is responsible for any benefits children acquire from friendships.

This conclusion, however, is weakened by evidence indicating that interactions between friends differ further from those of familiar peers. Masters and Furman (1981) found that children dispensed higher rates of positive (e.g., giving invitations to play and cooperative play) and neutral behaviors toward children they liked than toward either neutrally-liked or disliked peers, all of whom were familiar as classmates. Moreover, these rates were twice as great with liked peers as with the other two groups (i.e., neutral or disliked peers). Thus, children engage in more positive interactions with friends or liked peers than they do with other familiar peers.

Similar findings were reported by Raupp (1982) who found that mutual/best friends used more prosocial behaviors (helping, sharing, praise and reinforcement) with each other than did peers assigned to other friendship categories (e.g., one-sided friendship, some friendship, and acquaintances).

These findings are consistent with the contention that friendship may provide unique opportunities for children to observe and practice various types of social behaviors and skills, especially those that are of a positive or prosocial nature. However, the empirical question remains as to whether friendships and accompanying experiences influence children's social competence and adjustment.

The Howes (1983) study described earlier, offered some support for the contention that friendship facilitates competence. Howes (1983) evaluated maintained friendships (dyads which met the friendship criteria in one of the first three time periods, and continued to do so in every subsequent observational time period), sporadic friendships (dyads which met the friendship criteria only once or inconsistently), and nonfriendships over a six-month-period. Children within maintained friendships were increasingly successful at initiations, elaborated exchanges, complementary and reciprocal play, and positive affective exchanges. In contrast, children in sporadic friendships and nonfriend dyads showed no significant improvement for any of these measures. These data suggest that, although all types of friendships involve unique social interactions, particiption in a stable friendship facilitates the development of social competencies.

Additional support for this hypothesis is found in a recent study that related of preschoolers' peer networks to social and school adjustment (Ladd, Price, & Hart, in press). Ladd et al. (in press) observed playground behavior in the fall, winter, and spring of a school year. Network variables were constructed that included number of frequent play companions (i.e., playmates who were present in more than 30% of the subject's interactions) and network affinity (i.e., the proportion of a child's frequent play companions who also nominated a subject as a liked peer). Children's adjustment was assessed with sociometric measures (i.e., peer status in the classroom) and teacher ratings (i.e., perceptions of children's classroom peer status, overall social competence, and school adjustment). The number of frequent play companions was positively correlated with children's classroom peer acceptance (i.e., positive peer nominations, social preference, and average sociometric ratings) and all three teacher measures. In addition, the association between network affinity and the social/adjustment measures strengthened over the course of the year. In sum, the children who tended to be well-liked by classroom peers and viewed as well-accepted, adjusted, and socially competent by teachers, were those who were involved in a larger number of sustained playground relationships and those who were nominated as friends by their frequent play companions. In light of the correlational nature of these data, alternative interpretations are possible. While participation in sustained peer relationships may foster skills and competencies that are related to success in peer relations and school adaptation, it is also possible that the same competencies and abilities that enable children to develop and maintain peer relationships may also contribute to their social success, competence, and adjustment in the classroom.

Another manner in which friendships may contribute to preschoolers' social competence and adjustment is by serving as a source of emotional support. Although there is a paucity of research in this area, support for this hypothesis can be found in at least two studies (Ispa, 1981; Schwarz, 1972). Schwarz (1972) observed children in a novel situation (i.e., an unfamiliar room containing novel and familiar toys) with a close friend, with an unfamiliar peer (stranger), or alone. For a pair of children to be selected as friends, the head and assistant teachers both had to list and rate the partners as friends. Children in the friend condition exhibited more positive affect and greater mobility than did other children in the two remaining conditions (i.e., stranger or alone).

Ispa (1981) obtained similar results with familiar peers rather than friends. Children 2 to 3 years of age were observed in an unfamiliar room with either a familiar peer (classmate), an unfamiliar peer, or no peer present. An unfamiliar adult was present during two of the three observation periods. Children with a familiar peer displayed more positive affect, verbalization, and mobility. Moreover, children who were paired with an unfamiliar peer displayed more distress during the departure of the strange adult than did the children accompanied by a familiar peer.

The issue of whether friends offer more support than familiar peers has not been investigated. Intuitively, friendships may provide higher levels of social support because many of the behaviors that distinguish friendships from other peer relationships are of a supportive nature (e.g., helping and attention).

Thus far, it has been suggested that friendships contribute to children's social competence and adjustment, as contexts in which children learn and practice specific social skills, and as resources for emotional security. As a context for social learning, the interactions of friends apparently differ not only from those of strangers, but also from those of acquaintances. Specifically, friendships involve higher levels of social interaction, positive social exchange (e.g., helping, giving, and sharing), positive affect, and complementary and reciprocal play. At the very least, friendships may encourage children to practice and refine interactive competencies. In particular, findings reported by Howes (1983), suggested that social skills are best learned in stable as opposed to sporadic friendships.

In terms of social adjustment, Masters & Furman (1981) suggested that a child's overall liking by a peer group is a consequence of the child's ability to form specific dyadic relationships with a large number of peers. Similarly, the correlational data reported by Ladd et al. (in press) indicated that group acceptance was clearly related to a child's ability to negotiate a network of sustained relationships.

Attempts to draw conclusions about the role that preschool children's friendships play in the provision of emotional security and support would be premature and must await further research. However, a familiar peer can apparently have a positive effect on a child's emotional state in situations that might otherwise be perceived as threatening or frightening (Ispa, 1981).

School-aged Children

Current Assessments of Friendships

Whereas several strategies have been devised to identify friendships among preschool children, there has been an almost exclusive reliance on sociometric methods with school-age samples. Three factors may be responsible for this shift in methodology. First, the school-age child's conception of friendship has become more elaborate and stable. Second, more information regarding the nature of a specific friendship can be gained reliably from the participants themselves (Foot, Chapman & Smith, 1980). Consequently, there is less of a need compared with preschoolers to utilize alternative or corroborative assessments (e.g., direct behavioral observations) to identify school-aged children's friendships.

Third, the structure of children's social environment in elementary school makes it more difficult to obtain reliable direct observations. Compared with preschool, grade school provides fewer opportunities for social activities such as freeplay. Moreover, there is a shift in the range and consistency of the social contacts available to children during periods where peer activities are permitted (e.g., recess, or lunch). Recess periods at elementary schools often include children from a multiple grade levels on the same playground, and the specific classes present may vary from one occasion to the next.

Although sociometric procedures have been consistently chosen to define friendships with grade school children, there is considerable variation in the types of sociometric methods and criteria employed. Procedures range from relatively simple strategies based on mutual best friend nominations (e.g., Newcomb & Brady, 1982) to more complicated convergent methods that include nominations as well as measures of friendship stability and intimacy (e.g., Mannarino, 1976).

As a criterion for friendship with younger school-age children, researchers often used reciprocated friendship nominations which require children to list one or more "best" friends (e.g., Newcomb & Brady, 1982). From these data, pairs of children who mutually nominated each other as best friends (often only first or second choices are used) were identified. While the exact dimension of friendship assessed by these procedures might be debated, a shared perception of the relationship is clearly implied. It is also possible that this procedure reflects some degree of consensus in the dyad about the basis of the relationship. Presumably, when children nominate friends, they rely on certain concepts or experiences to distinguish among relationships. Previous research on children's friendship conceptions (e.g., Furman & Bierman, 1983) would suggest that dimensions such as mutual affection/liking, sharing, and the pursuit of common activities underlie early friendship choices. For older school-aged children, perceptions of characteristics such as intimacy and loyalty may also come into play (Bigelow, 1977).

Some nomination criteria imply that there are varying degrees of friendship, as in the case where the order of nominations is taken into account (e.g., whether a peer is listed as the first, second, or third best friend). In this case, children who are nominated first or second are often considered to be "closer" or "favorite" friends.

Some investigators have supplemented children's friendship nominations with information about liking or attraction. Berndt (1981a, 1981b) for example, first asked children to nominate their best friends and then requested that they rate all same-sex classmates on a 5-point "likability" scale. Dyads that met the criteria of mutual liking (partners whose average ratings on the 5-point scale was 4.0 or higher) and unilateral nomination (at least one member nominated the other) were considered to be friends. While not ensuring reciprocity of children's friendship perceptions, this procedure does imply mutual liking. Berndt (1981a) has suggested that this criteria may more accurately reflect a "good" friendship rather than a "best" friendship.

In research with older preadolescent children, some researchers have devised assessment approaches that used traditional nomination procedures and also measured intimacy and sensitivity. Mannarino (1976) first utilized this approach to investigate the relationship between preadolescent friendships and altrustic behavior. Children were first asked to name three best friends in order of preference; the same procedure was repeated two weeks later. Next, children were administered the "Chumship Checklist," an instrument designed by the author to evaluate whether or not a child communicates honestly with friends and is sensitive to their needs and interests. Finally, children were asked whether they would prefer to spend free time with their best friend or with a group of friends. To be included in the chumship group, three criteria were required: (a) the best friend nominated initially was also nominated as the best or second best friend in the second sociometric assessment; (b) 10 of the 17 items on the Chumship Checklist were endorsed; and (c) best friends rather than a group of friends were prefered for free time activities.

Since reciprocity was not a requirement for this particular definition of friendship, it is possible that the friendship partners identified in this study may not have perceived each other as friends. Although the extent to which reciprocity was present in the constituted dyads is unclear, this particular approach to friendship selection incorporates several other relationship dimensions. The Mannarino (1976) criteria imply that there are levels of friendship, and that types of friendship can be discriminated based on dimensions such as intimacy and open communication, the stability of the relationship, and partner's preference for spending time with the friend as opposed to a group. It is interesting to note that these dimensions underlie preadolescent conceptions of friendship (Bigelow, 1977).

In extending Mannarino's original criteria, McGuire and Weisz (1982) added reciprocity. In addition to slight modifications in Mannarino's criteria, McGuire and Weisz (1982), required that children in the chumship group nominated each other as either first or second best friends on the sociometric measure. Thus, friendship in this study was construed as a relationship in which the partners not only demonstrated specified levels of stability, intimacy, communication, etc., but also saw each other as friends.

A few investigators employed convergent or multiple sources of information to identify friendships among school-age children (e.g., Newcomb, Brady & Hartup, 1979; Ladd & Emerson, 1984). In the Ladd and Emerson (1984) investigation, reciprocated sociometric nominations, were corroborated with parent and teacher reports. With this particular approach, the goal was to verify consensus or reciprocity for the identified relationship while also confirming via external sources that mutual association was occuring.

Contributions of friendship. Compared with the research on toddlers and preschoolers, the functions of friendship during the school-age years has received more attention, primarily regarding the potential contributions of friendship to the development of social competence. The empirical work that is relevant to this topic has been conducted largely with preadolescent samples and has been designed to explore children's conceptions of friendship, to compare the interactions of friends and nonfriends, and to explore the relationship between friendship and prosocial behavior. Before reviewing this research, it is important to consider how school-age friendships have been viewed in the literature.

Sullivan (1953) has suggested that friendships, especially preadolescent friendships, provide children with unique interactional experiences that facilitate the growth of various social competencies. According to this view, children develop a greater need for intimacy as they approach preadolescence (beginning around nine years of age), and these feelings are often expressed within peer relationships. Preadolescent friendships are seen as qualitatively different from those of younger children in that they are characterized by intense closeness and open, honest communication. Presumably, intimate interactions that occur in friendships not only validate the self but also increase the individual's sensitivity to the needs of the friend. Sensitivity that is acquired in this manner is thought to generalize to subsequent peer relationships.

A similar thesis, developed by Youniss (1980) integrates elements of Piaget's and Sullivan's theories. He suggested that children's awareness of the unique interactions that occur with friends is an impetus for the elaboration of such concepts as cooperation, mutual respect, and interpersonal sensitivity. Once learned, these concepts are then generalized to other peer interactions.

Some support for these views can be found in research on children's conceptions of friendship (e.g., Bigelow, 1977). Generally, data from these investigations suggests that children at this age not only view friendships as being distinct from non-friend relationships but also conceive of friendship in more diverse and complex ways. While younger school-aged children tend to describe friendship in terms of affection, sharing, and helping (Furman & Bierman, 1983; Bigelow & LaGaipa, 1980), preadolescents are more likely to mention elements such as intimacy, loyalty and commitment (Bigelow, 1977).

There is also research on the behavior of school-age friends which may reflect on the hypothesized functions of friendship during this age period. Often these studies have been designed to compare the interactions of friends with those of nonfriends. In contrast to the naturalistic sites used with preschoolers, much of the research on school-age samples has been implemented in laboratory settings. The experimental setting is often arranged so that specific behaviors are observed in the context of a structured task or activity (e.g., game, movie, etc.). The behaviors or competencies assessed in these investigations included social responsiveness, mutality, and prosocial acts.

To examine the social responsiveness of 7- and 8-year olds in either friendship or stranger dyads, Foot, Chapman & Smith (1977) videotaped children while they were watching a comedy film. The duration and frequency of behaviors such as laughing, smiling, looking, and talking were greater between friends than strangers. Response matching, a measure of behavioral concordance between partners, was greater for friends than nonfriends. The findings are difficult to interpret because of the way Foot et al. (1977) operationalized friendship and selected the comparison group of nonfriendship dyads. Friendship was defined as dyads in which partners had mutually expressed a desire to be paired with each other for a subsequent visit to the laboratory. Rather than identifying friendship pairs, this criteria may have merely identified children who liked each other. Another difficulty is that strangers rather than acquaintances were in the comparison group. Thus, it is not possible to determine whether the social responsiveness of the ''friendship'' group was attributable to some level of familiarity as opposed to friendship.

The social responsiveness of friends and nonfriends were also compared in an investigation conducted by Newcomb, Brady, and Hartup (1979). In this investigation, children were observed while performing a block building task under either competitive or cooperative conditions. In addition, the overall level of social interaction, degree of equity, and types of interpersonal commands (e.g., mutual vs. individual) were examined. Compared to non-friends, the social contacts of friends were found to differ in both frequency and quality. Regardless of the incentive condition, friends expressed more affect (i.e., laughing, exclaiming, & teasing), reflected equity more often in discussions, and used more mutually-directed commands (which tended to elicit greater compliance).

The criteria used to define friendship in the Newcomb et al. (1979) study were more stringent than the Foot et al. (1977) criteria. Children were considered friends if they selected each other as preferred playmates (first or second choice) and if they were perceived by teachers to have a high rate of interaction. Non-friends were classmates who were willing to play with each other but who, according to the teachers, interacted infrequently. Thus, unlike Foot et al. (1977) the contrast achieved in this study would seem to be one of comparing "friends" with acquaintances. In the Newcomb et al. (1979) study, the social responsiveness of friends in a task performance situation was greater than that of familiar peers. The interactions of friends compared with nonfriends, involved greater mutuality, as expressed in verbal exchanges.

Newcomb and Brady (1982) examined the degree of mutuality and reciprocity found in the interactions of friends vs. nonfriends for a problem solving task that was presented under one of three incentive conditions: cooperative, competitive, or no reward. For this investigation, friendship was operationalized as boys who chose each other as first or second best friends. Nonfriends were acquainted pairs who indicated a mutual willingness to play with each other. The results indicated that across reward conditions, friends made significantly more problem solving discoveries than nonfriends, shared more task-related information through discussions, attended to a greater proportion of their partner's monologues, issued more mutually oriented commands, and complied more often with mutual commands. In addition, the interactions displayed by friends were characterized by greater affective expression and a greater likelihood to match or imitate the affective expressions of their partners.

Studies have also been designed to determine whether the dimensions that emerge from children's descriptions of friendship, such as helping and sharing, are reflected in their behavior. Perhaps the most extensive line of research on this topic has been conducted by Berndt (1981a, 1981b). In these investigations, pairs of children were considered to be friends if one or both partners named the other as a best friend and each partner's average rating on a 5-point liking scale exceeded 4.0. The comparison group included acquaintances (children who did not meet the friendship criteria and had not given the other child a "don't like" rating).

In the first of these investigations (Berndt, 1981b), the amount of sharing between friends and between acquaintances was examined in competitive situations where helping and sharing with a partner was likely to result in few rewards. The results indicated that friends did not share significantly more than nonfriends. There was, however, an interesting sex difference. While girls shared equally with friends and nonfriends, boys actually shared significantly less with their friends than with acquaintances.

Although a competitive situation was also employed in the second investigation (Berndt, 1981a), the reward structure of the task was changed to provide another alternative to winning and losing, namely equity in rewards. Pairs of children were observed in the fall and spring of the school year, and the friends with whom children were paired at the beginning of the year were also paired at the end of the year, even if they hadn't remained friends. Fourth graders helped their friends more often and refused to share with their friends less often than did first graders. The amount of sharing and frequency of refusals to help did not change from fall to spring for fourth graders. First graders, however, shared less with their friends and refused more often to help their friends in the spring as compared to the fall. Because many of the friendships among the fourth graders but not the first graders were maintained Berndt concluded that the changes in first graders' behavior from the fall to the spring were probably a result of weakening ties. One interpretation of this finding is that, even among first graders, children's responsiveness to each other's needs and requests is related to the strength of their friendship.

According to several theorists (e.g., Sullivan, 1953; Youniss, 1980), children learn prosocial competencies in friendship that, in turn, generalize to other peer relationships. Whereas little empirical work directly reflects on this hypothesis, there are at least two empirical studies that point to a relationship between friendship and altruism (Mannarino, 1976; McGuire & Weisz, 1982). Mannarino (1976) identified two groups of preadolescents, one group who had stable chums (friendships) and another who had no close chums (the criteria used to identify children with stable friendships were previously reviewed). Boys with close chums were found to be significantly more altruistic on a measure of their concern for others and on a prisoner's dilemma game. However, because children's behavior was not assessed in a naturalistic setting, it was not possible to determine the range of relationships in which altruism was expressed.

Expanding on Mannarino's investigation, McGuire and Weisz (1982) assessed altruism on a variety of measures including donations, teacher's ratings, and observations of children's freeplay behavior. Children with friends displayed higher levels of spontaneous altruism. However, since the target of altruism (i.e., friends or other peers) was not assessed, it was not possible to determine the scope or range of relationships in which altruistic behavior was expressed. According to Masters and Furman (1981), children are more likely to direct reinforcing behaviors toward their friends than nonfriends.

Although the results of these investigations are consistent with the hypothesis that children with friends are more altruistic, they do not support the contention that these behaviors tend to be acquired in friendships or generalize to other peer relationships. While it is possible that friendships may increase a child's interpersonal sensitivity and, in turn, their altruism, it is also possible that a child's interpersonal sensitivity and altruism may cause and sustain friendships.

Consistent with research on infants and preschoolers, studies conducted with school-aged children indicate that the interactions of friends differ from those of nonfriends (including both strangers and acquaintances). Not only do school-age friends demonstrate a greater frequency of social interaction, but they also evidence more positive affect and synchrony of affect, greater mutuality and reciprocity, and more prosocial behavior (helping and sharing). The latter difference becomes increasingly evident during middle childhood.

Although there is some evidence of situational variation for children's behaviors toward friends, many of the behavioral differences found between friends as compared to nonfriends were consistent across social situations (e.g., cooperative and moderately competitive tasks). Another general theme that can be abstracted from these findings is that reciprocity, in this case in the expression affect and positive social behavior, is present to a greater extent among friends than nonfriends. There is also evidence that mutual friends compared with unilateral friends at this age display greater reciprocity in their knowledge about one another (Ladd & Emerson, 1984). These differences, as Sullivan (1953) and Youniss (1980) have suggested, may attest to higher levels of intimacy and sensitivity in firendships.

Somewhat inconsistent are the findings of Berndt (1981a) indicating that, in highly competitive situations, boys are more competitive with friends than nonfriends. The author attributes this finding to the fact that children tend to view themselves as similar to their friends. Thus, in a highly competitive situation, males may compete as a way of demonstrating that they are equal to their friends.

In general, the interactional differences found between friends and nonfriends suggest that friendships may afford school-age children with a unique opportunity to engage in positive, reciprocal interactions with a peer. Although the question of whether friendships actually "cause" children to develop specific competencies remains open to debate and further research, the available data are consistent with the contention that friendships foster development of certain social skills. Were this the case, these competencies may promote the maintenance of present relationships and contribute to the formation of future relationships.

FRIENDSHIP ASSESSMENT AND FUNCTIONS: FUTURE DIRECTIONS

Historically, research on childhood friendships is in an early stage, and progress toward understanding the functions of friendship in child development is limited. Nonetheless, evidence from recent literature does not contradict the proposition that specific social competencies (i.e., those that may establish the foundation for future relationships or mediate interpersonal adjustment) are acquired and enhanced in friendships. There is also some evidence to suggest that children's friendships function as a resource for emotional security and support.

Although promising, these findings provide little basis for firm conclusions regarding the contributions of friendship to children's later relationships or subsequent adjustment. Clearly, the kinds of behaviors that occur in friendships (e.g., prosocial skills) and differentiate this type of social tie from other forms of peer relationships, are known to predict such social outcomes as popularity or status in the peer group (e.g., Dodge, 1983; Coie & Kupersmidt, 1983; Ladd et al., in press). Yet convincing empirical and causal connections between these variables have yet to be demonstrated.

A better understanding of these topics may depend in part on our ability to resolve a number of problematic issues. One such issue is the inconsistency across investigations in the assessment procedures and criteria used to identify friendships. For example, some investigators chose children's mutual preferences for activity partners as the criterion for friendship (e.g., Foot et al., 1977), while others used mutual nominations of friendship. These often subtle inconsistencies hinder comparisons across investigations. A second problem is the inconsistency found across investigations in the type of relationships (or "nonrelationships") used as a referent against which to compare friendships. In some instances, stranger dyads were used to create a comparison group, whereas, in other studies, pairs of acquainted children were compared, making it difficult to draw conclusions about the nature of friendship relative to other peer relationships. A related concern is the issue of generalizability or ecological validity of these relationships and comparisons. Participation in "nonfriendship" dyads may be a contrived phenomenon. The meaningfullness of comparisons between friends and "nonfriends" is open to question.

Other conceptual and empirical issues that warrant further research attention are associated with a need to further delineate: (a) the friendship processes (e.g., mutual trust, perceived similarity, interpersonal novelty or attraction, etc.) that foster specific types of interactions (see Duck, Miell, & Gabler, 1980; Bigelow & LaGaipa, 1980; Ladd & Emerson, 1984); (b) the specific social competencies that may be fostered in these interactions; (c) the relationship between these competencies and present and future peer relationships; (d) the qualitative aspects of friendships (e.g., familiarity, perceived support, etc.) that contribute to children's feeling of emotional security and support; and (e) the conditions under which friendships are most likely to have a supportive function. Furthermore, the question of whether there are differing forms or degrees of friendship must also be considered and incorporated into research on these issues.

It can be argued that progress in any of these areas is, to some extent, dependent on the development of consistent and "valid" definitions of friendship. Both the comparability of research findings and the resulting conclusions would be enhanced by systematic efforts to define (and eventually refine) the meaning of friendship at various age levels. There is a need to develop definitions and assessment procedures that are capable of distinguishing between various types or degrees of friendship. Such assessment tools would allow researchers to determine, for example, whether children's social interactions and competencies vary as a function of the degree or type of friendship they have established with their partner. The emphasis in current research on assessment procedures that distinguish between "friends" and "nonfriends" implies that friendship is a categorical rather than a continuous construct. As a consequence, our present knowledge of friendship may be restricted to friends-in-general or confounded across types or levels of relationships. This situation is further complicated by the fact that the criteria used to identify friendships vary across investigations.

When developing these assessments, special attention should be given to dimensions or measures used to define specific categories or levels of friendship (e.g., degree of mutual liking between members). Some of the current strategies for defining friendship may prove to be useful for this task. For example, the *degree* to which children say they like each other may reflect the level of friendship that exists in the dyad. It is also possible that the percent of time children spend together may reflect the quality of their friendship.

Two other dimensions of relationships that may prove useful for assessing friendship status are positive affect and reciprocity. These two dimensions are consistently revealed in studies designed to compare the interactions of friends with those of nonfriends. It is possible that closer or higher levels of friendship are marked by more frequent exchanges of positive affect between the partners and higher levels of synchrony in their interactions.

Finally, data reported by Howes (1983) suggests that stability may also be an important indicator of the level or quality or children's friendships (e.g., maintained vs. sporadic friends). Although it appears that stable friendships are more common among school-aged as opposed to younger children, there is some evidence to suggest that stable friendships also occur among infants and toddlers (Howes, 1983), and preschoolers (Gershman & Hayes, 1983; Howes, 1983).

With the exception of Raupp (1983), few researchers have defined friendship on a continuum and developed assessment procedures capable of discriminating among various forms or levels of friendship. In this particular study, however, Raupp (1983) attempted to distinguish various forms of friendship (e.g., mutual/best friendships, relationships involving some friendship, and unilateral friendships) from acquaintanceship using criteria based on teacher's reports of children's friendships, behavioral observations, and sociometric interviews. In this classification system, relevant criteria included the percentage of time dyads spent together, teacher's perceptions of the degree of friendship between the children, and children's perceptions of friendship.

Research is also needed to determine whether there is continuity across age levels in the dimensions that differentiate levels or types of friendship. Since it appears that the nature of friendship changes over the course of development, it seems likely that the dimensions that researchers use to define and discriminate between various forms of friendship may also change. For example, whereas the dimensions included in Raupp's (1983) procedure may be appropriate for assessing the degree of friendship in preschool dyads, these same dimensions may be inadequate or produce meaningless discriminations with older children. As theoretical accounts of friendship and research on children's friendship conceptions suggest, criteria such as intimacy, loyalty, and open communication may be more important or "valid" indicators of the quality of friendship between older children.

How researchers will choose among these potential criteria and integrate them into working definitions of friendship will no doubt depend on the theoretical model or paradigms deployed at each age level to specify this construct. We have suggested that friendship can generally be viewed as a multidimensional construct manifested in children's cognitions, affect, and overt behaviors. Acceptance of this premise would seem to dictate a multivariate approach to assessment, incorporating attributes from each domain as they may be relevant to one's definition of friendship at a particular age level.

Although it is premature to draw conclusions regarding the contributions of children's friendships to the development of social competence and adjustment, there is a growing body of evidence to suggest that friendships may serve important social functions during childhood. If this is the case, then children who fail to form friendships may be denied these experiences and suffer altered development. Although clear evidence of this possibility has not yet emerged in the empirical literature, the prospects of obtaining such a finding seem likely and may well serve as an impetus for further investigation.

REFERENCES

Allen, V. L. (1981). Self, social group, and social structure: Surmises about the study of children's friendships. In S. R. Asher & J. M. Gottman (Eds.), *The development of children's friendships* (pp. 182–203). New York: Cambridge University Press.

Berndt, T. J. (1981a). Age changes and changes over time in prosocial intentions and behavior between friends. *Developmental Psychology, 17,* 408–416.

Berndt, T. J. (1981b). The effects of friendship on prosocial intentions and behavior. *Child Development, 52,* 636–643.

Bigelow, B. J. (1977). Children's friendship expectations: A cognitive developmental study. *Child Development, 48,* 246–253.

Bigelow, B. J., & LaGaipa, J. J. (1980). The development of friendship values and choice. In H. G. Foot, A. J. Chapman, & Smith (Eds.), *Friendship and social relations in children* (pp. 15–44). Chichester, England: John Wiley & Sons.

Cobb, S. (1976). Social support as moderator of life stress. *Psychosomatic Medicine, 38,* 330–313.

Coie, J. D., & Kupersmidt, J. (1983). A behavioral analysis of emerging social status in boys' groups. *Child Development, 54,* 1400–1416.

Cohen, A., & Melson, G. (1980). The influence of friendship on children's communication. *Journal of Social Psychology, 112,* 207–213.

Dickens, W. J., & Perlman, D. (1981). Friendship over the life-cycle. In S. Duck & R. Gilmour (Eds.), *Personal relationships Vol. 2: Developing personal relationships* (91–122). New York: Academic Press.

Dodge, K. A. (1983). Behavioral antecedents of peer social rejection and isolation. *Child Development, 54,* 1386–1399.

Doyle, A. B., Connolly, J., & Rivest, L. P. (1980). The effects of playmate familiarity on the social interactions of young children. *Child Development, 51,* 217–223.

Duck, S., Miell, D. K., & Gaebler, H. C. (1980). Attraction and communication in children's interactions. In H. C. Foot, A. J. Chapman, & J. R. Smith (Eds.). *Friendships and social relations in children* (pp. 89–115). New York: Wiley.

Eckerman, C. D., & Stein, M. R. (1982). The toddler's emerging interactive skills. In K. H. Rubin & H. S. Ross (Eds.), *Peer relationships and social skills in childhood* (pp. 41–71). New York: Springer-Verlag.

Erikson, E. (1968). *Youth, identity and crisis.* New York: W. W. Norton.

Fine, G. A. (1981). Friends, impression management, and preadolescent behavior. In S. R. Asher & J. M. Gottman (Eds.), *The development of children's friendships* (pp. 29–52). New York: Cambridge University Press.

Foot, H. C., Chapman, A. J., & Smith, J. R. (1977). Friendship and social responsiveness in boys and girls. *Journal of Personality and Social Psychology, 35,* 401–411.

Foot, H. C., Chapman, A. J., & Smith, J. R. (1980). Patterns of interaction in children's friendships. In H. C. Foot, A. J. Chapman, & J. J. Smith (Eds.), *Friendship and social relations in children* (pp. 287–289). New York: Wiley.

Furman, W. (1982). Children's friendships. In T. M. Field, A. Huston, H. C. Quay, L. Troll & G. E. Finley (Eds.), *Review of human development* (pp. 327–339). New York: Wiley.

Furman, W. & Bierman, K. L. (1983). Developmental changes in young children's conceptions of friendship. *Child Development, 54,* 549–556.

Gershman, E. S., & Hayes, D. S. (1983). Differential stability of reciprocal friendships and unilateral relationships among preschool children. *Merrill-Palmer Quarterly, 29,* 169–177.

Gottman, J. M. (1983). How children become friends. *Monographs of the Society for Research in Child Development, 48*(3), serial no. 201.

Hartup, W. W. (1975). The origins of friendships. In M. Lewis & L. Rosenblum (Eds.), *Friendship and peer relations* (pp. 11–26). New York: Wiley.

Hartup, W. W. (1976). Peer interaction and the behavioral development of the individual child. In E. Schopler & R. J. Reichler (Eds.), *Psychopathology and child development* (pp. 203–218). New York: Plenum.

Hartup, W. W. (1983). Peer relations. In P. H. Mussen (Ed.), *Handbook of child psychology,* vol. 4 (pp. 103–196). New York: John Wiley & Sons.

Hartup, W. W. (in press). The peer context. In W. A. Collins (Ed.), *Basic research in middle childhood.* Washington, D.C.: National Academy of Sciences.

Hayes, D. S., Gershman, E., & Bolin, L. J. (1980). Friends and enemies: Cognitive bases for preschool children's unilateral and reciprocal relationships. *Child Development, 51,* 1276–1279.

Hinde, R. A., Titmus, G., Easton, D., & Tamplin, A. (1985). Incidence of "friendship" and behavior toward stong associates versus nonassociates in preschoolers. *Child Development, 56,* 234–245.

Hymel, S., & Asher, S. R. (1977). *Assessment and training of isolated children's social skills.* Paper presented at the biennial meeting of the Society for Research in Child Development. New Orleans.

Howes, C. (1983). Patterns of friendship. *Child Development, 54,* 1041–1053.

Ispa, J. (1981). Peer support among Soviet daycare toddlers. *International Journal of Behavioral Development, 4,* 255–269.

Ladd, G. W., & Asher, S. R. (1985). Social skill training and children's peer relations. In L. L'Abate & M. Milan (Eds.), *Handbook of social skill training and research* (pp. 219–244). New York: Wiley.

Ladd, G. W., & Emerson, E. S. (1984). Shared knowledge in children's friendships. *Developmental Psychology, 20,* 932–940.

Ladd, G. W., Price, J. M., & Hart, C. H. (in press). Preschooler's peer networks and behavioral orientations: Relationship to social and school adjustment. In S. R. Asher & J. D. Coie (Eds.), *Peer rejection in childhood: Origins, consequences, and intervention.* Cambridge: Cambridge University Press.

Lewis, M., Young, G., Brooks, J., & Michalson, L. (1975). The beginnings of friendship. In M. Lewis & L. Rosenblum (Eds.), *Friendship and peer relations* (pp. 27–66). New York: Wiley.

Mannarino, A. P. (1976). Friendship patterns and altruistic behavior in preadolescent males. *Developmental Psychology, 12,* 555–556.

Mannarino, A. P. (1980). The development of children's friendships. In H. C. Foot, A. J. Chapman, & J. R. Smith (Eds.), *Friendship and social relations in children* (pp. 45–63). New York: Wiley.

Masters, J. C. & Furman, W. (1981). Popularity, individual friendship selection, and specific peer interaction among children. *Developmental Psychology, 17,* 344–350.

McGuire, K. D., & Weisz, J. R. (1982). Social cognition and behavior correlates of preadolescent chumship. *Child Development, 53,* 1478–1484.

Newcomb, A. F. & Brady, J. E. (1982). Mutality in boys' friendships relations. *Child Development, 53,* 392–395.

Newcomb, A. F., Brady, J. E., & Hartup, W. W. (1979). Friendship and incentive condition as determinants of children's task-oriented social behavior. *Child Development, 50,* 878–881.

Oden, S., & Asher, S. R. (1977). Coaching children in social skills for friendship making. *Child Development, 48,* 495–506.

Raupp, C. D. (1982). *Preschooler's friendship status: Friendship cognitions, similarity, and interactions.* Paper presented at the biennial meeting of the Southeastern Conference on Human Development, Baltimore.

Raupp, C. D. (1983). *Classifying early peer relationships using convergent measures.* Paper presented at the Biennial Meetings of the Society for Research in Child Development, Detroit.

Richey, M. H. & Richey, H. W. (1980). The significance of best-friend relationships in adolescence. *Psychology in the School, 17,* 536–540.

Rubenstein, J., & Howes, C. (1976). The effects of peers on toddler interaction with mother and toys. *Child Development, 47,* 597–605.

Schwarz, J. C. (1972). Effects of peer familiarity on the behavior of preschoolers in a novel situation. *Journal of Personality and Social Psychology, 24,* 276–284.

Selman, R. L. (1981). The child as a friendship philosopher. In S. R. Asher & J. M. Gottman (Eds.), *The development of children's friendships* (pp. 242–272). New York: Cambridge University Press.

Smollar, J., & Youniss, J. (1982). Social development through friendship. In K. H. Rubin & H. S. Ross (Eds.), *Peer relationships and social skills in childhood* (pp. 279–298). New York Springer-Verlag.

Sullivan, J. S. (1953). *The interpersonal theory of psychiatry.* New York: Norton.

Tuveson, R. V., & Stockdale, D. F. (1981). The effects of separation from a friend on the social behaviors of preschool children. *The Journal of Genetic Psychology, 139,* 119–132.

Vandell, D. L. (1980). Sociability of peer and mother during the first year. *Developmental Psychology, 16,* 335–361.

Vandell, D. L., & Mueller, E. C. (1980). Peer play and friendships during the first two years. In H. G. Foot, A. J. Chapman, & J. R. Smith (Eds.), *Friendship and social relations in children* (pp. 181–208). Chichester: John Wiley & Sons.

Vandell, D. L., Wilson, K. S., & Buchanan, N. R. (1980). Peer interaction in the first year of life: An examination of its structure, content, and sensitivity to toys. *Child Development, 51*, 481–488.

Youniss, J. (1980). *Parents and peers in social development: A Sullivan-Piaget perspective.* Chicago: University of Chicago Press.

THE RELATION BETWEEN SOCIAL AGGRESSION AND PEER REJECTION IN MIDDLE CHILDHOOD

Karen Linn Bierman

ABSTRACT

Aggressive behavior and peer rejection are stable in middle childhood and predict a range of poor adult mental health outcomes. On the basis of substantial correlational evidence linking aggression with peer rejection, many investigators have assumed that children showing aggressive behavior or peer rejection represent a single, homogeneous group. Yet, several factors, such as the age, gender, and cultural background of the child and peer group, and the social skills of the aggressor, may affect the social impact of various aggressive behaviors. Hence, some aggressive children may not be rejected by peers. Conversely, nonconforming behaviors, such as hyperactive behaviors, may contribute to peer rejection in the absence of aggressive behavior. To examine the relation between aggressive

Advances in Behavioral Assessment of Children and Families, Vol. 2, pgs. 151–178.
Editor: Ronald J. Prinz

ISBN: 0-89232-481-3

behavior and peer rejection, teacher and peer ratings were collected on 170 boys in grades 1–3. Four groups of boys were compared: (1) Aggressive-Rejected boys (9% of the sample), (2) Aggressive (nonrejected) boys (6% of the sample), (3) Rejected (nonaggressive) boys (5% of the sample), and (4) Average (nonaggressive, nonrejected) boys. Teachers and peers ascribed similar aggressive behavior to Aggressive-Rejected and Aggressive boys, but boys in the latter group were well-accepted by peers and showed no other signs of social maladjustment. Rejected boys were comparable to the Average boys on measures of aggression, withdrawal, and hyperactive/disruptive behaviors; no behavioral basis for their peer rejection emerged. Implications of these findings are discussed for the study of aggressive behavior and the treatment of peer rejection.

DEVELOPMENTAL IMPLICATIONS OF AGGRESSION AND PEER REJECTION

Childhood is an exciting period of rapid growth and adaptation. New competencies and coping skills develop as children mature and struggle to meet and master environmental challenges. Behavioral problems inevitably emerge as part of normal adjustment and adaptation, although most diminish over time. Accumulating evidence suggests that two childhood problems are not transitional, however, and warrant clinical concern. Highly aggressive behavior and peer rejection are stable during middle childhood, are associated with poor social-emotional development, and are predictive of a range of poor adult mental health outcomes (Kohlberg, LaCrosse, & Ricks, 1972; Robins, 1972).

Aggression

Definition

Aggression is used generally here to describe a variety of acting-out behaviors that have in common an intrusive demand and aversive effect on others (Olweus, 1979; Patterson, 1982). Included are physically and verbally aggressive acts (e.g., observed behaviors such as attacks, threats, derogation; peer or teacher descriptions such as "starts fights," "says mean things to others"), disruptive behavior (e.g., inappropriate or off-task behavior; descriptions such as "bothers others," "gets into trouble"), and disagreeable and egocentric behavior (e.g., negative responses to others; descriptions such as "selfish," "demands attention"). While some definitions of aggression require hostile intentions and harm to others (Feshbach, 1970; Parke & Slaby, 1983), disruptive and disagreeable behaviors are included here because they often covary with the more direct forms of aggression (Patterson, Littman, & Bricker, 1967; Pekarik, Prinz, Liebert, Weintraub, & Neale, 1976) and were included in most of the studies reviewed in this chapter.

Developmental Course

Aggressive behaviors emerge early in children's peer interactions, but are quickly socialized. Instrumental, physically aggressive actions, such as hitting, pushing, or grabbing to get toys typically increase between the ages of 2–4, and occasional social and behavioral problems are typical in the preschool years (Van Alstnyne & Hattwick, 1939). Most instrumental aggression is transitional, however, and decreases substantially by the early grade-school years (Hartup, 1974).

By middle childhood, high rates of aggressive and disruptive behavior become stable and predictive of continuing problems. For eample, stability correlations for peer ratings of "starts fights" have been as high as .48 to .86 over three to four years, even across children's transitions from elementary school to middle school (Coie & Dodge, 1983; Olweus, 1977). In fact, in a comprehensive review of 16 studies, Olweus (1979) concluded that aggressive behavior shares a level of consistency similar to IQ, showing an average stability correlation of .63 over 10–14 year periods between middle childhood and adulthood.

Unlike internalizing problems (such as mentation problems, regressive anxiety, and isolation) which often improve over time, externalizing problems (such as conflict with parents, fighting, and delinquency) are likely to stay the same or increase in the direction of greater pathology (Gersten, Langner, Eisenberg, Simcha-Fagan, & McCarthy, 1976). Negative adult outcomes for highly aggressive youth include juvenile delinquency, adult antisocial personality disorders, poor interpersonal and marital relations, alcoholism, and other psychiatric disorders (Kohlberg et al., 1972; Robins, 1972). In fact, Robins (1972) has suggested that juvenile antisocial behavior may be the single most powerful known predictor of adult psychiatric status.

The self-perpetuating nature of aggressive behavior patterns may reflect a negative socializing cycle. Family factors such as high rates of parental coercive behavior, marital discord, inconsistent punishment for aggressive behavior, and low levels of praise for positive behaviors make it more likely that some children initially show high rates of aggressive behavior in their peer interactions (cf. Patterson, 1982). Then, peer responses become central variables maintaining and strengthening negative peer interactions in school settings (Patterson et al., 1967). Peers often respond selectively to the negative behaviors of "problematic" classmates, while ignoring the positive and appropriate behaviors of these children (Solomon & Wahler, 1967). In fact, Klein and Young (1979) observed that 20–70% of all classroom disruptions were reinforced by peers. Additionally, aggressive children may develop deviant social expectations and social-cognitive skill deficits, contributing to a maladaptive socialization cycle. For example, aggressive behavior has been linked to negative attributional biases, asocial goals, poor interpersonal perspective taking skills, deficits in social information processing, and agonistic social problem solving tendencies (cf. Parke & Slaby, 1983). Similar negative outcomes are experienced by peer-rejected children.

Peer Rejection

Definition

Children who are unaccepted by peers represent a heterogeneous group. Early investigators addressed this heterogeneity by sub-categorizing children on the basis of behavioral differences. For example, Northway (1944) described three types of unaccepted children: (1) recessive children, who were apathetic, listless, and poorly groomed, (2) socially uninterested children, who were uninterested in other children, being either shy of them or bored with them, and (3) socially ineffective children who were noisy, rebellious, and arrogant. On the basis of several case studies, Northway suggested that these personality patterns may reflect different etiologies and require different intervention strategies. Similarly, Olweus (1978) differentiated two groups of boys with poor peer relations on the basis of different behavioral patterns—"bullies," who actively aggressed against peers, and "whipping boys," who were often targets of their peers' aggression.

More recently, unpopular children have been sub-categorized on the basis of sociometric measures. Unaccepted children who have few friends (based upon low levels of positive sociometric nominations) are divided into two groups: rejected children, who receive many negative sociometric nominations and neglected children who receive few negative nominations. A number of sociometric classification systems have been developed, each different in terms of the statistics used to compute classification (Coie, Dodge, & Coppotelli, 1982; Newcomb & Bukowski, 1983). Little research is available yet concerning the overlap among these systems, although Hymel and Rubin (1985) suggest that, at least for preschool children, there is surprisingly little overlap. In this chapter, an inclusive definition of peer rejection will be used. Investigations that have differentiated actively disliked rejected children from neglected children will be included, regardless of the particular classification system employed.

The distinction between rejected and neglected children is important because these groups differ in clinical characteristics, behavioral patterns, and predicted outcome. For example, rejected status appears to be more stable over time than neglected status (Coie & Dodge, 1983), and more likely to continue across transitions into new peer groups (Coie & Kupersmidt, 1983). Rejected children are less preferred as playmates than neglected children (French & Waas, 1985; Hymel & Burin, 1985), and are more likely to report feelings of loneliness (Asher & Wheeler, 1983). Additionally, the parents of rejected children indicate greater pathology in their children than do parents of neglected, average, or popular children (French & Waas, 1985). Similarly, while teachers report greater than average academic problems and anxiety for both rejected and neglected children, they report abnormally high behavioral problems, problematic peer relations, aggression, and hostile isolation only for the rejected children (Foster & Ritchey, 1985; French & Waas, 1985). Rejected children are also at greater developmental risk than are neglected children, as described in the next section.

Developmental Course

Positive and negative nominations, upon which sociometric classifications are based, begin to stabilize during the preschool years and become quite stable by middle childhood. One year test-retest correlations for both positive and negative nominations are typically in the .50–.70 range for gradeschool children (Bukowski & Newcomb, 1984; Coie & Dodge, 1983) and sometimes as high as .90 (Bonney, 1943). Even over 3–4 years, reported stability coefficients remain around .30–.40 (Coie & Dodge, 1983; Roff, Sells, & Golden, 1972). Coie and Dodge (1983) specifically examined the stability of classification as a rejected child, and found that 45% of these children were still rejected one year later and 30% four years later. Fluctuation in sociometric choices appears to decrease during the gradeschool and preadolescent years; thus, children's sociometric status may become increasingly crystallized over time (Horrocks & Buker, 1951).

Rejected children may become deficient in important social competencies developed in the context of positive peer interaction. Peers may act as teachers or models and as sources of reinforcement and emotional support, facilitating children's development of cooperative, reciprocal, negotiation, and communication skills (Rubin & Daniels-Beirness, 1983). Additionally, peer interactions provide opportunities for fantasy play and role taking, enhancing social-cognitive development and the understanding of social roles and social norms (Ladd & Asher, 1985).

Correlational studies suggest that, in general, children who have poor peer relations are at increased risk for a range of poor mental-health outcomes as adults, including poor school adjustment, learning difficulties, and school dropout, juvenile delinquency, and referral for mental health services. For more complete reviews of this literature, the reader is referred to Ladd and Asher (1985), Kohlberg et al. (1972), and Putallaz and Gottman (1983).

When outcomes for neglected and rejected children are compared directly, the predictive risk appears much higher for rejected children. Kupersmidt (1983) examined the high-school records and juvenile delinquency status of children who were neglected or rejected by their classmates during their preadolescent and early adolescent years. While both rejected and neglected children were more likely to be truant than their well-accepted peers, only the rejected children were more likely to develop the serious problems of juvenile delinquency and school dropout.

Apparently, both aggressive interpersonal behavior and peer rejection are fairly stable childhood difficulties that predict a number of similar negative adult mental health outcomes. A variety of studies examining the relation between social aggression and peer rejection suggest that these problems often coincide. In fact, many reviewers treat aggressive-disruptive behavior and rejected sociometric status as isomorphic descriptors (Conger & Keane, 1981). In the following section, we will examine studies that link observations or peer descriptions of positive and negative social behavior to peer relations, in general, and to peer rejection, in particular.

Behavioral Correlates of Sociometric Status

Observations of peer interactions reveal only slight inverse correlations between children's rates of positive and negative peer interactions. For example, reported correlations between initiated positive and negative behaviors for preschool children range from .11 to −.29 (Hartup, Glazer & Charlesworth, 1967) and are only slightly higher (in the −.30 to −.40 range) for gradeschool children (Gresham, 1981; Ladd, 1983). Similarly, correlations between children's positive and negative sociometric nomination scores are often low. Correlation coefficients reported for preschool children are typically in the range of 0 to −.31 (Hartup et al., 1967), while among gradeschool children, coefficients are slightly higher, but still low ($r = -.21$, Coie, et al., 1982; $r = -.35$, Victor & Halverson, 1980). Occasionally, correlations above −.50 have been documented for children at both age levels (Kaplan & Kauffman, 1978; Moore & Updegraff, 1964). Given the mixed findings regarding linear relations between positive and negative behavior and between peer acceptance and rejection, correlations among these four variables will be considered separately. Evidence concerning the relation of positive behavior to peer acceptance and peer rejection will be reviewed first, followed by evidence concerning the relation of negative behavior to peer acceptance and rejection.

Positive Social Behavior

Correlational studies suggest that children who engage in high rates of positive social behavior, including friendly approach, conversation, smiling, cooperative interaction, and conforming behavior are likely to receive more positive behavioral responses from their peers and to have higher positive nomination and roster rating scores than children who engage in low rates of these behaviors (Bonney & Powell, 1953; Goldman, Corsini, & De Urioste, 1980; Gresham, 1981; Hartup et al., 1967; Masters & Furman, 1981; Rubin & Daniels-Beirness, 1983). Similarly, gradeschool children who are described by their peers as helpful, supportive, cooperative, friendly, likable, nice, calm, understanding, good leaders, good at games, and physically attractive, are likely to receive high roster ratings and many positive nominations (Coie et al., 1982; Hymel & Rubin, 1985; Victor & Halverson, 1980).

Thus, positive social behavior is clearly and consistently related to peer acceptance and popularity. One might expect, then, that low levels of positive social behavior would be related to peer rejection; however, evidence concerning the relation between positive social behavior and peer rejection is mixed. For example, Goldman et al. (1980), Hartup et al. (1967), and Masters & Furman (1981) all report nonsignificant correlations between observed positive social behavior of preschoolers and negative sociometric nominations. Similarly, the positive behavioral descriptions that Coie et al. (1982) found to correlate in the .40–.63 range with "like most" nominations showed correlations of much lesser magnitudes ranging from −.31 to .11 with "like least" nominations.

Apparently, positive interpersonal behavior goes hand in hand with high levels of group acceptance and popularity. Levels of positive behavior, however, appear to have only a low to mild negative relation with peer rejection, suggesting that socially unskilled children are rarely chosen as friends, but not necessarily actively disliked. Negative social behavior shows an opposite pattern, correlating with peer rejection but not inversely related to peer acceptance.

Negative Social Behavior

Among preschoolers, negative social behavior, such as noncompliance, interfering with others, derogation, attacks, and threats are correlated with negative sociometric nominations (Hartup et al., 1967; Masters & Furman, 1981). Similarly, classmates who gradeschool children describe as disruptive, snobbish, short-tempered, unattractive, and likely to brag, to start fights, to aggress against others indirectly, and to get in trouble with the teacher are likely to be actively rejected (Coie et al., 1982).

Surprisingly, aggressive-negative behaviors reveal no consistent relation to positive peer nominations. For example, reported correlations between observations of negative behavior and positive peer nominations among preschoolers range from .16 to −.18 (Hartup et al., 1967; Masters & Furman, 1981). Similarly, Bonney and Powell (1953) found that unpopular gradeschool children did not exhibit more aggressive acts or ignore or reject others any more frequently than their popular classmates, nor did they receive more criticism or aggression from teachers and peers.

Investigators likewise report little correspondence between negative peer descriptions and positive friendship choices. For example, using a "Guess who?" sociometric technique with 7- 8-year-old children, MacFarlane, Honzik & Davis (1937) found that, among boys, best friend choices were unrelated to descriptions such as "not quarrelsome," "not bossy," and "doesn't get mad easily." Also using a "Guess who?" technique, Tuddenham (1951) identified a cluster of items that third grade boys used to describe popular peers, including "good at games," "best friend," "real boy," "takes chances," "not bashful," and "leader." A second cluster of items involved refraining from negative behaviors, such as "not bossy," "not quarrelsome," "doesn't get mad," and "not a show off.'' No relation was found between the cluster of popular descriptors and the cluster of negative behaviors. Coie et al. (1982) also examined correlations between ''like most'' nominations and a host of negative descriptors (including fighting, indirect aggression, and getting in trouble with the teacher); the correlations were all low and nonsignificant.

Two other studies using somewhat different samples and methods also suggest little direct relation between negative behavior and social acceptance. On the basis of counselor descriptions, Campbell and Yarrow (1961) found that popular gradeschool children at a summer camp were both highly friendly and quite aggressive. Secondly, in a mainstreamed population of EMR children, Gottlieb, Semmel, and Veldman (1978) found that teacher and peer ratings of misbehavior, while significantly correlated with social rejection, were not correlated with social acceptance. Instead, teacher and peer ratings of cognitive ability predicted social acceptance.

When negative behaviors have been correlated with roster ratings, mixed findings emerge. For example, some observational studies have documented inverse relations between negative peer interactions and roster ratings while others report nonsignificant correlations (Gresham, 1981; Rubin & Daniels-Beirness, 1983). Similarly, correlations between peer descriptions of aggressive/disruptive behaviors and roster ratings have ranged from −.49 to −.09 (Hymel & Rubin, 1985). Olweus (1977) has reported low roster ratings to be more characteristic of victims than of instigators of aggression.

In general, positive social behavior is associated with peer acceptance and popularity but independent of peer rejection. Negative social behavior, in contrast, correlates with peer rejection but is less consistently related to peer acceptance. Coie and Dodge (1983) have suggested that this pattern of correlations may be explained by the existence of a group of low-accepted but nonrejected children—neglected children—who demonstrate low rates of prosocial behavior and low rates of aggressive behaviors. They suggest that a clearer picture of the behavioral correlates of various sociometric classifications emerges when the social behaviors of children classified as rejected, neglected, average, and popular are examined separately.

Behavioral patterns of rejected children. Based upon peer descriptions, Coie et al. (1982) suggested that neglected children were primarily shy and uninvolved socially, while rejected children were active, disruptive, more aggressive, and less cooperative than popular children. Three recent observational studies of children's classroom and playground interactions have corroborated these findings.

Observations of children's playground interactions reveal that rejected children engage in less peer interaction, less cooperative play, less social conversation, and more unoccupied behavior than popular and average children (Ladd, 1983). Additionally, rejected children engage in more aggressive acts (shoving, pushing, hitting, calling names, teasing, and arguing) and more rough-and-tumble play than children of average, popular, or neglected status (Dodge, Coie, & Brakke, 1982; Ladd, 1983). Neglected children, in contrast, engage in more solitary-appropriate activity and make fewer social approaches toward peers (Dodge et al., 1982). Rejected children, however, do not necessarily receive more aggression from their peers than children of other sociometric classifications. Compared to average and popular children, rejected children more frequently play in smaller groups, with younger or unpopular children (Ladd, 1983).

In structured classroom settings, the behavioral differences between rejected children and children of other sociometric classifications are less marked. Dodge et al. (1982) found rejected children to engage in more task-inappropriate behavior and less task-appropriate behavior, display more aggression, and experience more teacher interaction and more peer rebuff than neglected or accepted children. Foster and Ritchey (1985), in contrast, observed no classroom behavioral differences among rejected, neglected, and accepted groups, although both rejected and neglected children received fewer positive peer responses than accepted children.

Three other recent studies examined the behavior of rejected children in unfamiliar groups to reduce the possibility that prior reputational and relational experiences account for observed behavioral differences among children of various sociometric classifications. Coie and Kupersmidt (1983) observed boys of average, popular, neglected, and rejected status interacting in familiar and unfamiliar groups. Neglected children tended to be shy and uninvolved in the familiar groups only, but not in the unfamiliar groups. Rejected children, in contrast, tended to be more aggressive than popular and neglected children in both familiar and unfamiliar groups. Interestingly, rejected children were not more aggressive than boys of average sociometric status. However, the rejected children were more likely to be blamed for starting fights than were the average status children.

Studying unfamiliar groups of eight boys, Dodge (1983) found that boys who became rejected engaged in more aggressive and inappropriate behavior, making more hostile verbalizations, excluding and hitting peers more, and engaging in social conversation less than boys who achieved popular or average status. Boys who became neglected, on the other hand, conversed less and were more solitary than the average status boys. Similarly, in a group entry situation, Dodge, Schlundt, Schocken and Delugach (1983) found that rejected boys were more likely to use disruptive entry techniques than nonrejected boys, whereas neglected children were more likely to watch and wait.

The picture that emerges from this research, then, is that children who engage in high levels of aggression and negative-inappropriate behavior are likely to be rejected by their peers, while children who are inhibited and shy are likely to be neglected, and children who are positively interactive and agreeable are likely to be popular. Yet, this picture may be too simplistic. In the next sections, evidence will be presented suggesting that: (1) aggressive behavior is not always associated with peer rejection and (2) some children who do not behave aggressively are, nonetheless, rejected by peers.

FACTORS MODERATING THE SOCIAL IMPACT OF AGGRESSION

Aggression is a general class of behaviors, not all of which are socially unacceptable. The acceptability of aggressive behaviors may be influenced by demographic features, such as the child's gender and age, and the socioeconomic status, ethnic composition, and cultural background of the peer group. Topographical characteristics of the aggressive act may also affect its acceptability. Finally, the social impact of a child's aggressive behavior may depend upon the intra-individual context of that behavior; that is, a child who engages in aggressive behavior in the context of a range of socially, athletically, and academically competent behaviors may be evaluated differently than an aggressive child who generally behaves in an unfriendly and unskilled manner. Factors affecting the acceptability of aggression will be described briefly here; for a more comprehensive review, the reader is referred to Feshbach (1970) and Parke and Slaby (1983).

Demographic Features

Gender

Across observational studies, boys tend to behave more aggressively than girls (Hartup, 1974; McQuire, 1973). Teachers also describe higher levels and a greater range of aggressive behavior among boys than girls (LaGreca, 1981). Active, assertive behaviors are valued and aggressive behaviors are tolerated by boys more than by girls. Several investigators have used a "Guess who?" technique to examine the kind of traits or behavioral descriptions that relate to peer acceptance and rejection for boys compared to girls. Both Pope (1953) and Tuddenham (1951) found that descriptors reflecting dominance, daring, and leadership had positive connotations for boys, whereas these same characteristics were devalued by girls. Also using the "Guess who" technique, MacFarlane, Honzik & Davis (1937) found boys to be more frequently described by peers as wiggly, quarrelsome, better sports, and better at games than girls. Hence, positive peer ratings among boys support moderate levels of active and assertive characteristics. Hostile aggressive behavior, however, is devalued by boys as well as girls (Goertzen, 1959).

Interestingly, aggressive behavior appears to be a better predictor of unpopularity among boys than among girls (LaGreca, 1981; McQuire, 1973). This paradoxical effect may be due to differences in the level and quality of aggression displayed by each gender. Since aggressive behaviors are not socially acceptable for girls, rates of aggression are low, and correlations between aggressive behavior and peer acceptance may be attenuated. Moderate levels of assertive behavior are valued by boys, leading to higher rates and a broader distribution of aggressive behaviors than among girls. Boys are particularly more likely than girls to engage in hostile, person-oriented aggression (Hartup, 1974). The range of aggressive behaviors displayed by boys enables a clearer distinction between high, moderate, and low aggressors and allows a clearer relation between high aggression and peer rejection to emerge.

In addition to gender, the socioeconomic and ethnic composition of the peer group may affect the acceptability of aggressive behavior.

Socioeconomic Status and Ethnic Background

Children of different socioeconomic groups and ethnic backgrounds may value different social behaviors. For example, using a "Guess who?" format, Pope (1953) found that boys from high scoioeconomic backgrounds valued good classroom behavior (being assured with adults and in class and being intellectual), as well as leadership skills in play activities, while boys from low socioeconomic backgrounds focused solely on the latter attributes. Additionally, boys from the high socioeconomic group were less tolerant of restless behavior and fighting than boys from the low socioeconomic group. Using a similar technique, Feinberg, Smith, and Schmidt (1958) asked boys of three socioeconomic groups (which overlapped considerably with three ethnic groups—Protestant, Jewish, and Catholic) to list the characteristics of classmates that they would like to sit next to and classmates with whom they would feel uncomfortable or annoyed. All socioeconomic groups agreed on the positive characteristics of intelligent, plays fair, quiet, athletic, good company, conscientious, honest, can take a joke; all groups also agreed on the negative characteristics of pest, loud and noisy, conceited, silly and sissy. However, boys from the high socioeconomic groups were more likely to mention academic competence and active participation in sports and school activities as important positive characteristics and stupid, not athletic, not a leader, immature, and no activities as negative characteristics than boys from the middle or low socioeconomic groups.

Socioeconomic or ethnic differences have rarely been examined in observational studies. In one study, Hartup (1974) found that black children engaged in more instrumental (but not more hostile) aggression than white children. In another study, Gottman, Gonso, and Rasmussen (1975) observed children at a school serving a primarily working-class population to initiate and receive more negative behavior and to initiate less positive behavior than children from a school serving a predominantly middle-class population. More research is also needed to explore the possibility that the predictive correlates of aggression and peer rejection may vary among different socioeconomic or ethnic groups. Kupersmidt (1983) found that some of the relations between peer rejection and later outcomes held only for the majority white and not for the minority black sample. Similarly, Roff and Sells (1968) found that, for upper and middle socioeconomic levels, delinquency tended to occur in boys who had been rejected by other boys and there was almost no delinquency among any highly chosen boys. At the lowest socioeconomic level, however, delinquency occurred with equal frequency among the most rejected and the best liked boys.

Hence, the acceptability of aggressive behaviors and their social and predictive significance may vary as a function of demographic characteristics of the peer group, such as sex, socioeconomic status and ethnic background. Some forms of aggressive behavior may also be more socially acceptable than others.

Types of Aggression

In his 1970 review, Feshbach described several dimensions to characterize acts of aggression. Aggressive acts may vary in form; they may involve verbal or physical behavior and they may vary in amplitude, frequency, and context. Motives and affects accompanying the acts may vary. Some investigators believe that harmful intentions are essential features of behaviors defined as aggressive (Feshbach, 1970), while other investigators define coercive, aversive behaviors as aggressive regardless of whether or not an aggressive motive or angry affect is apparent (Patterson, 1982). Finally, the goal of various aggressive acts may differ. Aggressive behaviors are termed instrumental if the goal is impersonal, directed toward attaining some object or consequence. Hostile aggressive behaviors, in contrast, are person directed, designed to harm another. Instrumental aggression is more often elicited by goal-blocking and controlled by the contingent consequences (e.g., success or failure in attaining the goal), whereas hostile aggressive behaviors may be elicited by attack, derogation, or other threats to one's self-esteem and may be mediated more frequently by angry affect and controlled by the victim's expression of pain (Hartup, 1974; Patterson, 1982). Different types of aggression may be evaluated as more or less acceptable or reprehensible.

Using a "Guess who?" technique, Lesser (1959) found that preadolescent boys approved of provoked physical aggression, often attributing such behavior to well-accepted peers. In contrast, indirect aggression was least acceptable and highly negatively correlated with peer acceptance. Three other types of aggressive behavior, verbal aggression, unprovoked physical aggression, and outburst aggression tended to cluster together and to be moderately unacceptable. Across different classrooms, there was a range of variability in boys' responses to each of the items, which Lesser (1959) believes reflects the effects of different levels of socioeconomic status.

Parents also consider the motive and form of the aggressive behaviors, along with the age and sex of the aggressor, when judging the severity of an aggressive act. Aggressive behaviors are judged as more serious when the aggressor is an older child rather than a younger child, when the aggressive behavior is directed at a parent rather than a peer, when the act is physical rather than verbal, and when the act is unprovoked rather than provoked (Wenger, Berg-Cross, & Berg-Cross, 1980).

A few investigators have examined individual differences in the type of aggressive behavior displayed by various children. Dunnington (1957), for example, examined differences in the type of aggression demonstrated by children of high, medium, and low sociometric status during doll-play sessions (individual sessions with an adult). She coded total aggression displayed (including attacking, criticism, disorganization, threat, and negative affect), and then examined the proportion of this aggression that involved only a specific single play episode, or aggressive behavior within a story theme. A greater proportion of the aggression of children of high socioeconomic status involved specific or thematic aggression (70–100%) compared to the proportion of specific/thematic aggression in the play of children of low sociometric status (3–26%).

A somewhat different approach to the study of individual differences in the expression of aggressive behavior was taken by Harris and Reid (1981). Based upon earlier work by Patterson and Dawes (1975), they postulated that different types of aggressive behavior could be rank-ordered in terms of severity. Furthermore, they postulated that these behaviors would comprise a Guttman scale, such that children would not exhibit behaviors higher on the scale unless they also demonstrated behaviors lower on the scale. The heirarchy of behaviors identified included (in order of increasing severity): tease, noncompliance, disapproval, command negative, humiliate, physical negative, negativism, and defiance. Harris and Reid (1981) observed children in the classroom and on the playground and reported reproducability coefficients for this heirarchy of .92 and .93 respectively. Additionally, while boys' individual behaviors were not highly correlated across the classroom and playground settings, the rank-orders of the level of severity of their aggressive behavior in each setting did show significant cross-situtional correspondence.

Aggressive interpersonal behavior, such as fighting and quarreling, must be considered separately from delinquent behaviors, such as stealing. These two types of behavior appear to have different developmental courses and predictive outcomes (cf. Loeber, 1982). For example, Gersten et al. (1976) found that problems involving conflict with parents and peer-directed aggression tended to emerge early and become stable after age 6, while delinquent behaviors did not usually emerge until 10 years of age, and did not become predictive until age 14. Moore, Chamberlain, and Mukai (1979) compared the incidence of court-recorded nonstatus offenses for three groups of adolescent children who had been seen clinically 2–9 years earlier—social aggressors, stealers, and normative boys. Social aggressors were children referred primarily for disobedience, fighting, verbal aggression, and temper tantrums; stealers were children who had engaged in at least four stealing events in the two months prior to their intakes. Seventy-seven percent of the stealers acquired court records compared to 13% of the social aggressors and 21% of the boys in the normative sample.

Clearly the study of types of aggressive behavior and individual differences in the quality, as well as the quantity, of children's aggression warrants further study.

Intra-individual Context

A third factor mediating the social impact of aggressive behavior may be characteristics of the aggressor—the intra-individual context of the aggressive behavior. Patterson (1982) suggests that aggressive boys can be characterized by their position on two dimensions—one dimension reflecting the level of deviant, aggressive behavior and the other dimension reflecting social skills. He postulates that highly aggressive boys who additionally have serious social skill deficits are at a greater developmental risk than socially-skilled aggressors. While no direct evidence for this hypothesis is available, several studies suggest that the hypothesis has merit.

In two studies with preschool children, investigators examined the quality of the specific interactions that children had with classmates who they selected as especially liked or disliked (Hartup et al., 1967; Masters & Furman, 1981). Both investigations revealed that children tended to have more positive interactions with the classmates they selected as especially liked than with classmates they did not select. In neither study, however, were children found to have higher rates of negative interaction with classmates they selected as disliked than with unselected classmates. Perhaps this finding simply reflects attenuated correlations due to low rates of negative interaction, or perhaps children avoid interaction with classmates they dislike. Alternatively, children may be reacting negatively to some children on the basis of a general negative evaluation rather than specific negative exchanges. Children seem willing to tolerate negative behaviors from friends, while the same level of negative behavior from other children becomes a basis for rejection. Perhaps these negative exchanges differ in subtle ways, or perhaps children employ an "averaging" technique and thereby tolerate negative behaviors that occur in the context of positive interactions (Hendrick, Franz, & Hoving, 1975).

A second area of research concerning the effects of individual differences in patterns of behavioral skills and deficits comes from Ledingham and her colleagues (Ledingham, 1981; Ledingham, Younger, Schwartzman, & Bergeron, 1982). Based upon children's peer descriptions on the PEI, Ledingham (1981) identified three groups of children: aggressive children who scored above the 95% on the aggression scale and below the 75% on the withdrawal scale, withdrawn children who scored above the 95% on withdrawal and below the 75% on aggression, and aggressive-withdrawn children who scored above the 75% on both the aggression and withdrawal scales. Nondeviant comparison children, who scored below the 75% on both scales, were also identified. When these groups were compared on a variety of peer, teacher, and parent ratings, the aggressive-withdrawn group emerged as the most deviant. Peers rated aggressive-withdrawn children less likable than either aggressive or comparison children. Relative to withdrawn and comparison children, teachers rated both aggressive and aggressive-withdrawn children as more deviant on six scales of the Devereux Elementary School Behavior Rating Scale: classroom disturbance, impatience, disrespect-defiance, external blame, irrelevant responsiveness, and giving up on tasks. In addition, the aggressive-withdrawn group was rated more deviant than all other groups on external reliance, inattention-withdrawal, ability to change tasks easily, and time to complete tasks. Similarly, maternal ratings on the Devereux Child Behavior Rating Scale revealed aggressive and aggressive-withdrawn children to be rated significantly higher than withdrawn or comparison children on social aggression, and the aggressive-withdrawn children to be rated higher than all other groups on distractibility, pathological use of senses, and need for adult control. Apparently, children who engage in aggressive behavior along with other forms of immature, poorly skilled social behavior have a greater variety of problems and a more negative social impact across settings than do children who are aggressive but more socially skilled.

One pattern of socially-inappropriate behavior that often co-exists with aggressive behavior is hyperactive, impulsive and inattentive behavior. Hyperactive children, as a group, tend to show high levels of negative social behavior and to be disliked by their peers. They are less often on-task and exhibit more disruptive incidents and more negative peer interactions than "active" boys, although they do not show fewer positive social interactions (Klein & Young, 1979). Additionally, hyperactive boys receive more negative role nominations and fewer nominations as a "true friend" than do active boys (Klein & Young, 1979). Similarly, in their sample of hyperactive boys, Pelham and Bender (1982) report that 94% had negative nomination scores below their class means; 60% were as low as two to three standard deviations below their class means. Seventy-four percent of these boys had positive nomination scores below their class means. Hence, as a group, hyperactive boys appear to be disliked. Recent investigators have suggested that group data on hyperactive children may be misleading, since these children represent a heterogeneous group. In particular, some hyperactive children show high levels of aggressive behavior and receive high ratings on symptoms of conduct disorders, while other hyperactive children are low in aggression (Prinz, Conner, & Wilson, 1981). Boys who engage in high levels of aggressive behavior are likely also to show hyperactive behavior, while many hyperactive boys do not exhibit high rates of aggression (Prinz et al., 1981). Hence the peer rejection associated with hyperactivity may be due to the aggressive behaviors of a subgroup of these children rather than due to the hyperactive behaviors. Pelham and Bender (1982) examined this hypothesis by subdividing their sample into hyperactive boys who were high or low on the dimension of aggressive behavior. Surprisingly, the high hyperactive-low aggressive boys still appeared highly rejected by peers. Hence, hyperactive behaviors may elicit peer rejection even when they are not accompanied by high levels of aggressive behavior.

Taken together, these findings suggest that the social impact of aggressive behavior may depend upon the child's other social behaviors. Children who are socially awkward, hyperactive, immature, and obnoxious, as well as aggressive, may have fewer friends and be at greater risk for social-emotional development than socially skilled aggressive boys. Additionally, the presence of awkward, hyperactive, immature, and obnoxious behaviors may lead to peer rejection, even when no overt aggressive behavior is exhibited. Hence, social aggression and peer rejection may not necessarily co-exist. Rather, aggression and rejection may best be considered separate dimensions, with aggression leading to peer rejection when it is accompanied by a lack of social skills and the presence of other immature, socially-undesirable behaviors. To further explore this hypothesis, the following study was undertaken.

A STUDY OF AGGRESSION AND REJECTION AS SEPARATE DIMENSIONS

The purpose of the following study was to examine the proposition that aggressive social behavior and peer rejection represent separate dimensions, and that boys classified into groups on the basis of these two dimensions vary in their social reputations and adjustment. Gradeschool boys were classified as Aggressive, Rejected, Aggressive-Rejected, or Average on the basis of peer ratings, and then compared on several peer and teacher ratings.

Subjects

Fifty boys were selected from a sample of 170 first- to third-graders in four predominantly white, rural elementary schools. One of the schools served a population with primarily upper-middle to middle-class socioeconomic status, two schools drew from primarily working-class populations, while the other school served a population of mixed socioeconomic status.

Measures

Peer Ratings

Boys completed an abridged version of the PEI, which included 10 items assessing aggressive social behavior, 8 items assessing withdrawn social behavior and 5 items assessing likable social behavior. To simplify administration with the young elementary children, 9 items were deleted from the original PEI on the basis of lower factor loadings in the original Pekarik et al. (1976) study. Pilot testing suggested that almost no fidelity was lost by using this abridged version of the PEI when compared to peer ratings based upon the 35-item PEI. The number of nominations a boy received from other boys for the items on each subscale were totaled and divided by the number of raters, and then standardized for each class, giving each boy a standardized score for Aggression, Withdrawal, and Likability.

Boys were also asked to list up to three (but at least one) male classmates that they particularly liked and up to three (but at least one) that they did not like. Boys also rated how much they liked to play with each other on a 5-point scale (1 = not at all, never to 5 = a lot, all the time). Positive and negative nominations and play ratings were totaled and divided by the number of raters, and then standardized within each class.

Teacher Ratings

Teachers completed the 24-item PEI using a four-point scale (0 = behavior not at all characteristic of boy to 3 = very characteristic). Teacher rating scores were summed for each subscale and standardized within class to give each boy a standard score for Aggression, Withdrawal, and Likability.

Teachers also completed the abbreviated Conners Teacher Rating Scale (ATRS) (Conners, 1969), which is comprised of 10 items describing hyperactive and disruptive classroom behaviors. Each of these behaviors is rated on a 4-point scale (0 = child does not exhibit behavior at all to 3 = child exhibits behavior very much). A total score was computed for each boy and standardized within classroom. Teachers also rated each boy on a five-point scale, estimating how much classmates liked to play with him.

Procedure

Each boy was interviewed individually by an undergraduate student, who read aloud each PEI item. Each boy was given a roster of participating classmates and asked to name any classmates who fit each item desciption. If the boy listed no classmates, the interviewer systematically reviewed the names on the roster (e.g., "What about Mark, is he too shy to make friends easily?"). This procedure was adopted because many of the young elementary children answered "I don't know" or "none" without systematically considering all of the classmates. After the PEI, each boy provided positive and negative nominations, and play ratings, in that order. Teacher rating forms were given to teachers at the time of the peer interviews and were collected two weeks later.

RESULTS

Group Classification of Children

A boy was classified as Aggressive-Rejected if his peer PEI aggression score and peer rejection score were both one or more standard deviations above the class mean. He was classified as Aggressive if his aggression score was one standard deviation above and his rejection score was less than half a standard deviation above his class mean. A boy was classified as Rejected if his rejection score was one standard deviation above and his PEI aggression score was less than half a standard deviation above the class mean.

Using these criteria, 15 boys (9% of the sample) were Aggressive-Rejected, 11 boys (6% of the sample) were Aggressive, and 9 boys (5% of the sample) were Rejected. An additional 15 Average boys were identified who had peer rejection and aggression scores less than half of a standard deviation above their class mean.

Distribution and Intercorrelations Among Scores

Groups were compared with respect to peer aggression and negative nomination scores to determine the degree of discrimination on these selection measures. Post-hoc comparisons using Duncan multiple-range tests ($p < .05$) revealed that Aggressive-Rejected boys received higher aggression ratings than Aggressive boys, who, in turn, received higher ratings than Rejected and Average boys. Aggressive-Rejected boys also received higher rejection scores than Rejected boys, who, in turn, were more rejected than Aggressive and Average boys (Means are presented in Table 1).

A correlation matrix with all measures was computed for the entire sample and is presented in Table 2. Peer descriptions of likable social behaviors were highly correlated with positive peer nominations ($r = .73$) and with negative nominations ($r = -.59$). Teacher ratings of likability were significantly, though modestly, correlated with positive peer nominations ($r = .33$) but not with negative nominations ($r = -.22$). Peer ratings of aggression, on the other hand, were modestly correlated with negative peer nominations ($r = .32$), but were not correlated with positive peer nominations ($r = -.16$). Teacher ratings of aggressive and disruptive behavior were significantly correlated with negative nominations (rs = .41 to .44) and inversely correlated with positive peer nominations (rs = −.35 to −.44). Positive and negative nominations were strongly inversely correlated ($r - -.59$).

Group Acceptance

A MANOVA was conducted on the positive peer nominations, the peer roster ratings and the teacher roster ratings to examine the peer acceptance of boys in

Table 1. Mean Standard Scores for Aggressive-Rejected, Aggressive, Rejected, and Average Groups

Measures	*Aggressive Rejected* *(n = 15)*	*Aggressive* *(n = 11)*	*Rejected* *(n = 9)*	*Average* *(n = 15)*
Group Acceptance				
Peer positive nominations	$-.79^{a}$	$.04^{b}$	$-.73^{a}$	$.23^{b}$
Peer roster ratings	-1.14^{a}	$.10^{b}$	$-.64^{a,b}$	0^{b}
Teacher roster ratings	$-.71^{a}$	$.21^{b}$	$-.67^{a}$	$.26^{b}$
Likability				
Peer PEI Likability	-1.05^{a}	0^{c}	$-.92^{a,b}$	$-.39^{b,c}$
Teacher PEI Likability	$-.59$	$-.26$	$-.28$	$-.15$
Withdrawal				
Peer PEI Withdrawal	$.95^{a}$	$-.30^{b}$	$.39^{a,b}$	$.46^{a,b}$
Teacher PEI Withdrawal	$.40$	$-.30$	$.52$	$.07$
Aggression/Disruption				
Teacher PEI Aggression	1.43^{a}	$.89^{a}$	$.18^{b}$	$-.31^{b}$
ATRS	1.37^{a}	$.93^{a,b}$	$.27^{b,c}$	$-.21^{c}$
Group Selection Criteria				
Peer PEI Aggression	1.59^{a}	1.12^{b}	$-.28^{c}$	$-.17^{c}$
Peer Negative Nominations	1.70^{a}	$-.03^{c}$	1.30^{b}	$.07^{c}$

Note: Means with different subscripts are significantly different at the $p < .05$ level.

the four groups. This MANOVA revealed a significant effect for group membership, F (7,89) = 3.39, $p < .001$. Univariate ANOVAs revealed this significant group effect for each of the measures: positive nominations, F (3,46) = 7.91, $p < .001$, peer roster ratings, F (3,46) = 6.54, $p < .001$, and teacher roster ratings, F (3,46) = 5.12, $p < .01$. Mean scores are presented in Table 2. The Aggressive and Average boys were consistently more well-accepted than the Aggressive-Rejected and Rejected boys.

Likability

To examine group differences in reputations for likable behaviors, a one-way MANOVA was conducted on peer and teacher PEI likability scores, revealing a significant main effect for group status, F (6,90) = 2.67, $p < .05$. Univariate

Table 2. Intercorrelations Among Measures

	Measures									
Group Acceptance	2	3	4	5	6	7	8	9	10	11
1. Peer positive nominations	.68	.46	.73	.33	−.48	−.25	−.35	−.44	−.16	−.59
2. Peer roster ratings		.59	.66	.34	−.51	−.42	−.34	−.44	−.19	−.63
3. Teacher roster ratings		.53	.58	−.46	−.67	−.40	.85	−.22	−.22	−.50
Likability										
4. Peer PEI Likability				.42	−.31	−.41	−.46	−.58	−.16	−.58
5. Teacher PEI Likability					−.39	−.37	−.49	−.50	−.26	−.22
Withdrawal										
6. Peer PEI Withdrawal						.44	.06	.19	.10	.41
7. Teacher PEI Withdrawal							.12	.19	−.02	.35
Aggression/Disruption										
8. Teacher PEI Aggression								.85	.71	.41
9. ATRS									.62	.44
Group Selection Criteria										
10. Peer PEI Aggression										.32
11. Peer Negative Nominations										

Note: Correlations greater than .24 are significant at the $p < .05$ level, greater than .33 are significant at the $p < .01$ level, and greater than .42 are significant at the $p < .001$ level.

ANOVAs revealed this effect to be due to significant group differences on peer ratings of likability F (3,46) = 5.61, $p < .01$ rather than teacher ratings of likability ($p > .10$). Aggressive boys were viewed as significantly more likable than Rejected and Aggressive-Rejected boys (see Table 1).

To examine group differences for positive characteristics ascribed by peers, Duncan multiple-range tests were performed on each of the 5 items in the PEI Likability scale. The only item on which Aggressive boys clearly received higher scores than the other groups was the item "liked by all." Aggressive boys were significantly lower than the Average group (and equal to the Rejected and Aggressive-Rejected groups) on the item "especially nice." No group differences were revealed for the items: "helps others" and "best friends." Apparently, the higher likability scores of boys in the Aggressive group were due primarily to the items "liked by all" and "understand things." While no firm conclusions can be drawn from this data, a hypothesis worth further investigation is that Aggressive boys engage in an average level of prosocial behaviors but have academic or athletic competencies that enhance their acceptability.

Withdrawal

A MANOVA on peer and teacher PEI ratings of withdrawal resulted in a nonsignificant trend, F (6,90) = 2.00, $p < .10$. Univariate ANOVAs revealed no significant group differences on teacher ratings of withdrawal, but a significant effect for group on peer ratings, F (3,46) = 3.79, $p < .05$. As shown in Table 1, Aggressive-Rejected boys were rated significantly more withdrawn than Aggressive boys, with Rejected and Average boys intermediate in their withdrawal ratings.

Post-hoc tests were computed for the eight individual items. Four of the eight items showed no group differences. On two items ("too shy" and "feelings easily hurt"), the Aggressive boys were rated significantly lower than Average boys. For "chosen last" and "few friends," the Aggressive-Rejected boys had the highest scores. Aggressive-Rejected boys were almost twice as likely to be nominated as "chosen last" than the Aggressive and Average boys and more than three times as likely to be nominated as having few friends. A testable hypothesis for future evaluation is that Aggressive-Rejected boys do not necessarily engage in more withdrawn behaviors than other boys (e.g., shyness, unhappy, unnoticed), but rather suffer greater social ostracism.

Aggression

A MANOVA analyzing teacher ratings on the PEI aggression scale and the ATRS revealed a significant group effect, F (6,90) = 6.23, $p < .001$. Univariate ANOVAs revealed significant effects of group on the ATRS, F (3,46) = 7.35, $p < .001$ and on the PEI aggression scale, F (3,46) = 15.27, $p < .001$ (see Table 1). On the ATRS, Aggressive-Rejected boys had the highest scores and were significantly higher than Rejected or Average boys, while Aggressive boys scored significantly higher than Average boys. For the teacher PEI aggression scale, the Aggressive-Rejected and Aggressive boys were rated significantly higher than the Rejected and Average boys.

To provide a more specific description of the groups, individual peer-rated PEI aggression items were analyzed with Duncan multiple range post-hoc comparisons. On 8 of the 10 items, the Aggressive and Aggressive-Rejected groups did not differ and both scored higher than the Average group (''starts fights,'' ''messes around,'' ''rude,'' ''gives dirty looks,'' ''makes fun of others,'' ''bothers others,'' ''mean,'' ''shows off''). In general, Aggressive-Rejected boys had higher scores than Aggressive boys, but this difference reached significance ($p < .05$) on only 2 of the items—''tries to get others into trouble'', and ''gets mad when he doesn't get his way.'' Based upon this analysis, Aggressive and Aggressive-Rejected boys apparently engaged in similar types of aggressive behavior.

Comparison With Other Categorization Systems

Boys were recatagorized using the Coie et al. (1982) system into popular, neglected, controversial, and rejected groups, and were also recategorized in a manner comparable to Ledingham's (1981) into aggressive, withdrawn, and aggressive-withdrawn groups. For this latter analysis, a boy was considered aggressive if his PEI aggression score was more than one standard deviation above and his PEI withdrawal score was less than half of a standard deviation above his class mean, he was considered withdrawn if his withdrawal score was more than one standard deviation above and his aggression score was less than half a standard deviation above his class mean, and he was considered aggressive-withdrawn if his aggression and withdrawal scores were both more than one standard deviation above his class mean. These two classification systems are compared with the groups designated in the present study in Table 3. When the overlap between the obtained groups and the Coie et al. (1982) categories were considered, the Aggressive boys fell into no particular sociometric group (they were unclassified or average), the Aggressive-Rejected boys were, for the most part rejected, and the Rejected were about ⅔ rejected and ⅓ unclassified or average. When the obtained groups were compared to the Ledingham categories, most of the Aggressive boys were aggressive, ⅔ of the Aggressive-Rejected boys were aggressive-withdrawn and most of the others were aggressive, while most of the Rejected boys were unclassified.

DISCUSSION

When aggression and peer rejection were treated as separate dimensions, important differences emerged among boys who were high on one, both, or neither

Table 3. Comparisons of Alternative Peer Rating Classification Systems of High-Risk Children

	Present Groups			
	Aggressive-Rejected	*Aggressive*	*Rejected*	*(Nonclassified)*
Coie et al. (1982) Groups				
Rejected	7.6% (13)	0	3.5% (6)	5.3% (9)
Neglected	0	.6% (1)	0	9.4% (16)
Controversial	.6% (1)	0	.6% (1)	3.5% (6)
(Nonclassified)	.6% (1)	5.9% (10)	1.2% (2)	
Ledingham (1981) Groups				
Aggressive-withdrawn	5.9% (10)	0	0	1.8% (3)
Aggressive	2.4% (4)	5.9% (10)	0	1.2% (2)
Withdrawn	0	0	1.2% (2)	6.5% (11)
(Nonclassified)	.6% (1)	.6% (1)	4.1% (7)	

Note: Percentages represent proportions of total sample (n = 170). Number of boys in each group is in parentheses.

dimension. Peers and teachers ascribed similar aggressive behaviors to both Aggressive and Aggressive-Rejected boys, yet boys in the former group received fewer negative nominations, more positive nominations, higher teacher and peer play ratings, and higher peer likability scores than boys in the latter group. None of the Aggressive boys received a high-risk classification according to the Coie et al. (1982) or Ledingham (1981) systems (e.g., rejected or aggressive-withdrawn) whereas 94% of the Aggressive-Rejected boys received one of these high-risk classifications. Apparently, some aggressive boys achieve social acceptance; aggressive behavior may, but does not necessarily, contribute to peer rejection. Conversely, factors other than aggressive behavior may be associated with peer rejection. In this study, Rejected boys were comparable to Average boys on ratings of aggressive, disruptive, withdrawn, and hyperactive behaviors, yet they received more negative nominations, fewer positive nominations, and lower teacher play ratings than did Average boys.

Implications for the Study of Aggression

Patterson (1982) postulated that aggressive boys who have good social skills show fewer signs of social-emotional maladjustment and have a better prognosis for positive adult mental health than do aggressive boys who have social skill deficits. In this study, a substantial proportion of aggressive boys had established friendships and achieved peer group acceptance, suggesting that they had social skills and other competencies that made them attractive to peers in spite of their aggressive behavior. Anecdotal observations of the peer-accepted Aggressive boys suggested that these boys were more likely than the Aggressive-Rejected boys to direct their aggression toward peer-sanctioned targets. In one school, in particular, where war games were a common playground activity, Aggressive boys who fearlessly and skillfully led raids against the enemy forts were esteemed. Peers recognized that these boys could be mean bullies, but also described them positively as rough competitors and important battle allies.

Peer-accepted aggressive boys may not be at the same high-risk for poor adult outcomes as peer-rejected boys. First, as a function of their greater social awareness and interactional skills, peer-accepted aggressive boys may be responsive to socializing influences and more likely to reduce their aggressive behavior over time. Secondly, as a function of positive peer interaction opportunities, peer-accepted aggressive boys are not likely to suffer the negative effects of social ostracism nor to lack opportunities to develop positive skills. Future research on the characteristics and developmental outcomes of peer-accepted versus rejected aggressive children is needed to test these hypotheses.

Implications for the Study and Treatment of Rejection

Further research is also needed to examine the factors leading to the rejection of the Rejected, nonaggressive boys; the peer and teacher ratings used in this study did not reveal a behavioral basis for their rejection. Perhaps they are less attractive, have deficits in cognitive or athletic skills, fail to conform to social norms, or engage in immature, obnoxious behaviors that were not well-measured here. Apparently, peer rejection is multiply determined and rejected children do not represent a homogeneous group; research concerning subgroups of rejected children is needed.

One implication of this heterogeneity is that classification systems for high-risk children which are based upon sociometric scores alone (Coie et al., 1982; Newcomb & Bukowski, 1983) may obscure important behavior differences, such as those found between the Aggressive-Rejected and the Rejected groups. Classifications based upon behavior descriptions alone (Ledingham, 1981), however, may ignore children who are rejected for no obvious behavioral reason. The combination of sociometric and behavioral peer rating measures may provide a more precise classification of high-risk children.

A second implication of the heterogeneity among rejected children is that different etiologies may characterize aggressive and non-aggressive rejected subgroups. For example, aggression-prone parenting styles may be more characteristic of the families of aggressive rejected children than children rejected for other reasons. Additionally, aggressive rejected children may require different intervention strategies than non-aggressive rejected children. Social skill training programs, which have improved the positive social behavior and peer acceptance of unpopular children (Ladd & Asher, in press) may be less effective with aggressive-rejected children, since aggressive behavior is not targeted directly in these programs. Conversely, interventions that lead to reductions in aggressive behavior, such as contingency management procedures, may not necessarily improve the social skills or social acceptance of rejected, aggressive children (Drabman, Spitalnik, & Spitalnik, 1974). More comprehensive interventions may be required for aggressive rejected children designed both to reduce aggressive behavior and to enhance social skills and peer acceptance.

Finally, future research may clarify the relation between aggression and peer rejection at different developmental levels and in different populations. Normatively, the expression of aggression changes developmentally, as do the expectations and organization of the peer group. In general, overt aggressive behavior decreases with age. Hence, while a substantial proportion of aggressive boys in this young elementary school sample was accepted by peers, accepted aggressors may be less common at older age levels. Similarly, socioeconomic status and cultural background influence peer group values concerning aggression and, hence, may effect the likelihood of identifying peer-accepted aggressive children.

ACKNOWLEDGMENT

The preparation of this paper was supported, in part, by a Scholars in Mental Health of Children grant awarded by the W. T. Grant Foundation. Appreciation is expressed to the Bellefonte and State College Area School Districts for their assistance with this research, and to David Smoot for his comments on an earlier draft of this manuscript.

REFERENCES

Asher, S., & Wheeler, V. (1983). *Children's lonliness: A comparison of rejected and neglected peer status.* Paper presented at the Annual Meeting of the American Psychological Association, Anaheim, California.

Bonney, M. (1943). Personality traits of socially successful and socially unsuccessful children. *Journal of Educational Psychology, 34,* 449–472.

Bonney, M. E., & Powell, J. (1953). Differences in social behavior between sociometrically high and sociometrically low children. *Journal of Educational Research, 46,* 481–495.

Bukowski, W. M., & Newcomb, A. F. (1984). Stability and determinants of sociometric status and friendship choice: A longitudinal perspective. *Developmental Psychology, 20,* 941–952.

Campbell, J. D., & Yarrow, M. R. (1961). Perceptual and behavioral correlates of social effectiveness. *Sociometry, 24,* 1–20.

Coie, J. D., & Dodge, K. A. (1983). Continuities and changes in children's social status: A five-year longitudinal study. *Merrill-Palmer Quarterly, 29,* 261–282.

Coie, J. D., Dodge, K. A., & Coppotelli, H. (1982). Dimensions and types of social status: A cross-age perspective. *Developmental Psychology, 18,* 557–570.

Coie, J. D., & Kupersmidt, J. B. (1983). A behavioral analysis of emerging social status. *Child Development, 54,* 1400–1416.

Conger, J. C., & Keane, A. P. (1981). Social skills intervention in the treatment of isolated or withdrawn children. *Psychological Bulletin, 90,* 478–495.

Conners, C. (1969). A teacher rating scale for use in drug studies with children. *American Journal of Psychiatry, 126,* 152–156.

Dodge, K. A. (1983). Behavioral antecedents of peer social status. *Child Development, 54,* 1386–1399.

Dodge, K. A., Coie, J. D., & Brakke, N. P. (1982). Behavior patterns of socially rejected and neglected preadolescents: The roles of social approach and aggression. *Journal of Abnormal Child Psychology, 10,* 389–409.

Dodge, K., Schlundt, D., Schocken, I., & Delugach, J. (1983). Social competence and children's sociometric status: The role of peer group entry strategies. *Merrill-Palmer Quarterly, 29,* 309–336.

Drabman, R., Spitalnik, R., & Spitalnik, K. (1974). Sociometric and disruptive behavior as a function of four types of token reinforcement programs. *Journal of Applied Behavior Analysis, 7,* 93–101.

Dunnington, M. J. (1957). Behavioral differences of sociometric status groups in a nursery school. *Child Development, 28,* 103–111.

Feinberg, M. R., Smith, M., & Schmidt, R. (1958). An analysis of expressions used by adolescents of varying economic levels to describe accepted and rejected peers. *Journal of Genetic Psychology, 93,* 133–148.

Feshbach, S. (1970). Aggression. In P. H. Mussen (Ed.), *Carmichael's Manual of Child Psychology,* Vol. 2. New York: John Wiley & Sons.

Foster, S. L., & Ritchey, W. L. (1985). Behavioral correlates of sociometric status of fourth-, fifth-, and sixth-grade children in two classroom situations. *Behavioral Assessment, 7,* 79–93.

French, D. L., & Waas, G. A. (1985). Behavior problems of peer-neglected and peer-rejected elementary-age children: Parent and teacher perspectives. *Child Development, 56,* 246–252.

Gersten, J. C., Langner, T. S., Eisenberg, J. C., Simcha-Fagan, O., & McCarthy, E. D. (1976). Stability and change in types of behavioral disturbance of children and adolescents. *Journal of Abnormal Child Psychology, 4,* 111–127.

Goertzen, S. M. (1959). Factors relating to opinions of seventh grade children regarding the acceptability of certain behaviors in the peer group. *Journal of Genetic Psychology, 94,* 29–34.

Goldman, J., Corsini, D., & de Urioste, R. (1980). Implications of positive and negative sociometric status for assessing the social competence of young children. *Journal of Applied Developmental Psychology, 1,* 209–220.

Gottlieb, J., Semmel, M., & Veldman, D. J. (1978). Correlates of social status among mainstreamed mentally retarded children. *Journal of Educational Psychology, 70,* 396–405.

Gottman, J., Gonso, J., & Rasmussen, B. (1975). Social interaction, social competence and friendship in children. *Child Development, 46,* 709–718.

Gresham, F. M. (1981). Validity of social skills measures for assessing social competence in low-status children: A multivariate investigation. *Developmental Psychology, 17,* 390–398.

Harris, A., & Reid, J. B. (1981). The consistency of a class of coercive child behaviors across school settings for individual subjects. *Journal of Abnormal Child Psychology, 9,* 219–227.

Hartup, W. W. (1974). Aggression in childhood: Developmental perspectives. *American Psychologist, 29,* 336–341.

Hartup, W. W. (1983). Peer relations. In E. M. Hetherington (Ed.), P. H. Mussen (Series Ed.), *Handbook of child psychology:* Vol. 4. *Socialization, personality, and social development* (pp. 103–196). New York: Wiley.

Hartup, W. W., Glazer, J. A., & Charlesworth, R. (1967). Peer reinforcement and sociometric status. *Child Development, 38,* 1017–1024.

Hendrick, C., Franz, C. M., & Hoving, K. L. (1975). How do children form impressions of persons: They average. *Memory and Cognition, 3,* 325–328.

Horrocks, J. E., & Buker, M. E. (1951). A study of the friendship fluctuations of preadolescents. *The Journal of Genetic Psychology, 78,* 131–144.

Hymel, S., & Rubin, K. H. (1985). Children with peer relationships and social skills problems: Conceptual, methodological, and developmental issues. In G. J. Whitehurst (Ed.), *Annals of child development,* Vol. 2. Greenwich, CT: JAI Press.

Kaplan, H. K., & Kaufman, I. (1978). Sociometric status and behaviors of emotionally disturbed children. *Psychology in the Schools, 15,* 8–15.

Klein, A. R., & Young, R. D. (1979). Hyperactive boys in the classroom: Assessment of teacher and peer perceptions, interactions, and classroom behaviors. *Journal of Abnormal Child Psychology, 7,* 425–442.

Kohlberg, L., LaCrosse, J., & Ricks, D. (1972). The predictability of adult mental health from childhood behavior. In B. Wolman (Ed.), *Manual of child psychopathology.* New York: McGraw-Hill.

Kupersmidt, J. B. (1983). *Predicting delinquency and academic problems from childhood peer status.* Paper presented at the bienniel meeting of the Society for Research in Child Development. Detroit, April.

Ladd, G. (1983). Social networks of popular, average, and rejected children in school settings. *Merrill-Palmer Quarterly, 29,* 282–307.

Ladd, G. W., & Asher, S. R. (In press). Social skill training and children's peer relations: Current issues in research and practice. In L. L'Abate & M. Milan (Eds.), *Handbook of social skill training.* New York: Wiley.

LaGreca, A. (1981). Peer acceptance: The correspondence between children's sociometric scores and teacher's ratings of peer interactions. *Journal of Abnormal Child Psychology, 9,* 167–178.

Ledingham, J. E. (1981). Developmental patterns of aggressive and withdrawn behavior in childhood: A possible method for identifying preschizophrenics. *Journal of Abnormal Child Psychology, 9,* 1–22.

Ledingham, J., Younger, A., Schwartzman, A., & Bergeron, G. (1982). Agreement among teacher, peer and self-ratings of children's aggression, withdrawal and likability. *Journal of Abnormal Child Psychology, 10,* 363–372.

Lesser, G. S. (1959). The relationship between various forms of aggression and popularity among lower-class children. *Journal of Educational Psychology, 50,* 20–25.

Loeber, R. (1982). The stability of antisocial and delinquent child behavior: A review. *Child Development, 53,* 1431–1446.

MacFarlane, J. W., Honzik, M. P., & Davis, M. H. (1937). Reputation differences among young school children. *Journal of Educational Psychology, 28,* 161–175.

Masters, J. C., & Furman, W. (1981). Popularity, individual friendship selection, and specific peer interaction among children. *Developmental Psychology, 17,* 344–350.

McQuire, J. (1973). Aggression and sociometric status with preschool children. *Sociometry, 36,* 542–549.

Moore, D. R., Chamberlain, P., & Mukai, L. H. (1979). Children at risk for delinquency: A follow-up comparison of aggressive children and children who steal. *Journal of Abnormal Child Psychology, 7,* 345–355.

Moore, S. G., & Updegraff, R. (1964). Sociometric status of preschool children as related to age, sex, nurturance-giving, and dependence. *Child Development, 35,* 519–524.

Newcomb, A. F., & Bukowski, W. M. (1983). Social impact and social preference as determinants of children's peer group status. *Developmental Psychology, 19,* 856–867.

Northway, M. L. (1944). Outsiders: A study of the personality patterns of children least acceptable to their age mates. *Sociometry, 7,* 10–25.

Olweus, D. (1977). Aggression and peer acceptance in adolescent boys: Two short-term longitudinal studies of ratings. *Child Development, 48,* 1301–1313.

Olweus, D. (1978). *Aggression in the schools: Bullies and whipping boys.* Washington, DC: Hemisphere.

Olweus, D. (1979). Stability of aggressive reaction patterns in males: A review. *Psychological Bulletin, 86,* 852–875.

Patterson, G. R. (1982). *A social learning approach,* Vol. 3. *Coercive family process.* Eugene, OR: Castalia Publishing Co.

Patterson, G. R., & Dawes, R. M. (1975). A Guttman Scale of children's coercive behaviors. *Journal of Clinical and Consulting Psychology, 43,* 594.

Patterson, G. R., Littman, R. A., & Bricker, W. (1967). Assertive behavior in children. *Monographs of the Society for Research in Child Development, 32,* 1–43.

Parke, R. D., & Slaby, R. G. (1983). The development of aggression. In E. M. Hetherington (Ed.), P. A. Mussen (Series Ed.), *Handbook of child psychology:* Vol. 4. *Socialization, personality, and social development* (pp. 547–642). New York: Wiley.

Pekarik, E. G., Prinz, R. J., Liebert, D. E., Weintraub, S., & Neale, J. M. (1976). The Pupil Evaluation Inventory. A sociometric technique for assessing children's social behavior. *Journal of Abnormal Child Psychology, 4,* 83–97.

Pelham, W. E., & Bender, M. E. (1982). Peer relationships in hyperactive children: Description and treatment. In K. D. Gadow & I. Bialer (Eds.), *Advances in learning and behavioral disabilities,* Vol. 1 (pp. 365–436). Greenwich, CT: JAI Press, Inc.

Pope, B. (1953). Socioeconomic contrasts in children's peer culture prestige values. *Genetic Psychology Monographs, 48,* 157–220.

Prinz, R. J., Connor, P. A., & Wilson, C. C. (1981). Hyperactive and aggressive behaviors in childhood: Intertwined dimensions. *Journal of Abnormal Child Psychology, 9,* 191–202.

Putallaz, M., & Gottman, J. (1983). Social relationship problems in children: An approach to intervention. In B. B. Lahey & A. E. Kazdin (Eds.), *Advances in clinical child psychology,* Vol. 6. New York: Plenum.

Robins, L. N. (1972). Follow-up studies. In H. C. Quay & J. S. Werry (Eds.), *Psychopathological disorders of childhood.* New York: Wiley.

Roff, M., & Sells, S. B. (1968). Juvenile delinquency in relation to peer acceptance-rejection and socio-economic status. *Psychology in the Schools, 5,* 3–18.

Roff, M., Sells, S. B., & Golden, M. M. (1972). *Social adjustment and personality development.* Minneapolis: The University of Minnesota Press.

Rubin, K. H., & Daniels-Beirness, T. (1983). Concurrent and predictive correlates of sociometric status in kindergarten and grade 1 children. *Merrill-Palmer Quarterly, 29,* 337–351.

Solomon, R. W., & Wahler, R. G. (1973). Peer reinforcement control of classroom problem behavior. *Journal of Applied Behavior Analysis, 6,* 49–56.

Tuddenham, R. D. (1951). Studies in reputation. III. Correlates of popularity among elementary-school children. *Journal of Educational Psychology, 42,* 257–276.

Van Alstnyne, D., & Hattwick, L. A. (1939). A follow-up study of the behavior of nursery school children. *Child Development, 10,* 43–72.

Victor, J. B., & Halverson, C. F. (1980). Children's friendship choices: Effects of school behavior. *Psychology in the Schools, 17,* 409–414.

Wenger, S., Berg-Cross, L., & Berg-Cross, G. (1980). Parent's judgments of children's aggressive behavior. *Merrill-Palmer Quarterly, 26,* 161–169.

THE REVISED CLASS PLAY:

CORRELATES OF PEER ASSESSED SOCIAL BEHAVIORS IN MIDDLE CHILDHOOD

Kenneth H. Rubin and Janice S. Cohen

ABSTRACT

The concurrent and predictive correlates of the Minnesota Revision of the Class Play (Mastern & Morison, 1981) were examined in a longitudinal sample of second and third grade children. Peer sociometric, behavioral observational and self- and teacher-rating data were moderately related to the relevant Class Play factor scores of aggressive, sensitive/isolated, and sociable/leader behaviors. Interestingly, the correlational patterns varied by the age and sex of the children. Furthermore, the findings forced consideration of multiple pathways that determine children's social status within their peer group.

In recent years, researchers studying child development have begun to consider the significance of extra-familial socialization agents. Specifically, children's peers are recognized as important sources of influence on development. The

Advances in Behavioral Assessment of Children and Families, Vol. 2, pgs. 179–206.
Editor: Ronald J. Prinz

ISBN: 0-89232-481-3

impetus for the increased emphasis on the peer system emanates from at least two factors.

First, changing societal phenomena, such as the sharp increase in maternal employment, have necessitated the large-scale growth and expansion of child care facilities. The emergence of group care centers has thrust children into organized peer groups earlier than was the case in previous decades. It is natural to assume that the early and intensive exposure to the peer group in such settings has some impact on individual children's growth and development. Theoretical support for this assumption has emerged from the writings of Piaget (1926; 1932), Sullivan (1953), and Hartup (1970) who recognized that the peer network may serve as an important context for learning, consolidating, and practicing cognitive, social, and social-cognitive skills.

Second, it has been argued recently that children who fail to develop positive peer relationships may experience adaptational deficits in many basic developmental domains (Sroufe & Rutter, 1984). Support for this argument stems from reports of children with inadequate peer experiences who are vulnerable for academic failure and drop-out (Kupersmidt, 1983; Ullman, 1957), juvenile delinquency and conduct problems (Kupersmidt, 1983; Roff, 1961) and later psychological problems (Cowen, Pederson, Babigian, Izzo, & Trost, 1973).

The revitalized interest in children's peer relationships heightens the need to devise measures for identifying children who deviate from the norm, vis-à-vis their social behaviors and peer relationships. Investigators eager to inaugurate their research programs have developed a plethora of instruments, many of which have unknown psychometric strength. The major focus of this chapter is to evaluate, psychometrically, one of the more promising indices of social competence, the Minnesota Revision of the Class Play (Masten, Morison, & Pellegrini, 1985), an instrument used to obtain peer ratings of salient positive and negative social behaviors. We present data examining the concurrent and predictive relations between Revised Class Play ratings and (a) teacher ratings of social skills, (b) observations of social behaviors, (c) indices of perceived self-competence and (d) peer assessments of sociometric status in a longitudinal sample of children in Grades 2 an 3. However, prior to examining our data, we review those methodologies typically employed to identify children "at risk" for social skills and peer relationships difficulties. Our description of these methods is, of necessity, brief; consequently, readers interested in broader descriptions of targeting strategies are referred to recent reviews by Hymel and Rubin (1985) and Rubin, LeMare, and Lollis (in press).

BEHAVIORAL OBSERVATIONS AND TEACHER RATINGS

Researchers have long considered naturalistic observations of children's behavior to provide a wealth of information concerning social skills and peer relationships. Children who display both aggressive (e.g., Serbin, Lyons, Marchessault, & Morin, 1983) as well as anxious/withdrawn behaviors (e.g., Rubin, 1982; 1985) have been identified via naturalistic observation. Despite the apparent reliability and validity of these procedures, observational targeting techniques carry with them a number of practical problems. Primary among these problems is the fact that observational data are costly to gather in terms of effort, time, and financial expense. Furthermore, observational data are more easily gathered in preschool and kindergarten settings than in elementary schools since classroom free-play is virtually nonexistent in these latter settings.

Given these practical problems, researchers have searched for alternative means to assess children whose quality of peer relationships and social competencies deviate from their peers. Teachers are an alternative source of data. Teachers have been asked by researchers to rank order their pupils on the dimension of likeability (e.g., Connolly & Doyle, 1981; Green, Forehand, Beck, & Vosk, 1980) or they have rated children's social behaviors using one of many available rating scales (see Hymel & Rubin, 1985 for a thorough review). These latter scales typically distinguish between externalizing, aggression derived behavioral problems, and internalizing problems such as anxiety, fearfulness and withdrawal. Interestingly, the factor structure of most teacher rating scales is identical to that found for many peer rating scales of social behavior. Surprisingly, despite widespread use, many of the extant teacher rating scales have undergone limited psychometric evaluation. Typically, researchers report replications of given factor structures or test-retest replications of given ratings; however, it is rare for researchers to report inter-judge reliability or the relations between teacher ratings and other indices purporting to measure the same dimensions of behavior (Hymel & Rubin, 1985). Thus, despite the advantages of instruments that avoid classroom intrusion and that are completed by teachers who have considerable exposure to classroom and playground behavior, the reliability and validity for such teacher ratings are generally unknown.

An additional concern about most teacher rating scales is the problem of selective bias in the identification of problematic children. Teachers more readily identify children with conduct disorders than those who are withdrawn, anxious and fearful (Rubin et al., in press). The disruptive impact of aggressive behaviors is much more salient to teachers compared with more subtle demonstrations of social isolation and anxiety. As an interesting counterpoint, *peers* appear to be better able than teachers to identify both disruptive and withdrawn children (Rubin et al., in press). For example, in Rubin et al.'s (in press) recent report, peer ratings of aggression and withdrawal were more strongly related with observed agonistic and isolate play than were teacher ratings of these behaviors. Given these problems, researchers have turned increasingly to the peer group as the primary source of information concerning children's social skills and relationships.

PEER ASSESSMENTS

There are several advantages associated with the use of peer informants. First, peers through direct social experiences, function as ''inside'' sources of information about their social milieus (Hymel & Rubin, 1985). This insider's perspective allows peers to witness low frequency behaviors that may escape detection by observers and teachers who do not participate in the child's social group. Second, in contrast with *teacher ratings* which reflect a single viewpoint, peer assessments represent multiple perspectives about children's skills and relationships. Third, compared with *observational assessments,* peer assessments are applicable to a broad age range of children and are less costly. Finally, as noted earlier, peer assessments predict later mental health status better in comparison with adult-derived measures of adjustment (Cowen et al., 1973). For these and other reasons, the use of peer assessments to target children with skills and relationships problems has recently undergone wide adoption.

There are two major peer assessment techniques for targeting children experiencing social difficulties. The most commonly used index is the *sociometric* measure, which assesses the degree to which children are liked and disliked by their classmates. A major limitation of sociometric procedures is that they do not provide specific information about the behaviors or other factors that contribute to likeability. Recently, Dodge (1983), Coie and Kuperschmidt (1983), and Newcomb and Bukowski (1984) have argued that sociometric nominations (e.g., asking children to nominate classmates with whom they most like or dislike playing) provide some hints about the behaviors underlying sociometric status. Children who receive many nominations that are negative (''rejected'' children) are suggested to display aggressive, disruptive behaviors. In contrast, children who receive few, if any, positive and negative nominations (''neglected'' children) are described as somewhat withdrawn and basically nonproblematic. The equation of sociometric neglect and social withdrawal, however, cannot be assumed a priori. The extant data, in actuality, do not reveal that children who receive few nominations are observed consistently to be socially withdrawn (Rubin et al., in press). Furthermore, it appears as if not all rejected children demonstrate aggressive behaviors (Hymel & Rubin, 1985). The available published data suggest that we are not yet able to make clear links between sociometric nomination data and associated behavioral problems. In fact, the picture may be considerably more complex than originally assumed.

Given the above limitations of sociometric procedures, psychologists have developed measures by which children assess the social behaviors of their peers. This approach capitalizes on the unique opportunities that peers have to observe each other. Three measures gaining increased attention in the peer assessment literature include the Pupil Evaluation Inventory (PEI) (Pekarik, Prinz, Liebert, Weintraub, & Neale, 1976), the Class Play (Bower & Lambert, 1961) and its derivative, the Minnesota Revision of the Class Play (Masten et al., 1985). On these instruments, children are asked to nominate peers for a variety of behavioral roles or character descriptions. For the Class Play measures, the appeal of the task is maximized by telling children they are casting roles in an imaginary class play. The nominations received from peers are then summed to provide various indices of a child's typical social behavior or reputation within the peer group.

Although the Revised Class Play and the PEI are recent developments, the use of peer assessments actually antedates many of the commonly used sociometric techniques. For example, Hartshorne, May, and Maller (1929) in their classic studies of moral behavior used a "Guess Who" game to obtain peer assessments of social behavior. Thirty years later, Bower and Lambert (1961) devised the Class Play instrument as a measure of adjustment for use with elementary school age children. The original Class Play contained 20 items, 10 referring to positive behaviors and 10 referring to negative behaviors. The original form yielded a total "positive" and a total "negative" score and thus did not distinguish between aggressive and shy-withdrawn children.

In Bower and Lambert's (1961) study, the first to use the Class Play as an outcome measure, children in grades four through six identified by clinicians as "emotionally handicapped" were more frequently selected by peers for hostile, inadequate, and negative roles in the Class Play compared with normal classmates. More recently, the Class Play has been used as an adjustment measure in several longitudinal, predictive studies of children's vulnerability to psychopathology (Rolf, 1972; Cowen et al., 1973). For example, Cowen et al. (1973) found that negative peer reputation scores on the Class Play in third grade were more sensitive than teacher ratings, school reports, academic adjustment and performance data in predicting children's probable or actual future maladjustment.

Despite Bower's oft-cited conclusions concerning the predictive correlates of the Class Play, the instrument's psychometric properties have only been reported in the past few years. Use of the Class Play in the aforementioned longitudinal studies was based on the assumption that endorsement of an item accurately reflected the judged child's behavior. Clearly, such an inference is unwarranted. Class Play and other peer ratings may actually represent children's perceptual distortions of their classmates' personal and social characteristics rather than accurate perceptions of behavior. Nonbehavioral indices such as physical attractiveness, ethnicity, and dress may account, in part, for the behavioral labels peers assign to children (e.g., Dodge, 1983; Kleck, Richardson, & Ronald, 1974). These possibilities place even greater importance on the establishment of convergent and discriminant validity for the Class Play.

Anecdotal evidence for the validity of the Class Play was described by Bower (1969) who noted that hostile children were selected from Class Play roles consistent with their behavior. More recently, Butler (1979) found that fifth grade children who received a high number of negative Class Play nominations were observed to engage in fewer positive and more negative peer and teacher interactions than favorably rated classmates.

In a study of fourth and sixth grade boys, Asarnow (1983) found that children who were rated very negatively on the Class Play initiated and received fewer positive and more negative contacts from teachers and peers. Moreover, on occasions when positively evaluated boys became involved in negative interchanges, there was a tendency for the interaction to neutralize over-time. In contrast, the negative interchanges of negatively evaluated boys were maintained for the entire interaction.

Despite these attempts to examine correlates of the original Class Play, recent changes in the ideologies of longitudinal research programs have led to the revision of the measure (Masten et al., 1985). In the past, the Class Play was used as a screening device to detect early signs of maladjustment. Recently, large scale projects such as Project Competence (Garmezy, Masten, & Tellegen, 1984) have emphasized the ontogeny of competent or ''adjusted'' behavior. The Class Play, in its original form, included many negative items and few items for social competence. However, the absence of a negative reputation does not mean that a child is socially competent. As a needed improvement, one of the principle revisions made to the Class Play was the addition of several positive social role items.

In its present form, the Revised Class Play includes 15 positive and 15 negative behavioral roles. As well, several other revisions have been made to the original scale. These include the addition of items that are polar opposites of some of the existing social roles, the deletion of roles that involve academic and/or intellectual ability, the simplification of items so that each one refers to only one specific behavior and the elimination of any roles which might elicit sex-biased responding. Finally, the new instructions and format ensures that all children in the class will be considered in the role selection process. For a more thorough description of the revisions made to the Class Play the reader is referred to Masten et al., (1985).

Masten et al., (1985) offered preliminary data on the reliability, validity and factor structure of the Revised Class Play. The 30 items on the Revised Class Play load on three separate factors: ''sociability-leadership,'' ''aggressive-disruptive,'' and ''sensitive-isolated.'' These three basic factors are similar to those for the PEI (Pekarik et al., 1976) despite differences in the items included on both scales. Masten et al., (1985) have reported that the factor structure is internally consistent, stable, and replicable across different settings. Masten et al., found that teacher ratings of disruptive-oppositional behavior was the strongest social correlate of ''aggressive-disruptive'' peer ratings and that teacher ratings of cooperative-social initiating behavior was a strong inverse correlate of ''isolate'' peer ratings. These data support the validity of the Revised Class Play.

The three factors identified on the Revised Class Play are consistent with recent developments in the conceptualization of the social competence construct. Researchers are now dismissing simplistic dichotomies, such as peer ratings of sociometric popularity vs. unpupularity, or peer assessments of positive vs. negative behaviors. It is now assumed that rejected or negatively rated children comprise a heterogeneous sample and that we need to distinguish among subtypes of socioemotionally "at risk" children (e.g., Dodge, in press a). One can speculate that children rated by peers as aggressive may evidence difficulties in domains very different from those of children rated as highly isolated or withdrawn. For example, aggressive children may be impulsive, unable to think through the solutions to interpersonal dilemmas and they may be unpopular among their peers (Dodge, in press b; Rubin & Krasnor, in press). On the other hand, withdrawn children may not be unpopular or socially insensitive; rather, they may be insecure and anxious and they may have poor perceptions of their own competencies (Rubin, 1985; Rubin et al., in press). If these speculations are correct, then it would be appropriate to plan different intervention strategies for aggressive and withdrawn children who have, heretofore, been described simply as "negatively rated" by peers (e.g., Asarnow, 1983).

We feel that the Revised Class Play and its associated factor structure represents a move in a fruitful direction with respect to the targeting of children as socioemotionally "at risk." However, as with any index purporting to assess social behavior and predict psychopathology, it is necessary to derive validation data that go beyond the internal consistency and factor structure of its items. Little is currently known of the correspondence between observations of aggressive, withdrawn, and sociable behaviors and the relevant Revised Class Play factor scores. The relations between peer assessed likeability/rejection, self-ratings of competence, and peer ratings of behavior are not established. Finally, the correspondence between teacher ratings of aggression and withdrawal and Revised Play factor scores merits further evaluation beyond that provided by Masten et al. (1985).

A STUDY OF SOCIAL ASSESSMENT

To reiterate, the purpose of this chapter is to examine the construct validity of the Minnesota Revision of the Class Play. We will do so by evaluating the concurrent and predictive relations between peer assessments of social behaviors and (a) teacher ratings of social skills; (b) observations of children's social behaviors; (c) sociometric status; and (d) indices of perceived self-competence in Grades 2 and 3.

Children

Our sample was comprised of 86 second grade children (36 males, 50 females) who were participating in the Waterloo Longitudinal Project (Rubin, 1985), and who attended regular public schools in Waterloo, Ontario. In third grade, 69 of the original 86 children were re-assessed and an additional 27 third graders were assessed for the first time.

Predictions

We expected that the Revised Class Play would be a valid index of aggressive-disruptive and sensitive-isolated behavior patterns. Drawing on the findings of previous studies, we made the following predictions:

1. Children who received high ratings from peers on the Aggressive/Disruptive factor would receive high teacher ratings of aggression and impulsivity, would be disliked by peers (e.g., Dodge, 1983), and would demonstrate high frequencies of aggressive and negative peer interchanges, and immature, rambunctious and nonnormative play behaviors (Rubin & Clark, 1983).

2. Children rated by peers as sensitive-isolated would be characterized by teachers as anxious and fearful (Rubin, 1982; Rubin & Clark, 1983), would act withdrawn and engage in quiescent, sedentary activities, and would report self-doubt regarding perceived competencies (Rubin, 1985). Furthermore, in contrast to reports that low rates of interaction are not associated with sociometric status (see Asher, Markell, & Hymel, 1981 for a review), we predicted that high ratings on the Sensitive-Isolated factor of the Revised Class Play would relate significantly and negatively with sociometric popularity.

This latter prediction is based on a number of rationales. First, it is common to find that *non-normative* play behaviors are associated with peer rejection (e.g., Dodge, 1983; Putallaz, 1983; Rubin & Daniels-Beirness, 1983). Second, non-social play is actually quite normal for preschool and kindergarten-aged children (Parten, 1932; Rubin, 1982). Third, most studies in which nonsignificant relations have been found between social interaction rates and sociometric status were conducted with preschool and kindergarten children (e.g., Deutsch, 1974; Gottman, 1977). Thus, if the argument that low interaction rates are unpredictive of sociometric status is based upon data gathered from samples of young children, it rests on rather shakey developmental grounds. There is no reason, conceptually, to argue that normal behavior patterns should be associated with peer rejection.

Consequently, we believe that only when withdrawn/isolate behavior is perceived by peers as *nonnormative* and salient, will it become associated with peer rejection (Hymel & Rubin, 1985). In short, as with other forms of nonnormative behavior (e.g., aggression), a significant negative link between peer rated withdrawal and sociometric popularity is expected.

3. Children rated as highly sociable and as leaders would be popular among their peers, would engage in high frequencies of sociable and mature play behaviors, and would perceive themselves as competent.

4. Masten et al. (1985) found no sex differences in the factor structure and

correlates of the Revised Class Play. However, there is reason to believe that boys and girls do display different rates and perhaps different types of agonistic and prosocial behavior (Parke & Slaby, 1983). For example, boys have been found to display more aggressive behavior than girls (Maccoby & Jacklin, 1974). Consequently, we predicted a higher relation between observations and teacher ratings of aggressive behavior and peer rated aggression for boys rather than for girls (due to predicted greater variability in the observations and teacher ratings for boys).

The domain of isolation/sensitivity has received far less attention. Since girls are more likely to evidence internalizing problems than boys (Achenbach & Edelbrock, 1983), we predicted that observations of withdrawal, teacher ratings of anxiety and negative self-perceptions would be more highly related to peer rated isolation/sensitivity for girls.

A brief description of the measures used follows below.

Measures

The Revised Class Play. As aforementioned, this measure is comprised of 30 items that break down into three reliable dimensions of peer reputation: sociability-leadership; aggressive-disruptive, and sensitive-isolated. The measure was administered individually to all children. The children were asked to nominate up to three peers in their class who best fit each behavioral description. The number of votes received by each child for the items comprising each factor was divided by the number of children in each class who completed the Revised Class Play. A complete description of the Revised Class Play items is found in Masten et al. (1985).

Teacher ratings of social competence. Behar and Stringfield's (1974) Preschool Behavior Questionnaire (PBQ) was completed by each teacher. Drawn in large part from Rutter's (1967) Children's Behavior Questionnaire, the PBQ, is a 30 item scale that yields three reliable factors (hostile-aggressive, anxious-fearful, and hyperactive-distractible for preschool and elementary school aged children). The items comprising the factor loadings for elementary schoolers are slightly different than those for preschool and kindergarten age children (Rubin, Moller, & Emptage, in press); consequently, the elementary school factor loadings were used in this study.

Sociometric status. Sociometric popularity was assessed by a rating scale developed by Asher, Singleton, Tinsley and Hymel (1979). Each grade 2 and grade 3 child was individually presented with color photographs of each of his/her classmates. The children were asked to assign each picture to one of three boxes on which there was drawn either a happy face ("children you like alot"), a neutral face ("children you kinda like") or a sad face ("children you don't like"). As in Asher et al. (1979), each positive rating was accorded a score of 3, each neutral rating a score of 2, and each negative rating a score of 1. The sum of scores received by each child divided by the number of raters in the classroom yielded a total sociometric score.

Perceived self-competence. Children's perceptions of their own competencies were assessed by an individual administration of Harter's (1982) Perceived Competence Scale. The scale measures three competency domains, cognitive (e.g., "good at school work"), social (e.g., "have a lot of friends"), and physical (e.g., "do well at sports"). A fourth category, general self-worth (e.g., "happy the way I am") is also assessed. In addition to these four individual scores, a total score of self-perceptions was computed by summing scores across all four categories.

Behavioral observations. Each second grade child was invited to play with three same-sex age-mates for four 12-minute free play sessions in a laboratory playroom. The child's playmates differed in each of the four sessions, thus allowing observations to be made with 12 of different playmates.

During each play session, the children were observed following the procedures described in detail in Rubin (1982). Each child was observed for 42 10-second time intervals during each session. Behaviors were coded on a checklist that included the cognitive play categories of functional-sensorimotor, constructive, and dramatic play and games-with-rules. These categories form a development hierarchy with functional-sensorimotor play appearing first in infancy and games-with-rules last during the early elementary school years. These cognitive play categories were nested within the social participation categories as described by Rubin (1982), i.e., solitary, parallel and group activities. Other categories included unoccupied behavior, onlooker behavior, aggression, and conversations with peers. Drawing from Furman, Rahe, & Hartup (1979), the affective quality of each social interchange was noted as positive, neutral or negative. Reliability was assessed by pairing each observer ($n = 4$) with every other observer for a total of 30 minutes of coding each. The number of coding agreements/(number of agreements + disagreements) exceeded 85% for each pairing.

Procedure

All second grade children were administered the Revised Class Play, the sociometric rating scale, and the self-perception scale. Their teachers completed the PBQ and observations were made of their free play behaviors. Due to attrition, only 69 of the original 86 second graders were available for re-testing in grade three. An additional 27 children, however, were assessed for the first time in grade three. All measures administered in grade two were re-administered the following year. Unfortunately, due to funding constraints, behavioral observations could not be made on the 96 grade three children.

Results

Concurrent Correlations in the Second Grade Sample

Based on the predictions described earlier, selected correlations were examined separately for boys and girls. Significant correlations are presented in Table 1.

Aggressive/disruptive behaviors. Peer rated aggression was correlated significantly and positively with observed frequencies of nonsocial forms of play as well as with observed aggression for boys only. More specifically positive relations were evinced with solitary-constructive, and -dramatic play, solitary-games and all solitary play. It is important to note that solitary-dramatic play, when produced in a social setting, represents a highly immature and nonadaptive form of pretense (Rubin, 1982). Negative correlations, for boys and girls, were found with the observed frequency of onlooker behavior; a negative relation, for girls only, was evinced with unoccupied behavior.

As expected, teacher ratings of aggression were positively associated with peer rated aggression boys and girls. Teachers rated aggressive boys, but not girls, as hyperactive/distractible. Peer rated aggressive girls, but *not* boys, were rated negatively on the peer sociometric measure. No significant relations were found with the self-perception variables.

Sensitive/isolated behaviors. As with Aggression/Disruptive scores, Sensitive/Isolated scores produced stronger correlations for boys than for girls. Sensitive/Isolated scores were positively correlated with observations of solitary-constructive, -dramatic, total solitary play, total constructive, and total dramatic play, and negatively correlated with observations of peer conversations for boys only.

Boys and girls who received high ratings on the Sensitive-Isolated items were rated by teachers as anxious, were disliked by peers, and perceived themselves as lacking social skills. The total Harter scale score, computed by summing across all self-perception factor scores, was correlated negatively with peer ratings of sensitivity/isolation for boys and girls.

Despite these teacher-, peer-, and self-rating correlational consistencies for boys and girls, it was nevertheless the case that interesting sex differences were found. For example, teachers rated isolate boys as impulsive. Furthermore, negative relations with Sensitive/Isolated scores were found with the cognitive self-perception variable for boys and with the physical self-perception variable for girls.

Table 1. Significant Correlates of Revised Class Play Factors for Second Grade Children

	Males (n = *36)*		*Females* (n = *50)*	
	r	p	r	p
Source	*Dimension*			
	AGGRESSIVE			
OBSERVATIONS:				
Solitary—constructive	.28	.05		
—dramatic	.37	.01		
—games	.29	.05		
—total	.45	.003		
Onlooker	−.30	.04	−.28	.03
Unoccupied			−.23	.05
Aggression	.30	.04		
TEACHER RATINGS:				
Aggression	.38	.01	.24	.05
Hyperactivity	.46	.002		
SOCIOMETRIC:			−.30	.02
	ISOLATED			
OBSERVATIONS:				
Solitary—constructive	.60	.001		
—dramatic	.43	.005		
—total	.56	.001		
Conversations	−.35	.02		
Constructive total	.35	.02		
Dramatic total	.37	.01		
TEACHER RATINGS:				
Anxiety	.40	.008	.35	.006
Hyperactivity	.30	.04		
SOCIOMETRIC:	−.29	.05	−.27	.03
SELF-PERCEPTIONS:				
Cognitive	−.41	.006		

(*continued*)

Table 1 (continued)

Source	Males (n = 36) r	p	Females (n = 50) r	p
	Dimension			
Social	−.49	.001	−.38	.003
Physical			−.45	.001
General	−.34	.02		
Total	−.48	.002	−.38	.003
	SOCIABLE			
OBSERVATIONS				
Solitary total	−.27	.05		
Group—dramatic	−.32	.03		
—games	.35	.02		
—total	.32	.03		
Transitional			−.28	.02
Conversations			.25	.04
Isolate activity	−.38	.01		
TEACHER RATINGS:				
Hyperactivity	−.37	.01		
SOCIOMETRIC:	.49	.001	.65	.001
SELF-PERCEPTIONS:				
Social			.24	.05
General	.37	.01		
Total	.27	.05		

Sociable/leader behaviors. Once again, the correlational pattern differed for boys and girls. Peer ratings of Sociable-Leader behaviors for boys were correlated positively with observations of group-games and total group play, and negatively with observations of total solitary and group-dramatic play and isolate play (a composite of solitary + unoccupied + onlooker activity). For girls, positive relations were found with observations of peer conversations, group-exploratory activity, and the proportion of positive peer interactions; negative relations were evinced with the frequency of observed transitional behaviors (moving from activity to activity).

A negative relation with teacher ratings of impulsivity was discovered for boys only. For both boys and girls, however, a highly significant relation was found between ratings of Sociable-Leader behaviors and sociometric popularity. For self-perceived competency significant positive correlations were found with perceived "general" and "total" competencies for boys and with social competence for girls.

Concurrent Correlations in the Third Grade Sample

With the exception of observational measures, correlations with the Revised Class Play factors were analyzed for the third grade sample. Significant correlations are reported in Table 2.

Aggressive/disruptive behaviors. In general, the magnitude of the correlations with Aggressive/Disruptive assessments was higher in grade 3 than in grade 2. As in grade 2, teacher ratings of aggression were positively related with Aggressive/Disruptive scores for both boys and girls. In addition, peer-rated aggression for girls correlated positively with teacher ratings of anxiety while for boys teacher ratings of hyperactivity/impulsivity were positively associated with peer-rated aggression. Scores on the Revised Class Play aggression factor related negatively, for *both* boys and girls, with sociometric status. Aggression ratings were positively related with self-perceptions of social competence for boys only.

Sensitive/isolated behaviors. Peer assessments of Sensitive/Isolated behaviors for boys and girls were positively correlated with teacher ratings of anxiety and impulsivity, and negatively correlated with sociometric status, self-perceptions of physical competence and total self-perception scores.

Sex differences emerged for several variables. Isolated boys were rated by teachers as aggressive, and rated by themselves as less competent with regard to their own cognitive skills and general self-worth. Isolated girls rated themselves as less socially competent.

Sociable/leader behaviors. For boys and girls, peer rated Sociable/Leader behaviors were correlated with sociometric popularity and self-perceived social and cognitive competence, and negatively correlated with teacher ratings of aggression, anxiety, and impulsivity. The only sex differences noted were positive correlations, for girls, but not boys, with self-perceptions of general competencies and with the total self-perception score.

Factor Stability for the Revised Class Play

Year-to-year correlations ($n = 69$) between scores on the aggressive, isolated, and sociable factors were .73, .49, and .54 (all $p < .001$). The stability of ratings for boys and girls were virtually identical. As in previous reports concerning older children (see Younger, Schwartzman, & Ledingham, 1985), ratings of aggression were highly stable particularly in comparison with ratings of isolation. In view of the young age of the children in the initial assessment and given

Table 2. Significant Correlates of Revised Class Play Factors for Third Grade Children

	Males (n = *48)*		*Females* (n = *48)*	
	r	p	r	p
Source	*Dimension*			
	AGGRESSIVE			
TEACHER RATINGS:				
Aggression	.72	.001	.34	.009
Anxiety			.25	.05
Hyperactivity	.47	.001		
SOCIOMETRIC:	−.44	.001	−.51	.001
SELF-PERCEPTIONS:				
Social	.25	.05		
	ISOLATED			
TEACHER RATINGS:				
Aggression	.25	.05		
Anxiety	.45	.001	.38	.004
Hyperactivity	.34	.009	.24	.05
SOCIOMETRIC:	−.41	.002	−.49	.001
SELF-PERCEPTIONS:				
Cognitive	−.31	.02		
Social			−.32	.02
Physical	−.43	.001	−.28	.03
General	−.26	.04		
Total	−.38	.004	−.34	.01
	SOCIABLE			
TEACHER RATINGS:				
Aggression	−.26	.04	−.32	.01
Anxiety	−.27	.01	−.29	.02
Hyperactivity	−.33	.01	−.30	.02

(*continued*)

Table 2 (continued)

Source	Males (n = 48) r	Males (n = 48) p	Females (n = 48) r	Females (n = 48) p
	Dimension			
SOCIOMETRIC:	.44	.001	.75	.001
SELF-PERCEPTIONS:				
Cognitive	.24	.05	.24	.05
Social	.24	.05	.31	.02
General			.25	.04
Total			.29	.02

that quiescent, solitary activities are not salient for young children (Rubin et al., in press), modest stability for the isolated factor scores is not surprising.

One Year Predictions of Revised Class Play Scores

In our final analysis, measures assessed in second grade were used to predict peer ratings of aggression, isolation, and sociability in third grade. While stepwise multiple regression would have been the preferred statistical procedure, sex differences and a small sample of males ($n = 28$) and females ($n = 41$) who were available for testing in both grades precluded this possibility. Instead, a series of simple correlational analyses was calculated. Significant correlations are presented in Table 3.

Aggressive/disruptive behaviors. For boys only, significant positive predictors of subsequent aggression included teacher ratings of aggression and impulsivity, self-perceptions of competence (total score), observations of transitional behaviors, solitary-functional play and solitary-games, total parallel and functional play, and the proportion of negative peer interactions. The observed proportion of neutral peer interactions was negatively associated with aggression.

For girls, observations of solitary-, group-, and total dramatic play were negatively correlated with aggression. For both girls and boys, sociometric ratings and observations of onlooker behaviors negatively predicted aggression.

Sensitive/isolated behaviors. Sensitive/Isolate behavior in boys was significantly associated with grade 2 teacher ratings of impulsivity and with observations of solitary-dramatic, total solitary, group-constructive, group-dramatic, and total constructive play. Sensitive/Isolate behavior was negatively correlated with sociometric status, self-perceptions of social competence, and observations of group games.

Table 3. Prediction of Revised Class Play Factors for Third Grade Children using Measures from Second Grade

	Males (n = *28)*		*Females* (n = *41)*	
	r	p	r	p
Source	*Dimension*			
	AGGRESSIVE			
OBSERVATIONS:				
Solitary—functional	.35	.03		
—games	.48	.006		
—dramatic			−.28	.04
Group—dramatic			−.29	.04
Parallel total	.32	.05		
Functional total	.37	.02		
Dramatic total			−.31	.03
Transitional	.35	.03		
Onlooker	−.40	.02	−.34	.01
Proportion negative interactions	.55	.001		
Proportion neutral interactions	−.52	.002		
TEACHER RATINGS:				
Aggression	.32	.05		
Hyperactivity	.52	.002		
SOCIOMETRIC:	−.32	.05	−.29	.03
SELF-PERCEPTIONS:				
Total	.31	.05		
	ISOLATED			
OBSERVATIONS:				
Solitary—dramatic	.31	.05		
—reading			.49	.001
—total	.31	.05		
Parallel—dramatic			.44	.002
Group—constructive	.49	.004		
—dramatic	.57	.001		
—games	−.32	.05		
Constructive total	.38	.02		

(*continued*)

Table 3 (*continued*)

	Males (n = *28)*		*Females* (n = *41)*	
	r	p	r	p
Source	*Dimension*			
Dramatic total	.38	.02	.30	.03
Isolate play			.37	.008
TEACHER RATINGS:				
Hyperactivity	.37	.02		
SOCIOMETRIC:	−.35	.03		
SELF-PERCEPTIONS:				
Social	−.31	.05		
Physical	−.41	.02	−.28	.04
Total	−.34	.04	−.32	.02
	SOCIABLE			
OBSERVATIONS:				
Solitary—constructive	−.38	.02		
—total	−.43	.01		
Group—games	.48	.005		
—total	.43	.01		
Constructive total	−.32	.05		
Isolate play	−.38	.02		
TEACHER RATINGS:				
Aggression			−.27	.05
Hyperactivity	−.38	.02	−.41	.004
SOCIOMETRIC:	.56	.001	.38	.008
SELF-PERCEPTIONS:				
Social			.38	.008
General			.41	.004
Total			.39	.007

For girls, observations of solitary-reading, parallel-dramatic, and total isolate play (the sum of solitary + onlooker + unoccupied activity) correlated positively with Class Play ratings of Sensitive/Isolated behavior. For both sexes, grade 2 total self-perception and perceptions of physical competence were negatively correlated with grade 3 isolate scores. The frequency of observed dramatic play was positively predictive.

Sociable/leader behaviors. Boys who were observed to display a high frequency of group-games and group-total behavior were rated by grade 3 peers as highly sociable. Negative predictors included observations of solitary-constructive, solitary-dramatic, total constructive, and total isolate play.

For girls, observational data from the second grade did not predict peer ratings of Sociable/Leader behaviors. However, positive self-perceptions of social competence, general self-worth, and total self-perceptions predicted grade 3 peer ratings. Teacher ratings of aggression were negatively correlated with sociable/leader behaviors.

For both boys and girls, teacher ratings of hyperactivity/impulsivity were negative predictors of sociability while sociometric status was positively predictive.

DISCUSSION

The purpose of this report was to examine the concurrent and predictive correlates of the Minnesota Revision of the Class Play (Masten et al., 1985) as indices of the scale's adequacy for peer assessment of social behavior. Given the relative ease of administration, demonstration of validity for this instrument might lessen the need for multiple (and costly) assessment procedures to identify children "at risk" for socioemotional problems.

The general pattern of correlations was only moderately supportive of our predictions that the Class Play factors of Aggressive/Disruptive, Sensitive/Isolate, and Sociable/Leader behaviors would relate with conceptually associated variables. Sex differences were pervasive in our analyses and warrant further discussion.

An examination of the concurrent correlates of peer rated aggressive/disruptive behavior reveals that boys and girls receiving high scores on this factor were also rated by their teachers as aggressive. These data suggest that peers and teachers concur in identifying children who exhibit highly salient, aggressive behaviors. For the most part, children rated as aggressive and disruptive were also disliked by peers.

Interestingly, boys but not girls who were rated high for aggression by peers were rated as hyperactive and impulsive by teachers. These data are consistent with two sets of related findings. First, boys are more likely to be identified as hyperactive than girls (Whalen, 1983); second, it is common to find that hyperactive boys also demonstrate a relatively high frequency of aggressive behaviors (Cohen, Sullivan, Minde, Novack, & Helwig, 1981; Prinz, Connor, & Wilson, 1981). Perhaps the counterpart to the above relations in boys was our discovery that grade 3 girls who were perceived by peers as aggressive and disruptive were seen by teachers as anxious and fearful. Although the relation between aggression and anxiety is not immediately apparent, several psychologists have suggested that girls are more fearful and generally manifest greater anxiety than boys (Block, 1983; Maccoby & Jacklin, 1974). Girls may exhibit more behavioral evidence of anxiety while teachers may have sex-typed biases that lead them to ascribe atypical behavior in girls to anxiety. Additionally, theoretical support for the relationship between anxiety and aggression is evident in many theories of personality and psychopathology. Most recently, Sroufe (1983) and his colleagues have suggested that anxiety during infancy and toddlerhood may be predictive of aggressive displays in early childhood. The underlying operative assumption is that children who are experiencing anxiety which emanates from their insecure early relationships with their parents, may demonstrate their anxieties and insecurities via angry, aggressive displays with the peer group (e.g., La Freniere & Sroufe, 1985). Clearly, additional research is needed to explicate the relationship between these two domains, and to determine whether the association is sex-specific.

The sex differences that emerged with respect to the Aggressive/Disruptive dimension were most pronounced for observed behavior. For boys, peer related aggression was associated with observed aggression and immature, possibly disruptive forms of solitary play. For example dramatic play and games are usually observed to take place in group interactive, cooperative contexts (Rubin, Fein, & Vandenberg, 1983). It is unusual, within social milieus, to find children pretending or playing board games on their own. Yet, peer-rated aggressive boys were found to engage in greater frequencies of these nonnormative behaviors. Moreover, since the themes of pretense for boys often involve superhero action themes associated with violence (Rubin et al., 1983), one cannot dismiss nonnormal, yet solitary-pretense activities as quiescent, harmless and nondisruptive. It is quite probable that such activities are salient and disruptive in constrained social quarters such as those studied herein.

The only behaviors correlated with aggression for girls were those associated with solitude or remaining on the periphery of group activities. Peer-rated aggressive girls were less likely to watch other children (onlooker behavior) and more likely to be uninvolved in one form of activity or another (unoccupied behavior). Thus, unlike aggressive boys who spent a good deal of time alone, peer-rated aggressive girls were observed to engage in less nonsocial activity than their nonaggressive peers.

Perhaps the most interesting finding for girls was the lack of a relation between rated and observed aggressive or disruptive activity. Two possible factors may account for these findings. First, boys are reported to engage in more frequent aggressive encounters than girls (e.g., Parke & Slaby, 1983). Indeed, in our data set, boys were observed to be more aggressive than girls, $t\,(84) = 2.31, p < .02$. This quantitative difference in aggression was associated with a problem of restricted range for girls; that is, aggression for girls was observed at a low level with little variability. Thus, this infrequently observed behavior limited the magnitude of correlations with peer and teacher measures.

The procedure used for coding the naturalistic play of the children may have contributed to the nonsignificant relation between observed and rated aggression. The observational procedure tapped physical aggression; nonphysical forms of agonistic behavior like teasing, tattling, and blaming which have been reported to be more frequently observed in females (Parke & Slaby, 1983) were not coded separately from physical aggression on the play coding scale. The bottom line is that some Class Play items clearly involve physically aggressive roles, while others involve concepts like blaming and teasing. A differentiation between physical and verbal aggression may provide better concordance in future research.

The composite picture of aggressive-disruptive boys is completed when we examine their self-perceptions of competence. Grade 3 aggressive boys perceived themselves as socially more competent than their less aggressive classmates. Self-appraisals of competence across all domains in second grade significantly and positively predicted aggression ratings in third grade. In short, boys rated as aggressive perceived themselves as skillful; yet, given their unpopularity, impulsivity, and aggressiveness, their self-evaluations seem miscontrued and inaccurate.

Several possible explanations may account for these findings. It is possible that aggressive boys are deficient in the social-cognitive and attentional skills necessary to monitor the impact of their behavior on the peer environment. Such deficits may result in a failure to monitor social feedback cues in their environment. In recent research, Rubin & Krasnor (in press) and Dodge (in press, a) have identified social-cognitive deficits in aggressive children. Dodge, for example, found that aggressive children often judge other children's unintentional misbehaviors as being motivated by hostile intent. Once this hostile attribution is made, aggressive children are likely to respond agonistically. Implicit in these findings is the notion that aggressive children tend to externalize blame to an antagonist. Such defensive strategies may place the child in further conflict with peers and result in rejection (Dollinger, Staley, & McGuire, 1981). Defensive strategies may further allow the child to maintain a sense of self-worth and competence. Peer rejection may be of little consequence to aggressive children who attribute their interpersonal conflicts to sources other than themselves. Our finding with regard to the positive self-perceptions of aggressive boys may thus reflect social-cognitive and attributional deficiencies as well as ego-defense strategies.

Finally, sex differences in the correlational patterns with peer-rated aggression/disruption were evident in the concurrent correlations and the predictive results. For boys, grade 2 indices of immature and inappropriate play, sociometric rejection, hyperactivity, "inflated" self-perceptions, and of course, negative peer interchanges, predicted peer ratings of aggression in the third grade. This predictive composite is intuitively logical. Immature and probably disruptive solitary play coupled with ratings by teachers and observations of negative, aggressive, impulsive activity should predict ratings of aggression!

For girls the picture is more complex. As with boys, we found negative predictive relations with sociometric status and quiescent onlooker behaviors, which makes sense. However, solitary and social dramatic play in second grade correlated negatively with third grade aggressive behavior. This result, which is directly opposite to that found in the grade 2 concurrent (but not predictive) correlations for boys, may once again be explained by an examination of the themes generally found in the pretend play of males and females. For girls, it is typical to find domestic and school-related pretense themes (Rubin et al., 1983) that are played out quietly and nondisruptively. Consequently, a negative prediction of aggression from quiescent, nondisruptive behaviors would be expected for girls. The major troublesome note is that second grade observations of girls' aggressive and negative peer interchanges did not predict peer rated aggression in third grade, although the problem of range restriction may account for this result.

The main conclusion is that aggression/disruption probably has different meanings as well as different correlates and causes for girls and boys. The extent to which the Revised Class Play effectively captures these different meanings remains to be determined. Nevertheless, given the correlations described above, we do feel comfortable in offering this peer rating procedure for identification of aggressive children, particularly boys. However, we would strongly suggest the simultaneous use of a reliable teacher index of aggression to confirm the identification.

We turn now to a discussion of the correlates of the Sensitive/Isolated factor. Several of the observed relations were consistent with our hypotheses. Children rated by peers as sensitive and isolated were anxious according to teachers, generally rejected by peers, and perceived themselves as incompetent (although the specific domains of the negative self-perceptions varied for gender).

However, a closer examination of the findings revealed sex differences similar to those for aggression that clouded the conclusions. For boys, teacher ratings of hyperactivity were associated with sensitivity and isolation. Furthermore, grade 2 observations of immature, disruptive nonsocial play (e.g., solitary-dramatic play) as well as more sedate forms of solitary activities (construction) correlate concurrently with this factor. The disruptive, immature nonsocial dramatic play forms combine with sociodramatic activities to predict grade 3 ratings of sensitivity-isolation in boys. Given that the play themes of boys are more disruptive and hostile (Rubin et al., 1983), then it appears as if immaturity and disruptiveness, impulsiveness, peer rejection, and negative self-perceptions collectively predict grade 3 ratings of sensitivity-isolation for boys.

For girls, the composite differs somewhat. *No* observed behaviors were correlated with concurrently assessed peer-ratings of sensitivity and isolation, while teacher ratings of anxiety, peer rejection, and negative self-perceptions were concurrent correlates. The predictive analysis demonstrated that solitary or nonsocial quiescent (reading) and/or immature activity (parallel-dramatic play) as well as negative self-perceptions predicted grade 3 ratings of sensitivity-isolation. Unlike boys, the grade 3 ratings for girls are not predicted by teacher ratings of hyperactivity or peer rejection. In short, these correlations may be taken to suggest that for girls, quiet, sedentary, nonsocial activities plus negative self perceptions collectively characterize the Revised Class Play Sensitive/Isolated factor.

The divergent correlational patterns for males and females raise the issue of what the Sensitive/Isolated factor means for each sex. This factor from the Revised Class Play actually contains three sub-clusters of items: items referring to physical isolation from the peer group (e.g., ''rather play alone''), items reflecting ineffectual social skills (e.g., ''has trouble making friends''), and items referring to affective sensitivity (e.g., ''feelings get hurt easily''). Although represented by one factor score, the items seem to reflect several subtypes of isolated and withdrawn behavior, each potentially associated with a different etiology. For example, one can imagine a sequence whereby a child becomes rejected by peers, perhaps due to inappropriate, aggressive or impulsive behaviors, and consequently is isolated from the peer group (Coie & Kupersmidt, 1983). Our predictive correlational pattern for boys reflected this particular scenario. The significant behavioral correlations found for the boys in our study might reflect an association with those items concerned with ineffectual social skills (''has trouble making friends;'' ''can't get others to listen''). Interestingly, in Masten et al.'s (1985) presentation of the Revised Class Play's factor structure, these two items also loaded significantly on the Aggressive/Disruptive factor! In summary, it is not clear whether boys who obtain high scores on the Sensitive/Isolated factor are displaying high frequencies of nonsocial activity as a result of anxieties and sensitivities, or as a result of being rejected by the peer group.

A second plausible scenario may be described as follows. There may exist a subgroup of children who are initially insecure and anxious (perhaps because of early familial relationship histories, Rubin, et al., in press; Sroufe, 1983). As a result of their felt insecurities, these children may choose to remain on the periphery of the peer group and engage instead in quiet and sedentary activities. These children would not be expected to display assertive or aggressive behaviors; rather, they would be compliant with and deferent to their age-mates (Rubin, 1985). Given that these children may be responsive, submissive, and nondisruptive, there is little reason for peers to dislike them. One might expect that as their psychological difficulties become more apparent to the peer group, these children, at a later age, would be rejected by their class-mates. In fact, in our data a negative relationship emerged between the ''Sensitive-Isolate'' dimension and sociometric popularity across both grades and for both sexes. Furthermore, our data indicates that the magnitude of this relationship increases developmentally. These findings are consistent with a recent investigation by Moskowitz, Schwartzman, and Ledingham (1985) in which evidence was presented for the stability of withdrawn behavior across a three-year period. Moscowitz et al. (1985) also found that children initially identified as withdrawn become increasingly isolated over time.

The second scenario may be relevant to children who are "at risk" for internalizing problems. Moreover, it has been suggested that females are at greater risk for such difficulties (Achenbach & Edelbrock, 1983). The finding that sensitivity-isolation in girls was predicted by solitary and sedentary-quiescent behaviors (e.g., reading) in free-play settings, as well as by negative self-perceptions, but not by hyperactivity and peer rejection, fits well with our suggested second scenario. Finally, given that the Sensitive-Isolated factor on the Revised Class Play contains sub-clusters of items, we would hypothesize that the items most strongly related to indices of anxiety, quiescent, sedentary nonsocial play, negative self-perceptions, and social deference are those that tap sensitivity (e.g., "very shy;" "feelings get hurt easily") rather than social rejection ("has trouble making friends;" "can't get others to listen"). This hypothesis merits attention in future research endeavors.

In summary, we are suggesting the likelihood that there are multiple pathways for children to become isolated or withdrawn from the peer group. We are further suggesting that gender may be a significant determinant of these different pathways. Longer Longitudinal studies tracking the ontogeny of nonsocial behavior for boys and girls are sorely needed.

It is presently the case that considerable controversy exists concerning how to identify socially withdrawn children, whether these children represent a heterogeneous or homogeneous group, and whether they are "at risk" for later psychological difficulties. Our own bias leads us to suggest that there do exist different sub-types of withdrawn children who undoubtedly share some common behavioral variance, but who have distinctive histories (see also, Moscowitz, Schwartzman, & Ledingham, 1985; Rubin et al., in press). The Revised Class Play "sensitive-isolated" factor seems to capture some of the general variance common to all children identified as withdrawn. However, the instrument does not adequately discriminate between the different sub-types described in the aforementioned scenarios. Our recommendation, then, is that professionals who plan to identify children as withdrawn should be aware of the multiple pathways perspectives that we have described. We also do not recommend the Revised Class Play as a sole source of selection for isolated-withdrawn children.

The correlates of the Sociability-Leadership factor deserves brief discussion. As mentioned earlier, the sociable and leadership items were included in the Revised Class Play to permit study of competent functioning and invulnerability to stress. Despite these considerations, researchers typically still use peer assessments to identify children who deviate from normal behavior patterns in a negative way. Consequently, the correlates of Sociability-Leadership may not be as relevant to researchers as those for aggression and isolation/sensitivity.

In general, boys who received high scores on this factor were more likely to engage in group-cooperative activities involving specific rules and social roles (group-games) and less likely to engage in nonsocial activities. These boys were positively regarded by peers, teachers and themselves. Similar concurrent correlational patterns were found for girls, although this factor was related to conversations with peers rather than competitive, rule-governed social games.

The predictive correlates for boys included variables that centered around sociability (i.e., more group activities, fewer nonsocial activities) and likeability. For girls, the predictive correlates included likeability and positive self-perceptions. The observational scheme may not have captured the leadership or sociable behaviors that determine sociable-leadership peer status in girls. Nevertheless, the correlational patterns for girls and boys do make intuitive sense. We would argue, however, that the sole use of the Class Play to identify highly sociable children is not merited. We suggest that the combined use of the Revised Class Play plus positive sociometric peer ratings would be a reasonable strategy to identify children perceived to be socially skilled.

In our examination of the Revised Class Play we have discovered sex differences not originally anticipated or reported by Masten et al. (1985). We discovered subclusters of items that may tap different dimensions of sensitivity-isolation. Finally, the findings forced us to consider multiple developmental pathways that determine children's social status and psychological functioning. With further examination of the issues raised in this paper, investigators may be in a position to better identify, assess, and assist children who deviate in a debilitating way from the social norms of their peers.

ACKNOWLEGMENT

Preparation of this chapter and the collection of data reported herein were supported, in part, by Grant /6606-2302-04 from Health and Welfare Canada.

REFERENCES

Achenbach, T. M., & Edelbrock, C. S. (1981). Behavioral problems and competencies reported by parents of normal and disturbed children aged four through sixteen. *Monographs of the Society for Research in Child Development, 46* (1 Serial No. 188).

Asarnow, J. (1983). Children with peer adjustment problems: Sequential and non-sequential analyses of school behaviors. *Journal of Consulting and Clinical Psychology, 51,* 709–717.

Asher, S. R., Markell, R. A., & Hymel, S. (1981). Identifying children at risk in peer relations: A critique of the rate-of-interaction approach to assessment. *Child Development, 52,* 1239–1245.

Asher, S., Singleton, L., Tinsley, B., & Hymel, S. (1979). A reliable sociometric measure for preschool children. *Developmental Psychology, 15,* 443–444.

Behar, L., & Stringfield, S. (1974). A behavioral rating scale for the preschool child. *Developmental Psychology, 10,* 601–610.

Block, J. H. (1983). Differential premises arising from differential socialization of the sexes: Some conjectures. *Child Development, 54,* 1335–1354.

Bower, E. M. (1969). *Early identification of emotionally handicapped children in school.* Princeton, NJ: Educational Testing Service.

Bower, E., & Lambert, N. (1961). *A process for in-school screening of children with emotional handicaps.* Princeton, NJ: Educational Testing Service.

Butler, L. (1979). *Social and behavioral correlates of peer reputation.* Paper presented at the Biennial Meeting of the Society for Research in Child Development, San Francisco, California.

Coie, J. D., & Kupersmidt, J. (1983). A behavioral analysis of emerging social status in boys' groups. *Child Development, 54,* 1400–1416.

Cohen, N. J., Sullivan, J., Minde, K., Novack, C., & Helwig, C. (1981). Evaluation of the relative effectiveness of methylphenidate and cognitive behavior modification in the treatment of kindergarten-aged hyperactive children. *Journal of Abnormal Child Psychology, 9,* 43–54.

Connolly, J., & Doyle, A. (1981). Assessment of social competence in preschoolers: Teachers versus peers. *Developmental Psychology, 17,* 454–462.

Cowen, E. L., Pederson, A., Babigian, H., Izzo, L. D., & Trost, M. A. (1973). Long-term follow-up of early detected vulnerable children. *Journal of Consulting and Clinical Psychology, 41,* 438–446.

Deutsch, F. (1974). Observational and sociometric measures of peer popularity and their relationship to egocentric communication in female preschoolers. *Developmental Psychology, 10,* 745–747.

Dodge, K. A. (in press, a). A social information processing model of social competence in children. In M. Perlmutter (Ed.), *Minnesota Symposia on Child Psychology,* Vol. 18. Hillsdale, NJ: Erlbaum Press.

Dodge, K. A. (in press, b). Facets of social interaction and the assessment of social competence in children. In B. Schneider, K. H. Rubin, & J. Ledingham (Eds.), *Children's peer relations: Issues in assessment and intervention.* New York: Springer-Verlag.

Dodge, K. A. (1983). Behavioral antecedents of peer social status. *Child Development, 54,* 1386–1399.

Dollinger, S. J., Staley, A., & McGuire, B. (1981). The child as psychologist: Attributions and evaluations of defensive strategies. *Child Development, 52,* 1084–1086.

Furman, W., Rahe, D., & Hartup, W. (1979). Rehabilitation of socially-withdrawn preschool children through mixed-age and same-age socialization. *Child Development, 50,* 915–922.

Garmezy, N., Masten, A. S. & Tellegen, A. (1984). The study of stress and competence in children: A building block for developmental psychopathology. *Child Development, 55,* 97–111.

Gottman, J. (1977). Toward a definition of social isolation in children. *Child Development, 48,* 513–517.

Green, K. D., Forehand, R., Beck, S. J., & Vosk, B. (1980). An assessment of the relationship among measures of children's social competence and children's academic achievement. *Child Development, 51,* 1149–1156.

Harter, S. (1982). The perceived competence scale for children. *Child Development, 53,* 87–97.

Hartshorne, H., May, M., & Maller, J. (1929). *Studies in the nature of character: II. Studies in service and self-control.* New York: Macmillan.

Hartup, W. (1970). Peer interaction and social organization. In P. H. Mussen (Ed.), *Carmichael's manual of child psychology,* Vol. 2. New York: Wiley.

Hymel, S., & Rubin, K. H. (1985). Children with peer relationships and social skills problems: Conceptual, methodological, and developmental issues. In G. J. Whitehurst (Ed.), *Annals of child development,* Vol. 2. Greenwich, CT: JAI Press.

Kleck, R. E., Richardson, S. A., & Ronald, L. (1974). Physical appearance cues and interpersonal attraction in children. *Child Development, 45,* 305–310.

Kupersmidt, J. (1983). *Predicting delinquency and academic problems from childhood peer status.* Paper presented at the Biennial Meeting of the Society for Research in Child Development, Detroit, Michigan.

LaFreniere, P., & Sroufe, L. A. (1985). Profiles of peer competence in the preschool: Interrelations between measures, influence of social ecology, and relation to attachment history. *Developmental Psychology, 21,* 56–69.

Maccoby, E. E., & Jacklin, C. N. (1974). *The psychology of sex differences.* Stanford, CA: Stanford University Press.

Masten, A., Morison, P., & Pellegrini, D. (1985). A revised class play method of peer assessment. *Developmental Psychology, 21,* 523–533.

Moskowitz, D. S., Schwartzman, A. E., & Ledingham, J. E. (1985). Stability and change in aggression and withdrawal in middle childhood and early adolescence. *Journal of Abnormal Psychology, 94,* 30–41.

Newcomb, A. F., & Bukowski, W. M. (1984). A longitudinal study of the utility of social preference and social impact sociometric classification schemes. *Child Development, 55,* 1434–1447.

Parke, R. D., & Slaby, R. G. (1983). The development of aggression. In P. H. Mussen (Ed.), *Handbook of child psychology* (4th ed.), Vol. IV, *Socialization, personality, and social development* (Volume editor, E. M. Hetherington). New York: Wiley.

Parten, M. B. (1932). Social participation among preschool children. *Journal of Abnormal Psychology, 27,* 243–269.

Pekarik, E., Prinz, R., Liebert, D., Weintraub, S., & Neale, J. (1976). The Pupil Evaluation Inventory: A sociometric technique for assessing children's social behavior. *Journal of Abnormal Child Psychology, 4,* 83–97.

Piaget, J. (1926). *The language and thought of the child.* London: Routlege & Kegan Paul.

Piaget, J. (1932). *The moral judgement of the child.* Glencoe: Free Press.

Prinz, R. J., Connor, P. A., & Wilson, C. C. (1981). Hyperactive and aggressive behavior in children. *Journal of Abnormal Child Psychology, 9,* 191–202.

Putallaz, M. (1983). Predicting children's sociometric status from their behavior. *Child Development, 54,* 1417–1426.

Roff, M. (1961). Childhood social interactions and young adult bad conduct. *Journal of Abnormal and Social Psychology, 63,* 333–337.

Rolf, J. E. (1972). The social and academic competence of children vulnerable to schizophrenia and other behavior pathologies. *Journal of Abnormal Psychology, 80,* 225–243.

Rubin, K. H. (1985). Socially withdrawn children: An "at risk" population? In B. Schneider, K. H. Rubin, & J. Ledingham (Eds.), *Peer relationships and social skills in childhood,* Vol. 2, *Issues in assessment and training.* New York: Springer-Verlag.

Rubin, K. H. (1982a). Non-social play in preschoolers: Necessary evil? *Child Development, 53,* 651–657.

Rubin, K. H. (1982b). Social and social-cognitive developmental characteristics of young isolate, normal, and sociable children. In K. H. Rubin & H. S. Ross (Eds.), *Peer relationships and social skills in childhood.* New York: Springer-Verlag.

Rubin, K. H., & Clark, L. (1983). Preschool teachers' ratings of behavioral problems. *Journal of Abnormal Child Psychology, 11,* 273–285.

Rubin, K. H., & Daniels-Beirness, T. (1983). Concurrent and predictive correlates of sociometric status in kindergarten and grade one children. *Merrill-Palmer Quarterly, 29,* 337–352.

Rubin, K. H., Fein, G., & Vandenberg, (1983). Play. In E. M. Hetherington (Ed.), *Handbook of child psychology: Socialization, personality and social development.* New York: Wiley.

Rubin, K. H., & Krasnor, L. R. (in press). Social cognitive and social behavioral perspectives on problem-solving. In M. Perlmutter (Ed.), *Minnesota Symposia on child psychology,* Vol. 18. Hillsdale, NJ: Erlbaum Press.

Rubin, K. H., LeMare, L., & Lollis, S. (in press). Social withdrawal in childhood: Assessment issues and social concomitants. In S. R. Asher & J. D. Coie (Eds.), *Children's status in the peer group*. New York: Cambridge University Press.

Rubin, K. H., Moller, L., & Emptage, A. (1985). *Can the Preschool Behavior Questionnaire be used with elementary school-age children?* Paper presented at the Annual Meeting of the Canadian Psychological Association, Halifax, Nova Scotia.

Rubin, K. H., & Pepler, D. (1980). The relationship of child's play to social-cognitive growth and development. In H. Foot, T. Chapman, & J. Smith (Eds.), *Friendship and childhood relationships*. London: Wiley.

Rutter, M. (1967). A children's behavior questionnaire for completion by teachers: Preliminary findings. *Journal of Child Psychology and Psychiatry, 8,* 1–11.

Serbin, L., Lyons, J., Marchessault, K., & Morin, D. (1983). *Naturalistic observations of peer-identified aggressive, withdrawn, aggressive-withdrawn and comparison children.* Paper presented at the Biennial Meeting of the Society for Research in Child Development, Detroit, Michigan.

Shantz, C. (1983). Social cognition. In J. H. Flavell & E. Markman (Eds.), *Handbook of child psychology,* Vol. 3, *Cognitive development.* New York: Wiley.

Sroufe, L. A. (1983). Infant-caregiver attachment and patterns of adaptation in preschool: Roots of maladaption and competence. In M. Perlmutter (Ed.), *Minnesota Symposia on child psychology,* Vol. 16. Hillsdale, NJ: Lawrence Erlbaum.

Sroufe, L. A., & Rutter, M. (1984). The domain of developmental psychopathology. *Child Development, 55,* 17–29.

Sullivan, H. S. (1953). *The interpersonal theory of psychiatry.* New York: Norton.

Ullmann, C. (1957). Teachers, peers and test predictors of adjustment. *Journal of Educational Psychology, 48,* 257–267.

Whalen, C. K. (1983). Hyperactivity, learning problems, and the attention deficit disorders. In T. Ollendick & M. Hersen (Eds.), *Handbook of Child Psychopathology,* 151–199.

Younger, A. J., Schwartzman, A. E., & Ledingham, J. (1985). Grade related changes in children's perceptions of aggression and withdrawal in their peers. *Developmental Psychology, 21,* 70–75.

MULTIDIMENSIONAL ASSESSMENT OF SOCIAL ADAPTATION IN CHILDREN AND ADOLESCENTS

Geraldine A. Walsh-Allis and Helen Orvaschel

ABSTRACT

This article describes a multidimensional approach to the assessment of social adaptation in children and adolescents. The child's ability to respond constructively to pressures and expectations imposed by society reflects his or her social adaptational status. The authors advocate a multidimensional approach that covers the roles children play in the social environments inherent to their daily functioning. Reviews of several existing instruments provide examples of current approaches to the assessment of social adaptation in school-age children. Recommendations for further development of this area of measurement are discussed, particularly the need for instruments that describe positive behavioral attributes as well as maladaptive behavior patterns.

Advances in Behavioral Assessment of Children and Families, Vol. 2, pgs. 207–226.
Editor: Ronald J. Prinz

ISBN: 0-89232-481-3

This chapter reviews the assessment of social adaptation in children and adolescents. We will discuss the multidimensional approach needed to improve this area of measurement. Existing definitions of social adaptation in adults and children provide a foundation for understanding the assessment problem. The framework developed to promote an understanding of socially adaptive behaviors outlines the social systems that children and adolescents function within and the roles they play in each social system. A child's ability to perform developmentally appropriate roles within the normative expectations of each social system determines his or her level of adaptive functioning. A multidimensional assessment approach permits coverage of a range of relevant behaviors.

Although we begin with an overview of the conceptual aspects of this topic, a select sample of relevant instruments will also be reviewed. The presentation of these instruments focusses on how well the measures cover the social systems and role expectations corresponding to the age groups assessed. Two types of instruments are presented. The first provides specific information on the child's performance in two or more domains of social adaptation; the second type provides assessments of behavior disturbance or psychopathology in addition to either global or domain-specific measures of social adaptational status.

CONCEPTUAL DEFINITIONS OF SOCIAL ADAPTATION

An individual's social adaptational status reflects the degree to which he or she succeeds in fulfilling roles prescribed by the social environment. Investigators often use different terminology to describe constructs that are similar to, or overlap with social adaptation. Examples of terms used include social health, social adjustment, adaptive functioning and social skills.

In an earlier review of social adjustment measures designed for adult populations, Weissman (1975) described social adjustment as an interplay between the person and his or her social environment. More specifically, she refers to the ability of the individual to perform in roles he or she is expected to fulfill. This description mirrors a very early definition offered by Barrabee, Barrabee and Finnesinger (1955), who defined social adjustment as the degree to which the individual fulfills normative expectations of behaviors associated with his or her prescribed social roles. Using different terminology, and with a focus on child populations, Mercer (1977) described adaptive functioning as "the interface between the behavior of the individual and the norms of a particular group" (p. 86). Similarly, Kellam and Brown (1982) refer to a process of social adaptation that evolves over time and reflects the individual's level of success in social roles.

Although various investigators provide some variety in their definitions of social adaptation and related constructs, they share a common view that the individual's social functioning is externally judged. Social adaptation reflects the fit of the individual in social systems that are inherent to his or her daily functioning. Each social system contributes to determining appropriate roles and behaviors for individuals in that setting.

PAST AND PRESENT APPROACHES TO ASSESSMENT

Interest in social adaptation and its measurement in adults preceded a similar interest in children. In an updated review of social adjustment measures for adults, Weissman, Sholomskas and John (1981) pointed to a continuing lack of social adjustment measures available for child and adolescent populations. A recent review of the literature on the assessment of adaptive functioning in children (Orvaschel & Walsh, 1984) uncovered few well-developed instruments.

Many scale developers design instruments based on the assumption that the absence of maladaptive or pathological behavior indicates that the child is functioning adaptively. This approach provides a detailed assessment of negative adaptation, but ignores the range of positive behaviors inherent in adaptivity. It does not include a gradient of positive behaviors. A few existing instruments reflect a broader conceptual definition of social adaptation by focussing on what social adaptation is rather that what it is not. These instruments are limited in coverage to one or two social systems and often fail to consider the multiple roles children play within each system.

Many measures of social adaptation designed for use with adult populations assess the individual's performance in a variety of roles across several relevant social systems. These typically include the individual's performance in occupational, community, marital, parental and extended family roles. At the present time, measures of social adaptation in school-age children lack the same depth or comprehensiveness.

CLINICAL SIGNIFICANCE OF SOCIAL ADAPTATION

The impetus behind efforts to measure social adaptation in adults grew out of the shift from custodial care of psychiatric patients in institutions to outpatient treatment, community living and efforts aimed at the prevention of psychiatric disorders (Weissman, 1975). Practitioners became increasingly aware that the family life, friendships and work patterns of patients affected treatment and course of illness. Similar concerns regarding the social functioning of children include identifying children at risk for psychiatric disorder, and developing primary and secondary prevention strategies. Garmezy (1974) suggested that insights into the social functioning of children may contribute to our understanding of individuals prone to later disorders. Data presented by Cowen, Pederson, Babigian, Izzo, and Trost (1973) support the implication that social factors in childhood predict referral for mental health problems in adulthood. These investigators followed a cohort of children over a period of 11 to 13 years from ages 6 and 8 at initial intake (1958 to 1961). The children were identified in the primary grades as vulnerable to psychological disorder based on a variety of school adjustment problems. Mental health treatment histories of adults who had been identified in the primary grades as vulnerable were compared to the treatment histories of peers not reported as having school adjustment problems. School records, teachers, peers, and the target child provided information on school adjustment status at intake. At follow-up, children identified as having school adjustment problems at study entry appeared, as adults, in the Monroe County Psychiatric Register disproportionately more frequently than individuals not so identified in the primary grades. Among those in the cohort included in the psychiatric register, more than two-thirds experienced school adjustment problems in the primary grades.

In the study described, peer nominations predicted later psychiatric referral more powerfully than any other single variable. This suggests that children are quite sensitive to maladaptive behaviors among their peers. Perhaps of greater importance, however, is the fact that the children who received negative peer ratings were aware of how their peers perceived them. This observation led the investigators to speculate that when peers perceive maladaptive behaviors in other children, they behave differently toward these already vulnerable youngsters. Peer isolation or ridicule may exacerbate early problems and increase the probability of subsequent, more serious psychological disorder (Cowen et al., 1973).

Results from studies such as the one described above suggest that programs designed to diminish maladaptive behaviors and enhance more socially adaptive behaviors in children may serve as effective primary and secondary prevention strategies. At present our understanding of maladaptive behaviors in children far exceeds our understanding of competencies. We know how children fail to meet the normative expectations placed on them by society, but have little information on the behavior of children who succeed in meeting social expectations. As a result, data needed for the development of prevention efforts focussing on building social competence, as well as decreasing behavior problems, are lacking.

A potential method of identifying specific adaptive behaviors capable of offsetting disorder involves the study of individuals considered to be at risk for disorder for reasons other than early adjustment problems. For instance, children of parents with major depressive disorder are at higher risk for psychological symptoms, treatment for emotional problems, school problems, suicidal behavior and DSM III diagnoses than children of normal parents (Weissman, Prusoff, Gammon, Merikangas, Leckman, & Kidd, 1984). The evidence for this increased risk is supported by studies of adult depressives that find a higher prevalence of depression and other psychological disorders in these patients' parents and other family members (Orvaschel, Weissman, & Kidd, 1980). Information on adaptive or maladaptive traits that increase or decrease subsequent risk of disorder in the offspring of depressed parents can contribute to developing effective prevention strategies.

SOCIAL ADAPTATION AND MENTAL HEALTH

Definitions of social adaptation and related constructs share a common basis in what some investigators refer to as the 'adaptive fit' of an individual within the norms of the given social system. In the context of our current understanding of mental health, social adaptation reflects the component of the individual's healthy or unhealthy functioning measured against an external standard. Each social system provides normative standards for determining the individual's level of social adaptation. This externally judged component of functioning differs from the internally judged component, which Kellam, Branch, Agrawal and Ensminger (1975) refer to as psychological well-being. Psychological well-being is simply how the individual feels. Unlike social adaptation, evaluation of psychological well-being relies on normative standards intrinsic to the individual.

The approach to evaluating mental health that Kellam and his colleagues advocate includes both social adaptation and psychological well-being. Each of these conceptually distinct components of mental health contributes uniquely to the overall functioning of the individual. Psychologically disordered individuals observed in clinical settings often initiate treatment because of disturbances in their psychological well-being. These disturbances appear in the form of symptoms that differ from the normal experience of the individual and make him or her uncomfortable enough to seek therapeutic intervention. Individuals may also be referred for mental health care because of disturbances in social adaptation. Problems in social adaptation often cause discomfort to others, as well as to the patient. Although the two dimensions contribute separately to the individual's mental health, they are not mutually exclusive.

Social adaptation and psychological well-being operate in the determination of mental health status in both adults and children. Unlike adults, however, children rarely initiate their own referrals. Children usually enter treatment because of socially maladaptive behaviors observed by adults in their environment. Awareness of the child's problems and subsequent referral for intervention often do not occur until the child exhibits behaviors that clearly fail to meet the normative role expectations of one or more social systems.

The role of social adaptation in mental health and in the identification of childhood disorders is of particular significance in epidemiologic research. Kellam and Ensminger (1980) observed that social role performance and its relation to psychological disorders become more prominent in the epidemiologic site, such as the classroom, compared to clinical settings. Research in child psychiatric epidemiology relies heavily on externally determined ratings. In order to apply this component of mental health to research in child psychology and psychiatry, however, norms must be developed for both adaptive and deviant social behaviors in a variety of social systems. These norms should cover the various roles children play at different levels in their development.

ASSESSMENT OF SOCIAL ADAPTATION

Those who wish to assess social adaptation in children face the task of identifying specific behaviors that are adaptive in particular settings. We recognize deviant behavior easily, since it often causes discomfort to both troubled individuals and those around them. The range of positive adaptive behaviors, most of which go unnoticed, far exceeds the range of maladaptive behaviors. Developing an instrument that accurately assesses the position of an individual on a gradient of social adaptation, ranging from highly successful to highly maladapted, requires sampling positive as well as negative behaviors.

Adaptive behaviors differ across a variety of settings. Mercer (1977) suggested that all adaptive social behaviors be evaluated in terms of the normative structures of each social system. Similarly, the Life Course-Social Field concept presented by Kellam et al., (1975) includes both the social environment and the child's developmental level in evaluating social adaptation. Individuals undergo a continuous process by which they must modify their behavior to fit the demands or standards of the particular social system. As a child matures, demands and expectations for role performance increase along with the number and complexities of social roles. Effective assessment of role performance requires an understanding of all possible social roles children play, how age characterizes the roles in different ways, and what normative expectations determine effective performance at a given age. Consideration of the range of social roles and behavioral components that determine adaptive fit in children should precede development of social adaptation measures.

BEHAVIORAL COMPONENTS OF SOCIAL ADAPTATION

Recognition of social systems and roles children play assists in the identification of behavioral components relevant to the assessment of social adaptation. Several behavioral domains lend themselves to assessment of performance within each social role. Table 1 outlines the relationships among social systems, roles, and behavioral domains within three broad categories of social adaptation, namely social relationships, occupational roles, and leisure activities. The diagnostic system presented in the third edition of the *Diagnostic and Statistical Manual* (American Psychiatric Association, 1980) suggests the use of such categories in the evaluation of adaptive functioning. The evaluation of social adjustment in adults typically focusses on these areas of social adaptation. Similar categories

Table 1. The Structure of Social Adaptation in Children

Category of Adaptive Behavior	*Social System*	*Specific Role*	*Behavioral Domain*
Social	Home/Family	Son/Daughter	Parent-child relations
	School/Work	Student/Worker	Relationships with teachers, authority
		Peer	Peer relations
	Community/Neighborhood	Peer, playmate	Peer relations
		Neighbor	Relationships with neighbors
			Relationships with authority figures
			Respect for the law
Occupational	Home/Family	Responsible family member	Household responsibilities
	School/Work	Learner/Worker	Academic/work performance
			Conduct in classroom/workplace
Activities	Home/Family	Child	Use of leisure time, hobbies, etc.
	School/Work	Participant, leader	School or work-related clubs, athletics, government, etc.
	Community/Neighborhood	Participant, leader	Play activities, involvement in clubs, sports, scouts, church or synagogue
			Involvement in service-oriented groups

apply to the assessment of social adaptation in children, although the relevant social systems and many childhood roles differ.

Children typically function within three social systems that include home and family, school (or work), and neighborhood or community. The roles of children in social, occupational and leisure activity settings differ qualitatively from those of adults. As a child grows and develops, social roles change both in terms of the number of roles the child fulfills and the behaviors considered appropriate in carrying out those roles. Children's social systems change as they grow older. Some behavioral domains, such as peer relationships and relationships with authority figures, provide opportunities for observing children in roles which cross multiple social systems. For instance, peer interactions occur in the child's role as a student in addition to that of peer or playmate in the community. Likewise, the child's relationships with adults and responses to those in authority occur in all three social systems.

Each social system provides somewhat different normative expectations for determining the adaptive fit of the child. For instance, dancing and singing may be appropriate adaptive behavior in a dance, music or drama class. However, the child who presents these behaviors spontaneously in an arithmetic class exhibits maladaptive behavior. Since roles and behavioral expectations differ across social systems, evaluation of a child's social adaptation includes the ability to recognize norms, to behave accordingly, and to alter his or her behavior according to the situation and the expectations imposed by the social system.

At present, few measures of social adaptation in children include the assessment of a variety of behavioral domains and social roles. Most measures limit the evaluation of social adaptation to behaviors observed in only one social system. Moreover, most available instruments cover a limited age range. Instruments designed to effectively assess social adaptation in adolescents are practically nonexistent.

Comprehensive assessment of social adaptation in children calls for measures that consider the variety of roles children play in the different social systems relevant to their day-to-day functioning. Realistically, a single instrument covers only a sample of relevant behaviors. Individuals who wish to develop informative measures of social adaptation in children face the task of determining which behaviors best represent a child's overall adaptive functioning.

PROBLEMS OF MEASUREMENT

The conceptual framework for identifying behaviors within the context of roles and social systems provides a starting point in developing a strategy to measure social adaptation in school-age children. Measures of social adaptation should consistently and accurately evaluate a child's behavior in a variety of roles and social systems. Individuals familiar with both the child's functioning and the norms of the social system qualify as raters. Items should include behaviors that the rater has the opportunity to observe frequently. Brevity is desirable but not at the expense of the quality of information obtained. Response options must be clear and unambiguous. Efforts at instrument development must include estimates of reliability and validity.

Choice of Rater

Kellam et al. (1975) advocate the use of what they call natural raters in the assessment of social adaptational status in children. Some natural raters, such as parents and teachers, hold central roles in the social system. Natural raters often include those responsible for determining tasks expected of the child and the normative expectations for success in fulfilling assigned social roles.

Members of the peer group may provide ratings of social behaviors in children and adolescents (e.g., Pekarik, Prinz, Liebert, Weintraub, & Neale, 1976; Weintraub, Prinz, & Neale, 1978; Prinz, Swan, Liebert, Weintraub, & Neale, 1978; Cowen et al., 1973). The longitudinal analysis described previously (Cowen et al., 1973) suggests that peer status may be a more powerful predictor of later life adjustment than ratings of school adjustment made by teachers.

Children's self ratings and clinicians' ratings receive little attention in the literature on social adaptation and related constructs.

Child as Informant

Few currently available instruments assess social adaptation by soliciting information directly from the child or adolescent. Only two measures of adaptive functioning reviewed previously (Orvaschel & Walsh, 1984) collected information directly from child informants other than peers (Gammon, John, Prusoff, & Weissman, 1982; Lambert, Bower, & Hartsough, undated). The literature on child psychopathology includes numerous reports on the use of child informants. These discussions focus on parent-child agreement and the particular strengths and weaknesses of each informant. Literature on the assessment of social adaptation and related constructs in children provides little discussion on the use of children as informants.

Reports on parent-child agreement in the assessment of psychopathology vary between studies. Herjanic, Herjanic, Brown, and Wheatt (1976) reported high levels of agreement between parents and children using a structured interview technique. Orvaschel, Weissman, Padian, and Lowe (1981) reported moderate parent-child agreement using a semi-structured interview procedure that assesses current and past psychopathology. Orvaschel et al. (1981) noted that mothers more accurately reported on factual and time-related information while children reported more effectively on their internal states. Thus, optimal assessment of the child's psychological status requires information from both parent and child (Orvaschel et al., 1982). Similar investigations into the effectiveness of parent and child informants in the measurement of social adaptation are needed. Certainly the possibility of soliciting information from children regarding their behavioral and emotional life relevant to social adaptation should not be overlooked.

The child, as a natural rater, crosses all social system boundaries and is familiar with all of his or her roles. The child is also likely to be quite aware of the normative expectations for role performance within each social system and how well he or she performs each role. The previously cited work by Cowen et al. (1973) suggests that peer ratings effectively predict later disorder and that children are aware of their status with peers. Thus, it is likely that information obtained from children on their own adaptive behaviors will also predict later dysfunction. These observations support the plausibility of obtaining information on social adaptation directly from children and suggests that children's perceptions of their behavior are comparable to the perceptions of other natural raters.

One concern in the use of child informants is that children may distort responses in a socially desirable direction. A child may over-report positive social behaviors and under-report maladaptive behaviors. At the present time there is no evidence that children bias responses to questions on social adaptation in the direction of social desirability. A high level of agreement between the child's responses and those of other natural raters in each social system would support the feasibility of relying on the child to assess social adaptation across a number of social systems.

Clinicians as Informants

In contrast to the use of natural raters, one might consider engaging individuals who appear to be experts in collecting information on social adaptation. Few investigators have reported on the use of clinicians as raters of child adaptive behaviors. Clinicians' expertise lies primarily in areas of maladaptive behavior and psychopathology rather than the entire range of social adaptation and psychological well-being. As a result, one may question the role of the clinician as an expert in this area.

Under the circumstances, clinicians' awareness of behavioral problems likely exceeds their awareness of the child's positive attributes and overall adaptive functioning. From the standpoint of training and experience, clinicians provide an excellent resource for integrating information on a child's behavior and can often provide excellent assessments of a child's overall functioning. However, their relative lack of direct observation time limits their ability to provide more quantitative ratings of specific behaviors, similar to those obtained from parents and teachers. Information on the frequencies of specific adaptive behaviors may be obtained more directly from the same sources the clinician uses, namely the child, the parent and the teacher.

Lessing, Williams and Revelle (1981) reported low levels of agreement in parent-clinician and teacher-clinician comparisons of responses to items reflecting social competence and emotional stability. In contrast, they reported a fairly high level of agreement between parents and teachers. These findings provide evidence against the use of clinician ratings of social adaptation. However, the low agreement reported by these authors may stem from the use of psychodynamically oriented clinicians who may tend to report interpretations rather than observed behaviors. Further investigations into the use of clinician raters should take into account the paradigmatic orientation of the clinician.

Parents as Informants

Parents inform on virtually every aspect of child functioning, including physical and psychosocial development, health, symptoms of psychopathology, academic performance and, so on. In the assessment of social adaptation, a parent is the most obvious natural rater within the family. However, there are limitations to the information parents can provide on children's behaviors outside the home. As children grow older, they spend more time with peers and less time under the direct supervision of parents. Parental awareness of a child's behavior in the community and in the school setting diminishes as the child grows older unless problems occur. As a result one might suspect that the reliability of information obtained from parents on behaviors outside of the home will depend on the age of the child being assessed and the degree to which the behaviors are problematic.

Teacher Raters

The use of teachers as informants on children's social adaptation is most productive in elementary school, when children function within a limited environment. In elementary school one teacher usually presents most or all academic subjects to a group of children, and often oversees their behavior in other situations, including the playground and lunchroom. The elementary school teacher has ample opportunity to observe behaviors related to the child's academic performance, classroom behavior and peer relationships.

Once children reach middle and high school years, teachers have less opportunity to get to know each child well. Fewer opportunities occur to observe children in settings other than the classroom. In more advanced school years, one teacher rarely observes the same child in the variety of situations to which he or she must adjust. A child may adapt well in a situation such as woodshop or gym, where he or she may interact with others and move around. The same child may have difficulty in a more regimented and less interactive situation such as a history lecture. Similarly, some children do well in sports competition but interact poorly in more intellectually competitive situations, such as a debate. High school teachers lack the opportunity to observe this variety of behaviors. Although one might consider collecting information on social adaptation from multiple teacher informants, this alternative is cumbersome, time-consuming, and difficult to integrate.

Peer Raters

Children's peers serve as natural raters in school and in the neighborhood or community. A variety of investigators evaluated the social functioning of children and adolescents in school with peer measures (Lambert, Hartsough, & Bower, 1979; Pekarik et al., 1976; Prinz et al., 1978; Fisher, 1978; Rubenstein, Fisher, & Iker, 1975). Using peers to describe other children's adaptive functioning in the neighborhood is difficult because of the lack of structure in most community settings.

Miller and Maruyama (1976) found peer ratings of child behavior to be stable over time. As mentioned previously, peer ratings appear to be more powerful predictors of later dysfunction than information obtained from teachers (Cowen et al., 1973). Unfortunately many currently available sociometric instruments require considerable time to administer and score. Use of sociometrics is sometimes hampered by the reluctance of school officials and by the requirement of parental permission for each participating child (LaGreca, 1981). Many of the currently available sociometric instruments do not provide information on specific areas of social adaptation (Van Hasselt, Hersen, Whitehill, & Bellack, 1979). Nonetheless, peers provide useful information on interpersonal behavior and peer acceptance in other children.

Method of Administration

Among currently available instruments that measure social adaptation in children, informant-rated behavior checklists predominate. Scale developers must choose between the rapid and inexpensive administration characteristic of behavior checklists and rating scales, and the more lengthy and costly administration of structured or semi-structured interview procedures. The ultimate use of the data should dictate the method of administration chosen.

Most currently available measures of child social adaptation screen child behaviors to rule out maladaptation. More comprehensive assessments are needed which provide detailed profiles of children's adaptive functioning, so that information predictive of later adjustment can be obtained and utilized to develop prevention strategies. Although administering structured or semi-structured interview procedures requires a greater expenditure of time and energy, such procedures may be more effective in collecting detailed information.

Item Development

The multidimensional approach to measuring social adaptation in children advocated here requires the collection of data on behaviors observed by natural raters in a variety of social systems, including home, school and community. An effective approach to item development incorporates considerations of construct and content validity.

Construct validity reflects the degree to which a measure effectively assesses a theoretical construct or trait. Developers of social adaptation instruments must provide clear working definitions of social adaptation in children that are stated in positive terms rather than simply as the absence of psychopathology. In this review, social adaptation is defined as the child's ability to perform in expected roles characteristic of his or her day-to-day functioning.

Content validity refers to the representativeness of the items, coverage of major aspects of the theoretical construct, and whether that coverage is in appropriate proportions. Behavioral domains that characterize the child's adaptive functioning must be identified. Specific behaviors the child demonstrates in order to fulfill role expectations characterize his or her adaptation to the relevant social systems (Home/Family, Neighborhood/Community, School or Work). Natural raters within each social system may serve as resources for item development by providing information on behaviors which reflect various levels of adaptation in the particular social environment. The potential universe of behaviors which characterize social adaptation across different ages and in multiple social systems far exceeds the number of items one can reasonably include in a single measure. It becomes necessary to narrow the field to those behaviors which most effectively predict later adjustment and which adequately reflect the child's social adaptation.

Reliability and Validity

The reliability of an instrument is often determined by its temporal stability, internal consistency, and interrater agreement. Although evaluation of internal consistency and temporal stability present no special problems in the assessment of social adaptation, determining interrater agreement may be difficult.

The evaluation of interrater reliability requires two or more raters who, ideally, are exposed to the same behaviors relevant to the social adaptation domains of interest. Other than the child, only one natural rater may be available. Elementary school children usually spend most of the day with one teacher. A second rater with comparable information does not exist in this situation. In contrast, high school students have multiple teachers, but none of them are likely to know the child well. High school teachers spend relatively little time with each child and sample different behaviors and situations. These factors may decrease reliability between raters.

Validation poses particular problems for scale developers. Many investigators do not agree on what constitutes adaptive behavior in children. In addition, methods of scale administration, choice of raters, and the social systems and behavioral domains assessed often differ. It follows that no consistent comparison criteria exist for validating social adaptation instruments.

The choice of appropriate comparison measures in estimating the criterion-related validity of any instrument must consider the intended use of the instrument being developed. Social adaptation scales designed to predict future adjustment or psychiatric status may be compared to subsequently administered social adjustment and psychopathology scales. If the instrument evaluates the child's current level of social adaptation, the investigator must find an appropriate concurrent measure to use for comparison purposes. For instruments designed to assess the spectrum of positive and negative adaptive behaviors, valid concurrent measures are lacking.

CURRENTLY AVAILABLE MEASURES OF SOCIAL ADAPTATION

Brief reviews of several existing scales that measure social adaptation in children or adolescents are presented. Instead of presenting an exhaustive review of all relevant instruments, we offer examples of instruments with useful assessment properties and available psychometric data. Measures that either assess multiple dimensions of social adaptation or provide indices of both psychopathology and social adaptation are included. Increased awareness of the gaps in our understanding of social adaptation and effective measurement of this construct will hopefully stimulate more involvement in this underdeveloped area of research.

Child Behavior Checklist (CBCL) and Teacher Report Form (TRF)

The parent version of the CBCL is a brief self-administered rating scale initially designed to assess behavior problems in children aged 4 to 16. A Social Competence section was added because of the author's belief that systems for describing and classifying child psychopathology should reflect positive and adaptive competencies as well as maladaptive characteristics (Achenbach, 1978). The Social Competence section includes 16 items that cover interpersonal behaviors, activities and school functioning. Ratings are based retrospectively on behaviors observed over the previous six months.

The development of social competence items followed a review of the existing literature on indices of social competence. Item analysis and feedback obtained from parents, clinicians and paraprofessionals in child guidance clinics contributed to subsequent revisions of the CBCL Social Competence section. Social Competence items reflect involvement and attainment in areas of activities, social participation, and school. The Activities subscale reflects the amount and quality of the child's participation in sports, nonsport hobbies, leisure activities, games, jobs, and chores. The Social subscale covers membership and participation in organizations, number of friends and contacts with them, and behaviors with parents, siblings, and peers. The School subscale reflects a summary of the child's performance in academic subjects, type of school placement, promotion status, and presence or absence of problems in school. Normative data are available for all age-sex groups on behavior problem and social competence scales.

The authors assessed interrater reliability of the CBCL Social Competence scales by collecting ratings from both parents of 168 children referred for mental health services. The intraclass correlation coefficient for the Social Competence total score was .97. One week test-retest reliability for ratings obtained from 72 mothers of referred children produced an intraclass correlation of .99. Ratings completed by 12 mothers of non-referred children provided data to establish three month test-retest reliability. The intraclass correlation for Social Competence was .97 (Achenbach & Edelbrock, 1981). Highly significant differences ($p < .001$) between normal and clinical samples for all Social Competence scales of the CBCL provide evidence of their discriminant validity (Achenbach, 1978; Achenbach & Edelbrock, 1979).

The TRF parallels the parental CBCL. Teacher ratings are obtained for children 6 to 16-years-old. The Adaptive Functioning section includes four questions, each rated on a seven-point scale. These ratings reflect whether the stated attribute is characteristic of the child "much less" or "much more" than other children the same age. Teachers rate behaviors observed over the previous two months. The four items cover how hard the child is working, how appropriately he or she is behaving, how much he or she is learning and how happy he or she is. Each rating constitutes a subscale. The sum of individual item ratings provides a total Adaptive Functioning score. A separate school performance section reflects mean performance on up to six academic subjects. Normative data are currently available for all age-sex groups (Edelbrock & Achenbach, 1984; Edelbrock & Achenbach, 1985).

Preliminary estimates of interrater reliability compared ratings obtained from teachers and teacher assistants (Edelbrock, 1984, personal communication). Pearson correlation coefficients of .76 for Work, .84 for Behaving Appropriately, .76 for Learning, .71 for Happy and .81 for Adaptive Functioning Total Score were obtained. One-week test-retest reliabilities, expressed as Pearson correlation coefficients, are .99 for School Performance; .93 for Work Behavior and Learning; .78 for Happy, and .95 for Adaptive Functioning Total Score (Edelbrock, Greenbaum, & Conover, 1985). Significant differences ($p < .001$) between normal and disturbed boys, aged 6–11 on each of the Adaptive Functioning and School Performance scales provides evidence of discriminant validity (Achenbach & Edelbrock, 1984).

The parent version of the CBCL and the TRF are primarily psychopathology scales which include estimates of social competence and adaptive functioning. The scale authors recommend against use of the assessments of social competence and adaptive functioning apart from the remainder of the CBCL. These instruments produce only rough assessments of social adaptation in children. However, these scales assess the child's functioning in a number of specific behavioral domains relevant to social adaptation and complement the assessment of psychopathology.

Health Resources Inventory (HRI)

The HRI measures the presence of positive behavioral attributes which contribute to personal and social competence. This 54-item behavior rating scale was initially designed for completion by the classroom teacher of 6 to 8 year old children (Gesten, 1976). A subsequently developed composite scale, the CARS-HRI, includes 20 items from the HRI as well as several items from the Classroom Adjustment Rating Scale (Lorion, Cowen, & Caldwell, 1975). The CARS measures maladaptive classroom behavior. The CARS-HRI assesses maladaptive and positive adaptive behavior in children aged 10 to 12 (Wright & Cowen, 1982).

HRI items were initially derived from prior health scales, statements about healthy functioning in the literature and health characteristics suggested by teachers, mental health professionals and parents. An initial item pool of 79 items was reduced to 54 on the basis of teachers' perceptions of how easily they could rate the item and the amount of variability they expected among children they rated. Redundant and ambiguously worded items were eliminated. A principal components factor analysis produced a stable five-factor solution accounting for 71% of total scale variance. The HRI provides separate scores for each subscale and a composite index of social competence. The subscales include Good Student, Gutsiness, Peer Sociability, Rule Conformity and Frustration Tolerance.

Four to six-week test-retest reliability obtained from ratings on 60 children in first to third grade ranged from .72 (Peer Sociability) to .92 (Rules). Girls obtained significantly higher scores than boys ($p < .01$) on all but the Gutsiness factor. Urban children scored significantly lower than suburban and rural children ($p < .01$) on all but Frustration Tolerance. Gesten (1976) demonstrated the scale's ability to discriminate levels of competence in a normal population using an extreme groups contrast. One member in each of 10 teacher pairs rated their pupils as either most competent, middle competent or least competent. The second teacher independently completed HRI ratings on nine children in the class (three from each competence group). Mean competence differences among the criterion groups on all HRI subscales and total scores were significant at the $p < .001$ level using one way analysis of variance. The author presents significant negative correlations between HRI and CARS scores as evidence of concurrent validity.

Gesten (1976) stated that the HRI should not be considered a generalized measure of social competence and pointed to the need for further work in developing a less situationally based understanding of competence. He recommended sampling competence behaviors in settings other than the school, such as the home or neighborhood.

Adaptive Behavior Inventory for Children (ABIC)

The ABIC is a 243 item structured interview developed by Mercer and Lewis (1977), which assesses social role performance in 5 to 11 year old children. A trained interviewer records parent responses on a precoded interview form. The first 35 questions are asked for all children. Subsequent sections are age-graded. The interviewer begins with the section that corresponds to the chronological age of the child, but may move backward until a baseline of functioning is established. The interview proceeds through subsequent items until a ceiling is reached.

The ABIC provides a cross-sectional assessment of the child's adaptation in the social systems relevant to daily functioning. ABIC items are organized into six subscales defined a priori by the scale authors to represent the social systems in which the child functions. Scale items cover the child's role in the home and with family, as a citizen in the community, relations with peers, behavior in the school setting, ability to manage finances and self-maintenance, and coping skills.

The ABIC is used in making school placement decisions among children judged to be mildly mentally retarded. Item development was initially based on information obtained from mothers of children labeled as retarded by the school system as well as mothers of children in regular public school classes. Item ratings reflect the frequency of the observed behavior (never, sometimes, or often). Analyses of ABIC items showed that sex differences did not affect total scores, since items that favored males balanced those which favored females. Socioeconomic differences were similarly balanced, so that SES accounted for less than one percent of the variance on ABIC scaled scores (Mercer, 1977).

Normative data used to calculate standard scores and average scaled scores of ABIC subscales were collected on a sample of 185 children aged 5 to 11 (Mercer, 1977). The sample consisted of equivalent numbers of black, Hispanic and white respondents. Split-half reliability estimates obtained from the normative sample range from .76 (Peer Relations subscale for 11 year old children) to .98 (average scaled score for 10 year old children). Interrater reliability estimates were collected from 332 participants attending 10 different training workshops. Participants independently recorded parent responses from an unrehearsed interview conducted by the workshop instructor. Weighted mean standard deviations calculated across the 10 groups range from .9 (Earner/Consumer) to 2.2 (Self Maintenance). The scale authors reported that these results indicated high interobserver agreement on the scoring of parental responses. Agreement between parent informants were not reported.

The scale authors have not reported validity studies on the ABIC. Other authors (e.g., Oakland & Feigenbaum, 1980; Scott, Mastenbrook, Fisher & Gridley, 1982; Kazimour & Reschly, 1981) have questioned the applicability of the norms obtained in the California standardization sample to other populations.

Determination of the ABIC's applicability as an overall measure of social adaptation in children requires further investigations into its reliability and validity in nonreferred populations. Compared to most of the currently available instrumentation, however, the ABIC provides assessments which are more similar to those available for adult populations.

Conclusion

From both a theoretical and a practical perspective, the assessment of social functioning in children and adolescents is a significant though underdeveloped area. Gesten (1976) pointed out nine years ago that little was known about normal behavior, and even less about effective or optimal human functioning. Although more recent efforts have begun to fill the gaps in our knowledge of healthy adaptive functioning, our ignorance continues to far exceed our knowledge in this area.

Several questions must be addressed before we proceed in this area of assessment. We presently lack information on characteristics inherent to the child or the chosen raters that might bias measurement of social adaptational status. In the development of the CBCL and TRF, significant differences (all at $p < .05$ or better) were found between socioeconomic groups on Social Competence and Adaptive Functioning scales (Achenbach, 1978; Achenbach & Edelbrock, 1979; Edelbrock and Achenbach, 1984), suggesting that expectations placed on children differ according to their socioeconomic status. It is equally likely that adaptive behaviors vary among children with different ethnic, racial, and geographic characteristics. If significant differences exist, is it possible to develop informative measures that provide unbiased assessments of social adaptation in children from a variety of backgrounds?

We may begin to answer some of these questions by collecting cross-sectional data on large population groups. Such information can provide needed baseline data to improve our current understanding of the range of socially adaptive behaviors in school-age children. Longitudinal data may contribute to evaluating the impact of social adaptation on subsequent social functioning and psychiatric status among normal children as well as those known to be at increased risk for psychiatric disorder. The multidimensional nature of adaptive functioning should be considered in the development of effective assessment measures. These instruments will, in turn, provide the tools necessary for acquiring empirical data on human development and psychopathology so that primary prevention and intervention strategies can proceed.

REFERENCES

Achenbach, T. M. (1978). The Child Behavior Profile: I. Boys aged 6–11. *Journal of Consulting and Clinical Psychology, 46,* 478–485.

Achenbach, T. M., & Edelbrock, C. S. (1981). Behavior problems and competencies reported by parents of normal and disturbed children aged four to sixteen. *Monographs for the Society for Research in Child Development, 46,* 1–82.

American Psychiatric Association. (1980). *Diagnostic and statistical manual of mental disorders, third edition.* Washington, DC: APA.

Barrabee, P., Barrabee, E. L., & Finnesinger, J. E. (1955). A normative social adjustment scale. *American Journal of Psychiatry, 112,* 252–259.

Cowen, E. L., Pederson, A. Babigian, H., Izzo, L. D., & Trost, M. A. (1973). Long-term follow-up of early detected vulnerable children. *Journal of Consulting and Clinical Psychology, 41,* 438–446.

Edelbrock, C. S., & Achenbach, T. M. (1984). The teacher version of the Child Behavior Profile: I. Boys ages 6–11. *Journal of Consulting and Clinical Psychology, 52,* 207–217.

Edelbrock, C. S. & Achenbach, T. M. (1985). The teacher version of the Child Behavior Profile: II. Boys aged 12–16 and girls aged 6–11 and 12–16. Submitted for publication.

Edelbrock, C. S., Greenbaum, R., & Conover, N. (1985). Reliability and concurrent relations between the teacher version of the Child Behavior Checklist and the Revised Connors Teacher Rating Scale. *Journal of Abnormal Child Psychology, 13,* 295–303.

Fisher, L. (1978). Peer judgement of competence in junior high school classrooms. *Developmental Psychology, 14,* 187–188.

Gammon, G. D., John, K., Prusoff, B. A., & Weissman, M. M. (1982). *Assessment of social adjustment in children and adolescents: Development and testing of a semi-structured interview.* Paper presented at the 29th Annual Meeting of the American Academy of Child Psychiatry, Washington, D.C., December.

Garmezy, N. (1974). The study of competence in children at risk for severe psychopathology. In E. J. Anthony & C. Koupernic (Eds.), *The child and his family,* Vol. 3. *Children at psychiatric risk.* New York: John Wiley & Sons.

Gesten, E. L. (1976). A health resources inventory: The development of a measure of the personal and social competence of primary-grade children. *Journal of Consulting and Clinical Psychology, 44,* 775–786.

Herjanic, B., Herjanic, M., Brown, F., & Wheatt, T. (1976). Are children reliable reporters? *Journal of Abnormal Child Psychology, 3,* 41–48.

Kazimour, K. K., & Reschly, D. J. (1981). Investigation of the norms and concurrent validity of the Adaptive Behavior Inventory for Children. *American Journal of Mental Deficiency, 85,* 512–520.

Kellam, S. G., Branch, J. D., Agrawal, K. C., & Ensminger, M. E. (1975). *Mental health and going to school.* Chicago: University of Chicago Press.

Kellam, S. G., & Brown, C. H. (1982). *Social adaptational and psychological antecedants in first grade of adolescent psychopathology ten years later.* Presented at the Research Workshop on Preventive Aspects of Suicide and Affective Disorders Among Adolescents and Young Adults, Harvard School of Public Health and Harvard School of Medicine, Boston, MA, December.

Kellam, S. G., & Ensminger, M. E. (1980). Theory and method in child psychiatric epidemiology. In F. Earls (Ed.), *Studying children epidemiologically,* Vol. 1 (pp. 145–180), *International Monograph Series in Psychosocial Epidemiology* (B. Z. Locke & A. E. Slaby, Series Eds.). New York: Neale Watson.

LaGreca, A. M. (1981). Peer acceptance: The correspondence between children's sociometric scores and teachers' ratings of peer interactions. *Journal of Abnormal Child Psychology, 9,* 167–178.

Lambert, N. M., Bower, E. M., & Hartsough, C. S. (undated). *A process for the assessment of effective student functioning: Technical report.* Unpublished manuscript.

Lambert, N. M., Hartsough, C. S., & Bower, E. M. (1979). *A process for the assessment of effective student functioning: Administration and use manual.* Monterey, CA: Publishers Test Service.

Lessing, E. E., Williams, V., & Revelle, W. (1981). Parallel forms of the IJR Behavior Checklist for parents, teachers and clinicians. *Journal of Consulting and Clinical Psychology, 49,* 34–50.

Lorion, R. P., Cowen, E. L., & Caldwell, R. A. (1975). Normative and parametric analyses for school maladjustment. *American Journal of Community Psychology, 3,* 291–301.

Mercer, J. R. (1977). *System of Multicultural Pluralistic Assessment: Technical manual.* New York: Grune & Stratton.

Mercer, J., & Lewis, J. (1977). *System of Multicultural Pluralistic Assessment.* New York: The Psychological Corporation.

Miller, N., & Maruyama, G. (1976). Ordinal position and peer popularity. *Journal of Personality and Social Psychology, 33,* 123–131.

Oakland, T., & Feigenbaum, D. (1980). Comparisons of the psychometric characteristics of the Adaptive Behavior Inventory for Children for different subgroups of children. *Journal of School Psychology, 18,* 307–316.

Orvaschel, H., Puig-Antich, J., Chambers, W., Tabrizi, M. A., & Johnson, R. (1982). Retrospective assessment of prepubertal major depression with the Kiddie-SADS-E. *Journal of the American Academy of Child Psychiatry, 21,* 392–397.

Orvaschel, H., & Walsh G. A. (1984). *The assessment of adaptive functioning in children: A review of existing measures suitable for epidemiological and clinical services research* (Report No. 84-1343). Washington, DC: Department of Health and Human Services.

Orvaschel, H., Weissman, M. M., & Kidd, K. K. (1980). Children and depression: The children of depressed parents; the childhood of depressed patients; depression in children. *Journal of Affective Disorders, 2,* 1–16.

Orvaschel, H., Weissman, M. M., Padian, N., & Lowe, T. L. (1981). Assessing psychopathology in children of psychiatrically disturbed parents. *Journal of the American Academy of Child Psychiatry, 20,* 112–122.

Pekarik, E. G., Prinz, R. J., Liebert, D. E., Weintraub, S., & Neale, J. M. (1976). The Pupil Evaluation Inventory: A sociometric technique for assessing children's social behavior. *Journal of Abnormal Child Psychology, 4,* 83–97.

Prinz, R. J., Swan, G., Liebert, D., Weintraub, S., & Neale, J. M. (1978). ASSESS: Adjustment Scales for Sociometric Evaluation of Secondary School Students. *Journal of Abnormal Child Psychology, 6,* 493–501.

Rubenstein, G., Fisher, L., & Iker, H. (1975). Peer observation of student behavior in elementary school classrooms. *Developmental Psychology, 11,* 867–868.

Scott, L. B., Mastenbrook, J. L., Fisher, A. T., & Gridley, G. C. (1982). Adaptive Behavior Inventory for Children: The need for local norms. *Journal of School Psychology, 20,* 39–44.

Van Hasselt, V. B., Hersen, M., Whitehill, M. B., & Bellack, A. S. (1979). Social skill assessment and training for children: An evaluative review. *Behavorial Research and Therapy, 17,* 413–437.

Weintraub, S., Prinz, R. J., & Neale, J. M. (1978). Peer evaluation of the competence of children vulnerable to psychopathology. *Journal of Abnormal Child Psychology, 6,* 461–473.

Weissman, M. M. (1975). The assessment of social adjustment: A review of techniques. *Archives of General Psychiatry, 32,* 357–365.

Weissman, M. M., Prusoff, B. A., Gammon, G. D., Merikangas, K. R., Leckman, J. F., & Kidd, K. K. (1984). Psychopathology in the children (ages 6–18) of depressed and normal parents. *Journal of the American Academy of Child Psychiatry, 23,* 78–84.

Weissman, M. M., Sholomskas, D., & John, K. (1981). The assessment of social adjustment: An update. *Archives of General Psychiatry, 38,* 1250–1258.

Wright, S., & Cowen, E. L. (1982). Student perception of school environment and its relationship to mood, achievement, popularity and adjustment. *American Journal of Community Psychology, 10,* 687–703.

METHODOLOGICAL ISSUES IN THE USE OF SOCIOMETRICS FOR SELECTING CHILDREN FOR SOCIAL SKILLS RESEARCH AND TRAINING

Sharon L. Foster, Debora Bell-Dolan, and Ellen S. Berler

ABSTRACT

Sociometric assessment is commonly used to select children for social skills training and research. This chapter examines possible ways different uses of sociometrics can yield different subject samples. Comparisons of same-sex and opposite sex scoring of peer nominations and peer ratings yielded moderate correlations of scores but poor extreme-group overlap, using Coie, Dodge, and Coppotelli's (1982) method of selecting extreme groups. Similar findings were ob-

Advances in Behavioral Assessment of Children and Families, Vol. 2, pgs. 227–248.
Editor: Ronald J. Prinz

ISBN: 0-89232-481-3

tained when work and play sociometric data were compared. Weighted and unweighted scores were highly similar. Teacher nominations of children in need of social skills training and those who could serve as models overlapped poorly with peer-designated social status groups. Finally, comparisons of children who receive parental consent to participate in social skills research with those without consent indicated that nonconsenter groups may be less popular than consenter groups, according to teacher ratings.

Interest in children's peer relations and social skills has exploded in the past decade. As a result, large literatures examining both the behavioral correlates of peer status and the impact of social skills training have emerged. While various methodological approaches characterize these literatures, both social skills training and behavioral correlates studies frequently examine the characteristics of selected samples of children, often chosen because they are either well accepted or poorly accepted by peers.

One prevalent method of selecting such populations employs sociometric assessment, first popularized in the 1930s. Sociometric measures evaluate children's relative standing in the peer group, and commonly take one of three forms (Hymel, 1983). With *nomination sociometrics,* children name specific peers who fit designated positive or negative criteria (e.g., ''Pick three children with whom you would most/least like to play''). *Rating-scale sociometrics* require children to rate peers using Likert scales along specified dimensions (e.g., ''Rate how much you like each person on this list''). With *paired comparison sociometrics,* each child is presented with all possible pairs of classmates, and asked to choose between the two (e.g., ''Pick which one you would like to play with'').

Over 30 studies published in the last two decades have employed sociometric assessment to select samples of children either for social skills training or for known-groups comparisons (Berler, Allen, & Burge, 1985; Foster, DeLawyer, & Guevremont, in press). With large literatures come discrepant findings, and this area is no exception. Noncomparability of samples across studies is one obvious source of discrepancy, and subject selection procedures that are biased or idiosyncratic decrease the generality of research findings.

The purpose of this chapter is to explore three potential sources of subject selection bias related to selection of target populations for social skills research and training. Initial consideration focuses on whether variations in sociometric format and scoring lead to selection of different samples of children. The second section of the chapter examines how samples of children identified by sociometric assessment compare to those selected based on teacher assessment or referral. Finally, the potential influence of parental consent on subject selection is explored.

VARIATIONS IN SOCIOMETRIC FORMAT AND SCORING

Despite widespread use of sociometric measures, considerable procedural diversity characterizes their format, administration, and scoring: Berler et al. (1985)

identified over 25 different variations in sociometric assessment methods. This raises the disturbing possibility that such variations create major incomparabilities in samples across studies.

Sociometric procedures can vary along three general dimensions. The first involves the peer group who completes the assessment: should same-sex only or both-sex peers evaluate each child? should only classmates in the same class complete an assessment, or should each child be evaluated by peers who share only a few classes with him or her? The second domain involves the type of sociometric task employed, including general structure of the sociometric (nominations, ratings, or paired comparison), the types of questions asked (e.g., workmate vs. playmate vs. best-friend preferences), and, with nomination sociometrics, the number of nominations requested (e.g., two, three, or unlimited). The final dimension pertains to procedures both for tabulating scores to represent a child's social status and for using these scores to select members of particular social status groupings (e.g., weighted vs. unweighted scores, selection of popular children based only on positive nominations vs. based on a combination of positive minus negative nominations).

Here we examine three areas of comparability across variations in sociometric methods: (a) same-sex vs. both-sex computation of social status, (b) play vs. work preference scores, and (c) weighted vs. unweighted scoring procedures.

Gender of Raters in Scoring Sociometric Instruments

One area of diversity in sociometric assessment lies in whether scores are based only on the evaluations of same-sex peers, or the entire peer group. This issue arises from findings that, at least for older elementary school students, children receive more negative nominations and lower sociometric ratings from opposite-sex than from same-sex peers (Asher & Hymel, 1981; Edelson, 1980; Reese, 1962).

A few studies address this question. Landau, Milich, and Whitten (1984) compared positive and negative nominations of kindergarten boys provided by boys with those provided by girls. Correlations were fairly high for both total positive (r = .67) and negative (r = .74) nominations.

In other studies, investigators have allowed children to nominate or rate peers of both sexes, then compared scores based on same-sex only, opposite-sex only, and/or both-sex evaluations. Edelson (1980) presented data indicating that same-sex play ratings were only modestly correlated ($r < .38$) with opposite-sex ratings provided by children in grades 4–6. Asher and Hymel (1981) reported more extensive data based on nomination and rating scale sociometrics collected with children in grades 3–5. Although same-sex-only and opposite-sex-only scores for positive and negative nominations and play ratings only correlated between .41 and .54, much higher correlations emerged for comparisons of same-sex-only versus both-sex data (rs between .83 and .96). This increment is not surprising, given that same-sex data comprise a subset of the data used to compute both-sex scores. Nonetheless, the strongly positive relationship between these scores implies that the two scoring methods should yield comparable samples.

To replicate and extend these findings, we examined Foster and Ritchey's (1985) peer nomination data from 125 fourth through sixth-grade children along with peer rating data from a separate sample of 114 second-graders and 121 fifth-graders from 12 classrooms. Both samples of children provided play- and work-mate preferences. In the first study, children nominated two most and least preferred classmates, with no restriction on the sex of their choices. In the second study, participants rated each of the boys and girls in their classrooms using 5-point Likert scales. Using Coie, Dodge, and Coppotelli's (1982) method, four scores were derived from the nomination data: (a) ''like-most'' (LM) scores (z scores based on total numbers of positive nominations within each class); (b) ''like-least'' (LL) scores (z scores based on total negative nominations), (c) social preference (SP) scores (LM − LL), and (d) social impact (SI) scores (LM + LL). Rating scale data were averaged for each child and transformed to z scores within classrooms. Correlations among both-sex, opposite-sex, and same-sex scores for play and work nomination and rating data are presented in Table 1.

As Edelson (1980) and Asher and Hymel (1981) found, opposite-sex nomination and rating scores correlated only moderately at best with equivalent same-sex scores. Same-sex and both-sex scoring correlated more highly, for both work and play preferences for both nominations and ratings.

Despite these high correlations, groups of children selected using different scoring strategies might not be the same. To examine this, we computed how

Table 1. Correlations (rs) of Same-, Opposite, and Both-sex Scoring of Sociometric Measures

Variable	*Same-sex vs. Opposite Sex*		*Same-sex vs. Both-Sex*	
Peer nominations (n = 125)	Play	Work	Play	Work
Like-most scores	−.04	−.04	.94**	.93**
Like-least scores	.43**	.30**	.83**	.78**
Social preference score	.29*	.20*	.91**	.88**
Social impact score	.07	.05	.85**	.80**
Peer ratings				
Grade 2 (n = 114)	.13	.26**	.69**	.73**
Grade 5 (n = 122)	.26**	.31**	.67**	.74**

Note: $^*p < .05$
$^{**}p < .005$.

much similarity existed between accepted, rejected, neglected and controversial groups selected from same-sex vs. both-sex nominations. Coie et al.'s (1982) cutoffs were used: for "accepted" children, $SP < -1$, $LL < 0$, and $LM > 0$; for "rejected" children, $SP < -1$, $LL > 1$, $LM < 0$; for "neglected," $SI < -1$, $LL < 0$, $LM < 0$; for "controversial," $SI > 1$, $LL > 0$, $LM > 0$. To establish comparable criteria for peer ratings, accepted and rejected children were designated as those with z scores above 1 and under -1, respectively (neglected and controversial children cannot be selected using peer ratings). As indicated in Table 2, 12% to 69% of the children selected as members of extreme groups overlapped for same-sex versus both-sex scoring. Many comparisons indicated less than 50% agreement on selected children, in spite of the fact that Coie et al.'s (1982) scoring system produces relatively large numbers of children in each status group.

Examination of patterns of disagreement for play nominations indicated that 14% of the children classified as accepted by one method were classified as controversial by the other, with 36% classified into an "unclassifiable" group. Rarely were children cross-classified as both accepted and rejected (3%) or neglected (3%). Children designated as neglected were most likely to be unclassified (35%) or classified as rejected (18%) when disagreements occurred; rejected children were most likely to be classified neglected (34%). Controversial children were most likely to be cross-classified as accepted (36%) or unclassifiable (36%).

Disagreements on work nominations had similar patterns. Disagreements on accepted children occurred most often when these children were designated

Table 2. Percentage Overlap of Extreme Groups Selected by Same-sex vs. Both-sex Sociometric Scoring Procedures

	Social Status Group			
Variable	*Accepted*	*Rejected*	*Neglected*	*Controversial*
Nominations				
Play	58%	69%	53%	29%
Work	49%	45%	42%	35%
Ratings				
Grade 2: Play	29%	44%		
Grade 5: Play	12%	52%		
Grade 2: Work	36%	46%		
Grade 5: Work	38%	43%		

Note: Overlaps computed by formula: # overlapping children/total number selected for that group by either method. Neglected and controversial children were not discernible from peer ratings.

unclassified (33%), neglected (12%), or controversial (6%). Neglected children were most often cross-classified as rejected (24%) or unclassified (29%); rejected children were cross-designated neglected (30%) or unclassified (24%). Disagreements about controversial children took the form of cross-classification as unclassified (47%) or accepted (18%).

Thus, extreme group composition across studies may be quite different, depending on whether same- or both-sex scoring are used to form extreme groups using the Coie et al. (1982) method. These data indicate that reasonably large numbers of children classified as rejected in one study could be part of the neglected population in another investigation. Similar overlap exists between controversial and popular children. The extent to which this less-than-perfect overlap actually influences substantive findings of known-group comparisons, particularly regarding peer interaction styles, needs to be evaluated. However, to the extent that these disagreements imply within-group heterogeneity on the variables of interest, one could expect investigators to have difficulty finding between-group differences, especially when the number of subjects per social status group is fairly small.

In the absence of such data, Asher and Hymel (1981) recommend that investigators select one sociometric method over another based on the purposes of the assessment. The size of the peer group used to assess the child is another important consideration, especially if only same-sex peers supply the ratings. Even with moderate parental consent rates (e.g., 60–70%, the norm for our studies), sociometric scores based solely on same-sex scores in small classes or classrooms with uneven sex distributions would yield results based on an uncomfortably small number of peer responses. No systematic studies have established the minimum number of peers required to yield a stable and internally consistent index of peer acceptance and rejection. Nonetheless, from a psychometric standpoint, a larger number of peer evaluators is preferable to a small one for optimum stability.

Work vs. Play Preferences

A second area of potential incomparability across samples is the type of sociometric judgments researchers ask children to make. Sociometric questions range from asking children to name or rate who they generally like to requesting names or ratings of peers favored for specific activities (e.g., to go to a movie). At an intermediate level of specificity are questions about preferred playmates, workmates, or best friends.

The importance of comparisons of question types lies in the comparability of samples that use different sociometric questions to select subjects. If responses to sociometrics depend on the specific question asked (preferred playmates vs. workmates vs. best friends) less comparability would be expected.

Gresham (1982) reported a correlation of .88 between play and work ratings with a sample consisting solely of rejected third and fourth grade children.

Correlations between play and work scores for the nomination and rating data described previously (collected with more heterogeneous samples) are presented in Table 3. Work and play ratings correlated from .77 to .90 for both-sex and same-sex ratings. Correlations for nomination scores were significant but lower, ranging from .57 to .80. Comparisons of play and work extreme group overlap (see Table 4) indicate between 26% and 50% overlap for ratings with similarly poor group overlap for nominations.

Thus, although work and play evaluations yielded reasonably-correlated scores, extreme-group overlap was poor, regardless of whether ratings or nominations were employed. Examination of disagreement patterns for both-sex nomination data showed that when disagreements occurred, accepted children were most likely to be cross-classified as unclassified (44%), neglected (18%), or controversial (8%), while neglected children were likely to be designated unclassified (49%), rejected (19%), or accepted (14%). Rejected children were cross-classified as unclassified (24%), neglected (24%), or controversial (10%), while disagreements with the controversial children revolved around whether some belonged in the unclassified (47%), popular (18%), or rejected (18%) group. Patterns based on same-sex nominations were very similar.

Thus, known-group comparison studies may in fact be targeting markedly different samples of children. Whether these samples are behaviorally comparable is important to establish. Gresham (1982) found that behavioral predictors and correlates of play and work scores were similar for ratings, positive nominations, and best friend nominations. However, these findings should be replicated with a less select sample and a broader range of responses before concluding that work and play sociometric data bear functionally comparable relations to particular social behaviors. Similarly, comparability should be assessed among nomina-

Table 3. Correlations (*rs*) Between Work and Play Sociometric Measures

Variable	*Same-sex Scoring*	*Both-sex Scoring*
Peer nominations ($n = 125$)		
Like-most scores	.58*	.57*
Like-least scores	.65*	.80*
Social preference score	.65*	.73*
Social impact score	.57*	.61*
Peer ratings		
Grade 2 ($n = 114$)	.79*	.77*
Grade 5 ($n = 122$)	.81*	.90*

Note: $^{*}p < .0001$.

Table 4. Percentage Overlap of Extreme Groups Selected by Work vs. Play Sociometrics

	Social Status Group			
Variable	*Accepted*	*Rejected*	*Neglected*	*Controversial*
Nominations				
Same-sex	42%	26%	33%	11%
Both-sex	31%	52%	35%	18%
Ratings				
Grade 2				
Same-sex	38%	38%		
Both-sex	36%	46%		
Grade 5				
Same-sex	26%	50%		
Both-sex	50%	41%		

Note: Overlaps compared by formula: # overlapping children/total # selected for that group by either method. Neglected and controversial children were not discernible from peer ratings.

tions and ratings of liking, best friendship, favorite playmates, and other conceptually similar but semantically different dimensions of peers relations.

Computing Total Sociometric Scores

The usual way of summarizing peer ratings is to average the ratings. In contrast, nomination sociometrics can be scored several ways. Nomination scores can be weighted (based on order of choice) or unweighted, and then combined in various ways. According to Hymel (1983), the current practice is to compute unweighted scores because weighting of scores implies that first-choice peers are more salient to the child than later choices, an invalid assumption for some sociometric questions. Nonetheless, Marshall (1957) described two studies reporting correlations above .97 between weighted and unweighted nomination scores. Gottman (1977) found average correlations between weighted and unweighted scores of .86 for positive nominations and .74 for negative nominations. Similar analyses of the aforementioned Foster and Ritchey (1985) nomination data also yielded extremely high correlations (all rs $> .90$) between weighted and unweighted scores for like-most, like-least, and social preference scores.

While weighting apparently makes little difference in the interpretation of sociometrics, different systems of combining nomination scores into overall indices of peer status are less comparable. Hymel and Rubin (in press) describe four classification systems for social status based on peer nominations: Gronlund's (1959), Peery's (1979), Coie et al.'s (1982), and Newcomb and Bukowski's (1983). The categories of all four systems include accepted children (who receive many positive and few negative nominations), rejected children (who receive many negative and few positive nominations), and neglected children (who receive few positive or negative nominations). With the exception of Peery's, the systems also classify children who receive many positive and negative nominations as a "controversial" group.

Nevertheless, the systems differ, some markedly, in the methods used to select children for social status groups. For example, Peery (1979) used extreme absolute scores to select groups, Coie et al. (1982) computed standardized scores, and Newcomb and Bukowski (1983) determined whether individual scores exceeded chance values. These classification systems also differ in (a) the number of children classified into various social status groups (Hymel & Rubin, in press; Newcomb & Bukowski, 1983), (b) the groups into which children are placed (Hymel & Rubin, in press), and (c) the relationships of behavioral descriptors provided by peers to the social status grouping (Newcomb & Bukowski, 1983). The latter findings are particularly troublesome, as they indicate that different classification schemes lead to different conclusions about correlations of peer status.

COMPARABILITY OF TEACHER AND PEER ASSESSMENT

Sociometric measures have the major advantage of directly sampling the viewpoints of peers with whom the target child interacts. Recently, however, teacher assessment has been explored as an alternative to peer sociometric measures for several reasons. First, reported test-retest reliability scores, especially with younger children, are often as low as .29 (e.g., Asher, Singleton, Tinsley, & Hymel, 1979; Hartup, Glazer, & Charlesworth, 1967; Moore & Updegraff, 1964). Second, ethical questions have been raised about whether asking children to talk about liked and disliked peers adversely affects children's feelings and/or behaviors (Asher & Hymel, 1981; Foster & Ritchey, 1979). Third, teacher assessment takes less time to administer and score than sociometric measures. Finally, teachers are major referral agents for children with social skills problems.

It is not clear, however, whether data obtained from teacher and peer evaluations are comparable. A few studies compared peer sociometric measures to teacher rankings and ratings of children's social status and teacher nominations of children's friends. McCandless and Marshall (1957) found significant correlations ranging from .53 to .85 between pooled teacher measures of "closest" friends and preschool children's peer nominations of preferred playmates. However, teachers differed widely in their ability to predict children's friends. Green,

Forehand, Beck, and Vosk (1980) reported that third grade teachers' estimates of peer dislike significantly correlated with actual peer ratings of disliking (r = .59) and peer nominations of best friends and disliked peers (rs = −.44 and .48, respectively). Connolly and Doyle (1981) also found that teacher and peer measures of popularity of preschool children correlated .55. However, while teacher measures significantly predicted both teacher-rated and observed social competence, peer nominations did not. According to these results, teacher measures may be more than a substitute for peer sociometric measures; they may be an improvement—depending, of course, on what one wishes to predict. However, these results must be viewed with caution because of unusually close interaction and familiarity between teachers and children in this study.

Landau et al. (1984) have questioned the validity of teacher evaluation as a substitute for peer assessment. In this study, as in previous research, teacher rankings of popularity of kindergarten boys correlated significantly with peer nominations of popularity (r = .50) and rejection (r = −.59). Contrary to Connolly and Doyle's (1981) findings, however, Landau et al. found that peer nominations provided a unique contribution to the prediction of observed behavior, possibly because negative nominations (not included in the Connolly and Doyle study) were added.

Sociometric measures have also been compared to teacher questionnaires focusing on sociability or likability, aggression, withdrawal, and pathology (Green et al., 1980; LaGreca, 1981). In general, these studies found moderate correlations in predicted directions between peer rejection or peer ratings and: (a) the Conners Teacher Rating Scale (Conners, 1969) sociability and pathology factors, (b) the Pupil Evaluation Inventory (PEI; Pekarik, Prinz, Liebert, Weintraub, & Neale, 1976) withdrawal factor, and (c) for males only, PEI aggression and likability scores. Peer acceptance was not significantly correlated with teacher measures of any of these dimensions.

In a related study, Ledingham, Younger, Schwartzman, and Bergeron (1982) investigated the concordance of teacher and peer ratings on the Pupil Evaluation Inventory. Teacher and peer ratings correlated significantly on all factors (rs = .47 to .83), with highest agreement for aggression. Although these agreement figures are higher than those of other studies (e.g., Green et al., 1980; LaGreca, 1981), this may be due to the use of the same measure for both teacher and peer ratings.

To this point, research on the comparability of teacher and peer measures of social status has not determined whether teachers can identify children at the extremes of the social status continuum. While correlational information is useful for determining how well teachers evaluate the general pattern of social relations in a classroom, extreme group analysis is important for drawing conclusions about how well teachers can identify those who, according to peers, could benefit most from social skills training.

In conjunction with a larger study (Foster & Ritchey, 1985), Foster and

Ritchey collected pilot data relevant to this question with 125 children in five grade 4–6 classrooms. Each child gave first and second choice positive and negative nominations of play and work preferences. Without knowing the sociometric results, each teacher indicated, in order, three children in the classroom he or she thought could benefit most from a program to teach how to get along better with other children. Teachers also nominated, in order, the three children they believed got along best with peers and would be considered models for others.

Teacher nominations of "model" and "needy" children were compared with peer-identified accepted, rejected, neglected, controversial, and nonclassifiable groups, classified via Coie et al.'s (1982) procedures. Table 5 presents the Coie et al. categories into which the teacher-nominated children fell. For play and work nominations, the greatest overlap occurred between accepted children and models. Teachers selected no rejected children as models, but did occasionally choose controversial and neglected children. Teacher and peer convergence on "needy" children was also poor, with 13%–20% of the children selected by teachers as needing social skills training designated as accepted by peers!

Although the overlap between peer and teacher nominations of the extreme groups was low, teacher-nominated model children differed significantly from teacher-nominated needy children in terms of play and work social preference scores (one-tailed *t*-tests, all $ps < .05$). Model children received mean play and work social preference scores of 1.00 and .77, respectively, while needy children received mean play and work scores of −.17 and −.22.

Thus, teachers could only discriminate to a limited extent between chiluren at the high and low ends of the peer acceptance continuum. These results and those

Table 5. Percent Overlap Between Teacher Nominations of Model and Needy Children and Peer Nominations of Accepted, Rejected, Neglected, Controversial, and Nonclassifiable Children

	Peer Classification				
Teacher Classification:	*Accepted*	*Rejected*	*Neglected*	*Controversial*	*Other*
			Play Nominations		
Model	43%	0%	14%	14%	29%
Needy	13%	33%	13%	13%	27%
			Work Nominations		
Model	36%	0%	21%	21%	21%
Needy	20%	27%	27%	0%	27%

Note: Teacher-nominated model children, $n = 14$; teacher-nominated needy children, $n = 15$.

of other investigators (e.g., Landau et al., 1984) suggest that although teachers and peers may consider many of the same behaviors when determining children's social status, they are not basing their decisions on entirely the same information, especially when identifying unpopular children. Furthermore, the children teachers refer for social skills interventions may not be the same as children peers identify as rejected or neglected, thus raising the strong possibility that studies of children selected based on low peer acceptance are not generalizable to teacher-referred populations.

On the basis of these data, teacher measures of social status cannot be recommended as substitutes for peer sociometrics, especially if the goal of the assessment is to identify rejected children in need of intervention. However, teacher nominations might correspond more closely to an average of multiple sociometric administrations, or teacher ratings of children might match peer ratings more closely than nominations. Further research should compare different types of teacher and peer measures of social status for the purpose of identifying children either for treatment or for known-group research.

PARENTAL CONSENT: A BIASING FACTOR IN SOCIOMETRIC RESEARCH?

The national concern with individual rights is reflected in the number of regulations and guidelines established by the federal government, professional organizations such as the American Psychological Association, and Institutional Review Boards for the conduct of research with human subjects. A key element of these guidelines is the requirement that researchers obtain informed, voluntary consent from prospective subjects. Although ethical guidelines and the procurement of informed consent are unquestionably needed, they may have a significant impact on research outcome (Adair, Dushenko, & Lindsay, 1985). Parents and minors who voluntarily agree to the child's participation in research may not be representative of the total population of interest, resulting in a biased subject sample.

Ample evidence of bias due to volunteer status exists with adults and college students (see Rosenthal & Rosnow, 1975). Volunteers and nonvolunteers have been shown to differ on several dimensions, including sociability, intelligence, social class, and educational level. Differences in the sociability of volunteer and nonvolunteer adults suggest that researchers studying the social behavior of neglected and rejected children should at least be aware of the possibility of bias in their subject samples.

To date, research addressing the issue of volunteer bias in child research has been minimal, although the issue is certainly no less relevant than with adults. The ethics involved in conducting research with nonconsenting children (i.e., children from whom parental permission and/or child assent have not been obtained) severely limits the questions that can be pursued. Nevertheless, in one early investigation, Wicker (1968) found that students who had IQs above 100, recent grades of C or above, and parents in professional or managerial occupations were almost twice as likely to receive parental consent to complete a questionnaire than other students.

Similarly, Lueptow, Mueller, Hammes, and Master (1977) found that nonconsenting high school seniors had lower grades and intelligence scores than consenting students. Lueptow et al. (1977) also examined consent rates prior to and following the establishment of ethical guidelines for research with human subjects, obtaining a consent rate of nearly 100% when the project was presented as a school requirement but only a 69.7% consent rate for those 18 or over and a 42.4% rate for minors after voluntary consent regulations were implemented.

Severson and Ary (1983) directly compared consenters and nonconsenters in a study of self-reported frequency of alcohol, cigarette and marijuana use among seventh-grade students, and found that self-reported cigarette and marijuana smoking was related to consent rate: smokers were disproportionately represented in the nonconsenters group. Parental smoking habits and education level were also related to consent, but socioeconomic status was not.

Sample Bias in Social Skills Research

Beck, Collins, Overholser, and Terry (1984) assessed possible consenter bias with first and sixth graders in a study employing peer sociometric measures, classroom behavioral observations, teacher ratings of classroom behaviors, and children's self-report of interpersonal behavior. Teachers were given written descriptions of withdrawn and aggressive behavior and asked to indicate, first, how many children fit each description and second, how many of those withdrawn and aggressive children had returned permission forms signed by themselves and their parents. The authors found that withdrawn and aggressive children were underrepresented in the consenters group.

Contrary to the findings of Beck et al. (1984), Frame and Strauss (in press) found no significant relationship between consent and teacher ratings of psychological functioning. The authors examined the relationships among consent, peer-rated sociometric status, and teacher ratings of 149 elementary school children on the Revised Behavior Problem Checklist (RBPC). Only social status was significantly related to teacher ratings, suggesting that the consenter group was representative of the larger group.

Partial corroborating evidence for the findings of Beck et al. (1984) is available from studies conducted independently by the first and third authors of this chapter. The data were collected as part of four larger studies that described behavioral differences between socially accepted and unaccepted children (Studies 1, 3, and 4) and the stability of sociometric measures (Study 2). The first study was conducted in a public elementary school that served a catchment area of lower-middle and middle-class families in a southern suburban community. The remaining studies were conducted in public schools serving predominantly lower-middle-class and middle-class neighborhoods in a rural university community. Developmental differences were examined in the first three studies by comparing children in grades 2 and 5 in Study 1, grades 2, 5, 7 and 9 in Study 2 and grades 1, 3, 5 in the third study. Data for children in grades 4 through 6 were pooled in the fourth study.

All four studies used similar parental consent forms and procedures for obtaining informed consent. The consent forms specified: (a) the purpose of the research, (b) the procedural aspects of the study, (c) the confidentiality of the data, (d) the voluntary nature of participation, and (e) school approval of the procedures. As a requirement of the Institutional Review Board, the consent form used in Study 1 also stated that the sponsoring agency was not responsible for injuries that might be incurred as a result of the child's participation.

In each study, an experimenter entered the classroom, described the study to the children, distributed consent forms, and asked that the forms be taken home to the parents. In Study 1, children were instructed to return the signed forms to the teacher only if the child and parent agreed that the child could participate in the project. In the other studies, forms were to be returned whether or not the child was given permission to participate. In all studies, additional forms were given to children to take home to if they had failed to return them by a specified date. The nonconsenter group was comprised of children who repeatedly failed to return forms or whose returned forms indicated parent or child nonconsent for participation.

The percentages of males and females within each grade who consented to participate in Studies 1, 2 and 3 are presented in Table 6. Consent rates for Study 4, in which data from fourth, fifth, and sixth grade students were pooled, were 64% for boys (total n = 63) and 63% for girls (total n = 62). The rates were relatively consistent both across the four studies and with rates reported by other social skills researchers. Beck et al. (1984) received child and parental consent for 68% of the first graders and 63% of the sixth graders in their study; LaGreca and Santogrossi (1980) reported a 74% consent/assent rate for their sample of third, fourth and fifth graders. It is difficult to ascertain whether these percentages are truly representative of those obtained in the social skills literature, given the limited number of studies that report this information (Beck et al., 1984; Berler et al., 1985), and the necessity of obtaining a fairly high consent rate in order to carry out an investigation. However, it appears that approximately 50% to 75% of elementary school age children participate in social skills research when requested to do so. Consent rates may be somewhat higher for older students, as suggested by the consent rates found for the seventh and ninth graders in Study 2, and the fact that Ford (1982) also found participation rates of 76% to 90% for ninth and twelfth graders in a study of the relationship between social cognition and social competence.

Table 6. Percentages of Children with Parental Permission and Child Assent for Participation in Social Skills Research

	Study 1		*Study 2*		*Study 3*	
Grade	*Male*	*Female*	*Male*	*Female*	*Male*	*Female*
Grade 1						
% Consenting					57%	70%
Total *n*					35	33
Grade 2						
% Consenting	68%	68%	55%	66%		
Total *n*	78	84	33	30		
Grade 3						
% Consenting					64%	68%
Total *n*					28	19
Grade 5						
% Consenting	53%	63%	49%	62%	38%	67%
Total *n*	101	105	41	37	16	33
Grade 7						
% Consenting			73%	85%		
Total *n*			30	26		
Grade 9						
% Consenting			78%	74%		
Total *n*			18	23		

To examine possible sampling bias, consenters and nonconsenters from Studies 1, 2 and 3 were compared on a 5-point teacher rating of each child's popularity with his/her classmates. Teacher ratings were obtained between two and six months after the consent forms had been returned to the teachers. Teachers in Study 1 made their ratings on a class roster randomly listing every student's name, without designating consent status. Although this was conducted with the permission of the principal, confidentiality concerns led to a modification of these procedures for Studies 2 and 3. For these, teachers were given a roster listing the names of the consenting group and were asked to rate the popularity of these children. Children in the nonconsenter group were rated separately, and their names were removed from the list of ratings given to the investigator.

Teachers were not told the purpose of the ratings but were informed that it would be useful to have descriptive information on all children in the classroom. Although it is possible that teachers realized the purpose of the ratings, which may have biased their responses, none of the teachers' comments suggested biased responding.

A group (consenters vs. nonconsenters) X grade X sex ANOVA was performed separately with teacher ratings from each study. There was a significant Group main effect for Study 1, $F(1, 360) = 11.49, p < .001$, and Study 2, $F(1, 236) = 9.22, p < .01$, but not for Study 3. All interaction effects were nonsignificant. Inspection of the mean ratings shows that teachers in Study 1 and 2 rated the consenters (*M*s = 3.54 and 3.47) as more popular than the nonconsenters (*M*s = 3.20 and 3.07). While these group differences are statistically significant and support the results of Beck et al. (1984), the degree of bias represented by these findings may be limited, given the small absolute differences between means.

The fourth study used peer sociometric nominations to evaluate potential differences between fourth through sixth grade consenters and nonconsenters. In this study, the sociometrics were administered prior to sending home consent forms. At the time the study was conducted, school system personnel requested this procedure in order to minimize the salience of and the relationship of the sociometric measure to other parts of the study (which involved observations of accepted, rejected, and neglected children selected based on peer nominations), thus reducing the possibility that children would guess the purposes of the study and stigmatize other children. Further, most teachers indicated that they routinely gave soicometric assessments in their classrooms during the school year for their own use so the procedure was not novel to the students. Since the time this study was approved, further considerations involved in the ethics of research with children have highlighted the need to obtain the child's assent and to inform parents fully of procedures involved in the study prior to beginning the research. These procedures are followed in our current research.

Consenter differences for like-most, like-least, social preference, and social impact work and play scores were analyzed with Group (consenters vs. nonconsenters) X Sex ANOVAs for same-sex and both-sex scores. No significant consenter main effects or interactions between sex and consenter status were obtained for any of these variables (all $ps > .10$). LaGreca and Santogrossi (1980) reported similar nonsignificant findings. Using same-sex play and work peer ratings as a measure of peer acceptance, they found that the 34 third through fifth grade consenters received the same total mean rating as the 12 nonconsenters.

The studies discussed in this section provide only tentative support for the hypothesis that children with the most serious peer relationship problems are not participating in social skills research because of a lack of parental permission and/or child assent. The strongest evidence comes from studies using teacher evaluations of children's social competence (Studies 1 and 2; Beck et al., 1984), although there is some nonsupporting evidence (Frame & Strauss, in press). The reasons for Frame and Strauss's nonsignificant findings are difficult to determine, but one possibility may be differences between the RBPC and other teacher evaluations, as the RBPC assesses more global characteristics than social competence.

When peer evaluations are used (Study 4; LaGreca & Santogrossi, 1980), significant differences between consenters and nonconsenters generally have not been found. The discrepancy between peer and teacher measures is in accord with findings summarized previously, indicating that they may reflect different dimensions of children's social relations. Increasingly stringent ethical regulations exclude the use of peer evaluations in further assessments of sampling bias. We must therefore rely on teacher perceptions, using methods that protect the anonymity and privacy of nonconsenters and minimize the risk to these children.

Researchers will need to struggle increasingly with the concept of risk. As Keith-Spiegel (1983) notes, the definition of minimum risk is not clearly operationalized in research regulations. The degree to which teacher ratings of adjustment or labeling of a child as withdrawn or unpopular places that child at risk is not known. A critical issue is whether the possible risks to and invasion of privacy of nonconsenters outweigh the potential benefits of evaluating selection bias (Beck et al., 1984). While we believe that the potential benefits outweigh the risks when studies are conducted in an ethically sensitive and responsible manner, discussion of this issue is seriously needed.

Potential selection bias from low consent rates has serious implications for the social skills literature. First, it may be difficult to illuminate some of the differences in the behavior and characteristics of accepted, rejected and withdrawn children without a truly representative sample of children. Biased samples may account for the relatively high percentage of negative findings in social skills research. In most studies, it seems that only a few of the many behaviors examined are found to be significantly correlated with sociometric status, and these significant relationships do not necessarily hold up from one study to another (see Foster et al., in press). Although many alternative explanations can account for these inconsistencies, volunteer status should not be ignored as a plausible hypothesis.

Second, the children participating in descriptive research may differ from children with consent to participate in treatment studies or from children who are referred for treatment in applied settings. If these differences exist, then data on the components of social competence may not be directly applicable to children involved in treatment.

A third and final consideration is the impact of low consent rates on data produced by sociometric measures. Nomination and rating scale instruments are generally administered only to those children with parental consent. Although often not specified in published research, the roster of classmates may likewise be limited to those children who have received parental permission. However, the sociometric scores for this sample may not be representative of scores that would be obtained if the entire class had participated. The reliability, validity and utility of sociometric scores could thus be affected if the distribution of scores given by consenters and nonconsenters differed. Although ethical considerations limit systematic assessment of this issue, the question of minimum levels of consent, below which the sample size would be considered insufficient for establishing social status, certainly warrants further scrutiny.

In light of the evidence, research on variables affecting consent rates is needed. Identifying methods that increase consent and result in concomitant increases in the representativeness of subject samples would be valuable to all researchers working in the area of social competence. We should begin by gaining a better understanding of why parents refuse to have their children participate in research. Although this can only be determined for those parents who return consent forms indicating they do not want their children to participate, these parents could be asked to respond to a checklist which identifies a variety of possible reasons for refusal (Beck et al., 1984). The resulting information may change the ways in which researchers approach parents and children when recruiting research subjects. Parents in particular may be the most important group to target, because they are most likely the ones who refuse to give consent (Beck et al., 1984; Lueptow et al., 1977).

Analyses of situational determinants of consent may prove useful in the development of procedures to enhance volunteer rates. Directions for empirically-based research can come from two sources. First, researchers need to describe the procedures they use to procure consent fully, in addition to reporting the percentages of boys and girls for whom consent is obtained. Second, the adult literature may provide several directions. Rosenthal and Rosnow (1975) identify several situational determinants of adult volunteerism, including material incentives, expectations of being favorably evaluated by the investigator, sex and status of the person making the appeal for volunteers, and the optimal number of potential subjects with whom the researcher should discuss the project at a given time. Other variables worthy of investigation are the degree of teacher support and encouragement for research participation and the establishment of direct contact between parents and investigators (possibly at PTA meetings or school functions). In exploring such procedures, it will of course be important to avoid coercive or misleading tactics that limit subjects' access to fully informed consent.

In addition to examining both methods for increasing consent and the effect of differences between consenters and nonconsenters on the primary variables of interest, it may also be necessary to investigate possible mediating variables, such as school grades (which may be associated with the motivational level of students), sex, race, socioeconomic status, and the educational level of parents. It is possible that factors such as these may be better predictors of bias than consent rates alone (Lueptow et al., 1977; Wicker, 1968).

CONCLUDING COMMENTS

Increased emphasis on valid, reliable methods for assessing children's position in the peer group has accompanied increased research interest in children's social competence. Sociometric assessment has been touted as one such method (Asher & Hymel, 1981; Foster & Ritchey, 1979), and has been widely used to select subjects for known-groups comparisons between well- and poorly-accepted children and for social skills training.

Unfortunately, there is no single widely-accepted sociometric measure. Nominations, ratings, and paired-comparison sociometrics differ not only in format, but also in the types of children each can be used to identify (e.g., rejected and neglected children can be distinguished with peer nominations, but not ratings), in their psychometric properties, and in their relationships with other variables (see Hymel, 1983, for a review). Even within a particular format, variations in the kinds of questions that are asked or the ways the data are scored can lead to moderate to substantial variations in populations. With nomination sociometrics in particular, children may frequently be classified into different social status extreme groups, depending on the procedures employed. Unfortunately, systematic investigations of the impact of these variations on the relationships obtained between sociometric status and other variables, such as observed behavior, have not been done, so at this point it is difficult to ascertain whether these differences are functionally important. Nonetheless, the data reviewed here suggest that populations studied by researchers employing different sociometrics are not fully comparable.

Equally disturbing are the findings that different classification systems for grouping children based on sociometric scores have different classification rates (Hymel & Rubin, in press; Newcomb & Bukowski, 1983), probably a function of different cutoff scores—cutoffs which often seem to have little empirical foundation. Some writers have also questioned the long-term temporal stability (Newcomb & Bukowski, 1984) of even the most sophisticated sociometric classification systems.

Authors justify the use of sociometric measures with a litany that begins most studies of social competence, citing a series of studies that relate poor peer relations to a variety of negative long-term outcomes in later childhood and adulthood. Yet a close perusal of this literature reveals that very few of these studies used sociometric measures (DeLawyer, 1985). This raises the possibility that sociometrics may not all predict long-range adjustment equally well. An even more uncomfortable possibility is that none of the measures, as they are currently employed, will prove satisfactory for this purpose. The predictive validity of sociometrics is far from established, although longitudinal studies such as those conducted by Coie and Dodge (1983), Kupersmidt (1983), Newcomb and Bukowski (1984), and Rubin and his colleagues (see Hymel & Rubin, in press) provide important first steps in examining this issue.

It is also clear from examining the data that teacher and peer assessments of children's peer relations yield different views of who is and who is not socially successful, with concurrence depending upon the kind of questions teachers are asked to answer about their students. Sources of these differences remain to be established, and may have to do with teachers and peers engaging in different types of interactions with target children. Nonetheless, children referred by teachers for social skills training may not share the attributes of children selected for social skills research based on peer sociometrics.

A final issue has to do with overlap between the sociometrically-selected group of children with poor peer relations and other diagnostic groups. Problematic peer relations are a defining characteristic of conduct disorder (American Psychiatric Association, 1980), as well as common correlate of attention deficit disorder with hyperactivity (ADDH) (e.g., Milich & Landau, 1982). The rejected social status group and these diagnostic categories are not mutually exclusive. To begin to establish which children fit which criteria in studies of all of these populations would be a first step in establishing the degree of population overlap and increasing the integration of findings on what have heretofore been treated in the literature as distinctly different groups of children.

In sum, diverse findings from different empirical slants characterize the voluminous social skills literature. The major concern of this chapter has been the comparability of subject samples across studies, and in our selective examination of sources of bias, several potentially problematic factors have emerged (e.g., consenter bias, type of sociometric and scoring system). Others appear to be less major in their effects (e.g., weighted vs. unweighted scoring). Clearly, sociometrics are still a viable way of selecting subjects for further study, although the best ways of using these measures to enhance their long-term predictive validity remain to be established.

REFERENCES

Adair, J. G., Dushenko, T. W., & Lindsay, R. C. L. (1985). Ethical regulations and their impact on research practice. *American Psychologist, 40,* 59–72.

American Psychiatric Association. (1980). *Diagnostic and statistical manual of mental disorders,* 3rd edition. Washington, DC: American Psychiatric Association.

Asher, S. R., & Hymel, S. (1981). Children's social competence in peer relations: Sociometric and behavioral assessment. In J. D. Wine & M. D. Smye (Eds.), *Social competence* (pp. 125–157). New York: Guilford.

Asher, S. R., Singleton, L. C., Tinsley, B. R.. & Hymel, S. (1979). A reliable sociometric measure for preschool children. *Developmental Psychology, 15,* 443–444.

Beck, S., Collins, L., Overholser, J., & Terry, K. (1984). A comparison of children who receive permission and children who do not receive permission to participate in research. *Journal of Abnormal Child Psychology, 12,* 573–580.

Berler, E. S., Allen, K. D., & Burge, D. A. (1985). *Thirty years of sociometric methodology: Implications of procedural variability for assessment and treatment research in children's social skills.* Unpublished manuscript.

Coie, J. D., & Dodge, K. A. (1983). Continuities and change in children's social status: A five-year longitudinal study. *Merrill-Palmer Quarterly, 29,* 261–282.

Coie, J., Dodge, K., & Coppotelli, H. (1982). Dimensions and types of social status: A cross-age perspective. *Developmental Psychology, 18,* 557–571.

Connolly, J., & Doyle, A. (1981). Assessment of social competence in preschoolers: Teachers versus peers. *Developmental Psychology, 17,* 454–462.

Conners, C. K. (1969). A teacher rating scale for use in drug studies with children. *American Journal of Psychiatry, 126,* 884–888.

DeLawyer, D. D. (1985). *Predicting long-term adjustment from early peer relations: A review.* Manuscript in preparation.

Edelson, J. L. (1980). The effect of sex differences on sociometric data generated by a roster-rating scale instrument. *Journal of Behavioral Assessment, 2,* 249–254.

Ford, M. E. (1982). Social cognition and social competence in adolescence. *Developmental Psychology, 18,* 323–340.

Foster, S. L., DeLawyer, D. D., & Guevremont, D. C. (in press). Selecting targets for social skills training with children and adolescents. In K. D. Gadow (Ed.), *Advances in learning and behavioral disabilities,* Vol. 4. Greenwich, CT: JAI Press.

Foster, S. L., & Ritchey, W. L. (1979). Issues in the assessment of social competence in children. *Journal of Applied Behavior Analysis, 12,* 625–638.

Foster, S. L., & Ritchey, W. L. (1985). Behavioral correlates of sociometric status of fourth-, fifth-, and sixth-grade children in two classroom situations. *Behavioral Assessment, 7,* 79–93.

Frame, C. L.. & Strauss, C. C. (in press). Parental informed consent, child sociometric status, and sample bias in grade school subjects. *Journal of Social and Clinical Psychology.*

Gottman, J. M. (1977). Toward a definition of social isolation in children. *Child Development, 48,* 512–517.

Green, K. D., Forehand, R., Beck, S. J., & Vosk, B. (1980). An assessment of the relationship among measures of children's social competence and children's academic achievement. *Child Development, 51,* 1149–1156.

Gresham, F. M. (1982). Social interactions as predictors of children's likability and friendship patterns: A multiple regression analysis. *Journal of Behavioral Assessment, 4,* 39–54.

Gronlund, N. (1959). *Sociometry in the classroom.* New York: Harper.

Hartup, W. W., Glazer, J., & Charlesworth, R. (1967). Peer reinforcement and sociometric status. *Child Development, 38,* 1017–1024.

Hymel, S. (1983). Preschool children's peer relations: Issues in sociometric assessment. *Merrill-Palmer Quarterly, 29,* 237–260.

Hymel, S., & Rubin, K. H. (in press). Children with peer relationships and social skill problems: Conceptual, methodological, and developmental issues. In G. J. Whitehurst (Ed.), *Annals of child development,* Vol 2. Greenwich, CT: JAI Press.

Keith-Spiegel, P. (1983). Children and consent to participate research. In G. P. Melton, M. J. Koocher, & M. J. Saks (Eds.), *Children's competence to consent* (pp. 179–211). New York: Plenum Press.

Kupersmidt, J. B. (1983). *Predicting delinquency and academic problems from childhood peer status.* Paper presented at the meeting of the Society for Research in Child Development, Detroit, April.

LaGreca, A. M. (1981). Acceptance: The correspondence between children's sociometric status and teachers' ratings of peer interactions. *Journal of Abnormal Child Psychology, 9,* 167–178.

LaGreca, A. M., & Santogrossi, D. A. (1980). Social skills training with elementary school students: A behavioral group approach. *Journal of Consulting and Clinical Psychology, 48,* 220–227.

Landau, S., Milich, R., & Whitten, P. (1984). A comparison of teacher and peer assessment of social status. *Journal of Clinical Child Psychology, 13,* 44–49.

Ledingham, J. E., Younger, A., Schwartzman, A., & Bergeron, G. (1982). Agreement among teacher, peer, and self ratings of children's aggression, withdrawal, and likability. *Journal of Abnormal Child Psychology, 10,* 363–372.

Lueptow, L., Mueller, S. A., Hammes, R. R., & Master, L. S. (1977). The impact of informed consent regulations on response rate and response bias. *Sociological Methods and Research, 6,* 183–203.

Marshall, H. R. (1957). An evaluation of sociometric-social behavior research with preschool children. *Child Development, 28,* 131–137.

McCandless, B. R., & Marshall, H. R. (1957). A picture sociometric technique for preschool children and its relation to teacher judgements of friendship. *Child Development, 28,* 139–149.

Milich, R., & Landau, S. (1982). Socialization and peer relations in hyperactive children. In K. D. Gadow & I. Bialer (Eds.), *Advances in learning and behavioral disabilities,* Vol. 1 (pp. 283–339). Greenwich, CT: JAI Press.

Moore, S. G., & Updegraff, R. (1964). Sociometric status of preschool children as related to age, sex, nurturance-giving, and dependency. *Child Development, 35,* 519–524.

Newcomb, A. F., & Bukowski, W. M. (1983). Social impact and social preference as determinants of children's peer group status. *Developmental Psychology, 19,* 856–867.

Newcomb, A. F., & Bukowski, W. M. (1984). A longitudinal study of the utility of social preference and social impact sociometric classification schemes. *Child Development, 55,* 1434–1447.

Peery, J. C. (1979). Popular, amiable, isolated, rejected: A reconceptualization of sociometric status in preschool children. *Child Development, 50,* 1231–1234.

Pekarik, E. G., Prinz, R. J., Liebert, D. E., Weintraub, S., & Neale, J. M. (1976). The Pupil Evaluation Inventory: A sociometric technique for assessing children's social behavior. *Journal of Abnormal Child Psychology, 4,* 83–97.

Reese, H. W. (1962). Sociometric choices of the same and opposite sex in late childhood. *Merrill-Palmer Quarterly, 8,* 173–174.

Rosenthal, R., & Rosnow, R. L. (1975). *The volunteer subject.* New York: Wiley.

Severson, H. H., & Ary, D. V. (1983). Sampling bias due to consent procedures with adolescents. *Addictive Behaviors, 8,* 433–437.

Wicker, A. W. (1968). Requirements for protecting privacy of human subjects: Some implications for generalization of research findings. *American Psychologist, 23,* 70–72.

ISSUES IN THE ASSESSMENT AND TREATMENT OF SOCIALLY REJECTED CHILDREN

Gina Krehbiel and Richard Milich

ABSTRACT

Issues in the assessment and treatment of disordered peer relationships were reviewed. Special attention was directed toward the use of peer nomination procedures to identify the social status subgroups of isolated-withdrawn and rejected youngsters. Ethical issues associated with these assessment procedures were discussed, and alternatives to the peer nomination methodology were critically reviewed. It was noted that the two groups of isolated-withdrawn and peer rejected children may require different treatment approaches. Social withdrawal appears to involve primarily a social skills performance deficit whereas social rejection involves both behavioral excesses and skill deficits. Two intervention studies were reviewed demonstrating that a skill-deficit approach to the treatment of socially

Advances in Behavioral Assessment of Children and Families, Vol. 2, pgs. 249–270.
Editor: Ronald J. Prinz

ISBN: 0-89232-481-3

rejected youngsters may be of limited value. Instead, attention should be directed toward the behavioral excesses exhibited by these children.

INTRODUCTION

Within the last decade there has been a convergence of research interest in the area of social skills assessment and treatment of children with poor peer relationships. One line of research has attempted to identify behavioral correlates that account for disordered peer interactions, whereas other investigations have centered on developing treatment programs to enhance social adjustment. The initial appeal of these treatment regimes has been widespread as is evident in the plethora of social skills programs that are currently being marketed.

Although the initial treatment studies have been encouraging, a close scrutiny of the social skills assessment and training literature indicates inconsistent results that are difficult to interpret. The mixed findings may be attributable to several factors, the most significant of which are the methods of assessment and selection of subjects for participation in the training programs. Many of the interventions were designed and field-tested with socially isolated children, but the methods have been indiscriminately applied to groups of peer rejected youngsters.

In the training literature, peer rating scores are the most frequently employed measures of children's social status. By this method, children with low rating scores were selected for training programs. A single low rating score, however, does not differentiate between actively rejected and isolated children. As a result, social skill interventions were implemented with heterogenous samples of children rejected by the group and children isolated from the group, making a clear interpretation of the treatment efficacy difficult (Wanlass & Prinz, 1982). The confounding of subject assessment is critical because the peer relationship problems experienced by these two groups of children as well as their long-term outcomes are known to be quite different.

A related source of subject misidentification is the common assumption that children with poor social adjustment are all deficient in the same skills targeted for training, i.e., that the subjects are a homogeneous group of children who are unpopular for the same reasons. This assumption seems particularly faulty in light of recent data from two intervention studies suggesting that variables other than level of social skill may mediate peer acceptance (Coie & Krehbiel, 1984; Pelham, Schnedler, Miller, Ronnei, Paluchowski, Budrow, Marks, Nilsson, & Bender, in press).

The purpose of this chapter is to discuss the assessment of peer relationships, elucidate the differences between isolated-withdrawn and rejected youngsters, and to present implications for differential treatment approaches. Specifically, it will be argued that social withdrawal may involve primarily a social skills performance deficit whereas social rejection may tend to involve both behavioral excesses and skill deficits. The failure to recognize these and other differences may account for many of the disappointing findings in the skills-oriented treatment literature.

ISSUES IN ASSESSMENT

Peer Sociometric Methods

The evidence linking disordered peer relations and antisocial behavior in childhood with subsequent forms of maladjustment (for a review see Hartup, 1983) prompted the extensive development of two methods of assessing peer social status: sociometric questionnaires and observations. Sociometric questionnaires are procedures for measuring the personal appeal of individual members of a group, and they include a variety of techniques. The *positive nomination technique* (Moreno, 1934) requires children to nominate the names of other classmates who match specified positive interpersonal criteria. In studies using these techniques, children are asked to nominate those classmates they "like most." Each child's social status or popularity score is the number of positive nominations he or she receives. McCandless and Marshall (1957) developed a picture sociometric nomination technique for use with younger children in which each child is presented with a display of photographs of peers and is asked to point to and name peers in response to questions such as "with whom do you most like to play?" Estimates of the test-retest reliability of positive nominations by elementary school-aged children ranged from r = .83 to .96 after one week (Horowitz, 1962), to approximately .74 after three months (Bonney, 1943), from .53 to .56 after one year, and from .34 to to .42 after three years (Roff, Sells, & Golden, 1972). When the picture sociometric was used with pre-readers, the test-retest reliability of positive nominations was enhanced (Hartup, Glazer, & Charlesworth, 1967; Moore & Updegraff, 1964).

Some investigators seek *negative nominations* of those who are "least liked" in addition to positive nominations. In this case each child's social status or rejection score is based on the number of negative nominations ("like least") received. Roff et al. (1972) noted that the test-retest reliability is higher for positive nominations (r = .53 to .58 after one year) than for negative nominations (r = .44 to .46 after one year). Coie and Dodge (1983) found that the stability of negative and positive nominations is higher for large samples that include cross-sex choices.

A third sociometric procedure is the *roster rating method* in which all children rate all classmates on a five-point scale which asks a variant of the question "How much do you like each person?" (Oden & Asher, 1977). In this case a child's sociometric rating is the standardized average of the ratings he or she receives from the peers. This technique is considered to offer a general index of overall acceptability or likability (as opposed to number of friendships) and is thought to be more sensitive to changes in status than the scores which result from peer nominations (Asher & Hymel, 1981; Coie & Krehbiel, 1984). Additional advantages include the fact that each child is rated by all classmates, thereby providing a comprehensive index of each child's acceptance by every other classmate. Because the scale has positive and negative poles, children are not required to choose peers according to negative criteria. The procedure also reduces the possibility that a child is not selected because he or she was forgotten. The roster rating method has been found to correlate with positive nomination measures ($r = .63$ according to Hymel & Asher, 1977), and the test-retest reliability of the rating procedure is higher than that of the positive nomination method (.82 and .69 over six weeks according to Oden & Asher, 1977, and Thompson & Powell, 1951, respectively).

The three peer sociometric methods provide different indices of a child's social status. Positive and negative nominations children received were assumed in earlier studies to represent opposite poles of a single "acceptance continuum" with investigators choosing to measure only the positive pole (Hartup, 1983). However, positive and negative nominations are only moderately and inversely correlated with estimates ranging from $r = -.04$ to $-.50$ (Gottman, 1977; Hartup et al., 1967; Hymel & Asher, 1977; Moore & Updegraff, 1964; Roff et al., 1972). The low correlations suggest that positive and negative nominations are two relatively orthogonal dimensions of peer regard. The number of positive nominations only differentiates between children who are more versus less accepted. The use of positive nomination or rating scores alone ignores the distinction between neglected and rejected children since both groups receive few positive nominations or low ratings.

Although current procedures for social status assessment were devised in the 1930s, classification systems for describing peer relationships have emerged only within the last decade. The classification approaches of Gottman (1977), Peery (1979), Coie, Dodge, and Coppotelli (1982), and Newcomb and Bukowski (1983) have grouped children according to their scores on both popularity and rejection dimensions derived from peer nominations.

Perhaps the first investigator to identify children's social status groups was Gottman (1977). Using a cluster analysis of four observation categories plus scores of social acceptance and rejection dimensions, Gottman (1977) identified five groups of children (see also, Hartup, 1983): stars (high on peer acceptance and low on rejection), rejectees (high on rejection and low on acceptance), teacher negative (high on teacher negative but also high on peer acceptance), tuned-out (low on both acceptance and rejection), and mixers (high on both acceptance and rejection). Gottman's classification is especially interesting as it is the only system based upon multivariate statistical procedures.

Peery (1979), like Gottman, based his classification schema on peer acceptance and rejection, but he combines them to create two new dimensions. *Social impact* was defined by the sum of positive and negative nominations, while *social preference* equalled the number of positive nominations minus the number of negative nominations. These two new dimensions were used to generate four social status groups: populars (high impact, highly preferred), amiables (low impact, highly preferred), isolates (low impact, nonpreferred), and rejects (high impact, nonpreferred).

Classification procedures that have emerged subsequent to Peery's (1979) have primarily consisted of variations on the use of social impact and social preference dimensions. For example, Coie et al. (1982) used standardized scores on these two dimensions to create five social status groups: popular, rejected, neglected, controversial, and average. By setting relatively high criterion scores, Coie et al. successfully classified 57% of their 848 children into one of the five groups. In contrast, Newcomb and Bukowski (1983) applied probability theory to raw scores from peer acceptance and rejection nominations to classify children into the same 5 groups as employed by Coie et al., successfully classifying 100% of the children.

These classification procedures have been proposed based on either multivariate statistical methods or extreme group cutoff scores. There are subtle distinctions among these approaches, including qualitative differences among identified groups, differing proportions of children classified by each, and issues of reliability, stability, and validity (see Newcomb & Bukowski, 1983; Bukowski & Newcomb, 1984; Putallaz and Gottman, 1983). However, it may be more beneficial to focus on the commonalities of these approaches, since there appears to be considerable agreement in how peer relationships and the social status environment are conceptualized. Five basic social status groups emerged regardless of how the children are classified: (a) the child who receives many positive nominations and few if any negative nominations; (b) the child who receives few if any positive and many negative nominations: (c) the child who receives significant numbers of positive and negative nominations; (d) the child who receives few if any nominations, positive or negative; and (e) the child who receives nominations similar in number to the mean number of positive and negative nominations for the entire group (Coie et al., 1982). The use of these nomination-based classifications promotes the differentiation of children whose peer relations and problems differ significantly (Dodge, Coie, & Brakke, 1982).

Ethical Considerations

Although the value of obtaining peer sociometric data is now generally accepted (Asher, 1983), the use of these assessment procedures has caused considerable concern among school personnel. Concerns have centered around the potential harm that may result from asking peers to evaluate each other, and thereby sensitize children to think about whom they do not like or encourage them to compare whom they nominated (Asher, 1983; Hayvren & Hymel, 1984). The feared end result is that the use of sociometric procedures may lead to further ostracism of unpopular or disliked children. Thus, primary concern has been raised over the collection of negative (i.e., peer rejection) measures (Connolly & Doyle, 1981; Ladd, 1983), although many school districts are apparently moving toward an outright ban of the collection of any form of sociometric data.

Although easily understood, concerns about the impact of sociometric assessment procedures are not supported by empirical evidence. Sociometric data have been collected on literally thousands of school children (see, for example, Ledingham, 1981; Pekarik, Prinz, Leibert, Weintraub, & Neale, 1976), and researchers who have collected such information have reported no apparent problems (Asher & Hymel, 1981; Coie et al., 1982). Asher (1983) recommended putative safeguards that included using a balanced mix of positive and negative items, timing the sociometric administration so that recess or other free time (i.e., and opportunity to compare responses) did not immediately follow, and reminding the students of the confidentiality of their responses.

Recent evidence supports clinical impressions that administration of sociometric instruments has relatively benign effects. After gathering positive and negative sociometric information from preschoolers, Hayvren and Hymel (1984) recorded all verbalizations made in the classroom in the ten minute period immediately following the assessment. Peer interactions were observed the week prior to and the week following the sociometric assessment. The authors found no evidence to suggest that sociometric testing adversely influenced the children's peer interactions. The children did not alter rates of interactions with most-preferred and least preferred peers. Further, when they did talk about the sociometric, they revealed positive choices but did not mention negative choices to any peers.

Hayvren and Hymel's (1984) results are encouraging but not definitive. As Asher, Markell, and Hymel (1981) noted, rates of interaction are not valid indicators of social status. In addition, Hayvren and Hymels's study was conducted with preschoolers, whereas older children, with their greater abstracting ability, may question the reasons for the implications of the sociometric assessment. Further research using dependent variables that are sensitive to subtle changes in children's impressions about their peers is needed. If more evidence can be marshalled demonstrating the benign effects associated with sociometric assessment, then school districts might become less resistant to allowing the collection of this information. Recently, Asher and Dodge (1984) have explored another method of collecting peer social status data while circumventing ethical concerns associated with data collection. These investigators studied the value of using number of positive nominations and lowest ratings in combination and identified children who are rejected or controversial with good success. Although the method is less accurate in the identification of average, popular, and neglected children than the traditional classification method, it has an appealing advantage in that the solicitation of negative nominations is avoided.

Teacher Assessment of Social Status

Ethical concerns about the sociometrics as well as the recognized importance of understanding children's peer relationships have stimulated development of psychometrically robust alternatives to sociometric methods. The primary alternative is teacher evaluation of social status and peer relationships. Other possibilities (for example, self-reports, parental ratings, role-playing tasks) have consistently failed to meet generally accepted criteria for validity (Glow & Glow, 1980; Ledingham, Younger, Schwartzman, & Bergeron, 1982; Van Hasselt, Hersen, Whitehill, & Bellack, 1979).

Moderate correspondence between teacher and peer assessments has been demonstrated, with correlations ranging from .40 to .70 (Milich & Landau, 1982). This has been found for specific ratings of peer relations as well as assessments of behavioral adjustment. For example, Butler (1979) found a correlation of −.67 ($p < .001$) between peer nominations on the Class Play procedure and teacher ratings of adjustment. La Greca (1981) obtained good correspondence (i.e., all p values $< .001$) between teacher ratings on the three factors of the Pupil Evaluation Inventory (PEI) and a peer rating scale for boys but weaker correlations for girls. Matson, Esveldt-Dawson, and Kazdin (1983) obtained a correlation of .62 ($p < .001$) between teacher and peer rankings of popularity. In an extensive study, Meterko, Anderegg, and Budoff (1984) compared peer nominations on the Revised Class Play procedure with teacher ratings on the Bristol Scale of Adjustment and found evidence for convergent and discriminant validity. Peer nominations for sensitive-isolated behavior correlated significantly with teacher ratings of overcontrolled but not undercontrolled behavior. The opposite pattern of results held for peer nominations of aggressive-disruptive behavior. Peer nominations of sociability-leadership correlated significantly and inversely with both teacher scales.

Broad peer and teacher assessments of behavioral adjustment and social relationships are generally convergent. Several researchers have even argued that teachers offer more reliable and valid information about peer social status (Connolly & Doyle, 1981; Greenwood, Walker, Todd, & Hops, 1979). For example, Greenwood et al. (1979) developed a procedure whereby teachers rank order students in terms of popularity with their classmates. These investigators found greater retest reliability for the teacher measure than for a comparable peer measure, and the teachers were better able to identify socially withdrawn preschoolers. Similarly, Connolly and Doyle found this teacher ranking procedure to predict observed social behavior among a preschool sample to a greater degree than did peer positive nominations. In point of fact, the positive nominations from peers supplied no significant information (i.e., no incremental validity) beyond that supplied by the teacher rankings.

Information from teachers may be as useful as peer assessments, but we do not know how teacher ratings are related to observed negative behavior. To address this problem, Landau, Milich, and Whitten (1984) included peer rejection nominations and observed negative behavior in a replication of Connolly and Doyle (1981) with a sample of kindergarten boys. In comparison with teacher rankings, peer nominations contributed significant and unique information to the predictions of observed solitary play and negative interactions.

Although the results obtained by Landau et al. (1984) contrast with those of Connolly and Doyle (1981) and Greenwood et al. (1979), it may be the case that teacher assessments are more valid for preschool samples but not for older children. Furthermore, as Landau et al. (1984) pointed out, the fact that the teacher measure of peer popularity was weakly related to the observed negative interactions does not necessarily mean that teachers were insensitive to aversive classroom behaviors. In fact, teacher ratings of aggressive behaviors correlated .36 ($p < .01$) with observed negative interactions. Perhaps teacher rankings of popularity are not sufficiently comprehensive for the assessment of social relations.

A major criticism of teacher assessments is that, although consistent with peer assessments of broad categories of functioning, they have not proven sensitive to subtle behavioral distinctions of diagnostic and prognostic importance. For example, teacher assessment of social functioning often fails to distinguish between peer popularity and rejected status (Landau et al., 1984; Van Hasselt et al., 1979). More importantly, teacher ratings have not been as sensitive as peer measures to subtle distinctions among groups of children. Rolf (1976) found that peer nominations on the Class Play produced significant distinctions among subtle groups of vulnerable children (i.e., those with schizophrenic mothers vs. those with neurotic mothers) whereas teacher ratings did not. Similar differential results concerning peer and teacher assessments have been offered by Weintraub, Liebert, and Neale (1975), Weintraub, Prinz, and Neale (1978), Beisser, Glasser, and Grant (1967), and Rolf (1972). Peer nominations may also predict long-term outcomes better than teacher assessments (Cowen, Pederson, Babigian, Izzo, & Trost, 1973; Rolf, 1972).

The aforementioned research offers a pessimistic view of replacing peer measures with teacher assessments, especially if discrimination of social status groups is the goal. However, it may be premature to dismiss the utility of teacher ratings completely. One can argue that the appropriate teacher assessment instruments have not been developed or employed in these studies. For example, even though Landau et al. (1984) found teacher rankings of popularity to do a relatively poor job of identifying negative peer interactions ($r = -.25$), ratings of aggression by the teachers did a better job ($r = .36$), although still below the magnitude offered by peer rejection nominations ($r = .46$).

In a similar vein, Milich and Fitzgerald (1985) found that if the appropriate scales are employed teachers can make subtle behavioral differentiations, such as between the externalizing disorders of hyperactivity and aggression in the classroom, a distinction that earlier studies had dismissed as unreliable (see, for example, Lahey, Green, & Forehand, 1980). Milich and Fitzgerald found that teacher ratings of inattention/overactivity exhibited unique relationship with classroom academic behavior (e.g., fail to attend, disapproval received from teacher), whereas ratings of aggression were uniquely related to classroom social behaviors (e.g., negative with teacher, physically aggressive). In an earlier study, Milich and Landau (1984) found these same teacher ratings of hyperactivity and aggression, when used conjointly, to differentiate subgroups of children differing in both social status and observed social behaviors.

The combination of teacher and peer assessments to identify social status subgroups offers an alternative to using only one data source. Ladd (1983) collected peer acceptance data and then asked teachers to divide the low acceptance children into neglected and rejected subgroups. Playground observations verified that the behavior of teacher-identified rejected children was consistent with descriptions reported in studies based on peer nominations. The teacher-identified rejected children engaged in significantly higher rates of both arguing and 'rough and tumble' behavior, and spent greater amounts of time unoccupied, compared with both popular and average students. Since Ladd (1983) did not report results for the neglected group, it is not known whether the teachers successfully identified this subgroup. Nevertheless, the results suggested that teachers can accurately identify rejected children from a low peer acceptance group. Future studies need to incorporate peer rejection data to test this conclusion further.

Rejected and Neglected Status

Differentiating rejected and neglected children is an important topic of research despite the sensitive ethical issues associated with asking children to make pejorative comments about classmates. Rejected and neglected children have different patterns of social behavior (Dodge et al., 1982). Studies predicting adult outcome suggest that only the group of antisocial rejected children is at substantial risk for future adjustment problems (Cowen et al., 1973; Kupersmidt, 1983). Likewise, rejected status has shown stability from elementary school to high school, whereas neglected status has not (Coie & Dodge, 1983; Coie & Kupersmidt, 1983).

The search for observed behavioral concomitants seems the most promising in terms of an effort to devise a developmental hypothesis about social status among peers. Indeed, observations have been used to investigate behavioral correlates of rejected and neglected social status with interesting result. Early informal observation studies focused on behaviors of preschoolers associated with high peer acceptance (Bonney & Powell, 1953; Charlesworth & Hartup, 1967). The few studies of behavior and social status of older children provided clear behavior patterns associated with peer rejection and peer neglect. In order to determine specific behavior differences among social status groups, Dodge et al. (1982) observed third, fourth, and fifth graders for several behavioral categories including task appropriateness, aggression, and prosocial approaches. Rejected children engaged in less solitary task appropriate behavior than average and popular children and more aggressive acts toward peers. Rejected children attempted more social approaches in the classroom and fewer social approaches on the playground than all other status groups. These findings indicated that the rejected children did not alter the frequency of their approach behavior according to the appropriateness of the environmental context. In a second study, Dodge et al. (1982) enhanced interobserver reliability through the use of videotapes and were able to replicate the initial findings. Additionally, rejected children engaged in more child-teacher interactions than any other group, while neglected children made the fewest social approaches and were most task appropriate.

In Dodge et al. (1982), observations were conducted after social status was established. It is not possible from such data to determine if the significant observed behavior is the causes or consequence of a child's status (Coie & Kupersmidt, 1983). To clarify causal direction, Coie and Kupersmidt (1983) studied behavior associated with emergence of status in groups of unacquainted boys and maintenance of status in groups of acquainted boys. Each play group was composed of four black fourth grade boys: a rejected, popular, neglected, and average status boy. Five groups were composed of boys from the same classroom, and five were composed of boys from different schools who did not know each other. Each play group met in weekly videotaped sessions for six consecutive weeks. Social status ratings for all children were obtained at the end of each session. Analyses indicated that popular boys engaged in more active social interaction and less solitary appropriate activity than did the neglected boys. Average and rejected boys were intermediate to these two groups for both variables. By the final group sessions, familiar and unfamiliar rejected boys engaged in less parallel play and more solitary inappropriate behavior. Rejected boys also talked more while neglected boys talked less. Rejected boys exhibited the most aversive behaviors and neglected boys the least. Average boys also engaged in more aversive behavior than popular or neglected boys. The boys were interviewed at the end of each weekly session and were asked to rank-order their preferred playmates from the group. For familiar and unfamiliar groups after only three sessions, social status within the groups was highly correlated with the boys' school-based status.

These results are similar to findings by Dodge (1983), who has implicated social approach patterns and peer-directed aggression as the critical elements in determining peer status in groups. Focusing on sequences of behavior related to social approach and aggression, Dodge observed six play groups, each composed of eight unacquainted second grade boys of unknown social status who met together for eight weekly sessions. Children who became rejected or neglected spent much time in solitary play and little time in cooperative play or social conversation. The rejected children were more likely to attempt aggressive play interaction and more likely to engage in inappropriate play behavior than any other group. Rejected children engaged in more hostile verbalizations and hitting than did neglected children, who spent more time in solitary play. Rejected children initially approached peers frequently; however, their interactions were of shorter duration compared with popular children, and the frequency of approaches and social conversation decreased in later sessions.

Although the re-emergence of status in groups of unacquainted children is a compelling illustration of its stability over a period of weeks, no data are more significant than those indicating that rejected status is a phenomenon that remains stable for years. In an oft-cited longitudinal study, Roff et al. (1972) reported strong correlations of stability for social preference scores ("liked most"–"liked least") of .53 for one year, .48 for 2 years, and .45 for 3 years. Coie and Dodge (1983) offered even more compelling data in the most important study of social status stability to date. These investigators collected yearly sociometric data from groups of third and fifth graders for a period of 5 years and reported correlations from Year 1 to Year 5 of .36 for the third graders and .45 for the fifth graders. This is most impressive when one takes into account the fact that these children changed peer groups when they shifted into junior high school. "Liked least" scores had greater stability than "liked most" scores, and rejected social status stability correlations were highly significant for all five years of the older cohort and for Years 1–3 of the third grade cohort. In other words, rejected children tended to remain rejected. Children of neglected status were rare in elementary school but more common among older children. They tended to move toward more positive social status without intervention (Coie & Dodge, 1983).

The data consistently suggest that rejected children interact frequently with their peers and are more disruptive and aggressive than others, whereas neglected children are less socially interactive and are almost never disruptive or aggressive (Coie et al., 1982; Coie & Kupersmidt, 1983; Dodge, 1983; Dodge et al., 1982; Green, Forehand, Beck, & Vosk, 1980). Rejected children reacquire their status when placed among children who do not know them. Their status remains quite stable over a period of years. Antisocial rejected children are at risk for mental health or general adjustment difficulties in adulthood. Neglected children are in quite a different and more positive position. For example, Cantrell and Prinz (in press) found few significant differences between neglected and accepted children, leading the authors to question whether neglected status constitutes a clinically deviant entity in need of attention. These differences in behavior, tractibility, and outcome dictate differences in approaches to intervention for the two groups.

ISSUES IN TREATMENT

Behavior Shaping Procedures

Several intervention studies have been attempted with low-accepted children (Wanlass & Prinz, 1982). One group of studies was based on the assumption that children are unpopular because they interact infrequently with peers and are deprived of opportunities to learn social skills and to make new friends. Consequently, the approach for treating these children has been to increase the frequency of interactions with peers through the use of shaping procedures derived from operant learning theory (e.g., Allen, Hart, Buell, Harris & Wolf, 1964; Strain, Shores, & Timm, 1977; Walker & Hops, 1973). Several clinical researchers have applied modeling techniques derived from social learning theory to promote social approach skills and other appropriate behavior with peers such as friendly play (Evers & Schwarz, 1973; Evers-Pasquale, 1978; Evers-Pasquale & Sherman, 1975; Keller & Carlson, 1974; O'Connor, 1969, 1972; Weinrott, Corson & Wilchesky, 1979).

Among the several methodological problems that should be addressed in connection with the modeling and shaping techniques are their dependence on systematic and contingent reinforcement, the ease with which frequencies of behavior return to baseline levels, the reliance on the spontaneous occurrence of the behavior which is to be reinforced, the simplistic nature of the behaviors typically reinforced, and the lack of adequate follow-up data. A significant issue associated with the modeling/shaping approach to intervention, however, is the definition of poor peer adjustment solely in terms of low interaction rate, an issue aptly discussed by Asher et al. (1981). Measures of social status have demonstrated little correspondence with rates of interaction (Deutsch, 1974; Furman, Rahe & Hartup, 1979; Gottman, 1977; Jennings, 1975). Some children who interact infrequently demonstrate competence when they do interact and also engage in appropriate but solitary work and play (Moore, Evertson & Brophy, 1974; Rubin, Maioni, & Hornung, 1976). There is even evidence suggesting that increasing the interaction rates of low-frequency children can lead to negative consequences (Kirby & Toler, 1970; Walker, Greenwood, Hops & Todd, 1979). In addition, longitudinal studies of the long-term consequences of low interaction rates have not indicated that early social isolation leads to subsequent mental health difficulties (Asher et al., 1981).

Social Skills Training

A second group of studies is predicated on the assumption that social problems result from particular social skill deficits rather than from a low frequency of interaction. These social skill training interventions presuppose that a child who lacks certain social skills will experience little in the way of successful interactions with peers and will acquire a low social status. Therefore, low-status children are coached to emit positive behaviors.

These oft-cited studies of social skills training (e.g., Gresham & Nagle, 1980; La Greca & Santogrossi, 1980; Oden & Asher, 1977) vary broadly with regard to which children are targeted as subjects, what skills are trained, and whether or not behavior or status changes are demonstrated. It is not surprising that they have yielded mixed results. While most training interventions resulted in an improvement in roster-rating scores, at least three studies failed to demonstrate such improvement (Gottman, Gonso & Schuler, 1976; Hymel & Asher, 1977; La Greca & Santogrossi, 1980). Although improvements in social adjustment as assessed by roster-rater methods have been demonstrated, no one has documented significant improvements in peer nomination scores. Even though coaching is presumed to increase positive behavior (such as cooperation, participation, and conversation) and cause a change in status, some coaching studies do not demonstrate an increase in positive interactions (e.g., Gresham & Nagle, 1980; Hymel & Asher, 1977; La Greca & Santogrossi, 1980; Oden & Asher, 1977). Some investigations found a decrease in the frequency of aggressive behavior following social skills training but did not include a measure of social status (Gottman, Gonso, & Rasmussen, 1975; Zahavi & Asher, 1978). Overall, changes in skill levels have not been accompanied by changes in sociometric ratings, and changes in sociometric ratings have not been accompanied by changes in skill levels. This suggests that changes in status may not be mediated by changes in behavior associated with coaching (Putallaz & Gottman, 1983).

In view of the mixed results of these studies, it is important to restate that social skills treatment interventions arose out of a desire to increase the social interactions of withdrawn and shy children (Wanlass & Prinz, 1982). Given a 'social skills deficit' orientation, the training emphasized increasing behaviors and augmenting the child's behavioral repertoire. Such an orientation may have only limited utility for rejected children who have behavioral excesses in addition to social skills deficits. This conclusion is supported by two major investigations of social skills training with rejected children (Coie & Krehbiel, 1984; Pelham et al., in press).

Coie and Krehbiel (1984) noted that rejected youngsters often have the dual problems of aggressive/disruptive social interactions and academic difficulties. Since the authors hypothesized that a complete treatment program should address both difficulties, their study compared social skills training, academic tutoring, and the combination of both as treatments for social rejection. A sample of 40 black fourth graders met the following selection criteria for peer rejection: a standardized social preference score of less than -1.0, a 'liked least' standardized score greater than 0.0, and a 'liked most' standardized score less than 0.0. In addition, the children had math or reading achievement scores below the 36th percentile and were nominated by their teachers as having both serious academic and social adjustment problems.

The 40 children were randomly assigned to one of four treatment groups: (a) academic skills tutoring (AST modeled after the work of Wallach and Wallach, 1976); (b) social skills training (SST as developed by Oden & Asher, 1977); (c) combined academic and social skills training (AST/SST); and (d) no-treatment control (NT). The academic tutoring involved approximately 35 45-minute individual tutoring sessions with trained undergraduates. The tutors focused on those academic areas in which the subject seemed most deficient. The social skills training involved six one-hour coaching sessions in which each subject was paired with a nonrejected classmate to permit the practice of skills. Skills of participation, cooperation, communication, and support were emphasized. In the SST condition the six individual sessions were followed by six more coaching sessions in small groups to practice the same skills. The NT control group had no contact with the project staff during the intervention phases. The dependent variables for the study consisted of pre- and postintervention measures of classroom observations, classroom sociometrics, and academic achievement. The sociometric data and academic testing were also collected again at one year follow-up. The primary analyses consisted of 2×2 (AST $\times$ SST) analyses of covariance, with pretreatment scores serving as the covariates.

For the achievement measures, significant main effects for AST groups were obtained for reading comprehension and mathematics computation, and marginally significant effects for reading vocabulary and mathematics application. The only significant SST main effect was in reading comprehension. There were no significant interactions for any of the variables. In terms of social preference scores, there was a significant main effect for AST, with AST and AST/SST groups both improving in mean social preference scores beyond the cutting point for rejected status. At one-year follow-up, significant main effects for AST for the achievement and social preference scores were maintained. In contrast, there were no significant main effects for SST at follow-up, although there was a marginal improvement for reading comprehension. In terms of classroom behavior, solitary on-task behavior and solitary nondisruptive off-task behavior (two of five categories) showed significant improvements.

In summary, Coie and Krehbiel found that a relatively intensive academic tutoring program for rejected youngsters led to improvements in academic achievement, social preference scores, and on-task behavior in the classroom. The improvements exhibited in the first two categories were maintained at one-year follow-up (with no observational data collected at follow-up). Perhaps more importantly, their social preference scores moved them (as a group) from the rejected to the average status category. In contrast, social skills training produced improvement on only one measure (reading comprehension), a finding that was not maintained at follow-up. There were no significant improvements associated with SST in terms of either classroom behavior or social preference scores, the latter being the outcome measure for which this intervention is usually targeted.

The results obtained by Coie and Krehbiel are intriguing, both in terms of the encouraging results associated with the academic tutoring, as well as the relatively disappointing findings regarding social skills training. These results are consistent with those obtained by Pelham et al. (in press) in a multimodal treatment study of childhood attention deficit disorder with hyperactivity (ADDH). Specifically, Pelham et al. investigated the effects of behavior therapy, stimulant medication (i.e., methylphenidate) and social skills training, in various combinations, in the treatment of 30 ADDH children. In addition to meeting the usual diagnostic criteria for Attention Deficit Disorder with Hyperactivity, a majority of the children were found to receive negative peer nominations (i.e., peer rejection scores) greater than two standard deviations above the classroom means.

The 30 children were assigned to one of five treatment groups. Twenty of the children received standard behavior therapy. This involved, on the average, 9.7 parent training sessions and 10.3 teacher training sessions. In addition, these 20 children were randomly divided into four groups, involving two levels of medication treatment (.3 mg/kg of methylphenidate vs. placebo) and two levels of social skills training (SST vs. none). SST involved group meetings for three hours every Saturday for eight weeks. The training was again modeled after the work of Oden and Asher (1977). The remaining ten children (i.e., those who received no behavior therapy) were placed in a social skill training contrast-treatment group and received the same SST treatment as children who also received behavior therapy. The dependent variables for the study consisted of pre- and posttreatment measures of parent and teacher ratings, positive and negative peer nominations, and observations of classroom behavior. For children in the SST contrast-treatment group, only peer nominations and teacher ratings were available.

A 2 (medication) × 2 (social skills training) × 2 (prepost) MANOVA for the 20 children in the behavior therapy groups revealed a significant main effect for prepost differences, but no other significant effects. In other words, receiving behavior therapy improved the children's behavior but the adjunctive treatments (i.e., medication, SST) did not significantly improve upon this effect.

Univariate analyses of variances indicated significant improvements for all categories of dependent variables, including parent and teacher ratings, peer nominations, and classroom observations. However, despite these improvements, 15 of the 20 children were still at least one standard deviation above the class mean in terms of negative nominations, and none of the children fell into the 'normal' range on the teacher ratings. Thus, there was evidence of improvement but not normalization. The adjunctive treatments did not add significantly to the results obtained for behavior therapy for any of the univariate analysis.

Separate analyses were undertaken comparing the pre- and post scores for the SST contrast-treatment group. In terms of teacher ratings there was a nonsignificant trend (*p* .2) towards improvement, whereas for the negative nominations there was a nonsignificant increase from pre- to posttreatment. The mean rejection scores rose from 9.5 to 10.9. When the 20 children who received behavior therapy were compared with the 10 who received SST only, the former showed significant improvement for teacher ratings and negative nomination scores.

In summary, Pelham et al. found that intensive behavior therapy (i.e., parent and teacher training) significantly improved the behavior of ADDH children across a variety of outcome measures, including parent and teacher ratings, classroom observations, and peer nominations. A few individual children fell into the 'normal' range following treatment, but these improvements were not enhanced by the addition of medication and/or social skills training. Finally, and perhaps most importantly for the present discussion, SST alone did not significantly improve the behavior or social status of the ADDH children and was significantly less effective along both dimensions than was behavior therapy.

CONCLUSIONS

Taken together, the results obtained by Coie and Krehbiel (1984) and Pelham et al. (in press) offer valuable insights into the treatment of peer rejected youngsters. Both studies documented that it is possible to improve the social behavior and social status of such children, although neither study was successful in alleviating these difficulties entirely. More importantly, intensive social skills training did not significantly improve the children's social behavior or social status. Instead, treatments (i.e., behavior therapy and academic tutoring) designed to address behavioral or academic difficulties but not social status seemed to be effective in improving the children's social status.

As the Pelham et al. and Coie and Krehbiel studies demonstrated, interventions designed to decrease disruptive behavior and increase both compliant, on-task behavior and academic performance, appear secondly to have beneficial effects on the target child's peer relations. If this conclusion is valid, three treatments should be considered when intervening with a socially rejected child: systematic behavioral training, stimulant medication (Pelham & Murphy, in press), and academic tutoring. In the Pelham et al. study, the combination of parent and teacher training in behavioral techniques significantly reduced the target children's inappropriate behavior in the classroom, as well as concomitantly reducing the number of peer rejection nominations they received. Due to the design of the study, it was not possible to determine whether teacher training, parent training, or both were necessary. However, given that significant peer relations were assessed in the classroom, this would suggest that teacher training was the more effective intervention. Future research needs to address these methods of decreasing disruptive, aggressive behavior.

Although Pelham et al. (in press) did not find stimulant medication to add significantly to the efficacy of the behavioral interventions, the use of medication should be considered, especially in the treatment of socially rejected ADDH or aggressive youngsters. The Pelham et al. study collected its outcome measures approximately three weeks after the termination of the medication. Dependent variables collected during the course of treatment indicated that children who received methylphenidate in combination with behavior therapy were rated by teachers as 50% better than those children who received placebo and behavior therapy. This finding is consistent with a large body of research (see Pelham &

Murphy, in press) suggesting that the combined effects of methylphenidate and behavior therapy are greater than the effects of either alone.

The beneficial effects of medication upon peer interactions were evident in a study by Cunningham, Siegel, and Offord (in press). These investigators examined dyadic interactions of hyperactive and normal boys and found that methylphenidate not only improved the behavior of the hyperactive children but was also significantly related to improved responses by the normal peers. The normal children exhibited less controlling and domineering behavior toward the medicated hyperactive children than toward the same children when medication was not administered. It remains to be seen whether the positive effects of medication are visible on outcome measures dealing with peer relations and social rejection.

The final intervention to be considered here is systematic academic tutoring. As Coie and Krehbiel (1984) noted, many rejected children have both behavioral and academic problems in school. The results of the Coie and Krehbiel intervention study indicate that rigorous tutoring programs may not only improve both of these problem areas, but that the beneficial effects carry over into social relations and reduce nominations of rejection. Although it is impossible to pinpoint the actual mechanism involved in this social improvement, the results of this study strongly indicate that academic functioning and school work-related behavior may supply a vital link in the development of successful social relations. Assessment of academic functioning and, when appropriate, careful selection of interventions may be central in helping socially rejected children.

FUTURE DIRECTIONS

It has been the thesis of this chapter that the problems experienced by socially rejected youngsters go well beyond social skills deficits. Instead, these children exhibit a wide variety of behavioral excesses and deficits, including off-task, disruptive behavior (Pelham & Bender, 1982), academic difficulties (Coie & Krehbiel, 1984), aggressive attributional biases (Dodge, 1980) and impulsivity (Williams & Landau, 1983), among others. Interventions that focus primarily on social skills training are unlikely to be successful with this population, as the Coie and Krehbiel (1984) and Pelham et al. (in press) studies demonstrate. Instead, multimodal or prescriptive treatment approaches are needed to address the diversity of difficulties experienced by these children with behavioral excesses.

The past attempts at intervention which resulted in behavior change without sociometric status change pose a great dilemma. If behavior change is consistently effected in the absence of peer status change, then not only must the traditional approaches to intervention be reviewed but so must the use of sociometric status as an outcome variable. It remains unclear whether peers perceive subtle changes in behavior or whether perceived subtle changes in behavior can produce major changes in attitude and response set. Interventions focusing on reputation and the peer group as the target for change may provide key information about effecting social status change in the peer group.

Just as change in behavior may not lead to a change in peer group status, a change in status may not lead to a long-term change in behavior or to a positive adjustment. It does not necessarily follow that, if poor peer relationships is an indicator of future difficulty, then intervention which results in improved social status will prevent future adjustment problems. Longitudinal data are needed to explore further the correlates of status and the long- and short-term benefits of intervention. Until evidence is available, social skills training and other forms of intervention cannot be presented as preventive.

Finally, innovative work by Ladd (1983) and Asher and Dodge (1984) suggests that relevant groups (those at risk for future difficulty) can be identified without the use of peer rejection measures. The continued development of alternative approaches to the collection of peer social status data is essential.

REFERENCES

Allen, E., Hart, B., Buell, J., Harris, F., & Wolf, M. (1964). Effects of social reinforcement on isolate behavior of a nursery school child. *Child Development, 35,* 511–518.

Asher, S. R. (1983). Social competence and peer status: Recent advances and future directions. *Child Development, 54,* 1427–1434.

Asher, S. R., & Dodge, K. A. (1984). *The identification of socially rejected children.* Manuscript submitted for publication.

Asher, S. R., & Hymel, S. (1981). Children's social competence in peer relations: Sociometric and behavioral assessment. In J. D. Wine & M. D. Smye (Eds.), *Social competence* (pp. 125–157). New York: Guilford Press.

Asher, S. R., Markell, R. A., & Hymel, S. (1981). Identifying children at risk in peer relations: A critique of the rate of interaction approach to assessment. *Child Development, 52,* 1239–1245.

Bandura, A. (1969). *Principles of behavior modification.* New York: Holt, Rinehart and Winston.

Beisser, A., Glasser, N. & Grant, M. (1967). Psychosocial adjustment in children in children of schizophrenic mothers. *Journal of Nervous and Mental Diseases, 145,* 429–440.

Bonney, M. E. (1943). The relative stability of social, intellectual, and academic status in grades II to IV and the interrelationships between these various forms of growth. *Journal of Educational Psychology, 34,* 88–102.

Bonney, M. E., & Powell, J. (1953). Differences in social behavior between sociometrically high and sociometrically low children. *Journal of Educational Research, 46,* 481–495.

Bukowski, W. M., & Newcomb, A. F. (1984). The stability and determinants of sociometric status and friendship choice: A longitudinal perspective. *Developmental Psychology, 21,* 941–952.

Butler, L. J. (1979). *Social and behavioral correlates of peer reputation.* Paper presented at the meeting of the Society for Research in Child Development, San Francisco, CA, April.

Cantrell, V. L., & Prinz, R. J. (1985). Multiple perspectives of rejected, neglected, and accepted children: Relationship between sociometric status and behavioral characteristics. *Journal of Consulting and Clinical Psychology, 53,* 884–889.

Charlesworth, R., & Hartup, W. W. (1967). Positive social reinforcement in the nursery school peer groups. *Child Development, 38,* 993–1003.

Coie, J. D., & Dodge, K. A. (1983). Continuities and changes in children's social status: A five-year longitudinal study. *Merrill-Palmer Quarterly, 29,* 261–281.

Coie, J. D., Dodge, K. A., & Coppotelli, H. (1982). Dimensions and types of social status: A cross-age perspective. *Developmental Psychology. 18,* 557–570.

Coie, J. D., & Krehbiel, G. (1984). Effects of academic tutoring on the social status of low-achieving, socially rejected children. *Child Development, 55,* 1465–1478.

Coie, J. D., & Kupersmidt, J. B. (1983). A behavioral analysis of emerging social status in boys' groups. *Child Development, 54,* 1400–1416.

Connolly, J., & Doyle, A. (1981). Assessment of social competence in preschoolers: Teachers versus peers. *Developmental Psychology, 17,* 454–462.

Cowen, E. L., Pederson, A., Babigian, H., Izzo, L. D., & Trost, M. A. (1973). Long-term follow-up of early detected vulnerable children. *Journal of Consulting and Clinical Psychology, 42,* 438–446.

Cunningham, C. E., Siegel, L. S., & Offord, D. R. (in press). A developmental dose-response analysis of the effects of methylphenidate on the peer interactions of attention deficit disordered boys. *Journal of Child Psychology and Psychiatry.*

Deutsch, F. (1974). Observational and sociometric measures of peer popularity and their relationship to egocentric communication in female preschoolers. *Developmental Psychology, 10,* 745–747.

Dodge, K. A. (1980). Social cognition and children's aggressive behavior. *Child Development, 51,* 162–170.

Dodge, K. A. (1983). Behavioral antecedents of peer social status. *Child Development, 54,* 1386–1399.

Dodge, K. A., Coie, J. D., & Brakke, N. P. (1982). Behavior patterns of socially rejected and neglected preadolescents: the roles of social approach and aggression. *Journal of Abnormal Child Psychology, 10,* 389–410.

Evers, W., & Schwartz, J. C. (1973). Modifying social withdrawal in preschoolers: The effects of filmed modeling and teacher praise. *Journal of Abnormal Child Psychology, 1,* 248–256.

Evers-Pasquale, W. (1978). The peer preference test as a measure of reward value: Item analysis, cross-validation, concurrent validation, and replication. *Journal of Abnormal Child Psychology, 6,* 175–188.

Evers-Pasquale, W., & Sherman, M. (1975). The reward values of peers and prior social experience: An investigation of their influence on the efficacy of filmed modeling in modifying social isolation in preschoolers. *Journal of Abnormal Child Psychology, 3,* 179–189.

Furman, W., Rahe, D. F. & Hartup, W. W. (1979). Rehabilitation of socially withdrawn preschool children through mixed-age and same-age socialization. *Child Development, 50,* 915–922.

Glow, R. A., & Glow, P. H. (1980). Peer and self-rating: Children's perception of behavior relevant to hyperkinetic impulse disorder. *Journal of Abnormal Child Psychology, 8,* 175–188.

Gottman, J. M. (1977). The effects of a modeling film on social isolation in preschool children: A methodological investigation. *Journal of Abnormal Child Psychology, 5,* 69–78.

Gottman, J. M., Gonso, J., & Rasmussen, B. (1975). Social interaction, social competence, and friendship in children. *Child Development, 46,* 709–718.

Gottman, J. M., Gonso, J., & Schuler, P. (1976). Teaching social skills to isolated children. *Journal of Abnormal Child Psychology, 4,* 179–197.

Green, K., Forehand, R., Beck, J., & Vosk, B. (1980). An assessment of the relationship among measures of children's social competence and children's academic achievement. *Child Development, 51,* 1149–1156.

Greenwood, C. R., Walker, H. M., Todd, N. M., & Hops, H. (1979). Selecting a cost-effective screening measure for the assessment of preschool social withdrawal. *Journal of Applied Behavior Analysis, 12,* 639–652.

Gresham, F., & Nagle, R. (1980). Social skills training with children: Responsiveness to modeling and coaching as a function of peer orientation. *Journal of Consulting and Clinical Psychology, 48,* 718–729.

Hartup, W. W. (1983). Peer relations. In E. M. Hetherington (Ed.), *Handbook of child psychology: Vol. IV. Socialization, personality, and social development* (pp. 103–196). New York: Wiley.

Hartup, W. W., Glazer, J. A., & Charlesworth, R. (1967). Peer reinforcement and sociometric status. *Child Development, 38,* 1017–1024.

Hayvren, M. & Hymel, S. (1984). Ethical issues in sociometric testing: The impact of sociometric measures on interaction behavior. *Developmental Psychology, 20,* 844–849.

Horowitz, F. D. (1962). The relationship of anxiety, self-concept, and sociometric status among fourth, fifth, and sixth grade children. *Journal of Abnormal and Social Psychology, 65,* 212–214.

Hymel, S., & Asher, S. R. (1977). *Assessment and training of isolated children's social skills.* Paper presented at the meeting of the Society for Research in Child Development, New Orleans, March, (ERIC Document Service Reproduction Service No. ED 136 930.)

Jennings, K. (1975). People versus object orientation, social behavior, and intellectual abilities in children. *Developmental Psychology, 11,* 511–519.

Justman, J., & Wrightstone, J. W. (1951). A comparison of three methods of measuring pupil status in the classroom. *Educational Psychological Measurement, 11,* 362–367.

Keller, M., & Carlson, D. (1974). Use of symbolic modeling to promote social skills in preschool children with low levels of social responsiveness. *Child Development, 45,* 912–919.

Kirby, F., & Toler, H. (1970). Modification of preschool isolate behavior: A case study. *Journal of Applied Behavior Analysis, 3,* 309–314.

Kupersmidt, J. B. (1983). *Predicting delinquency and academic problems from childhood peer status.* Paper presented at the meeting of the Society for Research in Child Development, Detroit, MI, April.

Ladd, G. W. (1983). Social networks of popular, average, and rejected children in school settings. *Merrill-Palmer Quarterly, 29,* 283–307.

La Greca, A. M. (1981). Peer acceptance: The correspondence between children's sociometric scores and teachers' ratings of peer interactions. *Journal of Abnormal Child Psychology, 9,* 167–178.

La Greca, A., & Santogrossi, D. (1980). Social skills training with elementary school students: A behavioral group approach. *Journal of Consulting and Clinical Psychology, 48,* 220–227.

Lahey, B. B., Green, K. D., & Forehand, R. (1980). On the independence of ratings of hyperactivity, conduct problems, and attention deficits in children: A multiple regression analysis. *Journal of Consulting and Clinical Psychology, 48,* 566–574.

Landau, S., Milich, R., & Whitten, P. (1984). A comparison of teacher and peer assessment of social status. *Journal of Clinical Child Psychology, 13,* 44–49.

Ledingham, J. (1981). Developmental patterns of aggressive and withdrawn behavior in childhood: A possible method for identifying preschizophrenics. *Journal of Abnormal Child Psychology, 9,* 1–22.

Ledingham, J. E., Younger, A., Schwartzman, A., & Bergeron, G. (1982). Agreement among teacher, peer, and self-ratings of children's aggression, withdrawal, and likability. *Journal of Abnormal Child Psychology, 10,* 363–372.

Matson, J. L., Esveldt-Dawson, K. & Kazdin, A. E. (1983). Validation of methods for assessing social skills in children. *Journal of Clinical Child Psychology, 12,* 174–180.

McCandless, B. R., & Marshall, H. R. (1957). A picture sociometric technique for preschool children and its relation to teacher judgments of friendship. *Child Development, 28,* 138–147.

Meterko, M., Anderegg, D., & Budoff, M. (1984). *Teacher and peer assessment of children's social competence.* Paper presented at the meeting of the American Psychological Association, Toronto, August.

Milich, R., & Fitzgerald, G. (1985). Validation of inattention/overactivity and aggression ratings with classroom observations. *Consulting and Clinical Psychology, 53,* 139–140.

Milich, R., & Landau, S. (1982). Socialization and peer relations in hyperactive children. In K. D.

Gadow & I. Bialer (Eds.), *Advances in learning and behavioral disabilities,* Vol. 1 (pp. 283–339). Greenwich, CT: JAI Press.

Milich, R., & Landau, S. (1984). A comparison of the social status and social behavior of aggressive and aggressive/withdrawn boys. *Journal of Abnormal Child Psychology, 12,* 277–288.

Moore, N. V., Evertson, C. M., & Brophy, J. E. (1974). Solitary play: Some functional reconsiderations. *Developmental Psychology, 10,* 830–834.

Moore, S. G., & Updegraff, R. (1964). Sociometric status of preschool children related to age, sex, nurturance-giving and dependency. *Child Development, 35,* 519–524.

Moreno, J. L. (1934). *Who shall survive?* Washington, DC: Nervous and Mental Disease Publishing.

Newcomb, A. F., & Bukowski, W. M. (1983). Social impact and social preference as determinants of children's peer group status. *Developmental Psychology, 19,* 856–867.

O'Connor, R. D. (1969). Modification of social withdrawal through symbolic modeling. *Journal of Applied Behavior Analysis, 2,* 15–22.

O'Connor, R. D. (1972). Relative efficacy of modeling, shaping, combined procedures for modification of social withdrawal. *Journal of Abnormal Psychology, 80,* 327–334.

Oden, S., & Asher, S. R. (1977). Coaching children in social skills for friendship-making. *Child Development, 48,* 495–506.

Peery J. C. (1979). Popular, amiable, isolated, rejected: A reconceptualization of sociometric status in preschool children. *Child Development, 50,* 1231–1234.

Pekarik, E., Prinz, R., Liebert, D., Weintraub, S., & Neale, J. (1976). The Pupil Evaluation Inventory: A sociometric technique for assessing children's social behavior. *Journal of Abnormal Child Psychology, 4,* 83–93.

Pelham, W., & Bender, M. (1982). Peer relations in hyperactive children: Description and treatment. In K. D. Gadow & I. Bialer (Eds.), *Advances in learning and behavioral disabilities,* Vol. 1 (pp. 365–436). Greenwich, CT: JAI Press.

Pelham, W. E., & Murphy, R. (in press). Behavioral and pharmacological treatment of attention deficit and conduct disorders. In M. Hersen & S. E. Breuning (Eds.), *Pharmacological and behavioral treatment: An integrative approach.* New York: Wiley.

Pelham, W., Schnedler, R., Miller, J., Ronnei, M. Paluchowski, C., Budrow, M., Marks, D., Nilsson, D., & Bender, M. (in press). The combination of behavior therapy and methylphenidate in the treatment of attention deficit disorder: A therapy outcome study. In L. Bloomingdale (Ed.), *Attention deficit disorder,* Vol. 3. New York: Spectrum.

Putallaz, M., & Gottman, J. M. (1983). Social relationship problems in children: An approach to intervention. In B. B. Lahey & A. E. Kazdin (Eds.), *Advances in clinical child psychology,* Vol. 6 (pp. 1–43). New York: Plenum Press.

Roff, M., Sells, S. B., & Golden, M. M. (1972). *Social adjustment and personality development in children.* Minneapolis, Minn.: University of Minnesota Press.

Rolf, J. E. (1972). The social and academic competence of children vulnerable to schizophrenia and other behavior pathologies. *Journal of Abnormal Psychology, 80,* 225–243.

Rolf, J. E. (1976). Peer status and the directionality of symptomatic predictors of outcome for vulnerable children. *American Journal of Orthopsychiatry, 46,* 74–88.

Rubin, K. H., Maioni, T. L., & Hornung, M. (1976). Free play behaviors in middle- and lower-class preschoolers: Parten and Piaget revisited. *Child Development, 47,* 414–419.

Strain, P. S., Shores, R. E., & Timm, M. A. (1977). Effects of peer social initiations on the behavior of withdrawn preschool children. *Journal of Applied Behavior Analysis, 10,* 289–298.

Thompson, G. G., & Powell, M. (1951). An investigation of the rating scale approach to the measurement of social status. *Educational and Psychological Measurement 11,* 440–455.

Van Hasselt, V. B., Hersen, M., Whitehill, M. B., & Bellack, A. S. (1979). Social skills assessment and training for children. *Behavior Research and Therapy, 17,* 413–437.

Walker, H. M., Greenwood, C. R., Hops, H., & Todd, N. M. (1979). Differential effects of reinforcing topographic components of social interaction. *Behavior Modification, 3,* 291–321.

Walker, H. M., & Hops, H. (1973). The use of group and individual reinforcement contingencies in the modification of social withdrawal. In L. A. Hamerlynck, L. C. Handy, & E. J. Mash (Eds.), *Behavior change: Methodology, concepts, and practice* (pp. 269–308). Champaign, IL: Research Press Co.

Wallach, M. S., & Wallach, L. (1976). *Teaching all children to read.* Chicago: University of Chicago Press.

Wanlass, R. L., & Prinz, R. J. (1982). Methodological issues in conceptualizing and treating childhood social isolation. *Psychological Bulletin, 92,* 39–55.

Weinrott, M. R., Corson, J. A., & Wilchesky, M. (1979). Teacher-mediated treatment of social withdrawal. *Behavior Therapy, 19,* 281–294.

Weintraub, S., Liebert, D., & Neale, J. (1975). Teacher ratings of children vulnerable to psychopathology. *American Journal of Orthopsychiatry, 45,* 838–845.

Weintraub, S., Prinz, R. J., & Neale, J. M. (1978). Peer evaluations of the competence of children vulnerable to psychopathology. *Journal of Abnormal Child Psychology, 6,* 461–473.

Williams, T., & Landau, S. (1983). *Kindergarten overactivity, inattention, and impulsivity: Implications for social status.* Paper presented at the meeting of the National Association of School Psychologists, Detroit, MI, March.

Zahavi, S., & Asher, S. R. (1978). The effect of verbal instruction on preschool children's aggressive behavior. *Journal of School Psychology, 16,* 146–153.

SUBJECT INDEX

Research Annuals and Monographs in Series in the *BEHAVIORAL SCIENCES*

U.C.C. LIBRARY
70869938